# Napoleon's Military Machine

Guild Publishing
London

# Napoleon's Military Machine

## Philip J Haythornthwaite

In the Spellmount Military list:

*The Territorial Battalions – A pictorial history*
*The Yeomanry Regiments – A pictorial history*
*Over the Rhine – The Last Days of War in Europe*
*History of the Cambridge University OTC*
*Yeoman Service*
*The Fighting Troops of the Austro-Hungarian Army*
*Intelligence Officer in the Peninsula*
*The Scottish Regiments – A pictorial history*
*The Royal Marines – A pictorial history*
*The Royal Tank Regiment – A pictorial history*
*The Irish Regiments – A pictorial history*
*British Sieges of the Peninsular War*
*Victoria's Victories*
*The 1914 Campaign*
*Rorke's Drift*

In the Nautical list:

*Sea of Memories*
*Evolution of Engineering in the Royal Navy Vol 1*
*1827-1939*

In the Aviation list:

*Diary of a Bomb Aimer*

This edition published in 1988 by
Book Club Associates
by arrangement with
Spellmount Ltd,
12 Dene Way, Speldhurst,
Tunbridge Wells, Kent TN3 0NX

Design and picture research by Ravelin Ltd, Stamford, Lincs/G. Beehag.
Figure artworks by Richard Scollins.
Typeset by Vitaset, Paddock Wood, Kent.
Printed in Great Britain by Robert Hartnoll Ltd, Bodmin, Cornwall.

# Napoleon's Military Machine

'I used to say of him that his presence in the field made a difference of 40,000 men' was the comment made upon Napoleon by the Duke of Wellington, and is eloquent testimony from one of history's greatest generals upon the capabilities of another. Due to the character of the man, Napoleon would not have been so generous had the position been reversed, yet it was that character which turned an obscure Corsican artillery officer within six years into the leader, ultimately emperor, of one of the most powerful states of modern times.

That Napoleon was one of the greatest generals in history is unquestioned, probably second to none and ranking alongside Caesar, Frederick the Great, Gustavus Adolphus, Marlborough and Wellington, but he was far more than just a 'great captain'; he was equally celebrated for his administrative reforms and codes of law, some of which have survived until the present day. As a combination of soldier and creator of a vast and diverse empire, only Alexander and Ghengis Khan can compare with his achievements. Some of his concepts – especially that of a unified European state, of which France would be the leader – were so advanced that even at the present time they appear futuristic. It has been said that had Bonaparte not been Bonaparte, Moreau would have been; in other words, the French Revolution and the governments which resulted from it, especially the tottering Directory, were inevitably to end in military dictatorship, and that Napoleon Bonaparte was the most obvious candidate to fill the gap. This statement overlooks the fact that Napoleon was no ordinary general, no ordinary talent; for whilst Moreau was a brilliant and constantly under-rated soldier, his political skills were poor, whereas Napoleon was as adept a politician as he was a general, which is one reason not only for his meteoric rise to power but for the maintenance of an empire unprecedented in Europe since the days of Charlemagne. Napoleon's beginnings were in obscurity; born 'Napoleone Buonaparte' in Ajaccio, Corsica, on 15 August 1769, his father was an impoverished lawyer of minor aristocratic background; his edu-

cation was state-supported and after a year in the Paris military academy he was commissioned into the artillery. Though he showed an aptitude for science and mathematics, his spare time was spent in the study of military history and theory, and he benefited greatly from the influence of the great artilleryman Jean Pierre du Teil, his commandant in 1786. Protracted study, coupled with immense natural talent and energy for relentless hard work, reaped its benefits when his plan for the recapture of Toulon flung him into prominence, and despite a period of incarceration resulting from his friendship with Robespierre's brother his use of the 'whiff of grapeshot' to defend the Convention against a royalist mob assured him the support of the scheming politician Paul Barras (1755-1820). Once given command of the Army of Italy, Napoleon's future was assured, for in the field his natural talent made his rise almost inevitable. His removal from the immediate political scene left him largely untainted by the low tone of the Directory (largely set by the immoral Barras, whose rejected mistress Josephine de Beauharnais Napoleon married), so that when he returned from Egypt he was in a position to execute the *coup d'état* which replaced the Directory with the Consulate. The step from 'First Consul for Life' to Emperor was but a short one, and was founded upon his unprecedented military successes.

These triumphs were achieved by the efforts of countless thousands of ordinary soldiers, but the army from the late 1790s at least was to a degree Napoleon's creation, so an appreciation of the efforts of the anonymous masses who marched under his banner does not necessarily detract from Napoleon's greatness. It is possible to analyse the organisation of the army and the basic tactical and strategic patterns which Napoleon employed and to deduce from them the essence of Napoleon's 'art of war'; but such analyses are necessarily incomplete without a consideration of the character of the architect of these armies and strategies.

Central to Napoleon's character was a burning ambition, which from Lodi at least led him to 'believe myself a superior man' and to realise that the stamp of

greatness was, indeed, upon him. This ambition led him to power, and also to exercise power exclusively, not to be shared (from possible fear of usurpation). As early as 1796 any conception of a joint command was anathema to Napoleon, it must be admitted with good reason to a degree as several times during the Revolutionary Wars disasters occurred or opportunities were lost due to the failings in collaboration between two equal commanders; 'Better one bad general than two good ones' was his remark to the Directory when it was suggested that he share the Italian command with Kellermann. This 'unity of command' gave Napoleon an immense advantage over the majority of his opponents, especially after 1800, because as head of state in addition to commanding general he had complete control over his resources and the policy of his state; whereas his opposing generals might be beset with internal conflict and dissent or suffer from the interference of their sovereigns, Napoleon's will was paramount. (For example, the presence with the Allied army at Austerlitz of both the Czar and the Roman Emperor, each with their advisers, made Kutuzov's task immeasurably more difficult.) Though Napoleon's orders might be misinterpreted or even deliberately disobeyed, in theory at least he did exactly as he wished, with no masters to be placated and no interference from equals or superiors. This immeasurable advantage was coupled with a quite ruthless intention to execute his plans no matter what the cost, whether this involved widespread executions, assassination (which is virtually all the judicial execution of the duc d'Enghien was), the mass murder of the Ottoman prisoners at Jaffa or the death of countless thousands of his followers; his remark to Metternich, even if only intended to impress, that 'a man like me troubles himself little about the

*The meeting of Napoleon (left) and the Holy Roman Emperor Francis II, 4 December 1805, two days after the Austro-Russian army had been crushed at Austerlitz. Following Napoleon's dissolution of the Holy Roman Empire in 1806, Francis II (1768-1835) took the title of Francis I of Austria.*

lives of a million men' is testimony to the single-mindedness of his drive for power.

What marks Napoleon as a unique figure is not just his political and military talent, but his application of psychology to win not only the admiration of his army, but their adoration. Successful generals are usually popular with their followers, for their success if not for their person, but Napoleon's army regarded him with reverence, a combination of father and demigod. Napoleon possessed a charismatic appeal which inspired his men and compelled their unstinting loyalty, and he exploited that appeal with the ruthlessness he applied to politics: a calculated and deliberate policy which he described as, 'If I want a man I am prepared to kiss his ****'. Despite frequent dissent from the Marshals, the reverence he inspired caused the ordinary soldiers to make super-human efforts which at times seemed to raise them above the level of ordinary mortals, and stunned his enemies into defeat so that they were, as Wellington believed, already half-beaten before a shot was fired. And yet, set against

Napoleon's undoubted ruthlessness were glimpses of a more compassionate side to his nature, as expressed by his statement that 'The sight of a battlefield, after the fight, is enough to inspire princes with a love of peace and a horror of war'; and 'the soul is oppressed to see so many sufferers.' Such finer feelings, however, were sublimated to his ambition.

Napoleon was an improviser in much of his action, building upon what he found rather than creating foundations. Thus many of the military systems and developments of the Revolutionary Wars were invaluable factors in his system of war, and were equally significant toward his manipulation of morale factors to create the army he desired. Although it is doubtful whether Napoleon's rise could have been so spectacular without a share of good fortune, the system whereby promotion was open to talent which was a unique legacy of the Revolution – matched in no other state in Europe – was of vital significance. If Napoleon himself is the greatest example of the ability of natural leaders to rise by their own skills instead of by influential con-

tacts and social background, it was of equal significance to the morale of the French army, where (in Napoleon's phrase), every soldier did, potentially at least, carry the bâton of a Marshal of France in his knapsack. The knowledge that the ordinary soldier could indeed rise to high office if he were sufficiently talented cannot but have been inspirational, and the fact that at least ten of the Marshals had risen from the ranks put on one level, in one sense at least, the private trudging through the mud with knapsack on his back with the highest princes of the Empire. The prospects of promotion were allied with a system of rewards which Napoleon exploited: 'It is with baubles that men are led' was his somewhat cynical remark. The establishment of the *Légion d'Honneur* was central

*The French army on campaign, c. 1800: a typical scene showing a cuirassier of the 8th Cavalry and a mounted carabinier in a fur cap (centre), infantry (left), light infantry (right), and a baggage-train in the background.*
*(Print by Bartsch after W. von Kobell).*

to this theory: originally intended to be a 'legion' of the 5,250 most deserving members of the Empire, the award of 'the Cross' on its scarlet ribbon was widened to such a degree that an estimated 50,000 were distributed before 1815, sometimes by the handful to units which had performed some notable deed, yet despite its lavish award it never became debased in the eyes of the army, forming an almost mystical bond between Emperor and soldiers.

In addition to the morale and psychological value of such honours, Napoleon used his own personality to enforce the Napoleonic legend. A photographic memory for faces (probably aided by surreptitious enquiries among a unit's officers) led him frequently to pick a man from the ranks, on line of march, in battle or around a campfire: 'You were with me in Italy . . . I remember you from Egypt . . . I was with you at Arcola . . . How many wounds have you suffered . . . Haven't you received the cross yet, after so many campaigns? Why didn't you remind me . . .' Every one of these encounters would be told and re-told in the bivouacs – '*He* remembered me . . .' – so that the association between Emperor and soldier was reinforced time and again, building a mystique around him that though he might be the most powerful ruler in Europe, he was 'one of us'. Those who received the ultimate mark of imperial satisfaction, a pinch on the earlobe, recounted it to their grandchildren as the greatest day of their lives, a sign of the Emperor's unfailing care for their well-being. Napoleon's critics might claim that it was nothing but a psychological trick, a cynical sham to manipulate the emotions of his subordinates; yet probably there was some degree of sincerity in it, for no man could be unmoved by the prodigies performed on his behalf, even if heroism could be expected to bring more concrete rewards than the Emperor's approbation. The financial rewards of rank were considerable, especially if (like Augereau and Soult, for example), little was allowed to stand in the way of self-enrichment by plundering. In addition to his marks of affection and pecuniary reward (such as the bestowal of pensions), Napoleon used rages and censure as a further means of motivation. Harsh words – which were known to reduce even the most stalwart veteran to tears – were not

his only weapon; physical assault with his riding-crop upon the victim's head, or even kicks in the stomach, were further tactics employed to show his displeasure, or public disgrace such as the address to two unsuccessful *Demi-brigades* in Italy. 'Soldiers, I am not satisfied with you. You have shown neither bravery, discipline, nor perseverence . . . you are not French soldiers. General, chief of staff! Let it be inscribed on their colours: "They no longer form part of the Army of Italy!"' Such a tongue-lashing and public humiliation would have as much effect in making the men improve their conduct as would fine words and signs of affection. And a few words expressing confidence, addressed to a unit before it went into action, could transform a battalion. Napoleon recalled that 'the 32nd *Demi-brigade* was prepared to die for me because I wrote to them after Lonato, "the 32nd was there; I was tranquil"'; and when in 1807 he told the 44th Line that 'your three battalions count as six in my eyes', they shouted back, 'and we shall prove it.' Napoleon's addresses might be theatrically stage-managed, but they had the desired effect, and inspired his troops to suffer unceasing privation and violent death without complaint, so long as they had breath to shout '*Vive l'Empéreur!*' The reception he was given even by regiments filled with the 16-year-old conscripts of 1813-14, the 'Marie-Louises', is eloquent proof right to the end that his skills of morale-boosting and man-management were unequalled.

Vast numbers of men were required for Napoleon's campaigns; in 1812, for example, 630,000 were mobilised against Russia and a further 250,000 were serving in Spain. Although perhaps a quarter of the army in 1805 were seasoned soldiers, as ever more were required conscription was used to fill the gaps. Based on the 1798 Conscription Laws, all men between 18 and 40 years were obliged to register, and those between 18 and 25 (later 30) were liable to be called to the colours in annual 'classes', the required number being selected by ballot (until late 1813 exemption by purchasing a 'substitute' was permitted). Classes could be called before or after their date; in 1809, for example, hitherto-unrecruited classes of 1806-07 and part of 1810 were called up as well as the 1809 class. This practice of anticipating the class led to the teenaged

conscripts of 1813-14. Rarely were the annual quotas met in full, for as military service became increasingly unpopular, desertion and non-reporting for duty (the so-called *réfractaires*) became more prevalent, and their detection became an enormous problem. From January 1791 to July 1799 the republic conscripted 1,570,000 men; from that date to the end of the Empire, Napoleon ordered the levying of 2,545,357 men, of whom around 1,350,000 were actually called up. The annual requirement depended upon the state of the wars; for example, the only levy in 1810 was 500 men of the 'class of 1809', whereas 286,307 were called in 1811 (from the classes of 1808-11) and from January 1813 to January 1814 over a million were ordered. About three-quarters of the total came from 'old France', the remainder were from the annexed territories, 'French' only in name, yet despite their origin not classed as 'foreign' or 'allied' troops; in 1812, for example, the 5th *Tirailleurs* of the Imperial Guard included natives of Genoa, Erfurt, Mayence and Amsterdam. Service was for five years, but continual wars prevented discharge, and re-enlistment was encouraged by bonuses, better pay and privileges. Despite the escalating requirements, and including the levies of 1813-14, the number of men actually serving never exceeded 41 per cent of those eligible.

The recruit received little formal training, often departing to the front within a week of being mustered. Marching to their destination in short stages, being drilled during the afternoon halts, after 50 or 60 days' marching they arrived at the battlefront reasonably disciplined, when their combat training began. 'A soldier is trained after two months campaigning,' Napoleon stated, and by dispensing with long periods of induction the army received its recruits in the most rapid time, but it eventually led to a marked decline in standards, necessitating the change from elaborate manoeuvre to advance in large masses. By 1813-14 three-quarters of the men had little military training; Col Fezensac complained of his men being 'young soldiers who had to be taught everything', and of 'non-commissioned officers who did not know much more'. That their morale remained as high as it did is tribute to Napoleon's leadership, even if they fought simply to defend themselves, 'because it was impossible to do otherwise' as one officer claimed. Discipline was maintained in many European armies by the threat of corporal and capital punishment, either formal flogging (as in the British army) or extemporised beating and punching by officers and NCOs as practised in the Russian and some German armies. Corporal punishment was abolished in the French army in 1789, and though shooting or transfer to penal units was the punishment for capital crimes, lesser offences merited only loss of rank or fatigues. Much store was laid by Napoleon on the concept of 'La Gloire' and honour; to lose face was regarded as the greatest humiliation of all, and surprisingly it seemed to work: hope of reward (promotional or financial) and a belief in honour and fame kept the men to their duty, although it should be noted that in comparison with other armies, the French were appallingly undisciplined. In comparison with the British army, for example, where looting was punishable by death or flogging, in French service it was regarded as de rigeur; indeed, the marshals and generals were often the greatest plunderers of all. The attitude that 'if you leave a house and don't take something you feel to have forgotten something' was so commonplace that the slang term for a soldier's personal kit was butin, lit. 'booty'. As so many officers had risen from the ranks, relations between the ranks were remarkably free; as early as

1796 Ney complained that 'officers mingled with soldiers and drank with them in cabarets', contrary to the maintenance of discipline; but such freedom continued throughout the Empire.

The calibre of commissioned officers declined remarkably towards the last campaigns, for despite the influx of subalterns trained at one of the military academies and schools such as the Ecole de Mars of the technical Ecole Polytechnique, casualties among officers were appalling. Between 1805 and 1815 the army suffered some 50,000 officer casualties, including 15,000 killed, of whom 34,770 were infantrymen, against only 8,073 cavalrymen. The small engineer corps alone lost 501, and the staff an amazingly high figure of 3,024. Initially, the hard core of officers were those who had learned their trade in the Royal army, or who had been commissioned in the earliest days of the Revolutionary Wars. Seniority counted for little, and if favouritism inevitably had some effect, capability was the most vital criterion for promotion; 'I cannot abide promoting a desk officer,' Napoleon remarked; 'I only like officers who make war.' From about 1809 between a quarter and a fifth of all officers were promoted from the ranks (though their chances of advancement beyond the rank of captain were not good), and with the increasing loss of officers, standards had to be lowered in order to fill the gaps. Latterly, the original two years' course at the schools

such as that established by Napoleon at Fontainebleau in 1803 and moved to St Cyr in 1808 was reduced to a few months; even the technical courses at the artillery and engineer school of the Ecole Polytechnique were cut short, as Napoleon declared there to be 'no need that these men know all about ballistics . . . all that is necessary is that they serve in the field and in the trenches.' The establishment of active-service training units (vélites) was intended to produce more candidate officers and NCOs, though the system was not universally successful (one believed his promotion blocked after laughing out loud when his sergeant was wounded!). By 1813 the calibre of officer had deteriorated so much by the inclusion of untrained cadets, recalled invalids, unsuitably-promoted NCOs and even customs officers that Napoleon complained 'These Officers are the laughing stock of their men . . . I shall have to dismiss them all and send them home.' Casualties among generals were also severe due to their practice of 'leading from the front'; at Leipzig, for example, 16 were killed and 50 wounded.

Napoleon's Marshals were the highest of his subordinate commanders, and though many were capable tacticians in their own right, Napoleon's lack of will to delegate full authority, trying to fight far-flung campaigns almost by proxy, stifled most attempts to use initiative. There were only 26 Marshals of the Empire, and of them four (Lefebvre, Kellermann, Perignon and Sérurier) were honorary appointments. The Marshalate represents in microcosm the composition of the army; whilst the majority came from backgrounds which might loosely be termed middle-class, at least seven came from poor families (Augereau, Brune, Lannes, Lefebvre, Massena, Murat and Ney) and at least ten had risen from the ranks (Augereau, Bernadotte, Jourdan, Lefebvre, Massena, Moncey, Ney, Murat, Soult and Victor). Eight had been commissioned in the royal army before the Revolution (Berthier,

*Eylau, 1807: the horrors of war are depicted in Gros' painting of a battle in which perhaps 35,000 men fell. Napoleon (centre left) orders prisoners to receive medical attention; Murat (centre right) looks on, dressed in one of his flamboyant uniforms. The Russian grenadiers wear the old-fashioned mitre caps.*

Davoût , Grouchy, Kellermann, Macdonald, Oudinot, Perignon and Sérurier), and four were of aristocratic descent (Berthier, Davoût, Grouchy and Poniatowski); their backgrounds were as diverse as Bessières, who had fought defending the King at the Tuileries, and Massena, who had been a smuggler. Not all were even French: Ney was of German descent, Macdonald Scottish, Mortier half-English and Poniatowski Polish. Relations between marshals were beset by petty jealousy and mutual antipathy, which could have dire effects upon the smooth running of a campaign; as Macdonald lamented (who himself sued Moreau for defamation!), 'What matters any detriment to the public weal, so long as private spite can be gratified.' The fates were kind to some marshals who espoused the Bourbon cause, though Bernadotte (regarded as a turncoat) was the only one to found a dynasty, as King Charles XIV of Sweden. Three were killed in battle (Bessières, Lannes and Poniatowski), Ney and Murat were executed, and two were murdered (or three if Berthier did not throw himself from a window): Brune, by a royalist mob, and Mortier, by an assassin's bomb.

The abiding memory of the Napoleonic age, however, is not with the Marshals or even the 'little corporal' himself, but with the ordinary soldier who marched and died at his Emperor's commands. They were ordinary men, but redoubtable ones; men who could say, in the darkest days of the retreat from Moscow, 'We're cooked, but *Vive l'Empéreur* all the same', or as *Tirailleur* Delvau of the Guard remarked, 'When there's no-one left but us, there'll still be plenty.' Years of campaigning brought a philosophy of acceptance: as Faré of the Old Guard said, 'Whatever they say, life is a blessing, and we have learned through resignation and hope, if not how to be happy, at least how to eat horse meat with relish'; or to quote the Belgian grenadier Scheltens on the subject of worries, 'the soldier no longer has any;

he abnegates life; he couldn't give a b--- . . .' Such resignation is epitomised by the guardsman who lost a leg to a round-shot at Eylau, and hopped away using two muskets as crutches, remarking that as he owned three pairs of boots, they would now last twice as long as he had bargained for, so it was really lucky.

In retirement, Napoleon's soldiers gradually faded away, as the proverb states, their days of fear and glory behind them. Many found the transition to civilian life painful; and many, like General Jacob-François Marulaz, an old hussar who had enlisted as a trooper before the Revolution, carried more than their memories of a lifetime's service to remind them. Old Marulaz, *beau sabreur* par excellence, continued to suffer from his 19 wounds, and when at night he would be questioned about unceasingly pacing his bedroom would answer, 'There's nothing either of us can do; it's the Waldeck Dragoons reminding me of our acquaintance.' When Marulaz died, as in so many other cases, his death was reported only briefly in the press, for old soldiers in 1842, and especially old soldiers of Napoleon's regime (not popular under royalist rule), were of low priority. 'If he had been a deputy, the Press would have given the event great publicity. But he was merely one of our

bravest soldiers, and one of the most honourable men of our old army', a man retired from active service at the age of 39, crippled by wounds and rheumatism, with a bullet lodged in his liver since 1799. Some, like the *chasseur* captain Thomas Aubry, regarded their campaigning with shame: 'Who would have thought that such a soldier, a genius . . . would have ended by betraying the trust of France . . . that . . . followed him so proudly . . . he became mad with ambition, plunging Europe in fire and blood to satisfy his despotic whims . . . How many times have we groaned, we other poor soldiers, at the sack and ruin and devastation of countries whose people were so gentle, so harmless, so happy! How much I could say of all the things that I witnessed, and all the miseries caused by the despotism of one man!' But for the majority, the memory was not of the undoubted ambition and despotism of one man and the untold misery caused by the Napoleonic Wars; they remembered instead the banners, the trumpets, the jingle of harness and flash of sunlight on sabre, the excitement of the drums beating the *pas de charge*, the strains of glory sounding down through the mists of time, the shadow of the little man in the grey overcoat and the echoing calls of *Vive l'Empéreur*!

# Napoleon and his Staff

One of Napoleon's major achievements was the ability to control and direct up to half a million men under arms, an immense task when communications generally travelled at the speed of a dispatch-rider's horse. Though its efficiency varied and problems always existed, Napoleon's headquarters was the first fully comprehensive staff system in history, an organisation of gargantuan proportions: by 1812 it numbered no fewer than 3,500 officers and more than 10,000 other ranks (including line-of-communication troops and clerical staff). Napoleon's headquarters, like the army as a whole, was not an unchanging entity; the following description of the staff system in operation is applicable to the year 1805 and after, at the zenith of Napoleon's power.

The Imperial Headquarters or *Grand-Quartier-Général* was divided into three main branches: the *Maison* or household of Napoleon's personal staff; the General Staff of the Grand Army (*Quartier-Général de la Grande Armée*);

*Marshal Louis-Alexandre Berthier (1753-1815), Napoleon's indispensable chief-of-staff. Remaining loyal to the monarchy in 1815, he fell to his death from a window after watching Allied troops marching toward France, overcome by remorse or possibly pushed. (Engraving after Gros)*

and the General Commissary of Army Stores, which overlooked all matters of provision, transportation and distribution of stores. In addition to these three main branches, a host of subsidiary staffs accompanied Imperial Headquarters: representatives of the foreign ministry, often a Secretary of State, the separate headquarters of the artillery and engineer commanders, the staff of the Imperial Guard (itself a small army in size by 1812); so that the entire staff organisation of the *Grande Armée* in 1812 might take seven days to file past a single point, despite a sensible emphasis being placed upon decentralization.

The *Maison* was the nerve-centre of the Empire, though it is not correct to credit its operation to Napoleon alone. An invaluable member was Louis-Alexandre Berthier, Prince of Neuchâtel and Wagram, Marshal, Chief of Staff and (until he relinquished the post to Clarke in 1807) Minister of War. A scion of minor nobility, Berthier had served as a staff officer to Rochambeau in the American War of Independence, and impressed Napoleon with his administrative capability from 1796, when Napoleon wrote that it was impossible to surpass him in activity, good will, courage and knowledge, an opinion only reinforced by Berthier's services as Chief of Staff until 1814. Though Napoleon sneeringly referred to him as a mere 'chief clerk', he was the man responsible for enacting Napoleon's plans. The second closest aide was Geraud Christophe Michel Duroc (1772-1813), duc de Frioul, Grand Marshal of the

Palace, who supervised the organisation of the *Maison* until his death at Bautzen; and thirdly Armand Augustin Louis de Caulaincourt (1773-1827), duc de Vicenza and Master of Horse, perhaps Napoleon's most trustworthy servant who rode at his shoulder with the appropriate map hanging from a button on his coat. After these came a host of unattached generals (capable of performing most services), aides-de-camp (almost all generals) and a huge personal staff including Napoleon's senior bodyguard, the mameluke Roustam, and the staffs of all the senior officers.

The centre of the *Maison* was the 'cabinet', the secretarial body responsible for the transmission of orders and liaison with the remainder of the *Grande Armée*, and the line of communication between Napoleon and his ministers. More significant was the *Bureau Topographique* (Topographical Office), the planning-centre of the army, run by the indispensable Louis-Albert Bacler d'Albe (1761-1824), by profession a painter, who despite lowly rank (he became a general only in 1813) was Napoleon's constant companion in the Emperor's planning sessions, responsible for the map-table which showed the situation of the campaign by coloured pins, and for keeping up to date the *carnets*. These were a series of notebooks in which was recorded, in meticulous and quite astonishing detail, every relevant fact about every regiment in Napoleon's army and all intelligence possible about his opponents; revised daily and renewed completely every fortnight, the *carnets* gave Napoleon an accurate daily situation report. Working all hours with little help, Bacler d'Albe

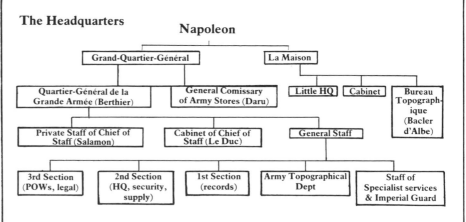

**The Headquarters**

**Napoleon**

- Grand-Quartier-Général
  - Quartier-Général de la Grande Armée (Berthier)
    - Private Staff of Chief of Staff (Salamon)
    - Cabinet of Chief of Staff (Le Duc)
    - General Staff
      - 3rd Section (POWs, legal)
      - 2nd Section (HQ, security, supply)
      - 1st Section (records)
      - Army Topographical Dept
      - Staff of Specialist services & Imperial Guard
  - General Comissary of Army Stores (Daru)
- La Maison
  - Little HQ
  - Cabinet
  - Bureau Topographique (Bacler d'Albe)

assisted by a number of generals, colonels and A.D.C.s of lower rank. The ordinary General Staff was split into three departments, though their tasks were not always defined rigidly: basically, the 1st Section was responsible for the clerical duties relative to issue of orders and maintenance of records. The 2nd arranged accommodation for the headquarters and was responsible for all matters of security, hospitals and the provision of food, the latter task in concert with the Grand Commissary of Army Stores, Pierre Bruno Daru, who maintained his own separate commissariat staff. The 3rd Section handled prisoners-of-war, conscripts and all legal matters. A fourth branch (though never officially recognised as such) was the Army Topographical Department, responsible for maps and allied matters.

'The General Staff is organized in such a manner that nothing is foreseen' Napoleon once complained; and in truth, the larger staff was an imperfect organisation, permitted no initiative, yet Napoleon was responsible for its creation. It was basically an administrative department which relieved Napoleon of the more mundane tasks; but at worst it misrepresented his orders, often with dire consequences. Though it was the weak link in the French military machine, Napoleon cannot be excused all blame, for his manner of keeping his staff in a state of constant anxiety, and of playing-off one subordinate against another, was hardly conducive to smooth and faultless operation. Even the faithful Berthier was found in tears in 1812, sobbing 'I am being killed by hard work; a mere soldier is happier than I', and whilst enjoying more familiarity with Napoleon than perhaps any other, even he was once seized by the throat and his head beaten against a wall during one of the Emperor's celebrated rages! Given the nervous strain often imposed by service on the general staff, it is perhaps surprising that the head-quarters operated as well as it did, flawed though the system was.

was of the greatest assistance to Napoleon in the planning of campaigns, but received scant reward for his invaluable services.

Whenever he commanded in battle or visited units in the field, Napoleon was accompanied by his 'little headquarters', his battle HQ of picked assistants: Chief-of-Staff, Master of Horse, the Marshal of the day (duty officer), two A.D.C.s, two orderly officers, an equerry, a page (bearing the imperial telescope), a groom, Roustam, a trooper of the escort carrying a folio of maps, and an interpreter. This small group was preceded by two orderly officers with an escort of an officer and a dozen cavalrymen, and followed by four squadrons of Guard cavalry about a thousand yards behind. Part of Caulaincourt's duties was to ensure that every formation down to Corps level maintained a relay of fresh horses so that the 'little headquarters' was always properly mounted. For longer journeys Napoleon used a light carriage, or his larger post-chaise which contained a folding bed and interior lighting, enabling it to be used as a mobile office when required.

The army staff was much less efficient than the *Maison*, curiously disunited and with inherent weaknesses such as duplication of some duties and omission of others. The staff, headed by Berthier, had but one task: to enact Napoleon's directives, with no capacity for independent action; Napoleon's authority was total, the planning and policy his alone. Berthier headed his own staff, which was divided into two offices: the Private Staff of the Chief of Staff, aided by his invaluable assistant, M. Salamon, and the Cabinet of the Chief of Staff, a dozen civilian officials headed by the Muster-Master-General, Le Duc. These bodies supervised the issue of all Napoleon's directives regarding troop-movements and operations, and were

# Administration of the Grande Armée

Napoleon inherited a system of army organisation which had originated in France with Marshal Broglie in 1761, which subdivided the army on campaign into permanent, self-contained formations. The importance of this, the 'divisional' or 'corps' system, cannot be over-emphasized in the advantage which it gave Napoleon over opponents who retained older-style organisation, though Napoleon must be credited with making great improvements and in perfecting the theory of the *corps d'armée*. Its evolution was a changing process, but the following describes the system at its most complete.

The smallest unit which could effectively act independently was the infantry battalion or cavalry regiment; but usually they acted in concert with similar formations, in the brigade. The smallest of the larger tactical formations, the brigade was composed of a number of infantry regiments or battalions (not all the battalions of a regiment necessarily served together), varying in size from two battalions up to seven or even eight; cavalry brigades normally comprised two or three regiments. The brigade was headed by a general officer, usually a *Général de Brigade*, though this term was a rank rather than an appointment: the holder of such a title might well not be in command of a brigade, and conversely the brigade might be

commanded by the senior field officer of the regiments which it comprised. The brigade possessed its own administrative staff and its commander, his personal aides-de-camp; it might have a battery of artillery attached, but transport was usually attached to the component parts of the brigade rather than to the brigade itself.

Two or more brigades combined to form the next formation in the organisational chain, the Division. Usually headed by a *Général de Division*, it had its own staff and was a more independent entity than the brigade, usually having a divisional transport train attached, and a divisional artillery reserve. (The term 'reserve' applied in this context does not imply a second-line formation or one used as a source of reinforcement, but simply an independent tactical unit not sub-divided among the component parts of the division, enabling the divisional artillery to be directed centrally by the divisional artillery commander to concentrate its fire upon any given point.) When accompanied by a unit of cavalry detached from the *corps d'armée*, the next link in the chain, an infantry division was the smallest force which could reasonably be expected to operate independently with success for more than a short period.

The *corps d'armée* was the keystone of Napoleon's military system, in effect a

complete self-contained army. It comprised two and often more infantry divisions, a cavalry division, and all the requisite supporting services, including a unit of engineers, corps transport supplementing that of the divisions, and the corps artillery reserve in which the heavier guns were usually concentrated. After the development of Napoleon's cavalry reserve, it was usual for the cavalry of a *corps d'armée* to consist of light regiments, more adept at skirmishing and scouting than the heavy cavalry, in order to provide the corps with its reconnaissance facility, massed cavalry actions involving heavier regiments usually occurring in a pitched battle when more than one *corps d'armée* was engaged. The mobile horse artillery which operated with the cavalry was attached to the cavalry division rather than part of the central corps reserve. The *corps d'armée* was usually commanded by a Marshal, with a full complement of staff to perform all the necessary clerical functions (the *corps d'armée* being an army in microcosm) as well as to maintain communication with the component divisions. The existence of the corps system permitted a great deal of strategic flexibility, for as each was a self-contained force it was perfectly feasible for a single corps to engage and contain a much superior enemy force for a short period, allowing Napoleon to

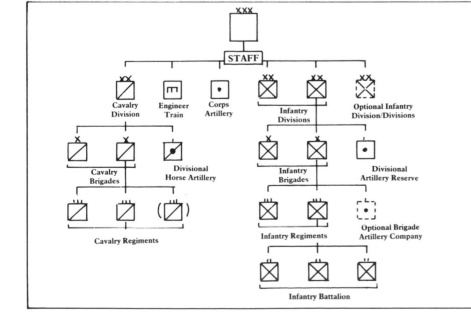

*This diagram represents the organisation of a* corps d'armée, *though it should be noted that the strength varied greatly depending upon circumstances, from fewer than 15,000 to 70,000. Commander usually a Marshal, with chief-of-staff and about 150 staff officers and ADCs. Cavalry division (average about 5,000 strong) was usually composed of 'light' regiments horse artillery normally had 6pdrs. (After 1812 many* corps d'armée *had only a single cavalry brigade). Engineers might include a pontoon-train. Corps artillery reserve had the heaviest guns, normally 12pdrs; divisional artillery usually armed with 8pdrs. Infantry divisions (typically 16,000 strong) comprised two or more brigades; one battalion in each brigade was usually light infantry.*

an abandoned
half an hour a
from loss of b
off.

The Guar
a total of 3,6!
the light inf:
one, later
Chasseurs à l
1802, the sa:
from Gar
Consulaire :
Impériale. I
were drawn
with ten
Guard Fus
late as 18
rigidly, N
or NCO 1
Old Guar
and foug
soldier m
Yet a co
most va
Guard w
to act a
remarke
them at
hundre
wreck
the dis
with ri
battle:
of the
gruml
shoul
Napo
vain
Wate
anec
com
Acc
to su
(17;
se r
not
act
res
'le
de
ep
O
th
g

I
t
l

*A general officer (centre) directing two staff officers: his adjoint or aide-de-camp (left) and an officer wearing the light blue uniform of Napoleon's officiers d'ordonnance. Although a dark blue staff uniform with gold embroidery was worn by general officers, many staff officers often wore regimental uniform.*

concentrate the remainder of his army in a flanking movement or to achieve superiority in numbers at another point in the enemy's cordon of defence. Knowing that a corps d'armée could hold its own against virtually any number of enemy troops for at least a day gave Napoleon a facility of manoeuvre not available to his opponents, and frequently the apparent weakness of a French corps d'armée tempted the enemy into rash assaults, only to discover when

committed that Napoleon's supports, initially too far away to be observed, had used the day's resistance of the corps d'armée to come into action, confounding the enemy's plans. Furthermore, the corps d'armée system allowed the army to operate in widely-spread areas, each corps being allocated its own route of march, ensuring that only one corps d'armée would have to live off the land in any given area; as each comprised all the necessary arms, any unexpected enemy attacks could be resisted until the other corps came up in support, Napoleon always arranging that corps should march at a maximum of two days' distance from each other. The corps d'armée had no fixed size but was structured according to the needs of its task, and indeed could be altered radically in mid-campaign, a device which confounded

the intelligence-gathering of the enemy, who though they might be aware of the location of a corps d'armée would have little idea as to its composition. In the 1805 campaign, for example, strengths varied from Augereau's corps of 14,000 men to Soult's 41,000.

At its inception the Grande Armée was intended to contain 200,000 men in seven corps d'armée, though a separate organisation of 'reserve' corps was also evolved. The heavier cavalry was concentrated into reserve cavalry corps (ideally with each of its divisions including a brigade of light cavalry to provide the reconnaissance and skirmishing capability), with horse artillery for fire-support. The existence of 'reserve cavalry' corps permitted the concentration on the battlefield of very much larger bodies of horsemen than was possible by the utilisation of the cavalry divisions of each corps d'armée. Similarly, a separate artillery reserve allowed the formation of huge batteries to bombard a single point in the enemy's line; and the 'Grand Reserve', in effect an élite corps d'armée (basically the Imperial Guard, sometimes with other attached élite units) provided the army's final resort.

Well though the corps d'armée system worked, it had one major weakness: with armies so huge in number and communication in the field dependent upon A.D.C.s bearing messages at the speed of a horse, their direction depended upon Napoleon's personal presence or in the capability of the Marshal in command. Unity of command, averred Napoleon, was 'the necessity of war', in which 'the commander in chief is the head . . . it was not the Roman army which conquered Gaul but Caesar.' Thus, although Napoleon issued the orders and devised the plans, he rarely encouraged subordinates to use initiative, with the result that few successful major actions were fought in which Napoleon was not present in person, or on which he exerted influence. Some of the Marshals, such as Davoût, were fine commanders in their own right; others were capable of following orders, until something untoward occurred; but none bore the mark of genius which was possessed by the Emperor. No matter how good the administration, the problem of distance and communication was insoluble even to Napoleon.

# The Ol

Napoleon's
place almos
corps d'élite
have been
deceptive;
sovereigns
usually be
leon's Gu
establishm
1814, an a
The M
was repl
number
great me
Directoir
escort fc
and 12(
with pe
after t

*Vivanc
1810.*
*who ac*
*with g*
*(carrie*
*(Prin*

*The* Premier Porte-Aigle *of the 9th Line,
of 1809-12, carrying the 'Eagle' of the
1st Bn. The flag is of 1804-pattern
(replaced by a tricolour in 1812), consisting
of a central white lozenge with red and
blue corner-triangles. The legend on one
side read*

### L'EMPÉREUR
### DES FRANÇAIS
### AU 9me RÉGIMENT
### D'INFANTERIE
### DE LIGNE

*and on the other*

### VALEUR
### ET DISCIPLINE
### 1er BATALLION

*The escorting NCOs (Deuxième and
Troisième Porte-Aigle) wore grenadier
caps.*

*Officer of the élite company of the 9th
Hussars, c 1812. The uniform is typical of
the kaleidoscope costume of the hussars,
each regiment having its own distinctive
colour-scheme. The fur cap was generally
restricted to the élite company. Despite the
rigours of campaign, such dress uniforms
were frequently worn in action, the
prevailing attitude being that 'one is never
too well-dressed when the cannon roars!'*

A Grenadier à Pied *of the Imperial Guard in campaign dress, in which blue overall-trousers usually replaced the white breeches and long gaiters. A typical* grognard *of the Old Guard, he wears the orange service-chevron on the left upper arm indicative of ten years' service. The fur cap or* bonnet à poil *was the most distinctive feature, but the 'queue' and ear-rings were similarly 'uniform' items. No official issue of canteens was ever made, each man providing his own flask or gourd.*

*The* Champ de Mars: *presentation of the 'Eagles', 1804. Napoleon, with the Marshals in court dress, holding their bâtons of office aloft, receives the salute of the 'Eagle'-bearers of the French army. The flag in the foreground is that of the 1st Line; at the extreme right is that of the 9th Line featured on the facing page. The two officers in the immediate foreground belong to the* Chasseurs à Cheval *and the* Grenadiers à Cheval (right) *of the Imperial Guard. (Painting by J. L. David.)*

*A grenadier of the French infantry, c 1812, in a typical 'campaign' uniform. The elaborate dress uniform became dishevelled and stained on campaign, when it was common (even in hot weather) to wear the greatcoat instead of the dress jacket (which was often carried in the knapsack), with the epaulettes of élite companies often transferred to the greatcoat. The shako has a waterproof oilskin cover and the tufted red pompom of the grenadiers.*

35

Light infantry musicians, c 1806. The uniform of musicians attached to companies (drummers or *voltigeur* hornists) was usually that of the ordinary soldiers with the addition of coloured lace and ornaments such as 'wings' on the shoulders; but regimental bandsmen often wore much more elaborate uniform, the only restriction on which was the amount of money available to be expended upon them, design and decoration being the responsibility of the regimental commander. The man at right wears a head-dress resembling a lancer's czapka, and a blue surtout with sky-blue facings; at left is a more 'regulation' costume, including trefoil epaulettes which were common for bandsmen. Both have the white plume of regimental staff. (Print after 'Job'.)

Napoleon's adieu to the Old Guard at Fontainebleau, 19 April 1814, following his abdication. In one of the most emotive scenes of the Empire, Napoleon took his farewell of his 'children', the Old Guard. His speech is not recorded verbatim, but it included a dramatic final gesture: 'I cannot embrace you all, but I shall embrace your general'; and, after General Petit, he kissed the 'Eagle' of the 1st Grenadiers, whose bearer, Lieut Fortin, covers his face in this painting by Horace Vernet. The officers at right are representatives of the Allied nations, considerably less affected by the scene than the Frenchmen!

prevent the flight of the companies in front.

The *ordre mixte* continued to be employed as in the Revolutionary Wars, battalions in column holding the flanks of battalions in line; sufficient space was left between battalions to allow the formation to change when required, to meet any eventuality on the battlefield; usually at least 150 yards would be left between battalions to allow each to deploy into line without impeding the neighbouring battalions. As formations became larger, *l'ordre mixte* could be employed up to divisional level, with brigades in column and others in line. Formations were so flexible that other alternatives could be utilised, for example the 'broad arrow' formations used by St. Hilaire's Division at Austerlitz, in which two 'arrowheads' were formed by the 1st and 2nd Bns 10th Light Infantry, behind each of which four line battalions were arrayed in echelon, forming a double-headed arrow-shape screened by skirmishers. With well-drilled infantry the adaptability of the system was such that at Auerstadt Morand's Division performed five separate changes of formation at the height of the battle, without ever relaxing their pressure on the enemy. As the quality of infantry deteriorated as the result of years of attritional warfare,

*'Eagle' of the 8th Line Regt, typical of the pattern carried by all line infantry. The 8th's 'Eagle' was captured by the British 87th Foot at Barrosa.*
*(Engraving after Lt. Pym, 87th)*

however, larger formations became more common, such as the massive columns used by Macdonald at Wagram and d'Erlon at Waterloo. For example, Marcognet's Division at Waterloo assembled its seven battalions in line, one behind the other, each battalion three ranks deep and four paces between battalions, giving a frontage of about 200 yards (200 men) and a depth of 21 ranks or 52 yards. Flexibility of manoeuvre was impaired greatly with such formations, and the effectiveness of infantry tactics declined as a result. (The relative merits of column and line, and the wider application of infantry tactics, are covered in pp 86-87.) As the universal defence against cavalry, infantry would form a square, in which the battalions would face outwards, presenting a rectangular formation giving a complete hedge of bayonets on all sides, virtually impervious to cavalry which could be driven off by controlled volleys of musketry. Hardly any squares were broken by cavalry during the Napoleonic Wars, and then under exceptional circumstances; but when the cavalry was accompanied by horse artillery, or when field artillery could be brought to bear upon closely-packed infantry formations, terrible losses could be inflicted. Similarly, column formations were especially vulnerable to artillery fire; whereas a roundshot passing through a battalion in line might strike down one man in each of three ranks, a roundshot striking the head of a column and passing through it could account for fifteen men or more.

Training in the infantry concentrated upon manoeuvre rather than marksmanship, which was difficult to improve given the low standard of firearm; but even the official skirmishers were given little instruction in target-practice, though *voltigeurs* often carried the lighter dragoon musket, ostensibly easier

*Field officer of the 52nd Line Regt, wearing the 1812 uniform; rank was indicated by the epaulettes, gorget at the neck and lace on the shako.*
*(Print after Détaille)*

to handle. In December 1805 Napoleon wrote that 'it is not enough that a soldier shoots, he must shoot well', but little was done to improve the standard: lack of training and the influx of constantly younger recruits caused the decline in calibre of the infantry from their peak in 1805. Allied to this was the subject of 'regimental artillery' or 'battalion guns', light fieldpieces crewed by members of the battalions intended to provide immediate fire-support, ensuring that artillery was always present when a battalion went into action. This had been a common feature of many armies in the late 18th century, but in general was found to be more of an encumbrance than an advantage; as General Lespinasse wrote in 1800, 'if you want to prevent your troops manoeuvring, embarrass them with guns', and consequently regimental artillery was generally withdrawn from the French army in 1798. However, the declining standard of infantry persuaded Napoleon to reintroduce regimental artillery in 1809, because 'The more inferior the quality of a body of troops, the more artillery it requires', as he wrote; 'Every day I become more con-

| Typical schedule of regimental weapons issued to the 14th Line, 1808-9 | | |
|---|---|---|
| **Rank** | **Number** | **Weapons** |
| **Officers** | 134 | 38 sabres, 96 épées, 9 rifled carbines (*voltigeurs*) |
| **Sergeant-Majors** | 27 | 27 sabres, 24 muskets, 3 rifled carbines (*voltigeurs*) |
| **Sergeants** | 108 | 108 sabres, 96 muskets, 12 rifled carbines (*voltigeurs*) |
| *Fourriers* | 27 | 27 sabres, 24 muskets, 3 rifled carbines (*voltigeurs*) |
| **Corporals** | 216 | 216 sabres, 192 muskets, 24 dragoon muskets (*voltigeurs*) |
| *Sapeurs* | 13 | 13 sabres, 13 fusils (light muskets) |
| **Grenadiers** | 167 | 167 sabres, 167 muskets |
| *Voltigeurs* | 241 | 241 dragoon muskets |
| **Fusiliers** | 2,307 | 2,295 muskets, 12 fusils (for musicians?) |
| **Drummers and** *voltigeur* **buglers** | 54 | 54 sabres, 54 fusils |

vinced that great damage was done to our armies by the abolition of the battalion guns.' As the 6pdrs with which the infantry had been equipped were too cumbersome to keep up with a battalion in combat, the first to be reissued were 3 and 4pdrs, enabling Napoleon to utilise many captured Austrian and Prussian guns. Initially two such guns were issued to the 1st Battalions of regiments serving in Austria (June 1809), the battalions forming three sections of 20 men, one section to man the guns and two to drive the vehicles which accompanied them. These teams were discontinued officially in April 1810, but in February 1811 the regiments of the *Corps d'Observation* of the Elbe received four guns, six caissons and eleven other vehicles, for which gun-teams were formed of 58 gunners, 54 drivers and 4 staff (including two officers). Other regiments in the 1812 Russian campaign received only two guns each, a more mixed assortment including Piedmontese pieces and even some 6pdrs. Virtually all regimental artillery was destroyed in Russia and could not be recreated.

In addition to the vehicles which served the regimental artillery and the two waggons allocated to each battalion (and cavalry regiment) for transport, an additional waggon was allowed to carry officers' baggage; though this was invariably exceeded on campaign, with enormous numbers of unofficial vehicles

accompanying and encumbering an army, both sutlers' waggons and carriages belonging to officers and camp-followers, who included a considerable number of women; 'a walking brothel' was how one French officer described the army!

A further consequence in the decline in standard of the infantry was the difficulty of replacing officer-casualties, which were probably higher than in other 'arms' due to the way in which the officers habitually led the assault: at Albuera, for example, the 34th Line lost 17 out of 23 officers present. Whereas in 1805 many regimental officers were veterans of great experience, including many who had risen from the ranks, in the later campaigns the subalterns were mostly inexperienced; a measure of the desperation with which experienced officers and N.C.O.s were sought is Napoleon's statement that he could use any pensioners from the Invalides 'whose disabilities are slight and who would serve again with good grace.' If these shortages extended even to the Guard – two N.C.O.s appointed to the 9th *Tirailleurs* had each lost an arm – the situation in the line regiments was worse. The great expansion of the Guard also served to deprive the line regiments of their most experienced men to comparatively little effect; instead of concentrating the best elements into the enormously-enlarged Imperial Guard, it

might have been of more value to allow them to continue to stiffen the line. Nevertheless, even in the dark days of 1814 morale remained remarkably high, despite the sources from which many of the newly-created regiments were drawn; for example, although some were created from odd battalions of other line regiments, and others from 'provisional' regiments of infantry, many were converted from the National Guard (135th-156th Regts), the 123rd-126th from Dutch troops, the 12th and 128th from the Hamburg and Bremen Guard, and the 129th from Westphalians.

Weapons and equipment remained reasonably standard throughout the period, though shortages were never fully overcome. The costume of the infantry altered little, the dark blue tail-

*A 'Marie-Louise', 1814: a typical teen-aged conscript in ragged campaign uniform consisting of a greatcoat and shako with 'foul-weather' cover. Such wretched uniforms were common in 1813-14.*

coat of the revolutionary armies giving way to tighter versions, and from 1812 to a short jacket with lapels closed to the waist for the first time. The main alteration in the uniform occurred when the bicorn hat was replaced by the shako in 1806, this head-dress giving additional scope for regimental distinctions in uniform, especially in the costume of the élite companies which traditionally were the most ornately-dressed. Weaponry was similar throughout the period, the main change being in the attempted withdrawal of the short sabre carried by *voltigeurs* in 1807, an order which was obeyed only partially; the weapon was retained by grenadiers, N.C.O.s and drummers throughout, but its utility in combat was minimal. The basic firearm remained the 1777-pattern musket –

*Infantry wearing the 1812 uniform including short jacket with closed lapels. In the foreground a man bites off the top of a cartridge; behind him is the 'flash in the pan' as a musket fires. (Print after Raffet)*

unofficially styled the 'Charleville' from an arsenal of its manufacture – with modifications in the Years IX and XIII of the republican calendar (1800-01, 1804-05), hence the patterns styled *An IX* and *An XIII*. Hardly any use was made of rifled muskets, despite their effectiveness in the hands of trained British and German sharpshooters; a few were issued to selected officers and N.C.O.s of *voltigeur* companies, but were withdrawn by Napoleon in 1807. Firearms were manufactured by private contractors – in all almost four million weapons during the period – but despite an annual output of muskets which rose to 125,000 in 1803, there were never enough. Purchases were made abroad, and thousands of captured weapons pressed into service (some of non-standard calibre), but the turnover was vast; for example, 12,000 muskets were lost at Austerlitz alone. By November 1813 Napoleon had to order the disarming of all the foreign contingents (save the Poles) in order to arm his

French infantry, but even this drastic measure was insufficient for the requirements. Similarly, the conscripts of 1813-14 were so short of clothing that many received nothing but a shako and a greatcoat, which they wore over their civilian clothes. As well as being defective in quantity, quality of weaponry was often not high; the gunpowder in the musket-cartridges (of which each man carried 50 in his pouch) was especially coarse, requiring the musket to be cleaned after about 50 shots. As this was not possible in the heat of battle, impromptu methods had to be used to clear the clogging, burnt powder; as drinking-water was always at a premium in battle, many resorted to urinating down the barrel as the only way of keeping their musket in operation.

*A* tête de colonne: *the* premier porte-aigle *and escort of a line regiment, wearing grenadier caps. On campaign the 'Eagle' was often carried without the flag. (Print after 'Job')*

# The Infantrie Légère

Light troops had been formed in the French army as early as 1743-44, but as in many European armies they were regarded initially as 'irregulars' and consequently were organised in a very different fashion from the line regiments, as independent volunteer corps or as part of 'legions', units which comprised both infantry and light cavalry. These multi-arm formations or *corps mixtes* were broken up in 1788, when the light infantry was put upon a 'regular' footing as twelve independent battalions of *chasseurs à pied*, each of four companies of six officers and 102 men, increasing in wartime by 21 men per company. In April 1791 the *chasseur* battalions were reorganised into eight companies each, each company of 40 *chasseurs* and six carabiniers. (As a mark of their status as the élite of the infantry, the light regiments throughout the period maintained a singular terminology: instead of fusiliers, their 'centre' companies were styled '*chasseurs*', and instead of grenadiers, the élite company were '*carabiniers*'). In April 1792 the total strength of each company was increased to 130 men, including eight *carabiniers*; having the battalion's 'élite' men split up among the *chasseur* companies appears to have been an administrative practice only; in the field it was usual for the carabiniers to be united into a special company, usually ranking as the battalion's first. At this time the number of battalions was increased to 14 by the incorporation of the old Paris National Guard.

In addition to the 'regular' light battalions, many of the provincial corps were organised as light infantry (maintaining the tradition of light troops being 'irregular', outside the line), including a number of 'legions' combining two or three 'arms'; for example, the *Légion des Allobroges*, formed in August 1792, comprised 14 companies of light infantry, three companies of dragoons and one of artillery. Most of these corps were of brief duration and had their personnel transferred elsewhere; for example, the 1st *Legion des Francs de l'Ouest*, also known as the *Légion Noire* (Black Legion), which was intended to participate in Hoche's invasion of Ireland, formed the basis of the 14th Light Infantry in 1798.

Many of the 'irregular' units were assimilated into the regular army when *demi-brigades* were formed by the *amalgame* system. By January 1794 22 *demi-brigades légères* existed, each comprising three battalions of one *carabinier* and eight *chasseur* companies each (the *carabiniers* now permanently concentrated into an élite company). Having risen to 32, the number of *demi-brigades légères* was reduced to 30 in January 1796; by September 1799 there were 26, each of four battalions, and by August 1800 30 of three battalions each, but those numbered 3, 5, 8, 16, 18, 20, 25, 26 and 29 reduced to two battalions. In August 1801 there were 31 *demi-brigades*, and as for the line they were re-titled as 'regiments', the full name '. . . *Régiment d'Infanterie Légère*' usually being contracted to '. . . *Léger*'. A number of units seem to have formed sections of scouts as early as 1801, but in March 1804 a company of *voltigeurs* was added to each battalion, each company of three officers and 120 men, with the two drummers of the ordinary companies being replaced by buglers (*cornets*), equipped with hunting-horns, which were easier to use for transmitting orders when skirmishing. Thereafter, all changes affecting line regiments applied equally to the light infantry, including the switch from nine to six-company establishment per battalion in 1808. The number of regiments increased as new units were formed (the 32nd and 33rd in 1808, the 34th from auxiliary battalions in Spain in 1811, the 35th and 36th from the Mediterranean Regt and Belle-Isle Regt respectively, and the 37th from reserve companies also in 1812).

Although, as previously noted, light

Voltigeur cornet (*bugler*) *wearing the light infantry's distinctive uniform including pointed cuffs and lapels, gaiters cut to resemble hussar boots, and blue breeches and waistcoat.*
(*Print after P. & H. Lecomte*)

---

**A *Chasseur* Battalion, 1791** comprising a staff and eight companies

**Staff:** 2 lieutenant-colonels,
1 quartermaster-treasurer,
1 *adjutant-major*,
1 surgeon-major,
1 adjutant, 1 drum-major,
1 master-tailor, 1 master-shoemaker, 1 master-armourer.

**Each company comprising:**
1 captain, 1 lieutenant,
1 *sous-lieutenant*,
1 sergeant-major,
2 sergeants, 1 *fourrier*,
4 corporals, 4 *appointés*
(junior N.C.O.s),
6 *carabiniers*, 40 *chasseurs*,
1 drummer.

In April 1792 each company was increased to a total of 130 men, including 4 sergeants, 8 corporals, 8 *appointés*, 8 *carabiniers* and 2 drummers, the remainder of the increment in *chasseurs*.

infantry tactics and skirmishing formed the keystone of the system of tactics adopted by the revolutionary armies, the role of the light infantry was much the same as that of the ordinary line regiments. Whereas in the 18th century 'line' troops were generally incapable of skirmishing and operating in 'open order' (duties which required a degree of initiative and intelligence not normally required of line infantrymen whose traditional role was to load, fire and march at the word of command like an automaton), which necessitated the light troops being specially trained for skirmish duties, in the Napoleonic armies line regiments became equally adept in tactics previously considered the preserve of the light infantry; and conversely the light regiments assimilated the discipline and steadiness of the line, so that by the early 1800s the actual difference between line and light infantry was largely one of uniform and *esprit de corps*. Throughout the period there also existed a number of smaller

'irregular' corps to supplement the regular light infantry regiments, such as the *Tirailleurs Corses* (Corsican Tirailleurs), *Tirailleurs du Po*, and 'specialist' corps such as the *Chasseurs des Montagnes* (mountain-troops used in the Peninsular War); the fact that such units and foreign corps were organised as light infantry may be a relic of the old maxim that any units outside the line organisation must of necessity be light infantry.

Although the tactical difference was slight, the light regiments were often brigaded with two or more line regiments in a manner which presumed the differences still existed, with a brigade's light infantry battalion ostensibly there to fulfil the skirmish-role, even though the line regiments might be quite capable of doing it themselves. This is evident at Austerlitz, for example, where in I Corps the two Divisions of five line regiments had the 27th *Léger* attached not as part of the ordinary brigade structure but as the Corps' 'advance-guard'. In practice it would

*Light infantry in campaign uniform, c1814, wearing greatcoats, covered shakos and full equipment, including privately-acquired water-canteens, an item not issued officially to the French army. (Print after Leopold Bayer)*

*A* Chasseur *of the 12th* Léger, *1811, a unit present at Albuera, wearing the dark blue, short-tailed light infantry jacket with green epaulettes with red 'crescents' (a distinction adopted by many light regiments) and pointed cuffs and lapels, which distinguished light infantry (though many regiments used the 'flapped' line-infantry cuff instead); collar and cuffs scarlet, and white piping. Blue breeches and waistcoat were similarly light infantry features, as were the short gaiters, which for many regiments were cut to resemble hussar boots, complete with tassels. The shako has a non-regulation (but common) eagle-on-crescent plate, white cords and a scarlet pompon with green tuft.*

seem that when the skirmishers were required light regiments often took on the duty in preference to line regiments, on account of their supposed superior training. Their equipment was like that of the line, though all companies carried sabres until they were withdrawn officially in 1807 from all except cara-

biniers, NCOs and musicians (though nonetheless continued in use with many *voltigeurs* and *chasseurs*). Where the light infantry was genuinely different was in superior *esprit de corps*; ranking senior to the line regiments, they wore more flamboyant costume, often emulating that of the light cavalry with gaiters cut to resemble hussar boots, some *voltigeurs* even wearing hussar busbies, and reflected their superior status in a dashing attitude. This air of *élan* is exemplified by Col. Pouset of the 10th *Léger* at Austerlitz, whose solution to an untenable position was to call to his superior, 'General, don't pull us back! . . . There's only one honourable way out – go bald-headed at whoever is in front of us, and above all don't give the enemy time to see just how few we are!': a successful tactic in this case. The 9th Leger, Napoleon's favourite regiment, was known as *l'Incomparable* after Marengo; near Ulm the regiment was assailed by five times its number of Austrians, and five times took and re-took Jüningen village, losing six 'Eagle' bearers in the process; as Napoleon remarked, there was nothing which could shake the regiment. Similarly, a simple carabinier sentry of the 17th *Léger* was responsible for lifting Napoleon's flagging spirits before the same battle; passing the sentry, Napoleon muttered to himself that 'Those Russian b----s think they can make us swallow anything'. 'Not on your life!' shouted the sentry to his Emperor: 'not if we have anything to do with it!'

# The Foreign Corps

A most important source of manpower for Napoleon's forces were regiments of foreign origin; in 1807 approximately one-third of his troops were foreigners, a proportion which rose to fully a half by 1812. Apart from the many contingents provided by allied and satellite states (see pp 68-77) a large number of foreign troops served in the French army itself. These may be divided into two basic categories: firstly, the inhabitants of territory which became part of metropolitan France as a result of conquest or negotiation, for example the area now occupied by Belgium, which was annexed by the French republic after it had been over-run by the revolutionary armies; and secondly the 'foreign corps' *per se*, which included regiments which might loosely be termed 'mercenary', such as the Swiss regiments which were contracted by their own states to serve in the French army. Due to the geography of the Empire, the army contained many regiments which were 'French' in name only; in 1812, for example, apart from the Polish, Dutch and Italian units in the Imperial Guard, the ordinary line included the 14th Cuirassiers and 11th Hussars (Dutch); 8th (Polish) and 9th (Hamburg) *Chevau-Légers*; 9th (part-Swiss) and 28th (Tuscan) *Chasseurs à Cheval*; 11th (Swiss and Piedmontese) and 33rd (Dutch) Light Infantry; 11th (Piedmontese), 113th (Tuscan), 123rd-126th (Dutch) and 129th (North German) Line regiments. Foreign recruits could be drafted into 'French' regiments regardless of nationality, for example the conscription of 1,000 Lithuanian peasants pressed into service during the 1812 campaign, half in the 129th Line and the remainder in the Illyrian Regt. In addition to conscriptions from occupied territory, recruits could be garnered from all sources, including the enlistment of deserters and prisoners-of-war (always a risky policy) and the taking-over of regiments from other armies, such as the Provisional Croatian Regiments formed in 1811 from border troops originally in Austrian service. Every nationality in Europe was represented: the colonel of the 'Dutch' Grenadiers of the Imperial Guard, Ralph Dundas Tindal, was Scottish!

Swiss regiments had enjoyed a long association with the French army of the Ancien Régime, and in the republican era three Helvetian *Demi-brigades* existed. Napoleon formed four Swiss infantry regiments (from troops supplied under contract by the Swiss states) in 1805-06, and wrote of 'their bravery, fidelity, and loyalty . . . it is not the number of soldiers that makes the strength of armies but their loyalty and good faith', which caused him to restrict their recruits exclusively to Swiss. Wearing the traditional Swiss red coats, the regiments consistently proved themselves second to none in the army; as Gouvion St. Cyr wrote of the retreat from Moscow, 'They were, right to the end of the retreat, invincible; they outdid nature, and they spread a radiance of heroism into this desert of snow'. In addition to the four numbered regiments of Swiss infantry were the

LEGION DE LA VISTULE
INFANTRIE 1808~1814

*Infantry of the Vistula Legion in the uniform worn during the Peninusular War and 1812 campaign, blue with yellow facings and a 'sunburst' shako-plate like that worn on a czapka.*
*(Print after 'Job'.)*

Valais Battalion (incorporated in the 11th *Léger* in 1811) and the Neuchâtel Battalion, the latter famous for the nickname 'canaries' taken from their yellow coats. A battalion of Swiss rallied to Napoleon in 1815, maintaining their tradition of sterling service.

Equally, Poland provided excellent troops to the French army, originating with the Polish Legion formed in 1799, which passed to the army of the Republic of Italy in 1802. From the remnants of these troops Napoleon formed the *Légion Polacco-Italienne* for the Westphalian army in Poland in 1807, which became the Vistula Legion in 1808, a corps of four infantry and two lancer regiments. The latter became the 7th and 8th *Chevau-Légers* in 1811, and after hard service in the Peninsula the

infantry was amalgamated into a single regiment in 1813. The most famous actions of this excellent corps were at Saragossa, where the infantry lost one-third of their number in street-fighting, and at Albuera, where the lancers annihilated Colborne's brigade.

Four numbered *Régiments étrangers* ('foreign regiments') were formed in 1811 from previously-existing foreign units: the 1st from the *Régt de la Tour d'Auvergne* (raised 1805 at Weissembourg); the 2nd from the *Régt d'Isembourg* (raised 1805); the 3rd from the Irish Legion (raised 1803) and the 4th from the *Régt de Prusse* (Prussian Regt) raised 1806. The Irish Legion or *Régiment d'Irlandaise* included a number of Irishmen who had fled after the 1798 rebellion, and some British prisoners of war from the Peninsula, though these were few in number.

Italy provided a number of regiments, including the *Légion Italique* (6,000 strong, 4 infantry battalions of 10 companies, 4 squadrons of *chasseurs à cheval* and a company of horse artillery), raised in 1799 and transferred to the army of the Cisalpine Republic in 1800; the Piedmontese Legion or *Légion du Midi* (1803-11), the light infantry corps or *Tirailleurs du Po*, the Mediterranean Regt and numerous smaller units. Corsica, Napoleon's birthplace, provided a number of light infantry corps, most famous being the *Tirailleurs Corses*, and also a *Légion Corse* and battalions of *Chasseurs Corses*. Of less value were the Spanish units, the *Régt Joseph-Napoleon* (formed from the debris of La Romana's force in Denmark) and the Spanish Pioneers. The Portuguese Legion (formed 1808 and reorganised in three infantry and one cavalry regiment in 1811) was heavily engaged in the 1812 campaign and, like the bulk of the foreign regiments, was disbanded in 1813. Greece provided such exotic units as the *Régiment Albanais* (Albanian Regt), 1807-14, which wore Balkan native costume including 'skirts'; the *Bataillon Septinsulaire* (1809-14); the Ionian *Chasseurs à Cheval*, or *Chasseurs Grecs à Cheval*; and the *Chasseurs d'Orient*, formed from Greeks and Egyptians, as was the Coptic Legion formed in Egypt. Though the quality of some 'foreign' regiments was low, their very existence represented the breadth of Napoleon's Empire.

*An officer of the* voltigeurs *of the 3rd Swiss Regt, wearing the red uniform which distinguished the Swiss regiments and the Hanoverian Legion, another 'foreign corps' raised in 1803, and reinforced by the survivors of another, the Westphalian Regt. The red uniforms caused confusion with the British redcoats in the Peninsular War, so that red-coated Frenchmen were ordered to wear their greatcoats in battle, concealing the red. The facings of the Swiss regiments were yellow (1st Regt), royal blue (2nd), black (3rd) and sky-blue (4th).*

## The Neuchâtel Battalion, 1808

**Staff:** 1 *chef de bataillon*,
1 quartermaster-treasurer,
1 *adjutant-major*,
1 recruiting-officer (lieutenant), 1 *porte-drapeau*, 1 *adjutant sous-officier*, 1 surgeon, 1 drum-major, 4 musicians,
1 master-armourer,
1 master-tailor,
1 master-shoemaker,
1 master gaiter-maker.

**Six infantry companies each comprising:**
1 captain, 1 lieutenant,
1 *sous-lieutenant*,
1 sergeant-major,
1 *fourrier*, 4 sergeants,
8 corporals, 1 *sapeur*,
2 drummers (cornets for *voltigeurs*), 140 privates.

**One artillery company:**
1 captain, 1 *adjutant sous-officier*, 1 sergeant-major,
2 sergeants, 1 *fourrier*,
4 corporals, 1 drummer,
32 gunners.

**Artillery train:**
1 *sous-lieutenant*,
1 sergeant, 2 corporals,
16 drivers.

**Engineers:**
1 lieutenant, 1 sergeant,
2 corporals, 16 *sapeurs*.

'Great battles,' wrote Napoleon, 'are won by artillery'; 'Fire is everything; the rest does not matter.' Whilst these remarks might be expected from a general whose initial training was as a gunner, they were especially true of Napoleonic armies, for whom the aggressive use of artillery was often the deciding factor. Napoleon strove continually to improve the quantity and performance of his artillery, whose personnel increased from 28,000 under the Consulate to 103,000 by 1813. The ratio of guns to men rose from two per 1,000 in 1800 to almost five per 1,000 in 1812, to compensate for the declining standard of infantry, troops of lower quality requiring more artillery support.

Requiring technical training, the artillery had not attracted many aristocratic officers under the *Ancien Régime*, and thus suffered less from emigration than any other branch of the French army. Their resulting professionalism was a major factor in the successes of the early Revolutionary Wars, and it was upon this experience that Napoleon built, aided by the earlier development of a most superior artillery by Comte Jean-Baptiste Vacquette de Gribeauval (1715-89), the 'Gribeauval System' which formed the basis of the artillery throughout the Napoleonic Wars. There were two basic types (or 'natures') of artillery: 'guns' (cannon) and howitzers. The cannon was a smooth-bored weapon which usually

fired a 'roundshot', an iron sphere varying in weight from 3lb, 12lb being the maximum weight normally used by field artillery (the French pound was approximately ¹⁄₁₀th heavier than the English). Propelled by a charge of gunpowder rammed down the muzzle of the cannon, the roundshot was a weapon capable of considerable accuracy in trained hands, most lethal when fired with a low trajectory when it would strike down anything it met until it touched the ground ('first graze') when, except on very soft terrain, it would bounce up and continue its flight. This propensity for bounce allowed artillerymen to calculate deliberately for 'ricochet', to inflict the maximum damage on the enemy. It was thus virtually impossible to fire effectively over the heads of friendly troops on the same level, which dictated the siting of artillery at intervals between units or in front of a line of battle. For close combat, cannon could fire 'canister' or 'case-shot', metal cans filled with musket-balls which ruptured upon leaving the muzzle, turning the cannon into a giant shotgun, a horrendous weapon at close range usually employed at a maximum of 300 yards, as the last resort in repelling an attack. The howitzer was a short-barrelled gun intended for high-angle fire (a weapon strangely little-regarded by Napoleon), which usually lobbed 'common shell', a hollow iron ball filled with gunpowder, ignited by a burning fuse to explode

among the enemy, fragmenting the casing. Effectiveness of shells depended largely upon the skill of the gunner in trimming the fuse (which was ignited by the explosion of the propellant charge) so that the shell exploded at exactly the correct moment.

Rate of fire and effectiveness were variable, dependent upon circumstances. Due to severe recoil, guns had to be re-aligned after every shot, the effective rate of fire being slower with heavier projectiles, two or three shots per minute being the practicable maximum. The artillerist Müller calculated an optimistic figure that a 6pdr attacked by infantry would kill 30 men and wound 90 in the time they took to charge the final 400 yards, but in practice well-handled artillery might expect to inflict one to 1½ casualties per shot fired. Actual casualties recorded range from the 400 of Lannes's troops lost at Austerlitz to 40 guns in three minutes, to four squares at Smolensk, under fire for three hours by 12 guns, suffering only 119 casualties, despite the square being the most vulnerable of all formations to artillery fire.

*Formed in April 1808, the Foot Artillery of the Imperial Guard adopted bearskin caps in May 1810. In this illustration a gunner is in process of ramming the propellant charge down the barrel of a 12pdr.*

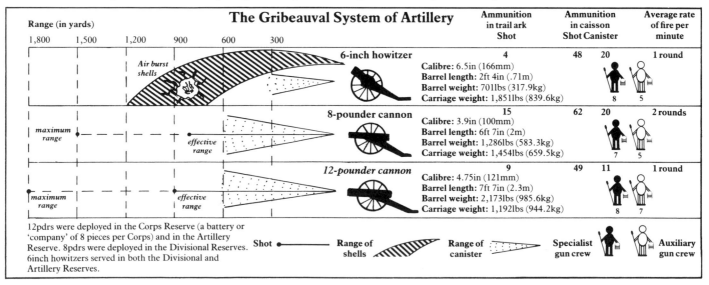

The Gribeauval System of Artillery

| Range (in yards) | | | | | | | Ammunition in trail ark – Shot | Ammunition in caisson – Shot | Canister | Average rate of fire per minute |
|---|---|---|---|---|---|---|---|---|---|---|
| 1,800 | 1,500 | 1,200 | 900 | 600 | 300 | | | | | |
| | | | **6-inch howitzer** Calibre: 6.5in (166mm) Barrel length: 2ft 4in (.71m) Barrel weight: 701lbs (317.9kg) Carriage weight: 1,851lbs (839.6kg) | | | | 4 | 48 | 20 (8 / 5) | 1 round |
| | | | **8-pounder cannon** Calibre: 3.9in (100mm) Barrel length: 6ft 7in (2m) Barrel weight: 1,286lbs (583.3kg) Carriage weight: 1,454lbs (659.5kg) | | | | 15 | 62 | 20 (7 / 5) | 2 rounds |
| | | | ***12-pounder cannon*** Calibre: 4.75in (121mm) Barrel length: 7ft 7in (2.3m) Barrel weight: 2,173lbs (985.6kg) Carriage weight: 1,192lbs (944.2kg) | | | | 9 | 49 | 11 (8 / 7) | 1 round |

*maximum range* / *effective range* / *Air burst shells*

12pdrs were deployed in the Corps Reserve (a battery or 'company' of 8 pieces per Corps) and in the Artillery Reserve. 8pdrs were deployed in the Divisional Reserves. 6inch howitzers served in both the Divisional and Artillery Reserves.

Shot ●——— Range of shells ◣ Range of canister ◁ Specialist gun crew / Auxiliary gun crew

# The Field Artillery

'Field artillery' was not a term in common use at the period, but is a convenient description to differentiate the guns generally used on campaign from those used in siege or garrison duty.

It is impossible to understate the effect of the reforms instituted by Gribeauval on the quality of the artillery which was inherited by Napoleon's army. Gribeauval redesigned all aspects of the French artillery, standardising the field-guns into 4, 8 and 12pdrs, supplemented by howitzers, all heavier pieces being relegated to siege and garrison work. New designs of the three basic types drastically reduced their weight and consequently improved mobility: by shortening barrels, introducing new methods of metal-casting, metal axles instead of wood, new patterns of carriage, wheels and limber, the weight of the heaviest field-gun, the 12pdr, was reduced from 3,200lb to 1,600lb. 'Pre-packed' (or 'fixed') ammunition (powder in a serge bag attached to the ball and a wooden *sabot* to act as 'wadding') increased the rate of fire; new gunnery tables and sights improved accuracy; and the development of the 8-gun battery and the attachment of batteries at Divisional level improved organisation and tactical efficiency.

A gun was composed of the barrel and carriage. In French service the barrel was cast in bronze (commonly called 'brass') with the centre of the tube bored out after casting; all artillery was smooth-bored. Brass guns were in one sense more unreliable than iron, for though they cracked less easily were more prone to distortion caused by repeated firing (known as 'muzzle droop') or to the widening of vents. At the sealed end of the barrel was a knob or 'cascabel' which was attached to the screw mechanism which elevated or depressed the barrel. At each side of the barrel was a projecting lug or 'trunnion' which fitted into a semi-circular depression on the wooden carriage, holding the barrel in place; in French guns there were two sets of trunnion-depressions, for the 'travelling' and 'firing' positions of the barrel, the former farther back so as to distribute the weight more evenly when the gun was on the march, though this slowed the speed at which the gun could discharge its first shot, as after unlimbering the barrel had to be manhandled into its firing-position. On top of the barrel near the cascabel was the 'vent', the hole by which a spark communicated to the gunpowder inside. The wooden 'carriage' upon which the barrel rested comprised an axle and two baulks of timber with a space in between, the so-called 'bracket trail'; the one-piece 'block trail' was not used in French service. The carriage was banded in iron to prevent it being shaken to pieces by firing, and painted an olive-green shade achieved by mixing yellow-ochre and black paint in a ratio of 80:1 (captured cannon were re-painted, though some Austrian yellow and Prussian grey-blue carriages were probably used). Each gun had a limber, a two-wheeled vehicle to which the horses were harnessed for transportation, attached to

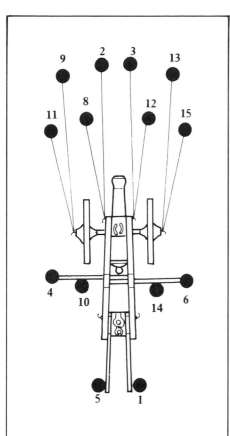

*Manhandling a cannon: advancing by* bricole. *To pull a cannon forward by hand, drag-ropes were attached to the front of the carriage and wheel-hubs and hauled by eight gunners; six more lifted the rear of the carriage by handspikes. For greater distances, the cannon could be attached to the limber by a rope* prolonge, *utilising horse-power but obviating repeated unlimbering.*

the gun by a 'pintle' which slotted through a hole in the gun-trail. The ammunition chest or *coffret* was carried on the trail, containing nine rounds for a 12pdr, 15 for an 8pdr, 18 for a 4pdr and 4 shells for a 6in howitzer; additional ammunition was carried by hand from four-wheeled ammunition-waggons or caissons, which for an 8pdr, for example, held 62 rounds of ball and 20 of canister.

The number of gun-crew varied, the heavier pieces requiring more 'servants',

*Napoleon aiming a gun at Lodi. Clearly visible is the bracket-trail of the cannon, the limber and ammunition-chest in the foreground, and the handspike used to correct the aim.*
*(Print after F. de Myrbach)*

though some of these were unskilled helpers and could be recruited *in extremis* from the nearest infantry unit; a 12pdr, for example, required 8 skilled and 7 unskilled men to work it effectively; fewer crew resulted in a lessening of the rate of fire. When the gun was unlimbered and its ammunition unpacked, it was aligned with the target by the senior gunner or 'aimer'. Traversing was done manually with 'handspikes', levers six or seven feet long inserted in bars in the trail; the barrel was elevated or depressed as necessary with the aid of a notched cross-bar sight on the gun which turned the once-haphazard gun-laying by 'naked eye' into a precise science, though the skill of the gunner was still vital in assessing the corrections needed after each shot. Before every shot the barrel was swabbed out with a wet 'sponge' (a rammer with fleece nailed on one end) to extinguish any smouldering powder from the previous shot, preventing premature firing of the next; to prevent any blow-back upon the 'spongeman', the third crew-member or 'ventsman' (who stood at the left of the breech) placed his thumb in a leather stall over the vent to stop the current of air. The 'loader', who stood at the left of the muzzle, then inserted the projectile and charge, which the 'spongeman' rammed down the barrel with the 'rammer' end of his double-headed sponge. The 'ventsman' then punctured the cartridge by inserting a wire down the vent, then plugged the vent with a quill or paper tube of gunpowder (or before about 1800 with a length of 'quick-match', cotton soaked in saltpetre and spirits of wine). The fifth gunner or 'firer' then ignited the charge by applying to the vent a lighted 'port-fire', a stick holding a length of smouldering 'slow-match'. The remaining members of the crew would then re-position the gun after recoil in preparation for the next shot.

Effectiveness of artillery-fire depended upon many variables, though numerous sets of test-data give a percentage of hits ranging from a theoretical 100 per cent at short range (450yd with roundshot) to 15 per cent at maximum range. Guns rarely fired at extreme range, gunners not wishing to waste ammunition; for the purpose of combat, 1,000yds was usually regarded as the maximum effective range for all sizes of gun: range was largely unaffected by the size of

shot, as the propellant increased to compensate for weight of ball. With case-shot or canister (which existed in two varieties, 'light' and 'heavy', the latter often mis-titled 'grapeshot'), Müller recorded tests which showed 55 hits per round at 200yds, 36 at 400yds and 6 with 'heavy case' at 600yds; 'light case' seems to have been fired at under 250yds, 'heavy' 250-500yds and roundshot (or shells for howitzers) at over 500yds.

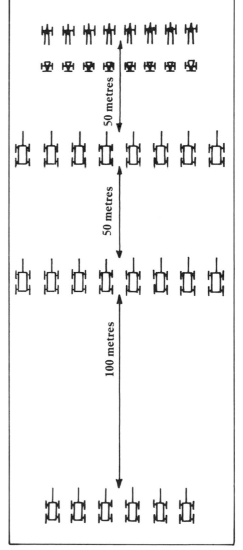

*A battery in action. The guns and limbers were positioned some 50 metres from the first row of caissons, one per gun, where ammunition was ferried by hand. 50 metres further back was a second row of caissons, which were driven forward when the first-line caissons were empty. 100 metres further back were the other battery vehicles.*

50 metres

50 metres

100 metres

Napoleon determined to improve the basic 'Gribeauval' artillery, Marmont's artillery committee producing the 'System of Year XI' (1803), but its recommendations were slow in introduction and though the *Grande Armée* in 1812 was equipped in the new manner, the forces in Spain continued to use pure Gribeauval ordnance. The main alteration was in the increasing of 12pdrs at the expense of the 8pdrs, and in replacing the 4pdr and some 8pdrs with a new 6pdr, intending a compromise between the hitting-power of the 8pdr and the mobility of the 4pdr; but the 6pdr was

*French gunners and Artillery Train attacked by Prussian cavalry at Hanau, 1813. The drivers of the* Train d'Artillerie *wore sky-blue or iron-grey uniforms faced dark blue. (Print after R. Knötel)*

inferior in design with a carriage which tended to shake to pieces, and was finally abandoned for the previous Gribeauval system which was re-introduced in 1818. New howitzers (24pdrs instead of 6in) were only a limited improvement. (Not only was hitting-power and mobility considered: one reason for discontinuing the 4pdr was that its noise was not suffi-

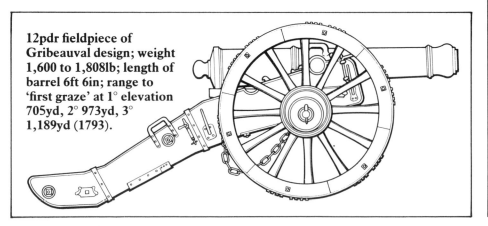

**12pdr fieldpiece of Gribeauval design; weight 1,600 to 1,808lb; length of barrel 6ft 6in; range to 'first graze' at 1° elevation 705yd, 2° 973yd, 3° 1,189yd (1793).**

---

### Foot Artillery of the Imperial Guard, 1808
comprising a staff, six artillery companies and one of pontooners

**Staff:** 1 major-commandant, 2 *chefs de bataillon*, 1 *capitaine-adjutant-major*, 2 *lieutenants-sous-adjutants-majors*.

**Each artillery company:** 1 captain-commandant, 1 2nd-captain, 1 1st-lieutenant, 1 2nd-lieutenant, 1 sergeant-major, 4 sergeants, 1 *fourrier*, 4 corporals, 4 artificiers, 20 gunners 1st class, 48 2nd class, 2 drummers.

**Pontooneer company:** 4 officers as artillery company, 4 master-artisans (corporals), 20 artisans 1st class, 24 2nd class, 24 apprentices, 2 drummers, 6 NCOs as artillery.

ciently demoralizing to the enemy, whereas the boom of the 12pdr was!) A further impetus for the introduction of the 6pdr was that it would utilise large numbers of captured ordnance; in 1807, for example, 42 out of 48 guns in Soult's Corps were of Austrian origin.

With the 4pdrs largely withdrawn or relegated to regimental artillery, the 6 and 8pdrs were normally allocated at brigade or divisional level, with the 12pdrs mostly in corps and army artillery reserves. Although Napoleon almost achieved his target of five guns per thousand men, this calculation included regimental pieces of limited value; in practice his greatest artillery power was assembled at Leipzig, where he fielded 600 guns (three per thousand); but even then was out-gunned by the Allies, who had 900: French armies rarely achieved numerical superiority of artillery on the

*A gunner of Foot Artillery wearing 1812-pattern uniform, blue with red facings, characterised by lapels closed to the waist; with the combined sponge-and-rammer used by the 'spongeman' of each gun crew.*

battlefield.

The gunners who manned the field artillery were members of the regiments of *Artillerie à Pied*. In 1791 there existed seven regiments, each of two battalions and a headquarters, each battalion composed of ten companies, regimental strength totalling 90 officers and 1,207 men, increased by an additional 400 men in wartime, and each regiment with its own depot and artillery school. Part of the artillery (but not employed in manning guns) were pontooneers and companies of *ouvriers* (artisans). Although organised in regiments, the basic unit was the company (or 'battery', though the latter term was not commonly used at the time), which invariably served independently, not in a regimental formation. At the end of 1799 the field artillery comprised a staff of 226 officers (not attached to regiments), 8 horse regiments, 8 foot regiments of 20 companies and 1,888 men each, two pontooner battalions and 12 *ouvrier* companies. A typical foot company comprised 1 1st-captain, 1 2nd-captain, 1 1st-lieutenant, 1 2nd-lieutenant, 1 sergeant-major, 4 sergeants, 1 *fourrier*, 4 corporals, 34 gunners 1st class, 43 2nd class and 2 drummers. Although a 9th Regt was formed in 1810 (from the Foot Artillery of the Kingdom of Holland), increases in strength were normally achieved by adding extra companies to the existing regiments (28 each by 1813) rather than creating new regiments. The eight-gun company remained the standard unit, usually consisting of six cannon and two howitzers. For each 12pdr and howitzer there were three caissons and two for lighter guns (many more caissons were present in the 'reserve parks' for re-supply), which when the other battery vehicles were included (spare gun-carriage, mobile forge, tool-cart and perhaps caissons with infantry ammunition) gave a total of around 30 vehicles with 140 horses. Each company was divided into four 'sections', each of which manned two guns (guns normally operated in pairs), plus a company of drivers. Guard and heavier batteries had even more vehicles, normally carrying

double ammunition. The Imperial Guard Foot Artillery was formed in 1808, six companies strong, which was added to the Guard Horse Artillery already existing, and was expanded rapidly so that the number of Guard guns rose from 96 in May 1811 to 196 in April 1813, with Young Guard companies formed from 1809 to bring the total to 22 Guard Foot companies. The available 12pdrs were concentrated into the Guard artillery park, so that it became the most powerful of all artillery units and was used as the army reserve.

Certain basic tenets governed the deployment of artillery; paramount was to site the guns as well as possible to give the best field of fire and maximum protection to the crew, ideally on the crest of a ridge with the caissons shielded from the enemy by the reverse slope. Stony ground was avoided, as the landing of the enemy's shot would throw up splinters and rocks, though 'counter-battery fire' (artillery firing upon artillery) was rare; the enemy's troops were a more practical target. The guns would be unlimbered in their firing-positions, with the limbers nearby (all vehicles faced to the rear). Operating in pairs, guns would rarely be deployed in a straight line to minimise the effect of enfilade fire (i.e. from the flanks) so that no more than one team would be hit by each bouncing round-shot. Batteries rarely fired in salvo, but each gun of a pair would discharge alternately, ensuring no hiatus in the battery's fire. The first line of caissons would be sited some 50yds behind the guns, a second line a further 50yds, and the spare caissons and other vehicles 100yds further, with ammunition ferried to the firing-line as required. If over-run by the enemy, the last resort was to 'spike' the guns by driving a nail into the vent, rendering the piece inoperable.

A contemporary maxim declared that the fire of a large battery was more effective than the sum of its parts, so in the later campaigns the artillery reserve (usually the Guard) was employed to concentrate its fire on critical points of the enemy line, which could decide a battle unaided; 80 to 100 pieces assembled in a 'massed battery' was a most formidable weapon, but Napoleon's shortage of guns never enabled him to utilise more than one such battery at a time on any battlefield.

# The Horse Artillery and Artillery Train

The concept of horse artillery was tried experimentally in the French army in the late 1770's, and in 1791 General Mathieu Dumas formed two 'flying batteries' at Metz, mobile artillery in which the gunners rode on caissons in the Austrian style. In the following year, three companies of true horse artillery (with all gunners mounted on horseback) were formed for each of the armies of the North, Centre and Rhine, manned by instructors from the Foot Artillery and rank and file from grenadier companies: consequently most were poor riders, but due to insufficient mounts all but one company in each army continued to ride on caissons.

The new army fought well at Jemappes and in 1794 the horse artillery – newly-styled as 'Light Artillery' – was increased to a strength of nine regiments of six batteries each, each with six or eight guns, often 8pdrs plus a light howitzer. Personnel remained a problem: most officers were cavalrymen, with scant knowledge of artillery, and the other ranks became known for quarrelling as much for their great fighting skills. The superior *esprit de corps* engendered by these élite formations was itself dangerous: in 1797 at Kehl, for example, a horse battery refused to construct defensive works to protect themselves ('We are horse artillery, meant to fight in the open field'), and were almost annihilated as a result.

In 1801 the number of regiments was reduced to six, a 7th Regiment being formed in 1810 by the incorporation of the horse artillery of the Kingdom of Holland, though the new unit was soon absorbed into the 1st and 4th Regts. Each regiment had three squadrons of two companies (or batteries) each, plus a depot company; and from August 1813 the 1st to 3rd Regts had a seventh field company. The Horse Artillery of the Imperial Guard originated in December 1799 with the formation as part of the Consular Guard of a company of *Artillerie Légère* (light artillery), 110 strong, manning eight guns. The unit was enlarged in March 1802 to a headquarters and two companies, each of 4 officers and 85 other ranks, reorganised into three 'divisions' in November 1803, each with two 6pdrs, two 12pdrs, two 6in howitzers and 20 vehicles (with a reserve of 25 vehicles). In April 1806 the corps was re-designated as *Artillerie à Cheval*, three squadrons of two companies each, each company of 97 men crewing four 4pdrs and two howitzers. The creation of the Guard Foot Artillery in April 1808 led to the reduction of the Horse Artillery to two squadrons of two companies each, which organisation remained unchanged until March 1813 when a third squadron was added, followed by a Young Guard company at the end of the year. For the 1815 campaign four companies were formed, each of six guns.

The tactical employment of horse artillery took advantage of their greatest asset, mobility, and for this reason it was usual for horse artillery companies to be attached to cavalry formations, to provide fire-support for charges, when the horse artillery could gallop quickly to within close range of the enemy: Murat's great charge at Borodino, for example, was accompanied by 100 horse artillery guns. Each company was equipped usually with four guns (generally 6pdrs) and two howitzers, though variations existed. At Jena, for example, the 3rd company of the 6th Horse Artillery crewed two 4pdrs and two 6in howitzers, and the 4th company of the same regiment had but four 3pdrs. The main reason for their ability for rapid deployment was not simply that the gunners were all mounted and the guns comparatively light; equally significant in the earlier years was the fact that from its inception all drivers of horse batteries were military personnel, which was not the case with the Foot Artillery, who until 1800 had to rely most unsatisfactorily upon civilian carters to drive the limbers and caissons.

Being employees of civilian contractors, such artillery drivers were not subject to military discipline and frequently were neglected by both military and civil authorities; ill-equipped and sometimes even left without rations, they declared in 1796 that although they were prepared to risk their lives in the service of the nation, they would prefer to be gaoled rather than continue under so wretched a system! Consequences of the lack of military control over these drivers were evident at Valmy, where the explosion of two caissons caused many drivers to flee, taking their horses with them. On the battlefield, though the drivers did come under fire, it was usual for all except horse batteries to unlimber out of the enemy's range and for the gunners to drag their cannon into position by hand (by *bricole*: dragropes), severely impairing their ability both to manoeuvre and to get their guns into action. To emulate the horse batteries, who could drive right up to the enemy before unlimbering, in 1800 at the suggestion of Marmont (who carried through most artillery reforms at Napoleon's behest) the artillery drivers were 'militarized', enlisted in the army

---

### A Horse Artillery Regiment, 1807
Comprising a staff plus three squadrons of two companies each, plus a depot company

**Staff:** 1 colonel, 1 major, 2 *chefs d'escadron*, 1 quartermaster-treasurer, 1 *adjutant-major*, 1 surgeon, 1 assistant-surgeon, 1 *adjutant sous-officier*, 1 veterinarian, 1 corporal-trumpeter, 4 master-artisans.

**Each company comprising:**
    1 captain-commandant, 1 2nd-captain, 1 1st lieutenant, 2 2nd lieutenants, 1 *maréchal-des-logis-chef*, 4 *maréchaux-des-logis*, 1 *fourrier*, 4 *brigadiers*, 4 artificiers, 1 master-ironworker, 4 ironworkers, 4 woodworkers, 2 trumpeters, 24 1st class gunners and between 45 and 60 2nd class gunners.

---

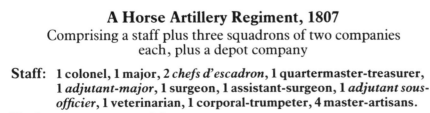

*Artillery in action in support of hussars crossing a river under fire from the Austrians at Dierhoff (18 April 1797), including a limbered gun-team about to cross the river. (Print after Coginet & Giradet.)*

and equipped at the state's expense (having previously been uniformed by their civilian employers). This change of status, wrote Marmont, 'had the happiest influence on the mobilities of batteries and their rates of fire', as gun-teams could now be driven directly to the positions in which they were to open fire, permitting the aggressive use of artillery such as Sénarmont's 'charge' at Friedland, in which he advanced by bounds until engaging the Russians almost point-blank.

Initially, eight battalions of *Train d'Artillerie* (Artillery Train) were formed, comprising a staff (captain-commandant, lieutenant and quarter-master) and five companies, each of 1 maréchal-des-logis-chef, 2 maréchaux-des-logis, 4 corporals and 60 men (80 in élite companies). The battalions never served en masse, but companies were separated and attached to individual artillery batteries, which explains the small number of commissioned officers in each battalion, the NCOs and men of the Train companies being commanded by the officers of the battery to which they were attached; originally, in each Train battalion one company was designated élite and was attached to horse artillery. By 1801 the battalions were enlarged to six companies each, each now comprising two officers and 76 men (with élite companies discontinued). The expansion of the corps was rapid: 10 battalions existed in 1804, 11 in 1805 and 13 in 1808, and in 1810 all were 'doubled', a wartime expedient by which each formed the cadre of two battalions, the newly-formed ones receiving 'bis' numbers (e.g. '10 bis'); and a 14th Bn was formed in Holland, making a total of 27 battalions. The expansion often exceeded resources, so that many were short of vehicles and horses, especially the 'bis' battalions. Upon the Bourbon Restoration in 1814 the Train was reduced to four squadrons, each of 15 officers, 271 men and 120 horses, increased to eight for the 1815 campaign.

The Consular Guard first raised its Artillery Train in September 1800, a single company which was increased to two in June 1802, and four in November 1803. In April 1806 it achieved battalion status by an increase to six companies, plus a depot battalion added in October 1807. The Guard's '*bataillon bis*', formed at the end of 1807, was transformed into the 13th line battn. in 1808. Three more Guard companies were added in October 1809, and in February 1813 the unit was reorganised as a regiment of three battalions, each of four companies; a fourth battalion, formed in March 1813, became the 1st Battalion of a new 2nd Guard Regiment in April 1813. For the 1815 campaign, the Guard *Train d'Artillerie* comprised a squadron of nine companies, one of which was designated as 'Young Guard'.

# The Siege Artillery

Protracted sieges of fortified places did not readily fit into Napoleon's scheme of rapid manoeuvre and the destruction of the enemy's field army; believing sieges unnecessarily time-consuming and wasteful of resources he was only directly concerned with four: Toulon, the citadel of Milan, Mantua and Acre, and indirectly with several more such as Danzig and Königsberg, though there were several in the Peninsular War in which French armies were concerned, such as Saragossa, Almeida and Gerona. Some sieges might better be termed 'blockades', in which the garrison was isolated in the hopes of being starved into submission, and others were even less closely-invested by troops who merely maintained a watch upon the garrison to warn of any breakout. A true siege, however, involved the bombarding of the *enceinte* (main outer wall) until a practicable breach was made, whereupon the garrison would be called upon to surrender, and if they refused be subjected to an assault, usually horrendously expensive to the attacker and catastrophic for the inhabitants of the defended city as storming-parties were traditionally allowed to plunder all who dwelt inside.

For a full siege, the most important factor was artillery of sufficient power to break down the *enceinte*, though unlike the armies of the early and mid-18th century those of the Napoleonic era were often poorly equipped with siege artillery. The very weight of the heaviest pieces meant that the siege-train (or 'battering-train') was the slowest-moving element of an army, and required a vast quantity of supporting services and ammunition. An army advancing at normal speed would thus out-march its siege-guns, and in retreat risked losing the entire train. Although guns capable of throwing enormous projectiles (42pdrs and 32pdrs) were sometimes utilised for sieges, Gribeauval retained the 'natures' of the earlier Vallière system for regular siege use, 24 and 16pdrs. The vast weight of these is evident from their specifications: whereas a brass 12pdr for field use had a length of 6ft 6in and a weight of 1,808 (French) pounds, a 24pdr siege gun was almost 10ft long and weighed 5,628lb; the 16pdr was only four inches shorter and weighed 4,111lb. The 24pdr was a formidable weapon, however, the British engineer Jones writing that its effectiveness when compared with the 18pdr (i.e. like a French 16pdr) 'is far greater than would be conceived . . . no engineer should ever be satisfied with 18 pounder guns when he can by any means procure 24 pounders.' Such huge pieces of ordnance had a very slow rate of fire.

Ordnance used almost exclusively for siege warfare were mortars, which resembled wide-mouthed howitzers and were restricted to high-angle fire with explosive shells, and were thus used for damaging the inside of a besieged fortress rather than against its walls. The barrels were affixed to wooden 'beds' without wheels, of the most sturdy construction, as the high angle of fire meant that the recoil had to be absorbed by the 'bed' and the ground beneath it, which would have destroyed an axle; mortars were transported on flat, wheeled carts and could only be unloaded by means of a 'gin', a legged structure with a block-and-tackle at the top. Elevation was by means of a wooden chock or quoin inserted underneath the front of the barrel, but it was usual for barrels to be angled permanently at 45° and variations in range achieved by varying the quantity of gunpowder used in the propellant charge; for example, a French 12in mortar (the diameter of its tube) with a charge of 1lb of powder threw its projectile 388yd at 45° elevation. With a charge of 3lb 8oz the range increased to 1,390yd. The usual shell (or mortar-bomb) was an iron sphere filled with powder and sealed with a tapered wooden fuze, similar to a howitzer-shell but usually with a thicker base to ensure that it landed fuze-uppermost and thus was not extinguished before it could explode; the effect of such projectile dropping almost vertically from their high trajectory upon a building could be startling, such as that which exploded the Almeida magazine. Bags of stones could be fired from mortars as anti-personnel devices, the guns designed for this service being termed 'stone mortars' or 'perriers'. Other projectiles of use almost exclusively in siege warfare were incendiary shells or 'carcasses', shells or tarred canvas bags filled with combustible mixture which was almost impossible to extinguish, for example 'Valenciennes composition' (50 parts saltpetre, 28 sulphur, 18 antimony and 6 pitch). For illumination (such as

*The bombardment of Lille, September 1792. A number of significant sieges occurred during the Revolutionary Wars; in this illustration Austrian heavy mortars are in action, protected by earth-filled wicker baskets or gabions. (Print after Bertoux).*

the discovery of a night assault or sally by a besieged garrison) 'light balls' were used, an iron framework covered with painted fabric and filled with a mixture of salpetre, mealed powder, sulphur, resin and linseed oil. There were also smaller mortars (light enough to be carried by two men) known by the generic term 'Coehorn' (or 'Coehoorn') after its designer. Napoleon retained Gribeauval's 12 and 18in mortars, but replaced the 10 and 6in.

There were no special corps organised to man the siege-train, ordinary foot artillery units being employed. For example, at Almeida in 1810 the siege-

*French guns in siege-position at Frankfurt, October 1792. Siege-batteries were always protected by field-fortifications, earthworks and gabions or sandbags, or in this case a 'blind' of brushwood erected to screen the gunners from enemy view. (Print after H. Lecomte)*

---

**A typical force of siege artillery was that present at the second siege of Saragossa:**

**Siege-train:**
    Staff: 16 officers
    3 coys, 3rd Foot Artillery
        13 officers 219 men
    3 coys, 6th Foot Artillery
        9 officers 176 men
    2nd coy, Pontooneers
        2 officers 69 men
    2nd coy, Artillery artisans
        2 officers 29 men
    1 coy, 6th *bis* bn Train
        2 officers 23 men

**Field Artillery from 3rd & 5th Corps:**
    Staff: 28 officers
    2 coys, 1st Foot Artillery
        4 officers 174 men
    4 coys, 3rd Foot Artillery
        5 officers 174 men
    5 coys, 5th Foot Artillery
        10 officers 325 men
    1 coy, 6th Foot Artillery
        1 officer 85 men
    1 coy, 5th Horse Artillery
        2 officers 69 men
    1 coy, 6th Horse Artillery
        3 officers 62 men
    4th coy, 1st Pontooneers
        2 officers 71 men
    2 coys, Artillery artisans
        1 officer 36 men
    3 coys, Guard Artillery Train
        3 officers 196 men
    18 coys, Artillery Train
        16 officers 1,209 men

---

train commanded by General Ruty comprised one company of the 1st Foot Artillery and two each from the 5th, 6th, 7th and 8th, with elements of seven battalions of artillery train, two artillery artisan companies, one company of pontooneers, one provisional pioneer company and one company of artillery train artisans; supplemented by field artillery including two companies of the 3rd Foot, one of the 1st, one company each from the 2nd and 5th Horse Artillery, two artisan companies and twelve artillery train companies, giving a grand total of 3,124 men (plus 27 staff officers) and 3,222 horses. The amount of ammunition expended in a regular siege could be equally vast; the British breaching-batteries at Badajos in 1812, for example, used 2,423 barrels of powder (227,070lb) and 31,861 roundshot, not including shells.

A siege was opened when the first trenches were dug, the 'parallels' (so called by being parallel to the *enceinte*) connected by the 'traverse' or zigzag saps; as the siege progressed 'parallels' were dug progressively nearer the defences, and the breaching-batteries (always 'dug in' to protect the gunners from the fortress's fire) closer to the walls. At the opening of a siege it was reckoned that each siege-gun should fire 5 rounds per day, with reduced propellant; later 20 rounds; and finally, when the breach was becoming evident, 60 rounds per day

with full charge (½ the weight of the shot); mortars should fire 20 shells per day throughout, and five light-balls per mortar every night. This vast amount of shot would beat down almost any defence (though was least effective against earthen fortifications which absorbed the shot), and would in theory persuade the garrison to capitulate rather than risk the horrors of a storm, the aftermath of which would be as costly to the defenders as the assault would be to the attackers. But with rapidly-moving armies of the types favoured by Napoleon, in which the field batteries might have to double as siege artillery, the field guns very likely would be insufficient for the task; for example, the medieval walls of Smolensk proved almost impervious to the fire of 12pdrs directed against them in 1812. With the vast amount of time and material expenditure necessitated by a siege, it is not surprising that Napoleon preferred not to employ siege-artillery but either isolate the garrison or, *in extremis*, launch an immediate assault despite the cost, such as that which captured Ratisbon in 1809.

# Chapter Three: THE CAVALRY

Unquestionably the most impressive element of Napoleon's army, the cavalry was the 'arm' in which Napoleon made the greatest improvements, for prior to about 1796 French cavalry regiments were in general greatly inferior to those of their opponents. The emigration of aristocratic officers which denuded the cavalry of leadership, the lack of time available to train recruits (cavalry training was naturally more extensive than that for any other 'arm') and the difficulty of procuring suitable mounts all contributed toward a general decline in quality following the revolution. Yet certain of the French regiment retained their *esprit de corps* and individual characteristics largely unbroken from the days of the monarchy.

Napoleon maintained a strict division between the various classifications of cavalry, each having its specialist role. Some of these were similar to the formations which existed prior to the revolution, but the distinctions were refined in the Napoleonic system. The keystone of the theory of employment of all classes of cavalry was Napoleon's belief that well-drilled horsemen were vital for the successful prosecution of a campaign: 'Cavalry is useful before, during and after the battle;' '. . . it is impossible to fight anything but a defensive war, based on field fortification and natural obstacles, unless one has practically achieved parity with the enemy

cavalry; for if you lose a battle, your army will be lost.' A vital role of cavalry, Napoleon believed, was 'shock' action: charges to hammer through the enemy line and to pursue a retiring opponent, but executed above all with discipline so that charges would not lose control and undo the initial successes; but, wrote Napoleon, 'Cavalry needs audacity and practice; above all it must not be dominated by the spirit of conservatism or avarice.' To execute the 'shock action' Napoleon perfected his heavy cavalry arm, primarily cuirassiers, powerful men on large horses, protected by iron body-armour and helmets, which were developed into the offensive force *par excellence* from the regiments which had existed in the revolutionary armies under the simple title 'Cavalerie'. The evolution of such regiments was accompanied by the consequent re-structuring of the field organisation, the heavy cavalry being concentrated into autonomous divisions, generally in corps of 'reserve cavalry', which enabled them to be assembled on the battlefield to act in huge, compact and most formidable masses. The rigorous standards applied to the cuirassiers, however, presented great administrative difficulties as the problems of finding suitable replacements and especially remounts of the requisite size were enormous.

The second category of Napoleon's cavalry were the dragoons, originally

mounted infantry but used increasingly as 'heavies', whilst retaining their capacity for fighting on foot. It may be argued whether the classification 'medium cavalry' ever existed, but although the dragoons were often used in a 'heavy' role, their unique capabilities separated them from the 'heavy' cavalry *per se*.

Numerically the largest and unquestionably the most dashing of the cavalry were the light regiments, *chasseurs à cheval*, hussars and later *chevau-légers-lanciers* (lancers). They were quite capable of executing the charge in a general engagement, yet their particular skills were directed towards acting independently, providing the reconnaissance facility for the army, raiding the enemy, serving as the army's advance-guard, rear-guard, protecting the flanks, communications and, most significantly, screening from enemy view the size and movements of the army. At the close of a major battle the light regiments would either skirmish with the enemy's advance-guard to cover the retreat of the French, or (more usually in the days of Napoleon's glory) be launched towards the retreating enemy, preventing him from re-forming, over-running his baggage, harrassing his rear-guard and destroying his morale. Such actions could in themselves have the greatest strategic effect, turning retirements into routs; as Napoleon remarked, 'After Jena, the light cavalry capitalized the victory all on its own,' capturing fortresses as well as rounding-up thousands of dispirited, straggling Prussian troops. The facility for independent action had an effect on the light cavalry's self-perception and esprit de corps; always the most gorgeously-dressed, they cultivated a swagger and bravado matching their heroism in battle. It is little coincidence that the most dashing of Napoleon's cavalry generals were originally light cavalrymen.

*Typical of the magnificent appearance of Napoleon's cavalry were the 2nd (Dutch) Chevau-Légers-Lanciers of the Imperial Guard, the so-called 'red lancers', from their scarlet uniforms.*
*(Print after Lalauze)*

---

### Typical organization of an army's cavalry: Massena's 'Army of Portugal', 1 January 1811

**Cavalry Brigade attached to 2nd Corps (General P. Soult):**
1st Hussars, 22nd Chasseurs, 8th Dragoons,
Hanoverian Chasseurs — 92 officers 1,048 men

**Cavalry Brigade attached to 6th Corps (General Lamotte):**
3rd Hussars, 15th Chasseurs — 48 officers 604 men

**Cavalry Division attached to 8th Corps (General St. Croix):**
Two sqdns each of 1st, 2nd, 4th, 9th, 14th
and 26th Dragoons — 86 officers 895 men

**Cavalry Reserve (General Montbrun):**
Brigade Lorcet: 3rd and 6th Dragoons — 51 officers 793 men
Brigade Cavrois: 11th Dragoons — 28 officers 557 men
Brigade Ornano: 15th and 25th Dragoons — 57 officers 1,178 men
Attached horse artillery — 4 officers 162 men
Headquarters: Gendarmerie — 7 officers 190 men

# The Cuirassiers

The cuirassiers originated with the 'heavy' regiments of the revolutionary wars, of which there were 25 in 1791, rising to 29 in 1793, and reverting to 25 in September 1799. Originally each regiment comprised three squadrons of two companies each, each company of 4 officers and 63 other ranks, plus a staff, giving a regimental total of 28 officers and 411 men, with 420 horses. Strength was increased in 1794 to 4 squadrons of two companies, but in 1796 the previous establishment was re-introduced, though with a higher strength of 24 officers and 507 men. These regiments were styled simply 'Cavalerie'; the transition to cuirassiers went hand-in-hand with the theory of accumulating large masses of cavalry in 'reserves' or autonomous divisions, capable of delivering a massed charge, instead of distributing heavy cavalry regiments piecemeal throughout the army.

Cuirasses (iron breast- and back-plates) had been common in the earlier 18th century, but had become redundant in many armies, their great weight requiring horses and men of exceptional strength, counter-acting their value in a cavalry mêlée in deflecting the sword-blows of the enemy. The only regiment to wear cuirasses originally, the 8th (styled 'Cavalerie-Cuirassiers', was used as a model, and in 1801 the 1st Regt was equipped similarly, at which time the 24th was amalgamated with the 1st. It was from this date that the cuirassiers began to be regarded as the élite of the cavalry, and thus the order which established an élite company in all cavalry regiments (corresponding to grenadiers in the infantry) did not apply to cuirassiers. As more regiments were converted to cuirassiers (and again increased to four squadrons) the number of Cavalerie regiments was reduced, the disbanded regiments providing the extra (fourth) squadrons. In October 1802 the 2nd, 3rd and 4th regiments were converted and the 25th disbanded; in December the 5th, 6th and 7th, with the 19th-23rd disbanded. In 1803 there existed eight cuirassier regiments (1st-8th) and 10 Cavalerie (9th-18th), and in September of that year the 9th-12th inclusive were converted to cuirassiers and the remainder to dragoons, giving a cuirassier arm

of twelve regiments. In 1806 each regiment comprised a staff and four squadrons of two companies each, with a total strength of 820 men and 831 horses; from October 1806 each added a fifth squadron before embarking on campaign, and on 10 March 1807 the five-squadron establishment was confirmed, regimental strength thus increased to 41 officers and 999 men. At the end of 1809 strength was again reduced to four squadrons of 240 men each. In addition to the twelve original regiments, a number of 'provisional' cuirassier regiments existed, two being formed in Spain from detachments of other units; from late 1808 one of these was taken into the line with the number 13, and the 14th Regt was converted in 1810 from the 2nd Cuirassiers of the army of the Kingdom of Holland. A 15th Regt existed briefly in 1814, formed from the depots of the first four regiments. At the Restoration the number of regiments was again reduced to twelve.

In addition to body-armour, cuirassiers wore an iron helmet with brass comb, supporting a horsehair mane; weaponry included pistols, ultimately

carbines, and principally the straight-bladed sabre designed for the thrust, the most lethal blow which could be delivered (light cavalry sabres with curved blades were designed for the cut or slash). Cavalry combat was decided by hand-to-hand fighting (unless the very sight of a cavalry charge caused one side to retire before blows were exchanged), and in such fights the advantage of the defensive armour of the cuirassiers was remarked upon, especially when opposed by unarmoured horsemen or those (like Austrian cuirassiers) who had no back-protection; at Eckmühl, for example, in a mêlée involving cuirassiers from both sides, the proportion of Austrian killed and wounded amounted to thirteen and eight respectively for each French casualty. Similarly, at Borodino the French Col Combe noted that the backless Russian cuirasses allowed the French 'to do great execution by thrusting at them as they fled.' The

*The massed charges at Waterloo were among the most spectacular but least effective actions of the French heavy cavalry; this illustration provides a dramatic but somewhat inaccurate view of cavalry attacking a British square. (Print after François Flameng)*

## A Cuirassier Regiment, 31 August 1806

Comprising a staff and four squadrons, each of two companies:

**Staff:** 1 colonel, 1 major, 2 adjutants-majors, 1 quartermaster, 1 surgeon-major and 3 assistants, 2 *adjutants-sous-officiers*, 1 corporal-trumpeter, 1 veterinarian, 1 tailor, 1 saddler, 1 breeches-maker, 1 boot-maker and 1 armourer.

**Each company:**
1 captain, 1 lieutenant, 1 *sous-lieutenant*, 1 *maréchal-des-logis-chef*, 4 *maréchaux-des-logis*, 1 *fourrier*, 8 brigadiers, 82 troopers, 1 trumpeter.

**Total strength 820 men and 831 horses.**

*A trooper of the 7th Cuirassiers in campaign dress, c 1812, the most visually formidable of all Napoleon's troops. The uniform was dark blue with regimentally-coloured facings (yellow for the 7th Regt); the large, stiff-topped boots were protection for the knees when charging in close formation. The 14th Regt wore their white ex-Dutch uniform for a period, and the 13th had makeshift brown coats made from local Spanish cloth.*

great weight of armour, however, had its disadvantages; unhorsed cuirassiers had difficulty recovering their feet on heavy ground, and the equipment necessitated both large men and powerful horses, replacements for which were difficult to find at times, though large numbers of captured steeds were pressed into service, large Prussian mounts being especially valuable to supplement the large Norman horses usually used. The large horses were comparatively slow, however, so that some charges (especially towards the end of an action) were actually executed at a trot rather than at full gallop *à l'outrance*. Their merit, however, was fully recognised by Napoleon, who wrote that 'Cuirassiers are more useful than any other cavalry' as a '*masse de decision*': a force which could win a battle on its own. To this end, cuirassiers were almost invariably brigaded into heavy divisions, stationed with the reserve cavalry, for use *en masse* in charges of enormous size, when they presented perhaps the most formidable appearance of any military formation. Only exceptional troops or bad tactics could cause them to fail, as proven by the gallant but unavailing mass charges at Waterloo, during which campaign 12 regiments served, concentrated in the 3rd and 4th Cavalry Corps.

In addition to the cuirassiers there existed two other regiments of armoured heavy cavalry, the Carabiniers, who wore *Cavalerie* uniform plus fur caps until 1809, when they adopted spectacular white uniforms and copper-brass combed helmets and cuirasses. They ranked as the senior regiments of line cavalry, but their organisation and function was exactly that of cuirassiers, and despite their title, their carbines were withdrawn in 1810.

# The Hussars

Of all Napoleon's regiments, it may truly be said that the hussars were less of an organisation than an attitude of mind. The 'hussar mentality', sustained by the most glamorous of all Napoleonic uniforms, incorporated a love of fighting (duelling if no battle were imminent!), women, horses, alcohol and tobacco, resulting in exceptional bravery and a professionalism which belied their outward air of swagger and braggadocio. Hussars were originally Hungarian irregular light horse (the name a Hungarian adaption of the Italian *corsaro*, a freebooter), whose tactics and costume were copied by many armies from the mid-18th century, hence the widespread use of garments originally of Hungarian 'native' origin, fur caps and fur-trimmed over-jackets or pelisses, which added to the distinctive and ferocious appearance of the typical hussar, cultivated by the regiments which encouraged such individuality. It even spread to their style of hair-dressing, fierce moustaches, 'queues' (pigtails) and *cadenettes* (braids at the temples) being jealously-guarded regimental distinctions; recruits too young to grow moustaches painted them on in burnt cork until able to produce the real thing!

Baron de Marbot described his troop-sergeant, Pertelay, who epitomises the genus: a 'typical hussar of the old school was a hard drinker, a brawler, always ready for a quarrel and a fight; brave, moreover, to the point of rashness. He was absolutely ignorant of everything that did not concern his horse, his accoutrements, or his service in the field . . . a jolly ruffian . . . with his shako over his ear, his sabre training, his florid countenance divided by an enormous scar, moustaches half a foot long waxed and turned up to his ears, on his temples two long locks of hair plaited, which came from under his shako and fell onto his breast, and withal such an air! – a regular rowdy air, heightened still further by his words, jerked out in the most barbarous French – Alsatian gibberish . . .' Within this regiment (the 1st Hussars, the old Bercheny Regt of the *Ancien Régime*) was an even wilder group, 'the gang', 'the most reckless and the bravest soldiers of the regiment' who addressed each other as 'joker' (*loustic*)

and were recognised by a notch cut in the top right-hand button of their jacket. Cliques of this nature, and the general attitude pervading the hussar organisation, produced the most audacious cavalry in Europe, governed by the mores which led the greatest hussar, Comte Antoine Charles Louis Lasalle, to remark, 'any hussar who isn't dead by thirty is a blackguard.'

Six regiments of hussars were in existence at the outbreak of the French Revolution, of which one (the Régt de Saxe) defected to the enemy in 1792; and in addition to the regular regiments there existed a number of smaller volunteer corps who styled themselves hussars, partly because they were light cavalry and partly, no doubt, to emulate the reputation of their more senior colleagues. Some of these units bore evocative titles reflecting their republican political sentiments, such as the *Hussards de la Liberté* (Liberty Hussars) and *Hussards de la Morte* (Death Hussars), the latter unit suitably clad in black and decorated with death's-head badges. Some of these corps were transformed into regular hussar regiments, increasing the establishment to 14 regiments by 1795, numbered 1–13 plus the '7 *bis*' regiment ('7 again' or '7½ regiment'). Of these, the first five were the original regular regiments of the

| **A Hussar Regiment** | |
|---|---|
| **1791:** | staff and four squadrons, each squadron of two companies, organised as *Cavalerie* at this time: regimental strength 36 officers, 544 men, 556 horses. |
| **1793:** | enlarged to 6 squadrons per regiment. |
| **1796:** | reduced to 4 squadrons; strength now 38 officers, 903 men, 935 horses. |
| **1807:** | still four squadrons of 2 companies each; staff 7 officers, 12 men; each company 4 officers, 124 men, 129 horses; regimental strength 43 officers, 1,000 men, 1,055 horses; senior company designated 'elite'. |
| **1814:** | staff 8 officers, 12 men; each company 4 officers, 74 men, 63 horses; regimental strength 40 officers, 604 men, 527 horses. |

*Hussars attempt, with characteristic ardour but without success, to penetrate British infantry formations at Fuentes de Oñoro (1811) in which battle the 1st, 3rd and 5th Hussars served. (Print after A. Dupray)*

*Ancien Régime*, the 6th was formed from a unit styled 'Defenders of Liberty and Equality', the 7th from Lamothe's Hussars, the 7th *bis* and 9th from the Liberty Hussars, the 8th from the *Eclaireurs de Fabrefonds* ('Col. Fabrefond's Scouts'), the 10th from the Death or Black Hussars, the 11th from the 24th *Chasseurs*, the 12th from the *Hussards de la Montagne* and the 13th from the *Hussards des Alpes*. The 13th Hussars were disbanded in 1796, and in 1803 the 7 *bis*, 11th and 12th were converted to the 28th–30th Dragoons, leaving ten hussar regiments. In 1810 a new 11th Regt was formed from the 2nd Hussars of the Kingdom of Holland and in 1811 a 9 *bis* (provisional) regiment in Spain, renumbered as the 12th in 1813, when the 13th and 14th regiments were also formed. (Two regiments bore the number 13 at this period: one of short duration, replaced by the French hussar regiment 'Jerome-Napoleon' of the Westphalian Guard.)

The tactical role of hussars was that of the other light cavalry, although (they would have averred) executed with a greater degree of audacity. Their existence was nomadic; as they said, when the village children learn your name, it's time to move on!. Though especially adept at reconnaissance, skirmishing (firing their short carbines from the saddle) and providing the army's cavalry 'screen', they were equally capable of executing the charge in battle (especially as the hussars claimed to be the best swordsmen in Europe!). The most astonishing exploits, however, were those performed when they had the opportunity of acting independently of the main army, such as Lasalle's pursuit of the Prussians after Jena with his famous *Brigade Infernale* ('Hellish Brigade'), the 5th and 7th Hussars. Harrying the Prussians unmercifully, Lasalle and his 700 men arrived before the garrison of Stettin on 30 October

*Trooper, 1st Hussars, campaign uniform, 1814, wearing the cylindrical* rouleau *shako which replaced the broad-topped version from 1812. The 1st Regiment wore sky-blue uniform with scarlet facings and white braid, without the pelisse in summer, which was carried in the valise at the rear of the saddle; in winter it was worn as a jacket, over the dolman. Fur caps were worn by élite companies.*

1806, a fortress of immense strength containing 120 cannon and 6,000 Prussian troops. With no means of mounting an attack or imposing a siege, Lasalle calmly demanded that the governor surrender or take the consequences of an assault and pillage. Stettin surrendered! If that were typical hussar audacity (Lasalle's reputation as a *beau sabreur* concealed the fact that he was a superbly professional general), then his comments were equally typical of the hussar philosophy: 'What's the point of living? To earn a reputation, get ahead, make your fortune? Well, I'm a General of

Division at 33, and last year the Emperor gave me an income of 50,000 francs . . . to have achieved it, that's satisfaction enough. I love battles, being in the noise, the smoke, the movement; so long as you've made your name, and you know your wife and children won't want for anything, that's all that matters . . . I'm ready to die tomorrow.' Shortly after, on the evening of 6 June 1809, at Wagram, Lasalle led a squadron in pursuit of a unit of Hungarian infantry. Hit between the eyes by a musket-ball, he was killed instantly, having exceeded by four years his stated maximum age for a true hussar.

# The Lancers and Chasseurs à Cheval

The *Chasseurs à Cheval* formed the largest element of the light cavalry, the ordinary line regiments which, like the hussars, were the army's reconnaissance force, cavalry skirmishers, those who provided the security-screens for advances or withdrawals, and the fast-moving pursuit squadrons who exploited a victory or break in the enemy forces. In tactical ability they were identical to the hussars, though were less impressively costumed and generally lacked the air of bravado which was possessed by the hussars; in effect, they were the solid and reliable element of the light cavalry, though were not without élan and audacity in action, and doubtless regarded themselves as equal to the more flamboyant hussars with whom they were often brigaded. Their disposition was as usual for light cavalry: generally allocated not to the 'reserve cavalry' corps which were concentrated for 'shock' action, but serving with the ordinary *corps d'armée* as either a 'corps reserve' or in smaller formations attached as divisional cavalry, to enable these formations to have a proficient mounted contingent capable of performing all the necessary cavalry duties in the field.

In 1791 there existed 12 regiments of *Chasseurs à Cheval*, each of 4 squadrons of 2 companies each plus a staff; throughout the period, organisation and establishment of the light regiments were like those of the hussars. In December 1792 three new regiments were created, and in 1793 eight more, from previous irregular corps of cavalry (including the 13th regt from the *Légion des Americains et du Midi*, 14th *Hussards des Alpes* and others, 15th *Chasseurs de Beysser*, 16th *Chasseurs Normands*, 17th *Chevau-Légers de West-Flandre*, 18th 1st *Chevau-Légers Belges* and Brussels Dragoons, 19th the *Légion de Rosenthal* and 20th *Légion du Centre*). The Belgian 17th and 18th were disbanded in 1794 (the numbers remaining vacant), and one

new regiment was formed, taking the number of regiments to 22, numbered 1 to 24. Regimental strength in 1796 stood at 38 officers and 903 men, with 935 horses. There also existed a short-lived organisation of 'legions' established in the west, one legion in each of the departments of Ille-et-Vilaine, Loire-Inférieure, Maine-et-Loire, Mayenne, Morbihan, Orne and Sarthe; each consisted of a light infantry battalion of one *carabinier*, one *sapeur* and 6 fusilier companies (each of 150 men) and a company of 124 *chasseurs à cheval*, a tem-

porary reversion to the old practice of combining light cavalry and infantry within the same unit.

In 1801 there were 24 *chasseur à cheval* regiments, numbered 1 to 26. The next additions to the *chasseurs* were made in May 1808, when the Belgian *Chevau-Légers d'Arenberg* were taken into the line as the 27th Regt, and the Tuscan Dragoons formed into the 28th *Chasseurs* at the same date. In August 1808 the 29th *Chasseurs* was formed from the 3rd Provisional Light Cavalry Regt (organised in Spain from small detachments), and in February 1811 new 17th and 18th regiments were organised at Lille and Metz, and the 30th Regt was created in

*A trooper of the 8th* Chevau-Léger Lanciers *in winter uniform, c1813. The 8th wore the blue uniform and* czapka *of the 'Polish' regiments, with yellow facings; the grey caped cloak illustrated here had facing-coloured lining. (Print after V. Chelminski.)*

Hamburg from the old Hanoverian Legion and other Germans. The final regiment of *Chasseurs* was created in September 1811, when the 1st and 2nd Provisional Light regiments were formed into the 31st *Chasseurs*. The *Chasseurs* wore green uniforms with the ubiquitous shako, though a number adopted items of hussar uniform to compete with their more colourfully-dressed comrades; the 27th, for example, wore full hussar dress for a period, and the 30th during their brief tenure as *Chasseurs* wore a mixture of garments, including much red cloth originally destined for the Hamburg Dragoons, hence their nickname of 'red lancers of Hamburg'. Items of hussar uniform, including fur busbies, were also adopted by the élite company of each regiment (designated as such from late 1803), who also wore red epaulettes like grenadiers as a mark of their status.

Equipment was that of the hussars, with the curved sabre being the principal weapon, though considerable use was made of the short carbines with which the *chasseurs* were armed for skirmishing. These were fired from horseback, and could even be used to greater effect on the battlefield, as evidenced by the 20th *Chasseurs* at Eylau, who were 'charged' by a body of Russian dragoons. Because of the driving snow and soft ground the Russians were unable to proceed at more than a walk, so instead of meeting the

charge in motion (the usual practice) the 20th stood their ground and volley-fired their carbines from the saddle, which destroyed the Russian leading rank, before engaging with the sabre.

Lances were a particularly Polish weapon, and had been used in small numbers by Polish troops who fought with France as early as the Revolutionary Wars; but only with the formation of the Vistula Legion did the French army possess its own corps of lancers. Following the proof of its tactical advantages, Napoleon created his own lancer 'arm', the first line regiment to be equipped with lances being the 30th *Chasseurs* who, for a brief time, were termed *Chasseur-lanciers*. In June 1811 the 1st, 3rd, 8th, 9th, 10th and 29th Dragoons were converted to six regiments of *Chevau-Légers Lanciers* ('light-horse lancers') numbered 1 to 6 and classified as 'French'; to which three 'Polish' regiments were added (numbered 7-9) by the conversion of the two regiments of Vistula Legion lancers and the 30th *Chasseurs*. The 'French' regiments wore green uniform and a brass dragoon helmet (with the horsehair mane replaced by a bearskin crest), and the 'Polish' regiments blue, with the traditional Polish *czapka* head-dress. The lance was a weapon requiring some skill to use, but in trained hands was a most lethal tool, especially in the first 'shock' of a charge against other cavalry, in pursuit, and even more against infantry. Proof is provided by the destruction of Colborne's brigade at Albuera when, hidden by smoke and a hailstorm, the 1st Vistula Lancers and the 2nd Hussars (800 strong) burst upon four British infantry battalions which were advancing in line, without time to form square to repel the cavalry. Infantry were at a tremendous disadvantage in such circumstances with ordinary cavalry, but with lancers (who could spear the infantry without ever coming within bayonet-range) they had no chance. One battalion, the furthest from the impact, was able to form square and save itself, but the other three were ridden-down in moments: the 1/3rd Foot lost 643 men out of 755; the 2/48th 343 out of 452; and the 2/66th 272 from 441. Survivors later reported the particular ferocity of the Poles, who gave no quarter; it was the most devastating destruction of infantry by cavalry in the entire Napoleonic Wars. Similarly,

Chasseurs à cheval, *c1807, wearing dark green uniform with regimental facings. Hussar items are evident in the fur busby and* sabretache *of the élite company man (right) and the braided waistcoat of the central figure. The red epaulettes are further distinctions of élite status.* (*Print after Berka.*)

lancers were the only cavalry who could hope to break an infantry square, but only if the weather was so wet as to prevent the infantry from firing. In close combat with cavalry, however, the lance could prove a hindrance, as a British officer noted during a fight with the German *Lanciers de Berg* in 1811: 'They looked well, and were formidable till they were broken and closed with by our men, and then the lances proved an encumbrance: they caught in the appointments of other men and actually pulled them off their horses.' The lancers were originally intended to serve as the light troops of the heavy cavalry corps, but were employed thus only in 1812.

In addition to the line lancer regiments there existed units of *Lanciers-Gendarmes* who served in the Peninsular War, part of the mixed cavalry and infantry *Gendarmerie* formed for anti-guerrilla and security duties in Spain, composed of veterans and organised (by late 1812) in six 'legions', totalling 20 squadrons. They were employed as *bona fide* cavalry and fought with great distinction, losing a total of 831 killed and 1,078 wounded.

---

**Allocation of cavalry**

The typical disposition of light and heavy regiments according to their capabilities is demonstrated by the organisation of the *Grande Armée* in 1812; numerals in parentheses indicate the number of squadrons

**Reserve Cavalry Corps:**

**I Corps**
  **1st Heavy Div: cuirassiers (12), lancers (3)**
  **5th Heavy Div: cuirassiers (12), lancers (3)**
  **1st Light Div: hussars (12), lancers (12), chasseurs (4)**

**II Corps**
  **2nd Heavy Div: cuirassiers (12), lancers (3)**
  **4th Heavy Div: carabiniers (8), cuirassiers (4), lancers (3)**
  **2nd Light Div: hussars (11), chasseurs (4), lancers (4)**

# The Dragoons

Dragoons originated in the 17th century as mounted infantry, soldiers who rode into battle and then dismounted to fight on foot. By the beginning of the Napoleonic Wars, almost all the dragoons in Europe had been transformed from this role into cavalry proper, with no greater capabilities of fighting on foot than those of other types of cavalry. The French dragoons, however, maintained an element of their historic origin whilst forming a major part of the cavalry as a whole. In this sense they were the most adaptable of Napoleon's horsemen and are sometimes described as 'medium' cavalry, though certainly from 1805 should be classed with the heavy cavalry rather than the light, able to execute equally the 'shock' of the charge as well as serve on the detached duty associated with the light cavalry. The most numerous of all the types of cavalry, the dragoons were also the most valuable, versatile and by 1813 probably of the highest calibre.

At the beginning of the Revolutionary Wars there were 18 regiments of dragoons, a number increased during the next decade as the value of the arm was realised: three regiments (numbered 19 to 21) were formed from volunteer corps in 1793, and in 1803 the 22nd to 27th Dragoons were converted from the old line cavalry regiments 13 to 18, with the 28th to 30th Dragoons converted from the 7th *bis*, 11th and 12th hussars. These thirty regiments served throughout the Napoleonic Wars, and saw extensive service in all theatres.

In 1791 each dragoon regiment comprised three squadrons, increased by 1798 to four squadrons with an overall establishment of 943 men. In 1803 the establishment of a regiment reflected the intended tactical use of dragoon regiments, by combining mounted and dismounted companies within the same squadron; from that date, each regiment comprised a staff (10 officers and 10 NCOs) and four squadrons, each of two mounted companies and two dismounted.

*A trooper of the 3rd Dragoons brandishing a captured British infantry Colour: a hypothetical scene, although this regiment did serve in Spain in 1808-11. (Print published by Pierre Martinet c.1810)*

The mounted companies comprised 3 officers, 12 NCOs, a trumpeter and 54 troopers, and dismounted companies 1 officer, 3 NCOs, a drummer and 26 troopers; thus the theoretical strength of each squadron stood at 8 officers and 194 other ranks, and each regiment at 32 officers and 776 other ranks, plus staff. This organisation varied: in 1805, for example, 24 regiments were organised in

three mounted and one dismounted squadron. The purpose of the dismounted companies was not to serve with their regiments in line-of-battle, but to add flexibility for detached service and principally to provide combined units of dismounted dragoons, such as the four regiments of *Dragons à Pied* organised in 1805, each regiment comprising a staff and two battalions of six companies each. These battalions were formed from the dismounted companies of the dragoon regiments; for example in

1806 the 1st Bn 1st *Dragons à Pied* (formed at Mayence by Dorsenne) was drawn from the 2nd, 14th, 20th and 26th Dragoons. On these occasions the dragoons carried infantry equipment and wore infantry gaiters, though all dragoons habitually carried muskets (and usually bayonets) to enable them to fight as infantry even when officially mounted. (The firearm used was the 'Dragoon musket', shorter than the infantry pattern, for greater convenience when carried on horseback, but much longer and more effective than the short-range carbine of other cavalry; they also carried pistols and the straight-bladed sabre of the heavy cavalry). The concept of 'infantry dragoons' was disliked by both officers and men and in 1807 a new organisation was introduced, by which each regiment comprised four squadrons of two companies each, each company of 4 officers and 123 men, all mounted (when there were sufficient horses). Regiments were sometimes expanded to five squadrons, giving a grand total of some 1,200 men. Though increasingly used as 'heavy' cavalry – whose major tactic was the charge *à l'outrance* – the dragoons remained invaluable for detached service, protecting lines of communication, providing flank-guards, conducting couriers, escorting transport and still (especially in the Peninsular War) serving as mounted infantry when required.

Proof of the utility of the dragoons is the fact that for the invasion of Russia in 1812, only four complete regiments could be spared, forming the 6th Heavy Cavalry Division; plus a composite regiment formed in four squadrons whose eight companies were provided by the 2nd, 5th, 12th, 13th, 14th, 17th 19th and 20th Regts., which served as the cavalry of Augereau's XI Corps. In the Peninsular War (a campaign especially suited for the dragoons' capabilities, especially in anti-guerrilla operations when a combined infantry/cavalry role was invaluable), they formed the backbone of the French cavalry service, despite suffering at times from inferior mounts. At Vittoria, for example, dragoons represented over 55 per cent of the total Franco-Spanish cavalry.

*Dragoons were instantly recognisable by their green uniform (usually with facing-coloured lapels, though the Peninsular War trooper illustrated here wears the single-breasted, plain surtout popular on campaign), and especially by their brass helmets, which resulted in the nickname 'golden heads' bestowed upon them by the Spaniards. The 19th Regt, shown here, had yellow facings and piping.*

---

### Dragoon Regiment, 1807
Comprising a staff and four squadrons of two companies each

**Staff:** 1 colonel, 1 major, 2 *chefs d'escadron*, 2 *adjutants-majors*, 1 quartermaster-treasurer, 1 surgeon-major 2 assistant-surgeons, 2 *adjutant sous-officiers*, 1 veterinarian, 1 corporal-trumpeter and 5 master artisans.

**Each company comprising:** 1 captain, 1 lieutenant, 2 *sous-lieutenants*, 1 *maréchal-des-logis-chef*, 4 *maréchaux-des-logis*, 8 *brigadiers*, 2 trumpeters and 108 dragoons.

# Chapter Four: TRANSPORT AND SUPPLY

'An army marches on its stomach' is perhaps the most famous of Napoleon's maxims; yet for many of his campaigns, the commissariat arrangements of the French armies were extremely bad, and to the very end of the Napoleonic Wars French soldiers had, to a considerable extent, to rely upon their own ingenuity to feed themselves.

From the early Revolutionary Wars, foraging was the hallmark of French armies: 'living off the land' by the forcible requisition of food and forage, instead of the established practice of supplying the army by waggon-train drawing upon storage depots. Foraging was initially adopted as a necessity, it being impossible to supply the hugely-expanded armies by conventional means; and the result was of great strategic importance, as it released the army from the stricture of supply depots. Thus, in the operations leading to Valmy, the Prussian army halted regularly for bread to be baked, and then renewed operations only until another baking-halt; whilst the French (though they were usually hungry) could manoeuvre at will. This system allowed Napoleon to neglect temporary breaks in lines of communication which, allied to increased mobility, formed the foundation of his system of warfare. Although by 1805 the Empire *could* have fed all its troops, normally only between four and seven days' rations were carried with an army, for issue when the enemy was in such close proximity as to preclude foraging.

Counter-acting this freedom of manoeuvre were strictures imposed by barren country, the movements of an army often being decided by the amount of provisions which could be garnered, and usually requiring wide dispersal: as Napoleon wrote, 'We must separate to live and unite to fight'. Commanders were often prevented by the spectre of starvation from manoeuvring where they desired, as late as 1812 Marmont reported to Napoleon, 'If the army marches against Rodrigo now we should not be able to stay there for three days for lack of food. We should achieve nothing as the enemy knows we cannot stay there.' Foraging served to impair discipline and damaged relations with occupied territories; and in inhospitable terrain, especially during the Eylau campaign when the condition of the roads prevented the issue even of what supplies were available, the army starved. As Napoleon wrote, '. . . the fate of Europe hinges on the question of food. If only I had bread, it would be child's play to beat the Russians . . .'; and this experience led him to make a thorough overhaul of the transport system.

Napoleon had not neglected his commissariat, but often made arrangements for the establishment of magazines from which supplies could be drawn (he was especially concerned with the provision of adequate footwear); but even where these depots existed, the perennial problem was distribution. A system of waggon-supply was already in existence, but the waggons, horses and carters were civilian, hired from civil contractors, whose personnel were reviled by the army, who bestowed upon them such sobriquets as 'Royal Cart Grease'. The system was especially prone to corruption (which was severe enough within the army itself), and eventually broke down entirely. The Breidt Company, which provided most of the army's transport, was castigated by Napoleon: 'It would be difficult to organise something worse . . . a band of rascals who do nothing and it is better to have no one at all than bother with such people'. After the débâcle of the Eylau campaign, Napoleon took over the waggons of the Breidt Company and militarized the supply service by the formation of the *Train des Equipages* (Equipment Train), initially eight battalions of four companies and approximately 140 waggons each. This organisation was expanded so that 13 battalions of six companies existed by 1810, with nine more raised in 1812, plus two provisional battalions in Spain and a light battalion of pack-mules, but even in these numbers the Train was inadequate for the task in hand, and the loss of almost all the army's transport in Russia in 1812 compounded the problem (after the Russian campaign the Train was reorganised into nine battalions, to which three more were added). Usually, four waggons from each company were allocated to ambulance work, the remainder being allotted to individual units (two waggons per infantry battalion or cavalry regiment), to provide a shuttle between the unit and supply-depot; or to a centralized Train under the aegis of army headquarters to carry reserve rations or munitions.

Although Intendant-General Daru (responsible for the army's logistic support) was a gifted administrator, and no matter how assiduous were the commissaries he commanded, there was always insufficient transport to move the vast amount of food and ammunition required. Despite Napoleon's constant concern over the feeding and equipping of his men, the problem of distribution was never solved; his cry to Daru in 1813 was one heard throughout the era: 'The army is not being fed. It would be an illusion to regard matters otherwise . . .'.

*The Imperial Guard had its own* Train des Equipages *battalion, wearing sky-blue uniform with dark blue facings; the line Train wore iron-grey with brown facings. (Print after Berka, c1810).*

---

**Organisation of A Battalion of *Train des Equipages* in 1807:**

**Staff:** 1 captain-commandant, 1 lieutenant *adjoint adjutant-major*,
1 quarter-master (*sous-lieutenant*), 1 surgeon-major, 1 veterinarian
(ranking as *maréchal-des-logis-chef*), 1 *maréchal-des-logis*,
2 *fourriers*, 1 trumpet-master, 1 master-saddler, 1 master-farrier,
1 master-wheelwright, 1 master-tailor, 1 master-bootmaker.

**Four companies, each comprising:**
1 *sous-lieutenant*, 1 *maréchal-des-logis-chef*, 2 *maréchaux-des-logis*,
4 *brigadiers*, 1 trumpeter, 80 privates, 1 harness-maker, 2 farriers
and 1 wheel-wright. Each company was equipped with 34 caissons,
1 forage-waggon, 1 forge, 9 saddle-horses and 152 draught-horses.

# The Engineer Services

At the beginning of the Revolutionary Wars there existed only a small permanent staff of engineer officers, the artisans who carried out the work being organised in six companies of specialist miners (*mineurs*), and six companies of *sapeurs* who formed part of the artillery, and who were so little regarded that they were converted to Foot Artillery. In 1793 a proper Engineer Corps was formed by detaching the miners from artillery control and combining them with the engineer officers and new *sapeur* battalions, each of eight companies. In 1795 the total comprised 437 officers, 6 miner companies and 9 *sapeur* battalions; in 1798 the *sapeurs* were reduced to four battalions, and a further reorganisation in 1799 gave an establishment of 637 officers, 6 miner companies and two *sapeur* battalions of 1,807 men each, each company comprising 4 officers, 9 NCOs, 4 master-artisans (*maîtres-ouvriers*), 12 *sapeurs* 1st class, 36 2nd class and 1 drummer; this increased to 4 officers and 95 men in 1803 and 4 officers and 154 men in 1806. In 1806 an Engineer Train (*Train du Génie*) was formed to provide independent transport, formed into a battalion of seven companies in 1811. In 1808 the miners were reorganised into two battalions of five companies, later six, and in November 1811 a specialist company of engineer artisans (*ouvriers*) was formed, 4 officers and 122 men, increased to 182 in war-time. In 1812 there were two miner battalions and eight of *sapeurs* (one was Italian, one Dutch and one Spanish; the 6th and 7th were known as the *Bataillon de sapeurs de Walcheren* and *Bataillon de l'Ile d'Elbe* respectively); but losses in the Russian campaign caused the number of battalions to be reduced to five.

In addition to these engineers (whose training was extensive and their skill considerable) there existed a number of *ad hoc* units of less-skilled pioneers to provide manual labour, many of whom were foreign. These included the *Pionniers Noirs* (9 companies of 4 officers and 106 men each, formed into a battalion in 1803, composed of Negro refugees from San Domingo and Egypt, transferred to Neapolitan service the 'Royal African' regiment in 1806); two battalions of *Pionniers Blancs* organised in February 1806 from Austrian prisoners of war, re-organised in five companies (later eight) in 1811 and styled *Pionniers volontaires étrangers*; and two units of Spanish pioneers, one of four companies formed in March 1812 titled *Pionniers espagnoles à Nimègues*, and another in November 1813 styled *Pionniers espagnoles*. Other corps included *Compagnies de pionniers* whose duty was restricted to fortification and public work, formed from conscripts who had deliberately mutilated themselves to avoid serving in the combatant branches of the army, and battalions of seamen assembled for a particular campaign to perform the least skilled tasks. From 1810 the Imperial Guard possessed its own engineer companies, enlarged to a battalion in 1814. There was also a corps of Geographical Engineers (*ingenieurs géographes*) or 'Topographical Engineers', whose duties were surveying and the production of maps, a most vital service on campaign; this unit was composed exclusively of officers, and though the original corps was disbanded in 1791 they remained attached to the general staff, and the unit was resurrected as an independent body in January 1809, with an establishment of 90 officers, the subalterns being drawn from the *Ecole Polytechnique*.

The engineers were responsible not only for digging the trenches around besieged garrisons and for fortifying French positions, but also for road-works in the field, and for the construction of field-defences and gun-emplacements (or for overseeing and planning while the infantry did the manual labour). Pontoon bridges were constructed by the army's pontoon-train, which was a separate formation under army control, but all permanent bridges and trestles were the responsibility of the engineers. (This illogical arrangement originated because only the artillery had the transport sufficient to handle the pontoon equipment; latterly the engineers also had their own bridging-train.) On campaign, all major projects were under central control of the Chief Engineer; field-

*Engineers preparing the way for an assault on a fortification, under fire from the defenders. The* sapeur *in the centre carried a gabion, the men at right fascines; the armoured* sapeur *cuts footholds in the glacis for the storming-party.*

works were usually sited by divisional, corps or artillery commanders. Engineer companies were deployed as and when required, though from 1809 each Corps had a battalion of *sapeurs* and a company of miners attached, complete with a train of 35 waggons containing 1,700 pickaxes, 170 miners' picks, 1,700 spades, 680 felling-axes, hand-tools, demolition stores and field forges. This was the most sophisticated engineer organisation of

*A sapeur in siege-armour. Though the engineers were dressed like the artillery (but black facings piped scarlet), their working-dress probably consisted of their sleeved waistcoat and loose trousers; for work under fire, enormously-heavy iron cuirasses and bascinet-style helmets, usually painted black, afforded some protection from enemy musketry.*

any European army, and the equipment of such excellent quality that in the Peninsular War British engineers equipped themselves with French tools at every opportunity. Training was extensive and the engineer school, greatly enlarged by Napoleon, produced 150 graduates a year after 1803. In addition to the engineer detachments present with each corps, there existed a central 'army park' such as that organised for the 1809 campaign (in which each corps had two *sapeur* and one pontoon company and 6,000 tools with which additional labourers from the infantry could be equipped). The central 'park' comprised two 6-company engineer battalions (formed from 9 *sapeur* and 3 miner companies), 3 pontoon companies, 4 pioneer companies and 3 battalions of seamen (total 2,000), four ambulance and 2 artillery companies with 6 guns.

Unlike some generals, Napoleon placed much importance on engineer services and fortifications; he even wrote a treatise, *Essai sur la fortification de campagne*, and asked 'how is it possible to manoeuvre with inferior or equal forces without the assistance of positions, fortifications and all such accessories of our art?' Field-works as such were not used extensively (in contrast to the Russian army, for example, which made great use of hastily-erected field-defences such as the famous 'Raevsky redoubt' and 'Bagration *flèches*' at Borodino), but villages and buildings were frequently strengthened before combat, though such was usually the responsibility of the infantry and artillery, with engineer advice. (Another expedient attempted in Egypt was the resurrection of 17th-century 'swine-feathers', iron shod stakes carried by each infantryman to form a portable palisade; not surprisingly they proved extremely unpopular and were thrown away, and the palisades never erected!) Siege-work, however, was where the engineers excelled, building their own fortifications for the breaching-batteries and digging the trenches (or mining, using the miners' skills), works of exceptional hazard as the besieged bombarded the engineers or launched sallies to attack them. Though much of the less-skilled manual labour was provided by infantrymen, the engineers were always most exposed and suffered heavy casualties; at Saragossa, for example, 28 engineers officers

| A typical engineer organisation | | |
|---|---|---|
| The second siege of Saragossa, 1808-09 | | |
| **'ARMY TRAIN'** | | |
| **Staff:** | | |
| 1 general (Count Lacoste, killed in the siege). | | |
| 1 colonel, 1 major, 2 *chefs de bataillon*, 23 captains, 13 lieutenants. | | |
| **Miners:** | | |
| 7th coy: | 3 officers, | 70 men |
| 8th coy: | 4 officers, | 84 men |
| 9th coy: | 3 officers, | 74 men |
| **Sapeurs:** | | |
| 6th coy 1st bn: | 2 officers, | 89 men |
| 7th coy 1st bn: | 2 officers, | 90 men |
| 1st coy 2nd bn: | 3 officers, | 90 men |
| 3rd coy 2nd bn: | 3 officers, | 91 men |
| 4th coy 2nd bn: | 3 officers, | 85 men |
| 2nd coy 3rd bn: | 3 officers, | 103 men |
| 4th coy 3rd bn: | 2 officers, | 103 men |
| 6th coy 3rd bn: | 2 officers, | 108 men |
| **5TH CORPS ENGINEERS** | | |
| **Staff:** | | |
| 1 colonel, 1 *chef de bataillon*, 3 captains, 2 lieutenants, 1 adjutant. | | |
| **Sapeurs:** | | |
| 5th coy 2nd bn: | 3 officers, | 62 men |

were killed or wounded during the second siege. Engineers constructed the gabions (wickerwork baskets filled with earth which shielded the breaching-batteries and their own entrenching) and fascines (bundles of brushwood used to fill the bottom of ditches), and in the event of an assault being necessary, guided and accompanied the storming-parties. Equally important was the work of the pontooneers; General Eblé's men who built and maintained the bridges over the Berezina, for example, under the most atrocious conditions, effectively saved the remnants of the *Grand Armée* in 1812, and similar heroic efforts bridged the Danube at Lobau, allowing the escape of the army after the check at Aspern-Essling, and permitting Napoleon's advance before Wagram. Though the whole engineer corps never numbered more than 10,000, its importance was out of proportion to its numbers and its contribution to the success of Napoleon's campaigns cannot be over-stated.

# Chapter Five: FRANCE'S ALLIES

A vital part of Napoleon's forces were his 'Allied' contingents, non-French troops who served under French command, usually as integral parts of the Napoleonic army. Apart from the many foreigners who served in French regiments, and the 'foreign' regiments which were on the strength of the French army, the 'Allies' fell into two categories: those states which were under total Napoleonic domination, and those allied by treaty. The extent to which Napoleon was dependent upon the allied contingents to provide the manpower for his campaigns can be deduced from an analysis of the *Grande Armée* in 1812, 'the army of twenty nations' which was the greatest force he ever assembled for one campaign. Although calculating an army by numbers of battalions and cavalry regiments is deceptive (as not all units were of the same size), if the *Grande Armée* is considered in this way the total number of units was approximately as follows: France was represented by 327 battalions or cavalry regiments, plus 53 'foreign' units as part of the French army. Warsaw provided 70, Bavaria and Austria 35 each, Saxony 33, Westphalia 30, Italy 28, Prussia 25, Württemberg 22, Naples 15, the smaller Confederation of the Rhine states 14, Berg and Baden 8 each and Hessen-Darmstadt 7; in other words, to 380 French units, the allied contingents contributed 330; if the 'foreign corps' are counted as non-French, the proportion was 383 allied to only 327 French. Allied contingents were sent to serve wherever the French army was on campaign. The force which besieged Gerona in 1809 may be taken as an example, again calculated by battalion or cavalry regiment, and including the covering army: France and Italy, 18 units each; Westphalia 7, Berg 6, Naples 4, Würzburg 2: 37 allied units to only 18 French. Although it was unusual for allied contingents to be in such preponderance, it demonstrates that without their contribution Napoleon could not have waged many of his later campaigns.

A number of allied contingents were enrolled unwillingly or under duress, but many fell under Napoleon's spell. Whatever the shortcomings of the Empire, in many cases French rule or influence was a vast improvement upon the régime it supplanted, and coincided with the national aspirations of the states concerned; this explains the loyalty with which the Poles, Italians and Westphalians served the Napoleonic cause. In addition to the states enrolled by treaty or political alliance, a number were under direct rule, either by Napoleon himself or by members of his family. Napoleon himself was King of Italy; his brothers Louis (1778-1848) was King of Holland, Jérôme (1784-1860) King of Westphalia, and Joseph (1768-1844) King of Naples; and his brother-in-law Joachim Murat was King of Naples after Joseph had been transferred to the throne of Spain. Of these states, most remained loyal until they were physically dismembered by enemy occupation, though the Bonapartist rule in Spain was always only tenuous and its military contribution small. The exception was Naples, when Murat's desire to retain his throne overcame his loyalty to his brother-in-law and he negotiated with the Allies. In January 1814 he agreed to provide 30,000 men to serve against France in return for a guarantee of his possessions, and though some fighting occurred in north Italy (against Eugène) Murat discovered that neither the Austrian Metternich nor the British were prepared to keep their part of the bargain. Attempting to regain Napoleon's favour in 1815 he was shunned, and executed after returning to Calabria.

The Kingdom of Holland developed out of the Batavian Republic, the satellite state created by the republican government from the previous United Provinces of the Netherlands. The Batavian Republic possessed its own army and the naval ships of the previous United Provinces, which served alongside French forces in the Revolutionary Wars. Louis Bonaparte (with the title 'Constable of the Empire') was given command of the troops in Holland in September 1805, and on 24 May 1806 was crowned as King of the new state. He commanded the Dutch forces during the British expedition to Walcheren in 1809, but quarrelled with Napoleon over economic policy (refusing to accept the full imposition of the 'Continental System'), and on 1 July 1810 abdicated the throne and retired to private life. Instead of appointing a new king, Napoleon absorbed the kingdom into France, so that like the Austrian Netherlands (Belgium) it became an integral part of the state. Consequently, the Dutch forces were integrated into the existing French army, with their 13 ships-of-the-line, 10 frigates and many smaller vessels being transferred to the French navy. The Dutch 2nd Cavalry became the French 14th Cuirassiers, and the 2nd Hussars the French 11th Hussars; the Dutch Guard Hussars became the 2nd *Chevau-Légers* of the Imperial Guard, and the Dutch Royal Guard infantry became the 2nd (later 3rd) Grenadiers of the Imperial Guard. The first four of the nine Dutch infantry regiments were re-numbered 123rd-126th French line regts, with the remaining five being broken up and distributed amongst them; the three Jäger battalions formed the French 33rd Light Infantry, the Foot Artillery became the 9th French Regt, and the Dutch Horse Artillery, intended to form the 7th French Regt, was instead transferred to the 1st French. The supporting services were transformed into the 14th Battalion of the Artillery Train, and the engineer corps absorbed into its French counter-part.

The least reliable politically of the allied contingents were the Prussian and Austrian units compelled unwillingly to participate in the 1812 campaign. The Austrians, under Austrian command (Field-Marshal Karl Schwarzenberg, 1771-1820), were allocated the right flank of the *Grande Armée*, and withdrew before they came into contact with the Russians; the Prussians, under French command (Marshal Macdonald) were largely concentrated in the Corps which protected the left flank. Acting under the senior Prussian commander, Johann Yorck von Wartenburg (1759-1830) they agreed to a convention with the Russians by which they became neutral, this action precipitating the Prussian change of allegiance for the 1813 campaign. But the actions of Austria and Prussia were exceptional: for the most part Napoleon's allies gave him faithful and indispensible service.

*Lieut Col, Westphalian Garde du Corps, c1810, Jérôme Bonaparte's personal bodyguard: blue French-style uniform with red facings and gold lace, the 'JN' on the gilt helmet and cuirass-decoration and on the holster-caps signifying 'Jérôme Napoleon'. The corps went to Russia in 1812 but returned home with Jérôme. (Print after Alexander Sauerweid.)*

# The Italians

Large numbers of Italians served under Napoleon, many in French regiments but the majority in allied contingents. Napoleon formed the Cisalpine Republic from Lombard possessions in North Italy on 29 June 1797, which state (with others formed under the aegis of republican France) actively supported France.

Upon the formation of the Kingdom of Italy in 1805 (the Cisalpine Republic enlarged by additional territory) Napoleon became king of a state whose army was a valuable contribution to his forces. (The Cisalpine Republic had maintained a Polish Legion in its army in addition.) As Napoleon observed in 1805, 'The Italians are full of spirit and passion, and it should be easy to make them good soldiers.' Although soldiering was held in low esteem by the educated classes of north Italy, the area had been under French influence since 1796, the centuries-old mercenary tradition was still remembered, and the relief of the population from the previous despotic rule made the French establishment popular, and thus the north Italian soldiers were generally not unwilling to march with Napoleon's armies. In 1805 Napoleon appointed his stepson Eugène de Beauharnais (1781-1824), son of Josephine and her first husband, as Viceroy of Italy, giving him powers to control the army of the Kingdom. An able general, loyal to Napoleon and a capable organiser, Eugène transformed the army of 23,000 conscripted peasants into a force of high calibre, which rose in number to 44,000 in 1808 and 90,000 in 1812. Capitalising on rising nationalism, Eugène gained support throughout the population, who viewed the alternative government – a return to Austrian or Sardinian rule – with abhorrence. By creating military academies at Pavia, Bologna and Lodi, Eugène provided a trained and efficient officer corps; organised on French lines, the Italian Army maintained high morale, especially the Royal Guard (formed 1805) and had a most creditable fighting record. About 30,000 served in the Peninsular War (where the 2nd Dragoons achieved great fame at Sagunto, 1811, by routing three Spanish battalions and capturing 800 prisoners), but only about 9,000 of the troops sent to Spain ever returned. About 27,000 served with the *Grande*

*Both the Italian and Neapolitan infantry wore white uniforms (the cavalry green), but the Neapolitan light infantry wore dark blue, this carabinier of the 1st Regt with yellow facings and the shako-cover commonly worn in Spain.*

*Armée* in the Russian campaign of 1812, of whom 20,000 perished; the Royal Guard won great renown at Maloyaroslavets, but was virtually annihilated. Amazingly, Eugène managed to re-create the army in 1813, sending a division to aid Napoleon in Germany, and also formed three corps of two divisions each to defend Italy against Austria.

Contrasting with the fine Kingdom of Italy troops, the second main Italian contingent was fielded by Naples. The forces of the 'Kingdom of the Two Sicilies' had fought against republican France but with a very undistinguished record; as the king is supposed to have remarked when considering a new uniform for his army, 'dress them in red or blue, dress them in green, they will run away just the same.' When France invaded in 1798 only the peasantry made any real resistance, and after French occupation the Bourbon monarchy controlled only Sicily, the mainland part of the kingdom being transformed into the Kingdom of Naples, ruled first by Joseph Bonaparte and later Murat. Conscription was introduced in 1807 and the army formed on the French model, but though considerable numbers of Neapolitan troops were dispatched to the Peninsular War and to the *Grande Armée* in 1812, their value was generally abysmal. Recruited mainly from unwilling peasants, criminals and impressed radicals, the army had a horrendous record of desertion. For example, early in 1810 the Neapolitan 1st Light Infantry escorted 1,000 conscripted convicts to Spain as reinforcements for the 1st Line Regt, already serving in the Peninsula; over half these had deserted before the Pyrenees were even crossed, whilst the 1st Light Infantry itself lost 148 deserters in June 1810 and 130 in July! Despite the efforts of the officers and a handful of reliable troops, the Neapolitans remained the weakest link in all Napoleon's forces, and he himself had no illusions about their worth. When his brother, King Joseph, requested that the Neapolitans be awarded 'Eagles' in 1807, Napoleon refused, because 'you must be aware that . . . these troops are no better than none at all.' In July 1810 Napoleon wrote to War Minister Clarke: 'Let the King of Naples know that all his troops in Spain desert, and are in a wretched state, and that I will have no more of them. Order Marshal Perignon not to send any more, and General Miollis to let none pass. They are a gang of thieves, and poison the country through which they pass'; and in the following month, regarding a

reinforcement sent from Naples: 'Order this battalion to be stopped as soon as it is met with, to be examined and kept back till further orders. I have no wish to crowd Catalonia with bad soldiers, or to increase the troops of banditti . . . Write to the King, for his guidance in future, that I do not want any more Neapolitan troops in Spain, and that I will have no more.' The wretched desertion-record culminated in a suggestion that the 2nd Line Regt should be disarmed, so that *when* they deserted at least their weapons would not be lost! A mark of the comparative value of the Neapolitan troops is found in the case of their 7th

Line Regt, known as the 'Royal African'; originally the unit was raised for the French army in 1803 from Negroes and mulattoes from San Domingo, under the title *Pioniers Noirs* (Black Pioneers). The corps was regarded as the most inferior in French service, yet when transferred to Neapolitan service in August 1806 they were superior to any existing unit of the Neapolitan army! Marshal Macdonald summed up the French attitude: 'My blood boils! . . . as I write these lines, and think to what a degree of abasement I should have fallen had I been desired to command Neapolitan soldiers!'

*Eugène de Beauharnais, Viceroy of Italy, uniformed as the Colonel-General of the* Chasseurs à Cheval *of the Imperial Guard. A worthy general, he served with distinction at Wagram, Borodino and Lützen, and assumed overall command of the* Grande Armée *from Murat in the close of the 1812 campaign. (Engraving after Henri Scheffer)*

# The Spanish 1804-1813

Spain contributed considerably to Napoleon's forces during the years in which that country was allied to France, the most effective elements being the naval squadrons. Although the Spanish fleet was considerable, at least on paper, in reality it had suffered exactly like the army from many years of neglect, mismanagement and corruption; so that, for example, in 1792 though the Spanish navy included 76 sail of the line, only 56 were in seaworthy condition and the naval dockyards were so bad as to be described as derelict! Nevertheless, Spanish naval strength was a valuable asset to Napoleon's forces during the period of alliance, and the mere presence of the Spanish fleet exerted considerable strategic influence, persuading Britain to evacuate the Mediterranean after the Treaty of San Ildefonso, for example.

Spanish military power was of much less significance to Napoleon, its collaboration being divided into two different episodes. Corruption and neglect had left the Spanish army in a dreadful condition, riddled with incompetence

---

## King Joseph's Army

**Royal Guard:**
1st Regt (Grenadiers); 2nd Regt (Tirailleurs); 3rd Regt (Fusiliers); Guard Hussars; Guard Artillery (one Foot, one Horse company); Guard Train (2 coys); Halbardiers (one coy, palace guard); Sapeurs (formed 1812).

**Line Infantry:**
Regts No 1 (Madrid), No 2 (Toledo), No 3 (Seville), No 4 (Soria), No 5 (Granada), No 6 (Malaga), No 7 (Cordova).

**Light Infantry:**
Regts No 1 (Castile), No 2 (Murcia)

**Cavalry:**
6 heavy regiments; 7th Regt (Lancers)

**Foreign Regts:**
Regt Royal-Etranger, Royal Irlandais

**Regt Joseph-Napoleon**

---

and largely demoralised. The venal rule of Manuel Godoy (1767-1851), who rose from a private in the Spanish Guard to chief minister of the state after becoming the 'favourite' of Queen Maria-Luisa, served only to wreck what remained of Spanish military competence. The sinister Godoy, one of the most disreputable politicians in Europe, almost bankrupted Spain in the 1793-95 war against France and, as a result of French bribes and blackmail, allied Spain with France against the Third Coalition, a decision which cost the destruction of the fleet at Trafalgar. In 1806, despite the alliance with France, Godoy attempted to intrigue with Prussia, as a result of which Napoleon demanded a military contingent from Spain for garrison service in northern Europe, ostensibly as a guarantee of Spanish good behaviour in the future, but probably also as a way of removing from Spain the cream of her army, in preparation for the deposition of the Spanish royal house in favour of a Bonapartist king, for which role the reluctant Joseph was selected.

Throughout the Napoleonic Wars, the Spanish army never recovered from the years of neglect and demoralisation. In sharp contrast with the courageous resistance of the civilian population, which sustained appalling hardship in sieges such as Saragossa and Gerona, the occasions on which the Spanish army fought even passably well were very limited in number; as William Warre of the Portuguese staff recorded in 1809, the regret was not that the Spanish continually ran away, but 'The loss I most regret on these occasions are the arms, which the fools throw away in their flight.' Always ill-organised, Spanish regiments were clumsy in size, recruited from the lowest orders, without even any official drill, colonels instructing their men in whatever way they chose. Units were invariably under-strength, the cavalry so short of horses that not one man in three could be mounted, and the officers uninterested and incapable, 'the most contemptible creatures that I ever beheld . . . utterly unfit and unable to command their men' according to one British officer. Excepting a few officers mostly of foreign descent, principally

Irish, the high command was no better, as exemplified by the utter incompetence of Cuesta. No army in the world could maintain high morale under such conditions, even less when half-starved and ill-equipped, and in general not until the later stages of the Peninsular War, when some Spanish forces were reorganised on Anglo-Portuguese lines, did they ever become even moderate in quality. There were notable exceptions: the artillery was renowned for its fighting qualities, though as its support usually ran away numbers of guns were captured after their crews had died in their defence; and one brigade fought heroically at Albuera, though significantly these were not ordinary regiments but Spanish Guards and the Irish Regt.

The force which Napoleon dragooned into service in northern Europe contained the best elements of the army, four infantry regiments, two light battalions, three cavalry and two dragoon regiments, with artillery, train and engineer units, the whole under the command of Spain's most capable general, the Marqués de la Romana (1761-1811), who ultimately became the supreme commander of the Spanish army which operated in Portugal alongside Wellington. The story of the escape of La Romana's army from its garrison-duty is one of the most remarkable episodes in the Napoleonic Wars, and was entirely due to the British agent and spy James Robertson, a Scottish Benedictine monk from Ratisbon, 'Brother Gallus'. Robertson was recruited from his clerical duties through Sir Arthur Wellesley and the Duke of Richmond, and he was sent to the Spanish troops serving in Denmark and Hamburg under the alias of Adam Rohrauer, a commercial traveller from Bremen who sold cigars and chocolate to the Spanish officers. Contacting La Romana in person, and making sure that the Spanish contingent's pro-French second-in-command, the Irish mercenary General Kindelan, was not privy to the negotiations, Robertson arranged for the Spanish contingent to be evacuated by British ships back to Spain, as almost to a man they supported the Spanish royal family instead of Joseph Bonaparte. The Spanish loyalists acted too soon, however, and two regiments mutinied when requested to swear allegiance to Joseph, shooting the French officer presiding at the oath-taking ceremony and threaten-

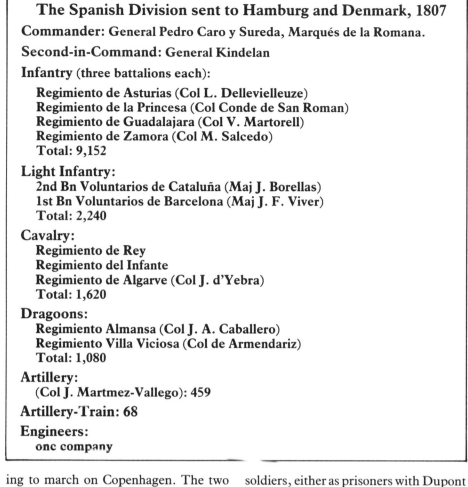

## The Spanish Division sent to Hamburg and Denmark, 1807

**Commander: General Pedro Caro y Sureda, Marqués de la Romana.**

**Second-in-Command: General Kindelan**

**Infantry** (three battalions each):

    Regimiento de Asturias (Col L. Dellevielleuze)
    Regimiento de la Princesa (Col Conde de San Roman)
    Regimiento de Guadalajara (Col V. Martorell)
    Regimiento de Zamora (Col M. Salcedo)
    Total: 9,152

**Light Infantry:**

    2nd Bn Voluntarios de Cataluña (Maj J. Borellas)
    1st Bn Voluntarios de Barcelona (Maj J. F. Viver)
    Total: 2,240

**Cavalry:**

    Regimiento de Rey
    Regimiento del Infante
    Regimiento de Algarve (Col J. d'Yebra)
    Total: 1,620

**Dragoons:**

    Regimiento Almansa (Col J. A. Caballero)
    Regimiento Villa Viciosa (Col de Armendariz)
    Total: 1,080

**Artillery:**

    (Col J. Martmez-Vallego): 459

**Artillery-Train: 68**

**Engineers:**

    one company

*Officer of the Spanish Royal Guard. The predominant uniform-colour of the Spanish army was white, dark blue for cavalry and yellow for dragoons; King Joseph's Royal Guard wore uniforms resembling those of their French counterparts, and his infantry and cavalry brown coats with regimental facings. (Print by Martinet.)*

ing to march on Copenhagen. The two regiments (Guadalajara and Asturias) were surrounded and disarmed, but La Romana managed to concentrate the remainder of his force and join the British Baltic fleet, less the Algarve Cavalry which was intercepted by Kindelan and Dutch troops en route to their rendezvous; their commander, Major Costa, shot himself and the remainder surrendered. Nevertheless, La Romana had extricated 9,000 of his men, who were shipped home to join the fight against Napoleon.

The second of Napoleon's Spanish contingents was the army raised by Joseph Bonaparte during his reign as King of Spain. In general, these were even more wretched in quality than the Spanish regiments opposing the French, but the Bonapartist army did include a number of reasonable units, most especially Joseph's Royal Guard which was composed of Frenchmen! As Napoleon advised, 'Admit no one into it except the French conscripts whom I have ordered from Paris and Bayonne, and French soldiers, either as prisoners with Dupont or otherwise, who have been for less than a year in the Spanish service. Of these you may be sure . . .'; in other words, the 'native' Spanish troops were guaranteed to be unreliable! This is supported by Napoleon's comments regarding the formation of the rest of Joseph's army, which comprised seven line and two light infantry regiments, six heavy cavalry and one lancer regiment. Napoleon wrote that 'These regiments are indispensible as a refuge for numbers of people who would otherwise become bandits'; 'They should not be allowed to approach within 10 leagues of Madrid': In addition to these, Joseph was advised to form 'foreign' battalions, principally the Regt *Royal-Etranger* ('Royal Foreigners'), to be composed of Austrians, Italians and Prussians; as Napoleon noted, 'One of the advantages of this will be to clear off the crowd of strangers who swarm in Madrid, and who may be put to some use when they are provided with officers and non-commissioned officers out of your guard.' A further unit was the Regt Joseph-Napoleon which served with the *Grande Armée* in the 1812 Russian campaign, along with Spanish pioneer units recruited in part from the Spanish prisoners who were unable to escape with the bulk of La Romana's force. In general, though the Bonapartist forces were organised and equipped on French lines (the Royal Guard, for example, wore the uniform of Napoleon's Imperial Guard save for a change of cockade), they were of little military value. The total strength of King Joseph's Spanish army at Vittoria, for example, was only 248 officers and 5,390 men, of whom they lost probably between 700 and 800, either casualties, prisoners or 'missing' (run off).

# The German States

Napoleon placed great reliance upon his German allies, who contributed large numbers of troops to his armies and, even though Napoleon's cause was not their own, served valiantly in many actions. The fact that most deserted the French in the later months of 1813 should not be allowed to diminish their contribution; in fact many were outstanding soldiers and some German contingents suffered the highest percentage losses for the entire Napoleonic Wars. Without doubt one reason for their stalwart and reliable conduct is that prior to the Napoleonic empire, many of the German states had maintained good, professional armies with long traditions, which allowed for the maintenance of high morale and *esprit de corps* even when the professional cadres were supplemented by large quantities of conscripts to provide the numbers required by Napoleon. In general, the German contingents co-operated amicably with the French, though at times complained about French arrogance. They trusted and preferred their own leaders, however, and understandably lacked the national fervour and corresponding élan in action which infused the French army; they did their duty as good, solid professionals and usually maintained high discipline, but never felt the fire of enthusiasm which Napoleon kindled in the French army. Whilst conforming to the French corps and divisional system (into which the German units were integrated fully), many retained their own national traditions and characteristics and gave ground only reluctantly, such as when the Bavarians were compelled to adopt the French method instead of maintaining their huge and comprehensive transport system which they had enjoyed previously.

The *Rheinbund* or Confederation of the Rhine formed the basis for the organisation of Napoleon's German contingents, but he had numbered German allies before the *Rheinbund* was formed. The Holy Roman Empire, which maintained feudal overlordship upon the majority of the small, independent German states, was not popular with the leaders of the states in question, especially when demanding military contingents to help fight the war against France. Bavaria, for example, mobilised her troops in 1792 but soon declared neutrality. Napoleon saw the advantage of establishing a *cordon sanitaire* of satellite states between France and her enemies, and took his opportunity in 1805 when Austria attacked Bavaria, during which campaign Bavaria, Württemberg and Baden all allied themselves to France. After Austerlitz, Napoleon proposed the federation of German states to be known as the Confederation of the Rhine, and on 12 July 1806 some 16 heads of state announced their repudiation of the Holy Roman Empire, promising France a contingent of 63,000 men. Opposition to the Confederation was one of the causes of the 1806 war between Prussia and Napoleon, but after Jena the organisation was secure and formed an important link in Napoleon's Continental System, by which the states over which Napoleon exercised control or influence closed their markets to British trade. Further states joined the Confederation, and until it fell apart in 1813 as one after another of the German princes deserted to join the Allies, virtually the whole of Germany (exclusive of Prussia) might be described as a French satellite.

Under Maximilian Josef, Elector and later King (1756-1825) – who was the son of a French general – Bavaria was one of the most reliable of all Napoleon's allied contingents (and like many German states, was connected by dynastic marriage to the Bonaparte family). The Bavarian army owed much to the reforms of the American émigré Benjamin Thompson, ennobled as Graf von Rumford. Reorganised in 1799 (and successively), the army consisted of up to 14 infantry regiments, seven light battalions and seven cavalry regiments, the latter undergoing a process of 'lightening' so that the previous cuirassier regiments became dragoons by 1804, and the dragoons chevaulegers (light horse), six regiments of which partici-

*An officer (left) and privates of Bavarian infantry, c 1806, wearing the distinctive crested* Raupenhelm, *the men carrying the unusual hide knapsack of the Bavarian army, slung at an oblique angle across the back. (Print after Volz)*

pated in the 1812 campaign; a regiment of lancers was raised in 1813. The Bavarian army was distinguished by distinctive light blue uniforms (green for chevaulegers, dark blue for artillery) and the high, crested leather *Raupenhelm* helmet. Bavarian contingents served in the 1805 campaign, played a minor role against Prussia in 1806-07, formed the VIII Corps of the *Grande Armée* in 1809, fighting at Eckmühl, Aspern-Essling and Wagram, and formed the VI Corps in the invasion of Russia in 1812, during which about 80 per cent of the Bavarian forces perished. In addition, Bavaria was engaged in pacifying three revolts in the Tyrol, which involved much arduous service, after which many Tyroleans conscripted into Bavarian service accounted for the Bavarian contingent in 1812 having the highest desertion-record of any German force. After changing sides in 1813 the Bavarians fought against Napoleon at Hanau and in the campaign of France.

Württemberg, like Bavaria, was an Electorate of the Holy Roman Empire upgraded by Napoleon to the status of Kingdom, after having originally fought against France. Their army was reorganised in 1798, consisting of up to eight infantry regiments (in dark blue) and two *Jäger* (rifle) and light battalions (in dark green), up to five cavalry regiments (two chevauleger, two *Jäger zu Pferde* (chasseurs) and one dragoon regiment), foot artillery and two horse batteries (in light blue). Their service was similar to that of Bavaria, including the provision of some 15,800 men to the 1812 campaign against Russia, where they fought with distinction but suffered terribly; as early as August 1812 their effective strength was reduced to 4,000 and on 10 November Napoleon remarked on the remnant of the Württemberg contingent still marching in formation, about 30 strong.

The Kingdom of Westphalia was created by Napoleon in November 1807 from the previous states of Hanover, Brunswick, Hessen-Kassel and parts of Prussia, with his youngest brother Jérôme Bonaparte (1784-1860) appointed king. Though not devoid of talent, Jérôme was not an inspiring leader, something of a profligate (once arrested for drunkenness by his own police!) and, especially in the 1812 campaign when he originally commanded VIII Corps, notably lethargic, leading to his dismissal from command after a row with Napoleon. The Westphalian forces comprised a Guard (created in imitation of Napoleon's Imperial Guard), six infantry regiments, three light infantry battalions and five cavalry regiments (two of cuirassiers, one of chevaulegers and two of hussars); the infantry wore white (dark green for light infantry and Guard *Jäger*), the cavalry green (cuirassiers white, later dark blue) and artillery dark blue. Westphalians served in the Peninsular War, in Saxony in 1809 and in Russia in 1812; generally composed of good troops, they were unfairly treated in the latter campaign (being allocated the horrendous task of clearing the battlefields of Borodino and Smolensk, for example) and suffered appallingly; from its establishment of 27,000 the contingent was down to 240 by the end of November 1812, of whom only 60 cavalry and 50 infantry escaped across the Berezina.

The Electorate of Saxony fought against Napoleon in the 1806 campaign, but their alliance with Prussia foundered after Jena and the Elector, promoted by Napoleon to king in December 1806, changed sides and thereafter fought with the French, at Friedland, Wagram and in the 1812 campaign. In return for his support, King Friedrich August received nominal overlordship of the Duchy of Warsaw, but lost half his state to Prussia in 1814 as a penalty for supporting Napoleon so determinedly. The Saxon army was typical of a reliable, professional German force and performed much good service under Napoleon's banner, and as they were largely concentrated in VII Corps in the 1812 campaign they escaped many of the horrors of the retreat from Moscow which befell other German units. Regiments in other formations suffered dreadfully, and the Saxons were especially distinguished at Borodino where their Gardes du Corps and cuirassier regiments were the first to storm the Raevsky redoubt, losing half their men in the process. An anecdote arising from this most heroic action is perhaps significant in determining Napoleon's view of the allied contingents; when Berthier saw the white uniforms of the Saxon cavalry enter the redoubt, he exclaimed 'The Saxon cuirassiers are inside!' Napoleon, seeing the blue coats of the Polish and Westphalian cuirassiers who seconded the Saxons in their attack, said that as they were dressed in blue, 'they must be *my* cuirassiers.' Such failures to acknowledge the full achievements of

*Private, 4th Bavarian Regt, 1812. The Bavarian infantry was distinguished not only by their 'cornflower'-blue jackets, but equally by the enormous, boiled-leather* Raupenhelm *helmets with woollen crest (bearskin for officers) which were so large that the men's cleaning-kit was carried in it! Prior to the 1812 campaign, French-style equipment had been introduced to replace the previous, somewhat untidy Bavarian pattern.*

the allied contingents was doubtless very dispiriting to the troops in question. The Saxon army consisted of a Guard (grenadiers wearing scarlet coats and bearskin caps), up to twelve infantry regiments (wearing white), two light infantry regiments and a *Jäger* battalion (in green), the Garde du Corps and three other heavy cavalry regiments (two after 1810), a hussar regiment (in white), four regiments of chevaulegers (dressed in scarlet) and foot and horse artillery (in dark green).

Probably the best of the Allied contingents (who though not German *per se* were part of the Confederation of the

Rhine) were the Poles of the Duchy of Warsaw. Inhabitants from that unfortunate country had supported France virtually since Poland had been partitioned, serving as mercenaries with the French forces in Italy and in the French army itself. The desire for a re-establishment of their homeland as an independent state caused the Polish nation to support Napoleon more faithfully than any other of his allied forces, though the sovereignty they received fell far short of their expectations. The state which was created by the Treaty of Tilsit was the 'Grand Duchy of Warsaw', smaller than the territory desired by the Polish leaders and under the nominal control of the King of Saxony; but in the hopes that Napoleon would eventually restore Poland to her borders of 1795, thousands of Poles enlisted, fought and died in Napoleon's service, without ever achieving their desire. A new 'Polish' army was created for the Duchy (separate from the Polish units which were integral parts of the French army), comprising initially 20 infantry, 18 cavalry and 2 artillery regiments, organised on French lines but maintaining many traditional Polish features, especially the unmistakable *czapka* head-dress which was a feature of Polish uniforms from the late 18th century to the present day, and provided the model for the Polish-style lancer regiments which ultimately were formed by virtually all European armies. Most of the cavalry of the Duchy of Warsaw were lancers (the number of regiments rose to 21), but three were *chasseurs à cheval*, two hussars and one cuirassiers, plus an

additional light cavalry formation of '*krakus*'. The infantry and cavalry wore dark blue (the *chasseurs à cheval* dark green), and the foot and horse artillery dark green; the artillery train dark blue and the equipment train (in the form of the French *Train des Equipages*) grey. From the creation of the Duchy, Polish troops played a major role in Napoleon's campaigns, never serving less than admirably, at Friedland, throughout the Peninsular War (though many of these were members of the Polish regiments in the French army), and especially in 1812. Even though the rapid expansion of the army resulted in a considerable proportion of the Warsaw forces being new recruits, the Polish V Corps in 1812 provided the strongest national contingent in the *Grande Armée* after the French, and the highest percentage of troops compared to the population of any. None entered the 1812 campaign with more enthusiasm or conducted themselves with more heroism, but suffered severely during the campaign. Epitomising the valour of the Polish troops was their commander, Prince Josef Anton Poniatowski (1763-1813), the 'Polish Bayard', who though born in Vienna, son of a senior Austrian commander and originally commissioned in the Austrian army, joined his uncle the King of Poland prior to the final partition. A figurehead for the Polish national hopes of independence, he served Napoleon with skill and bravery, commanding the right wing at Borodino, being wounded at the Berezina and reconstructing the Warsaw forces after the retreat from Moscow. Wounded by a

lance shortly before the battle of Leipzig, on 16 October 1813 he received the Empire's highest accolade, the bâton of a Marshal; wounded four more times during the fighting at Leipzig, he was drowned attempting to swim on his horse over the river Elster.

Baden was one of the smaller members of the Confederation of the Rhine, and consequently their military contribution was not extensive; though the 9,000 men they provided for the *Grande Armée* in 1812 has sometimes been regarded as the very best of all the German contingents. The army consisted of four infantry regiments, dressed in dark blue with combed helmets, a *Jäger* battalion (in green), two cavalry regiments, one of light horse (in light blue) and one of hussars (in green), foot and horse artillery in dark blue and the artillery train in grey. The hussar regiment, together with the Hessian Chevaulegers, performed the immortal 'charge of death' at Studianka, when attempting to secure the line of retreat for the *Grande Armée* from Russia in 1812, from which charge only about 50 men of each regiment returned.

Kleve-Berg was the duchy bestowed by Napoleon on Murat as the 'Grand Duchy of Berg', a principality on the right bank of the Rhine, its chief town being Düsseldorf. Its forces were small (only four infantry regiments, dressed in white) and two cavalry regiments (chevaulegers, the 1st regiment being attached to the French Imperial Guard), but of excellent quality; they served in Spain and mostly as part of IX Corps in the 1812 campaign, where the contingent was destroyed. Even after the horrors of the retreat from Moscow, however, the Berg troops still marched in formation around their colours, though the seven infantry battalions were reduced to some 200 men.

Hessen-Darmstadt was elevated to a 'Grand Duchy' upon the formation of the Confederation of the Rhine, its forces being reorganised on French lines, to consist of three infantry regiments (a fourth was raised in 1813), a provisional light infantry regiment (all wearing blue), a single light cavalry regiment, chevaulegers (in green, with a *Raupenhelm*), and foot artillery (in dark blue). Hessians served in the Peninsular War (the Regt Gross-und Erbprinz formed part of the garrison of Badajoz

when the city was stormed by the Anglo-Portuguese army in 1812), at Wagram and 5,000 in the 1812 campaign, when the chevaulegers won their great fame at Studianka.

Many of the smaller states which formed part of the Confederation of the Rhine had no 'armies' as such, or just individual regiments without the associated services of artillery and transport which were part of the forces of the larger states. Oldenberg, for example, which was forced to join the Confederation in 1808, had only possessed a company of infantry; now a battalion was required, but in May 1810 the state was annexed into Metropolitan France and the unit became part of the French 129th Line Regt. The Duchy of Nassau (formed from the principalities of Nassau-Usingen and Nassau-Weilburg) raised two infantry and one *chasseur à cheval* regiments for the Confederation forces (wearing green), both infantry regiments serving in Spain. Their career typifies the history of the Confederation as a whole: not over-enthusiastic about the concept, their troops served with some distinction until 1813, when the situation in Germany caused them to throw off the Napoleonic yoke. The 2nd Nassau Regt defected to the British en masse in Spain in December 1813 (with another Confederation unit, the Frankfurt Bn), whereupon to prevent a repetition, the 1st Nassau Regt was disarmed by the French and interned. Coming under the control of the newly-established Kingdom of the Netherlands, in 1815 the Nassau troops (many still dressed in the uniforms they had worn when fighting for Napoleon) were among the best of the Netherlandish units which fought against Napoleon in the Waterloo campaign. The very small Confederation states could not even raise sufficient troops to form a single battalion, so to accommodate their contribution to Napoleon's forces, a number of 'Confederation' regiments were formed, combining the contingents of the smaller states. The two Nassau regiments formed two of the Confederation regiments, Frankfurt and Würzburg one each; the remainder were multi-state units, allowing the employment of tiny contingents like the 150-strong Schaumburg-Lippe unit in the 5th Confederation regiment. These composite units (especially that formed by the Saxon Duchies) were extremely colourful, each state's companies wearing their own uniform.

The change of allegiance following the collapse of the Confederation in 1813 seems to have made no difference to the military capabilities of the German forces, who fought against Napoleon in late 1813 and 1814 with as much professionalism as they had fought with him. A typical individual career is that of Field Marshal Carl Philipp Wrede (1767-1838), the leading Bavarian soldier of his age. Under the Archduke Charles, he covered the retreat of the Austrian army after the defeat of Hohenlinden; then fought for Napoleon from 1805 to 1813, including commanding the 20th (Bavarian) division in the 1812 campaign. After Leipzig he turned against Napoleon, was badly defeated at Hanau and later fought at La Rothière and Bar-sur-Aube. This professional attitude to soldiering which allowed a change of allegiance without compromising military capability is probably the reason why Napoleon's German allies were so valuable during the time they marched under Napoleon's colours.

---

### The multi-state 'Confederation' regiments which served with the *Grande Armée* in the 1812 campaign

**3rd Regt: Frankfurt-am-Main** (dark blue uniform, faced red).

**4th Regt: Saxon Duchies,** comprising: Saxe-Weimar and Saxe-Hilburghausen (green uniform), Saxe-Coburg (green faced yellow), Saxe-Gotha-Altenburg and Saxe-Meiningen (dark blue faced red).

**5th Regt: Anhalt-Lippe,** comprising: Anhalt-Dessau (350 men), Alhalt-Bernburg (240) and Anhalt-Köthen (green uniform faced rose-pink); Schaumburg-Lippe (150) and Lippe-Detmold (500) (white faced green).

**6th Regt: Schwarzburg-Rudolstadt and Schwarzburg-Sonderhausen** (350 men each; green faced red), Waldeck (400, white faced dark blue), Reuss (450, white faced light blue).

**7th Regt: Würzburg** (white faced red).

**8th Regt: Mecklenburg-Schwerin** (1,900 men) and **Mecklenburg-Strelitz** (900); both dark blue faced red.

# The United States

The United States was not one of Napoleon's allies *per se*, but merits consideration due to the War of 1812 arising at least in part out of the British naval actions in support of the 'Orders in Council', the war of commerce designed to wreck the French economy. Although the war in north America was miniscule in terms of the number of troops involved

*A U.S. Infantry private, 1813. The American army began the war wearing a 'stovepipe' shako and a dark blue jacket with red facings and white lace, with overalls or one-piece 'gaiter-trousers'. In 1813 a new false-fronted shako was issued. Shortages meant that many units were equipped with makeshift grey jackets or the white summer waistcoat. Militia and volunteers had a variety of uniforms ranging from elaborate full dress to backwoods hunting-shirts and slouch hats.*

in even the major battles when compared to the leading actions in Europe, it served ultimately to divert considerable British resources, both naval and military, from the war against Napoleon, and is thus often regarded as a separate but inter-related theatre of operations of the Napoleonic Wars.

Despite the defeat by the US Army of a veteran British force in the final battle of the war at New Orleans, the naval forces of the United States were probably the most effective elements. The US Navy was tiny in size and quite inadequate to fight a conventional war against Britain, but compensated for lack of size by excellent training, seamanship and general audacity. Like the army, the navy was totally unprepared for war in 1812: there was no permanent dockyard (though this was being established at Norfolk, Virginia), there was not even a single ship-of-the-line on the establishment, and only 17 vessels of any consequence. The US Navy had been properly established only in 1798, and at the outbreak of war numbered only 5,750 men, three-quarters American citizens, 8 per cent British and the remainder Scandinavians, French, German and other European nationalities. The largest ships were frigates, but the biggest of these were very much larger and more heavily-armed than their British counterparts, so that fine ships like the USS *Constitution*, *President* and *United States* almost carried the firepower of a frigate; hence the stunning successes which occurred on several occasions when engaging British ships of ostensibly the same type.

The military force of the United States was equally small; in 1808 Congress had authorised a regular army

of just 175 officers and 2,389 other ranks. It was enlarged greatly in the months prior to the outbreak of war, the regulated strength rising to 35,603 in January 1812, though by May the actual strength had grown to 6,744. Such rapid increase in strength, with men enrolled on varied terms of enlistment from one to five years, whilst it might produce impressive numbers, resulted in much of the regular army being woefully trained, totally inexperienced and lacking competent leadership; no matter how stalwart the men, such deficiences were impossible to remedy at short notice, and the inspection report on the 14th Infantry is typical of the newly-formed part of the army: 'The 14th is composed entirely of recruits; they appear to be almost as ignorant of their duty as if they had never seen a camp, and scarcely know on which shoulder to carry the musket. They are mere militia, and, if possible, even worse; and if taken into action in their present state, will prove more dangerous to themselves than to the enemy.'

In addition to the regular army, much of the American military force was composed of militia, local volunteer companies for which all able-bodied men between 16 and 60 years were liable for service, providing their own muskets. Many of these corps were of little practical value when opposed by British regulars; as an officer of the District of Columbia militia wrote, 'as a cowl does not make a monk, to dress and equip a body of men as light infantry or dragoons does not make them what they are called . . . A company of cavalry, formed in the heart of a large commercial city, might choose to assume the name of "Cossacks" and provide themselves with lances and other suitable equipments, but they would remain in reality, just what they were before – a parcel of inoffensive clerks or journeyman mechanics.' But though many of these raw units were of limited combat value, some were composed of frontiersmen who had some experience of campaigning, and were extremely effective, such as Johnson's Kentucky Mounted Volunteers who performed so well at the Thames in 1813.

Leadership from the lowest ranks to the highest was unimpressive, with officers initially as inexperienced and incapable as their men. The improvement from the first débâcles of the war was marked; as a Baltimore newspaper remarked in August 1813, 'Gen Hampton is busily employed in making *soldiers* of the *officers* of the army at *Burlington*. They are frequently and severely drilled; and are given to understand that they *must* and *shall* ascertain and perform their several duties. This is

---

## U.S. forces at New Orleans, 1815

exact numbers are uncertain

**Commanding officer: Major-General Andrew Jackson.**

**Headquarters escort: Mississippi Dragoons (half troop).**

**7th U.S. Infantry (Maj H. D. Peire): 465**

**44th U.S. Infantry (Maj I. L. Baker): 331**

**1st U.S. Artillery: 132 plus small detachment of unknown strength.**

**Marines (Maj D. Carmick): about 60**

**U.S. Navy (Cmdt D. P. Patterson): maximum 500**

**Irregulars**

**Tennessee Mounted Infantry (Brig Gen J. Coffee): 800**

**Kentucky Militia Brigade (Maj Gen J. Thomas; actually commanded by Brig Gen J. Adair): 2,340**

**Tennessee Volunteers (Maj Gen W. Carroll): 806**

**Chootaw Indians (Chief Dujeat, alias Push-Ma-Ta-Ha): 62**

**Natchez Volunteer Riflemen (Capt J. C. Wilkins): about 40**

**New Orleans Rifles (Capt T. Beale): about 60**

**New Orleans Volunteers (Maj J. B. Plauché): 364 to 421 (included Carabiniers d'Orleans,**

**Compagnie Franche, Dragons d'Orleans, Chasseurs à Pied, Louisiana Blues)**

**Pirates: 43**

**Louisiana Militia (Maj Gen J. de Villére): clements from 18 regts, strength unknown.**

**'Bn of Free Men of Color' (Maj P. Lacaste): 280**

**Bn of Santo Domingo Negroes (Maj L. Daquin): 150**

**Three independent Negro companies (Col M. Fortier): 126**

---

striking at the very root of our disasters. The best materials for an army that the world could furnish, have been sacrificed to the pompous ignorance or inconsiderable courage of those who should have applied them to victory.' The high command was a major factor in American reverses in the early stages, with central direction confusing officers who were already incapable; as was observed of President Madison and his generals, 'Madison's orders to Hull and Dearborn passed beyond the bounds of ordinary incapacity, but Dearborn's answers passed belief.' A description of General Hull, who surrendered Fort Detroit and a garrison of at least 1,700 and 33 guns to a British force of 300 regulars, 400 militia and about 500 Indians, demonstrates the incapacity of the high command: awaiting the British advance, Hull 'sat on an old tent on the ground, leaning his back against the rampart. He kept, apparently unconsciously, filling his mouth with tobacco, putting in quid after quid, till the spittle, coloured with juice, dribbled out on to his neck-cloth, cravat, and vest. He seemed preoccupied, his voice trembled, he was greatly agitated and anxious, believing that ultimately the fort would fall, and dreading massacre . . .' Added to such factors were conflicts within the high command itself, regular officers resenting the command of militia generals, as exemplified in the operations which led to Queenston. The regular Major-General Alexander Smyth quarrelled bitterly with the militia Major-General Stephen van Rensselaer (they belonged to opposing political parties), and when Van Rensselaer began an advance on his own initiative (because his militiamen were demanding that they be employed or allowed to go home), Smyth with a strong brigade of regulars made no attempt whatever to assist, a shameful betrayal of his countrymen.

A further factor which hampered the American war effort was a chronic shortage of equipment. By declaring war well before the state was in a position to support it, Madison had initiated the problem, and it was never fully overcome. Some of the militia units were wretchedly equipped, as demonstrated by a description of the Kentucky Militia at River Raisin in 1813: 'Their appearance was miserable to the last degree. They had the air of men to whom cleanliness was a virtue unknown, and their squalid bodies

*Major-General Andrew Jackson (1767-1845), the outstanding U.S. military commander of the War of 1812. A quarrelsome man of Irish descent, Jackson inflicted on Britain the severest defeat of the war, at New Orleans. On top of his success in the Creek War, Jackson's military reputation carried him to the Presidency in 1828 and 1832.*

were covered by habiliments that had evidently undergone every change of season and were arriving at the last stage of repair . . . an air of wilderness and savageness which in Italy would cause them to pass for brigands of the Appenines . . .'

The combined effect of such maladministration, poor leadership and lack of training and *matériel* was the demoralisation of many American units; as Van Rensselaer wrote of Queenston, 'The ardor of the unengaged troops had entirely subsided. I rode in all directions, urging the men by every consideration to pass the river, but in vain . . . one-third of the idle men would have saved all!' Nevertheless, under the capable officers possessed by the army, who became more prominent as the war revealed the inadequacies of the political appointees, training and morale improved markedly, especially in the regular army. As the commander of the 25th Infantry wrote, the consequence of a course of instruction initiated by General Winfield Scott 'was, that when we took the field in July our corps manoeuvred in action and under fire of the enemy's artillery with the accuracy of parade.' No higher testimony can be given to the Americans than to state that towards the end of the war they could take on the British veterans on almost equal terms.

# Chapter Six: STRATEGY AND TACTICS

Napoleon was not, essentially, a great strategic theorist; he often wrote and talked of the 'principles of war' but never enumerated them, and even stated that there were 'no precise or definite rules' of warfare, but that 'like all beautiful things . . . the simplest manoeuvres are the best'. Such a statement is deceptive and perhaps tends to conceal the amount of study and calculation which Napoleon put into his theory and practice of the art of war; he read widely of the 'great captains' of the past (from Alexander to Caesar, Gustavus Adolphus, Eugene, Charles XII and Frederick the Great) and acknowledged his debt to them, especially Frederick, and to the theorists of his own era such as Du Teil and Guibert. His own strategic and tactical concepts were not principally innovative, but built upon the experiences of the past, overlaid with the developments of the revolutionary wars: mass conscription and a resulting 'national' war effort, and a huge simplification of logistics leading to the capacity for manoeuvre more rapid than anything seen in the immediate past, against which the stereotyped, 'traditional' armies of more pedestrian commanders initially had little answer.

Apart from a finely-tuned and professional army, Napoleon had two advantages not available to most of his opponents: unity of command and a fixed strategic objective. As head of state, he held both supreme political and military power, and thus his will was absolute. A consequence, however, was the lack of capable subordinate commanders: as armies grew in size, and when wars were conducted simultaneously on two fronts, it was impossible for Napoleon to retain the personal control over every aspect of his army as in the early campaigns, and delegation of power he avoided perhaps partly from hidden fears of deposition, especially when success began to elude him (in 1812, for example, General Malet's republican plot gained some support). Nevertheless, when Napoleon was able to control an army in person he was a dynamic and ruthless leader with an insatiable appetite for work. His second great advantage was his singularity of

purpose of destroying the enemy's field army; acquisition of territory or capture of cities was never high on his list of priorities. As he once observed, 'There are in Europe many good generals, but they see too many things at once. I see only one thing, namely the enemy's main body.' This was the essence of his strategy: a meticulously-planned campaign which would result in a single, decisive battle which would decide the war at a stroke, conducted at a speed which might genuinely be termed the Napoleonic *blitzkrieg*; to be followed by a relentless pursuit which prevented the defeated enemy from re-forming, and by destroying their morale removing the will for further resistance. Such a war was costly in terms of the lives of his men, but Napoleon rarely showed overconcern for the safety of his followers – 'a man like me troubles himself little about the lives of a million men' – yet the *blitzkrieg* style which ended a war rapidly, however costly in lives, might in the long term be less horrendous than a protracted campaign of attrition which slowly ground down the army. That, at least, might be the view of Napoleon's apologists; and until the final years, he had a fund of conscripts upon which to call to replace his losses.

All Napoleon's plans were thus directed towards the single, decisive blow, with the movements of his army at all times hidden from the enemy, initially by tight security and, once on the march, by screens of light cavalry. The organisation of the army into autonomous *corps d'armée* enabled each corps to take a separate route of advance which, apart from allowing them to forage off the terrain traversed, again tended to confuse the enemy as to Napoleon's primary objective: the advance into Russia in 1812 was on a front of 300 miles! When the enemy's

*The 'strategic battle', as illustrated in these diagrams, embodied the elements of Napoleonic 'grand tactics', duplicating on a smaller scale the essence of Napoleon's strategy including envelopment and breakthrough. Typical are the cavalry screening a flank march and the 'masse de rupture'.*

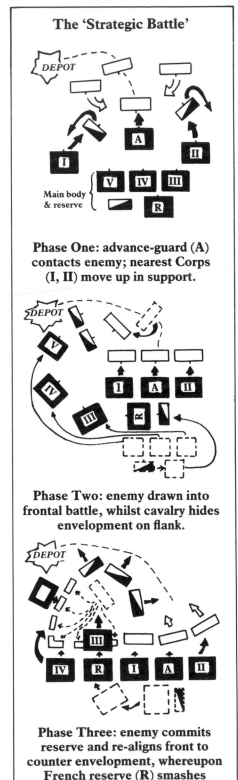

### The 'Strategic Battle'

**Phase One: advance-guard (A) contacts enemy; nearest Corps (I, II) move up in support.**

**Phase Two: enemy drawn into frontal battle, whilst cavalry hides envelopment on flank.**

**Phase Three: enemy commits reserve and re-aligns front to counter envelopment, whereupon French reserve (R) smashes through weakened line, destroying enemy.**

*Much depended upon the initial intelligence
and reconnaissance, which was founded
upon the light cavalry screen and advance
staff officers, such as the one illustrated
opposite. (Print after Meisonnier)*

main body was located, the advance would be drawn together into the formation known as a *bataillon carré*. This involved the various *corps d'armée* marching as the corners of a loose square, mutually supporting, with ideally no more than a day's march between corps; one corps in the lead, two further back on either flank, and one in the rear, with any additional corps tagged on behind. Though mutually supporting, the fact that each corps was a self-contained entity enabled any one to fight a holding action on its own; and by virtue of the 'square' formation, a rapid change of direction was possible, one of the flanking 'corners' becoming the vanguard if a 90-degree change of direction was required. When the enemy was encountered, a rapid concentration would take place, assembling most of the army together, intended to give the French numerical superiority at one point; Napoleon did win victories when outnumbered (most notably Austerlitz) but the essence of his system was to achieve 'local superiority'.

With this in view, Napoleon used two basic strategies, which may be termed the 'central position' and the 'rear manoeuvre'. The first of these was used when confronted by a numerically-superior enemy. Napoleon's theory was simple: in order to achieve 'local superi-

ority' with an inferior force, he must separate the enemy into two wings and defeat each in turn: hence the 'central position', i.e. interposing himself between the two enemy wings. Having established where the enemy's weakest point lay, he would then fall upon it with lightning speed and over-run the defenders of the 'central position'. Having selected his primary target, Napoleon would then detach at least one *corps d'armée* to engage and 'pin' the secondary target, whilst he with the rest of his army, including the reserve which he normally commanded in person, fell upon the wing selected for first destruction. By massing the majority of his army against this wing he achieved his desired local superiority, and was thus able to overthrow half the enemy. As soon as this force was defeated, Napoleon would detach two elements of his army, one to pursue the retiring enemy wing, and one to force-march in aid of the corps engaging the other wing, whose delaying actions would give him time to bring up the remainder of his troops, once again achieving local superiority and destroying the second enemy wing. A vigorous pursuit prevented any immediate reformation of the enemy forces.

The second stratagem, used more often in the heyday of the Empire as

Napoleon often enjoyed numerical superiority, was the 'rear manoeuvre', an envelopment of the enemy's rear again made possible by screening his real intentions from the enemy. Using a minor portion of his force, Napoleon would demonstrate in front of, or engage, the main enemy army, whilst

*The 'strategy of envelopment' illustrated on an imaginary terrain. The range of high ground acts as a 'curtain of manoeuvre' (which could equally well be a river) behind which Napoleon's main force advances, hidden from the enemy by a screen of light cavalry. The enemy army is preoccupied by Napoleon's 'covering force' and a diversionary attack, whilst Napoleon's main body crosses through the 'curtain' to threaten the enemy's lines of communication; advance bases are established and a corps d'observation detached to guard against any reinforcement for the enemy. With communications severed, the enemy must divide their force (part to contain the French diversion) and the remainder engage Napoleon's main army in the rear, on ground of Napoleon's choosing and cut off from assistance.*

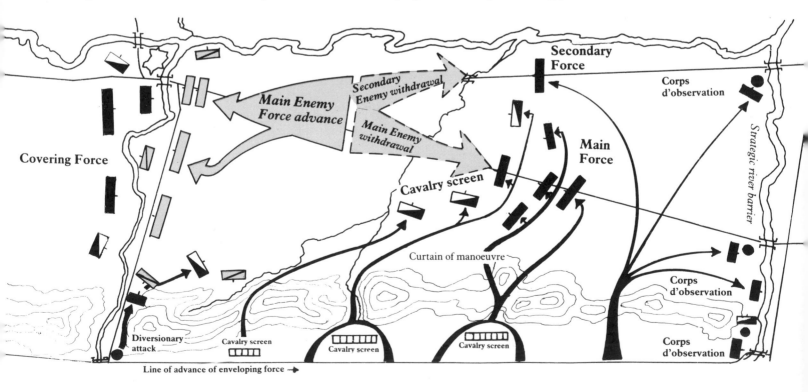

Covering Force

Main Enemy Force advance

Secondary Enemy withdrawal

Main Enemy withdrawal

Cavalry screen

Curtain of manoeuvre

Diversionary attack

Cavalry screen

Cavalry screen

Cavalry screen

Line of advance of enveloping force →

Secondary Force

Corps d'observation

Main Force

Strategic river barrier

Corps d'observation

Corps d'observation

marching with the majority of his army around the enemy's flank, severing his line of communication with his bases, thus compelling the enemy to fight upon Napoleon's terms and Napoleon's ground, and also to divide his force, for to concentrate his entire army upon Napoleon's main body would leave his rear open to attack from the corps which had originally occupied the enemy's attention. To prevent any reinforcement of the enemy army, Napoleon would detach a *corps d'observation* to interpose itself between the likely route of enemy reinforcement and the area in which the main battle would be fought. This plan of 'rear manoeuvre' or envelopment was potentially the most decisive, and most likely to result in the single, crushing blow which Napoleon always sought. A third manoeuvre, not in itself decisive, was the 'strategic penetration': by smashing rapidly through the enemy's 'cordon of defence' and marching deep into enemy territory, seizing a town or city for use as 'centre of operations', Napoleon at once threw the enemy's rear into confusion and set up the conditions for the employment of one or other of his two principle strategies.

Napoleon's tactics on the battlefield again were centred on attack, *toujours l'attaque*; in only three battles did he defend (Leipzig, La Rothière and Arcis-sur-Aube) and then only when initial offensive movements had failed. Battlefield 'grand tactics' involved three basic manoeuvres which mirrored his strategic theories: the 'central position' to divide the enemy's army; the envelopment of the enemy's flank; and, if all else were impossible, a frontal attack. As with strategical manoeuvres, however, these were not necessarily separate operations but could be combined together: flexibility was one of the greatest virtues of Napoleon's system of operations. The 'strategic battle' was typical of such a combination: by which the French advance-guard would engage the enemy as soon as contact was established, reinforced by the nearest supporting troops who extended the front of operations and thus drew in more of the enemy forces. Shielded by a screen of light cavalry, a further supporting element would manoeuvre around the enemy's flank to threaten his line of communications, necessitating either a change in the enemy's disposi-

tions or drawing in his last reserves to protect his communications. Two variations were possible from this stage: either a concentration of Napoleon's efforts to crush the exposed flank, or more classically, to launch the French reserve, after a huge preliminary bombardment, to burst through part of the enemy's over-committed line, ripping the enemy's army in half. Finally, if terrain or circumstances would permit no other manoeuvre, a frontal attack had to be used, but even here Napoleon would attempt to pressurize one wing in the hope that the enemy would sustain it by drawing reserves from his centre, so that the main assault by the '*masse de rupture*' could fall upon the weakened part of the enemy's line; but frontal assaults were always costly and potentially disastrous: Borodino was a draw and Waterloo a defeat. But once the break in the enemy's line was achieved, it would be exploited at top speed, heavy cavalry smashing through the gap and light cavalry pouring after to pursue the fugitives. In 'minor tactics' – the mechanism of handling individual formations on the battlefield – Napoleon had little interest, though he did express a liking for *l'ordre mixte* as the most flexible of formations.

From about 1807 Napoleon's task became more difficult due to a combination of circumstances, including perhaps a lessening of his own powers; as armies grew larger he had to rely more upon allied contingents and the ability of subordinates. As all Napoleon's strategy required good co-ordination and rapidity of movement, poor roads or unadvantageous terrain could confound his schemes: if the various stages of a plan could not be performed with meticulous timing, there was always the chance of failure. (The ineptitude of timing attacks correctly contributed to so many defeats in the Iberian peninsula.) As his strategies had become somewhat predictable, Napoleon's opponents were able to apply counters to them: to defeat the 'central position' move, the defeated wing of an army would retire towards or

parallel to the undefeated wing; to counter the envelopment required supplies to be kept with the army (thus reducing reliance on distant depots and lines of communication) and maintaining steady pressure on the frontal French 'pinning' force. If an enemy were able to avoid the battle Napoleon craved, the French could be in trouble, as Napoleon's lack of concern with logistics could undo his plans by lack of supplies, as occurred with the retirement of the Russians in 1812, drawing him forward in search of the single decisive battle which he was unable to achieve. Perhaps the supreme irony was the manner of Napoleon's final defeat, when at Waterloo the French army was engaged frontally and compelled to commit ever more troops to the main assault, leaving them vulnerable to the Prussian attack on the flank. How appropriate that the supreme commander of the age should finally fall to the use of his own tactics against him.

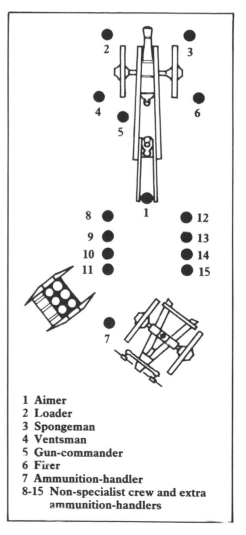

1 Aimer
2 Loader
3 Spongeman
4 Ventsman
5 Gun-commander
6 Firer
7 Ammunition-handler
8-15 Non-specialist crew and extra
    ammunition-handlers

*The most basic tactical element was the platoon or section; or as here, the gun-crew. This illustration shows the positions adopted by the crew of a French 12pdr field-gun during the firing-drill, with the* coffret *(ammunition-chest) and limber.*

# The Speed of Manoeuvre

The keystone of Napoleon's system of warfare was the ability of his armies to march at a speed which made possible his system of *blitzkrieg*: to out-march his opponents and fight a battle at the end of the most gruelling of forced marches. The character of the men he led played as large a role in the success of Napoleon's campaigns as did his tactical genius, for without the determination of the army, his plans were inoperable. The armies of the revolutionary wars had originated the French reputation for out-marching their enemy, originating from the system of victualling adopted out of necessity: by 'living off the land' armies were no longer constrained by slow supply-trains. But many Napoleonic armies *were* encumbered by vehicles; what was significant was not the 'average' speed of an army but the fact that at times large numbers of troops were able to travel considerable distances at great speed: it was this capability for rapid movement over a short period which confounded their opponents.

Theoretical speeds of manoeuvre are of little relevance in gauging what might occur on campaign, for such theoretical calculations were performed under ideal conditions, not over wretched roads or open country. This theoretical infantry pace measured 26½in, 76 paces to the minute in ordinary time and 100 paces to the minute in quick time; horses walked 400 yards in 4½ minutes, trotted the same distance in 2 minutes 3 seconds, and galloped it in 1 minute. A horse-drawn gun-team walked at 93 yards per minute, trotted at 204 and galloped at 216. On campaign, however, 10 to 12 miles per day might be an acceptable average, taking into account the many variables such as conditions of terrain, weather, quantity of baggage and hours of daylight, and the halts required to allow the pace to be maintained. The British artillerist Adye stated that the cavalry's usual rate of march was 17 miles in six hours, though this could be increased to 28 miles in that time for short periods, but cavalry in particular could not sustain such a pace without respite; infantry was far more resilient in maintaining a punishing schedule. Sustained effort could wreck an army; for example, at the beginning of the Peninsular War Junot's army marched from the French border to Lisbon, taking 43 days to cover 640 miles, the first 300 at twelve miles a day on main roads, and the balance at eighteen miles a day, over minor roads; but the cavalry and artillery had to be left behind and re-horsed en route, arriving in Lisbon ten days after the infantry!

Many troops were capable of making rapid marches of brief duration; the most famous of the Napoleonic Wars was performed by the British light brigade en route for Talavera, 42 miles in 26 hours, plus perhaps an additional four or five miles beyond Talavera; but for sustained pace, the French could not be equalled. There are many examples of prodigious feats which could turn a campaign, and which demonstrate the amazing endurance of the army: when executing the manoeuvre at Ulm, the *Grande Armée* moved from the Rhine to Danube and east in 11 days, Soult's

*The* Grande Armée *in columns of march crosses the Niemen to launch the invasion of Russia in 1812, watched by Napoleon in the distance (left).*
*(Print after F. de Myrbach)*

corps covering 275 miles. Davoût's corps marched to Austerlitz covering over 70 miles in a little over 48 hours, and the same general entered Berlin on 25 October 1806 after marching 166 miles as the crow flies, and having fought the battle of Auerstädt en route, in fourteen days. Marching to Russia in 1812, two Young Guard regiments covered 468 miles in 23 days. In his 1796 campaign Napoleon fought two battles in the week 5-11 September, during which time Massena's division covered 100 miles (including crossing a river by ferry) and Augereau's 114 miles; as Yorck von Wartenberg remarked, 'It is only a genius who can compel ordinary human beings to perform such feats', and that Napoleon did not 'vanquish his enemies so much by the battles of Ulm and Jena, however disastrous these were, as by his incredible marches'. Forced marches, however, were gruelling in the extreme for the troops, to appreciate which it is necessary to read a first-hand account such as that provided by Jean-Roch Coignet:

'Never was there such a terrible march. We had not a moment for sleep, marching by platoons all day and all night, and at last holding on to each other to prevent falling. Those who fell could not be wakened. Some fell into the ditches. Blows with the flat of the sabre had no effect on them. The bands played and the drums beat; nothing got the better of sleep. The nights were terrible. I was on the right of a section. About midnight I fell down the bank at the side of the road. I turned over and over, and went rolling down, never stopping till I reached an open field. I did not let go my musket, but I rolled into the other world. My brave captain sent someone down to look after me. I was badly bruised. They took my knapsack and musket. I was now thoroughly awake . . .'

The mechanics of the march were very different on campaign from the formations adopted on parade. On service, it was usual for formations to be very loose indeed; Comeau, a French émigré in Bavarian service, was astonished by the march from Ulm to Vienna, the French appearing 'no longer anything but an army in rout, but in rout in advance instead of in retreat. This torrent took the direction of Vienna, and henceforth there was nothing but an 'arrive qui peut' by roads full and encumbered. Our

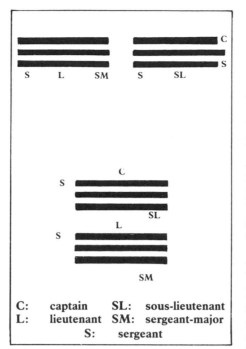

*Formation of the basic infantry unit, the company. Above: in line, 1st section right, 2nd left, three ranks deep. Below: a company in column, each section three ranks deep. These were the standard formations for manoeuvre on parade and in action; much looser organisation was utilised on the march.*

German army alone marched like regular troops'; but, he noted, at the first alarm the disorder was replaced at once by regiments assembled in formation. Such loose formations, however, encouraged marauding, so that orders had to be issued like that in May 1809: 'Every straggler who, under pretext of fatigue, leaves his corps for the purpose of marauding, will be arrested, tried by court martial, and executed on the spot.' Normally, troops would assemble at dawn and march at about three miles per hour, halting in the early afternoon with time to forage, cook and rest, the camping-ground having been selected by advance parties. Bands and drummers were essential in maintaining morale and, in the thick dust raised on dry terrain, in keeping the men on the correct route; in the advance into Russia in 1812 only the drums beating at the head of battalions enabled men to keep their bearings, so thick was the dust. Even where decent roads existed (and many traversed by Napoleon's armies were wretched in the extreme, becoming

mudpits in wet weather which sucked off boots), so vast were the armies that many had to march over open country; for example, 30,000 infantry on the march occupied five miles of road, 60 guns and caissons took up 2½ miles, and 6,000 cavalry, riding four abreast, 4 miles. Infantry might file alongside the guns but a number of parallel routes would be required to move anything more than a division. In 'minor tactics', movement on the battlefield was best performed in column; line-formations tended to move more slowly due to the greater difficulties of maintaining cohesion in line than in column.

Comparatively little use was made of waggon-transport for troops, partly because of the shortage of waggons and horses, as there were never sufficient to meet the needs of the supply-trains, especially when the state of the roads deteriorated so much that, as in Poland in 1806-07, nothing could move without a double or treble team. On decent roads, however, troop-transports could be utilised, for example the Imperial Guard column sent from Paris to Strasbourg in 1805 by 'post', troops packed four or five to a two-wheeled cart or twelve to a four-wheel waggon, covering 60 miles a day by changing horses at 'posting-stages' ten miles apart, but this was both exhausting for the men and very wearing on equipment. River-boats and barges might be used when possible, and sledges utilised in winter, the latter even taking a defensive function: in 1812 Marbot dismounted the 23rd and 24th *Chasseurs à Cheval* and formed a sledge-transported brigade, the sledges drawn into a square laager at night, behind which the men (each armed with two muskets) were secure from attack by marauding cossacks. The army's marching capability declined in the later campaigns, however, and Napoleon tended to expect too much of his men after 1812; the 1813-14 campaigns might have ended differently had Napoleon's troops possessed the capabilities of the *Armée d'Italie*. At the peak, however, the system was amazing: in 1805 Napoleon moved 210,500 men (226 battns, 29,500 cavalry in 233 squadrons, 161 engineer and artillery companies) and 396 guns (including 58 12pdrs and 146 8pdrs and 5,430 draught horses) with supplies more than 200 miles in 13 days, a most formidable achievement.

# The Attack in Column

Much has been written regarding the tactic of infantry attack in column, and a number of misleading conceptions have resulted. As described already, attack in column was adopted originally as the most efficacious method of utilising the largely undrilled conscript units of the revolutionary wars, who were incapable of more sophisticated tactics; yet this crude device was not intended to be employed on its own once training has been achieved, but instead to be utilised merely as part of more elaborate man-oeuvres. Much misconception occurs over the very term 'column', the popular vision of an immensely-long mass of men only a few files wide being accurate only for marching columns. In essence the 'attack column' was a rectangle, its front far wider than its depth: a 'battalion column', for example, with the French nine-company per battalion establish-ment, was 50 yards wide and about 21 yards (twelve ranks) deep; with the later six-company establishment it has a frontage of 75 yards and a depth of 15 yards. Even a 'column of companies' (each company arrayed behind another) might have a frontage of 25 yards. Only in the most restricted terrain (mountain warfare, street-fighting and siege-opera-tions) did 'attack columns' resemble marching columns.

The advantages of the column, in addition to mobility, were flexibility (in that other formations could easily be formed from column), the maintenance of greater cohesion at speed than pos-sible with a line, and also a psychological advantage over the enemy, many of whom, in Wellington's words, were half-beaten before the battle began, overawed by the great victories won by the French in previous years. The major

*French infantry formations. (Above): A 'battalion column' under the six-company establishment, led by the* voltigeurs *(V) and grenadiers (G), with the four fusilier (F) companies behind. Each company three ranks deep; frontage of 75 yards and depth of 15 yards. (Below): An alternative 'column of companies' adopted when the* voltigeurs *were deployed ahead of the column in a skirmish-screen. Grenadiers would bring up the rear if the other companies were likely to falter.*

disadvantage of the column was that only the first two, or at the maximum three ranks, were able to use their muskets; thus a unit in column would be at a severe disadvantage when opposed by an equally-sized unit in line, where all men would be able to bring their muskets to bear simultaneously. But this is a simplification which over-looks the essential purpose of the column as employed from the late revolutionary period onwards: that it was a method of allowing units to approach the enemy rapidly but not primarily a method of engaging them in combat; for if the enemy were not sufficiently shaken by a preliminary or accompanying artillery bombardment, or by the horde of skirm-ishers which ideally preceded on attack column (in which case the enemy might begin to break before the column came within bayonet-range, allowing the column to punch through the enemy line as in the early days of the revolutionary wars), when approaching musket-range the column then halted to deploy into

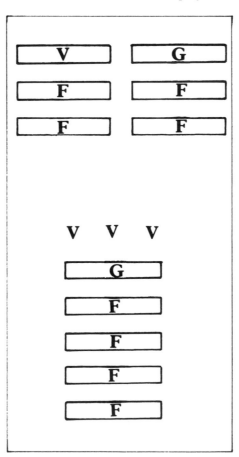

line, to utilise its maximum firepower. It was when the column failed to deploy that it began to be beaten with regu-larity, most notably by the British in the Peninsular War.

In assessing the weakness of the column formation it is useful to quote General Bugeaud's vivid description of a typical attack in the Peninsular War, which in its early stages is typical of column-attacks against any army:

'. . . we marched straight on, taking the bull by the horns. About 1,000 yards from the English line the men became excited, called out to one another, and hastened their march; the column began to become a little confused. The English remained quite silent with ordered arms, and from their steadiness appeared to be a long red wall. This steadiness invari-ably produced an effect on our young soldiers. Very soon we got nearer, crying *"Vive l'Empéreur! En avant! A la baionette!"* Shakos were raised on the muzzles of muskets; the column began to double, the ranks got into confusion, the agitation produced a tumult; shots were fired as we advanced. The English line remained silent, still and immovable, with ordered arms, even when we were only 300 yards distant, and it appeared to ignore the storm about to break. The contrast was striking; in our innermost thoughts we all felt the enemy was a long time in firing, and that this fire reserved so long would be very unpleasant when it came. Our ardour cooled. The moral power of steadiness, which nothing can shake (even if it be only appearance), over disorder which stupifies itself with noise, overcame our minds. At this moment of intense excitement, the English wall shouldered arms; an indes-cribable feeling would root many of our men to the spot; they began to fire. The enemy's steady, concentrated volleys swept our ranks; decimated, we turned round seeking to recover our equili-brium; then three deafening cheers broke the silence of our opponents; at the third they were on us, pushing our disorganised flight.'

Some historians have argued that the French delivered column attacks of this nature by design, remembering the revolutionary wars and intending to use the impetus of the charge and the psychological advantage to crash right through the enemy line. This may have been true in some cases; but probably

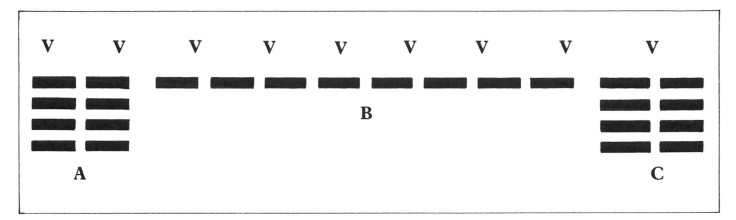

*The classic formation of* l'ordre mixte, *which could be employed at every level from battalion up to division. Three battalions are shown, with the nine-company establishment: 'A' are two battalions each deployed in 'column of divisions' (two-company frontage), and 'B' is the third battalion, deployed in line. The* voltigeur *company (V) from each battalion precedes the advance in a skirmish-line. Each company occupied a frontage of about 25 yards, three ranks deep. Depth of battalion column about 21-25 yards.*

the regular defeats of French columns in the Peninsular War resulted instead from poor co-ordination (not supporting attacks with artillery, without which failure was already half-certain) and in the inability to deploy into line at the required moment. Wellington's practice of keeping his main body on the reverse slopes of a ridge not only protected them from the preliminary artillery and skirmish-fire (and the French skirmishers found their British counterparts more than a match), but also prevented the French commanders from knowing where their enemy was, and thus from gauging the moment at which it was necessary to deploy from column. Keeping the columns formed until the crest of the ridge was reached, they saw the British when it was too late to deploy; raked by musketry, often from three sides, the head of the column would disintegrate and the whole be swept back down the hill by the threat of the succeeding British bayonet-charge. Even

*Grenadiers of the Imperial Guard in column of march, 1813-14; such formations were used for combat only in restricted terrain. Napoleon is visible at the right. (Print after A. Bligny).*

the Imperial Guard at Waterloo fell into this trap: they attempted to deploy when the British troops in their front stood up and began to fire, but deployment under such a volume of fire was impossible, and destruction was assured. Nevertheless, it was only by the British that the column was defeated regularly: to use Wellington's phrase, coming on in the old style, and being beaten off in the old style; in other theatres its flexibility overthrew virtually every army which it encountered, providing the necessary support was co-ordinated.

With the declining standard of infantry, more massive columns tended to be used, less flexible and consequently less successful than before. Macdonald's enormous formation at Wagram was

typical, a vast square of 23 battalions, 8,000 strong, led by two ranks of four battalions in line with a frontage of 1,200 yards and a depth of 750 yards. Unable to manoeuvre as freely as before due to the declining quality of training and experience as ever more conscripts were pushed into the infantry to replace casualties, such unwieldy formations had only a limited chance of success when attacking uphill against troops whose morale was not already shaken. The failings of these vast columns when compared with the *ordre mixte* are demonstrated by the defeat of d'Erlon at Waterloo, when columns were employed of 6, 7, 8 and 9 battalions, each battalion in line behind one another, 200 yards wide and 30 yards deep.

# The Cavalry's Tactics

Napoleon's use of his cavalry throughout his campaigns serves to emphasize that not only were they the most visually impressive part of his army, but also one of the most decisive. Whilst the three basic varieties of cavalry (heavy, light and dragoons) had their own individual characteristics, as already described, many aspects of cavalry service and tactics were similar for all branches.

Training was crucial, and involved not only the ability to handle weapons and to act as part of a cohesive body, but included the additional requirment of horsemanship, of the ability to control an animal which under combat conditions might be driven to panic by noise or wounds. Consequently, cavalry training was more extensive than that of infantry, and imperfections in training more apparent. The marked decline in the heavy cavalry in particular following the catastrophic Russian campaign of 1812 was due in part to the difficulty of procuring sufficiently large horses to carry a cuirassier, and partly to the lack of time available for training recruits: De Gonneville's account of the assembly of a raw regiment in 1813 is extreme, but demonstrates the problem. The first time the commanding officer assembled the regiment for drill, the order to draw swords caused scores of horses to bolt, 200 men were unseated, one squadron careered out of control for a mile, and it was two hours before the unit could be re-assembled. With the previous élite heavy cavalry, the cuirassiers, half-trained and mounted on unsuitable horses, it is easy to appreciate why the

veteran dragoon regiments withdrawn from Spain to the campaign in Germany and France were the best of Napoleon's heavy or 'medium' cavalry. Even earlier than the last campaigns, however, cavalry had taken the field in an imperfect state of training, as demonstrated by the action at Burkersdorf on 14 February 1807, in which the experienced and capable General Edouard Jean Baptiste Milhaud (1766-1833) was retiring with his dragoon division after a reconnaissance in force, followed by a much inferior force of Russian light cavalry. A single Russian hussar regiment suddenly fell upon his flank unexpectedly, and Milhaud ordered the nearest brigade to face the attack. It failed to do so before the Russians hit, and broke and fled; whereupon the other two brigades, seeing the rout, turned about and galloped away and could not be rallied until they had gone three miles to the rear. Milhaud was so appalled at this unaccustomed behaviour that he tried to commit suicide by charging the Russians accompanied by only four companions, but miraculously was not even captured; he then asked to be relieved of the command of troops who were so incompetent – 'je ne veux pas commander de pareilles troupes'. The explanation for this singular behaviour was that the six regiments in question had mostly begun the campaign as infantry-trained dismounted dragoons, and had only been converted to cavalry during the campaign.

Such behaviour, however, was most unusual: in general Napoleon's cavalry performed prodigies and on several

occasions (as at Eylau) were responsible on their own for saving the army from defeat. Horse-management, however, was never a high priority: it was said that French cavalry formations could often be detected before they came into view, by the smell of the infected saddle-sores; yet this is an unjust generalisation as some cavalry leaders, most especially Lasalle, paid the greatest attention to the well-being of their corps' mounts. Napoleon's view, despite his difficulty at times of finding suitable remounts, was allied to his theory of the offensive use of cavalry: 'I do not wish the horses to be spared if they can catch men . . . Take no heed of the complaints of the cavalry, for if such great objects may be obtained as the destruction of a whole hostile army, the state can afford to lose a few hundred horses from exhaustion.' The second element of cavalry training was swordsmanship, to which considerable importance was attached, but individual skill took a subsidiary place to discipline and the ability to act in a formed body, which increased in importance the greater numbers involved: Napoleon considered that although two mamelukes

*A squadron of cavalry in line or 'battle order', preceded by the regiment's adjutant and trumpeters. Assembled in two ranks, the frontage was about 52 yards and the depth about 6½ yards, though this would naturally depend upon the strength of the squardron. Note the disposition of the NCOs throughout the ranks, with officers and senior NCOs in the front and rear of the squadron, ensuring that not all would become casualties in the first moment of a charge. Succeeding squadrons would follow at about 17½ yd distance.*

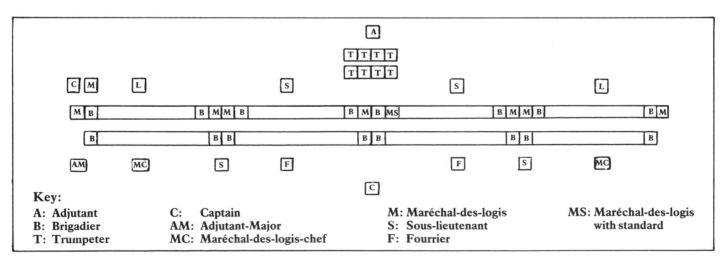

Key:
A: Adjutant
B: Brigadier
T: Trumpeter

C: Captain
AM: Adjutant-Major
MC: Maréchal-des-logis-chef

M: Maréchal-des-logis
S: Sous-lieutenant
F: Fourrier

MS: Maréchal-des-logis
with standard

could out-fight three Frenchmen, 300 French could defeat an equal number of mamelukes, and 1,000 French rout 1,500 mamelukes. A similar opinion was held by the Duke of Wellington: 'I considered our cavalry so inferior to the French for want of order, that although I considered one of our squadrons a match for two French, yet I did not care to see four British opposed to four French, and still more as the numbers increased, and order (of course) became more necessary.'

Cavalry formations resembled those of the infantry, in that they could operate both in line and column, and whilst the charge in line was the most classical formation, charge in column was used increasingly throughout the period and was, on balance, probably the more effective. The basic tactical unit was the squadron (of two companies), which in 'battle order' would assemble in two lines, with about half the officers and NCOs deployed at the rear, so that not all would become casualties in the first 'shock' on contact with the enemy, the squadrons of a regiment assembling either in one continuous line, in echelon, or one behind the other, or combinations of line and echelon. The depth of a two-rank line was about 6½ yards and the frontage of an average squadron (not including officers and NCOs on the flanks) about 52 yards. When drawn up in column (*colonne serré*) the squadrons would assemble in line, one behind the other, at a distance of 17½ yards. There were in addition three other types of column which were employed: firstly, 'column of divisions', in which the two companies of each squadron were ranked one behind the other, both arrayed in two lines, giving a single-company frontage of about 26 yards and a depth of about 40 yards. Secondly, 'column of platoons', in which each company was arrayed in four ranks, one behind the other, giving a frontage of about 13 yards, and with a 14 yd gap between each platoon of two ranks. Finally, for the march only, was the column of fours, where the men rode four abreast, the length of a squadron travelling in this manner being about 86 yards. In each case the NCOs and officers were distributed along the length of the column, many not being part of the lines but riding separately in order to maintain maximum control. Sufficient space was maintained between all these formations for the units to change from column to line and back again at a canter, flexibility being vitally important: the facility to 'change face' (i.e. change the direction in which they were proceeding) being imperative in action, if debâcles like that of Burkersdorf were to be avoided.

As conceived by Napoleon, the primary function of the cavalry – certainly the heavy cavalry, which he refused to disperse or wear-out by allowing them to operate as part of the reconnaissance-screens – was the charge, whether it be directed against infantry or other cavalry. The most important factor was timing the moment of the charge, both in its launch and in ensuring that its impetus was at a maximum at the moment of contact with the enemy. In this, discipline and experience were all-important. Under normal circumstances, a charge would begin at a walk, moving quickly to a trot until one-third of the distance to the enemy had been covered, when the pace would be increased to a canter. Only when the enemy was but 150 yards distant would the canter increase to a gallop, and only in the last 50 yards would the horses be allowed their head and the full-speed charge *à l'outrance* develop. Incorrect timing could result in the horses being 'blown' before the enemy had been reached, or the speed not having been increased to the maximum. This fact was appreciated by most French cavalry leaders; as Lasalle remarked when confronted by enemy cavalry coming towards him at full gallop, 'Look at those mad sods! Let them wear themselves out!'

Discipline was equally important after the first 'shock' of the charge had occurred, when the formations were broken and the fight had developed into a large number of personal combats. Two factors were of vital consequence: first, that the cavalry kept their heads and did not continue to charge, pursuing the fugitives, which could result in gallops of several miles of little tactical value (the perennial failing of the British cavalry); instead, once the enemy had been overthrown, it was imperative that the victorious cavalry rallied and re-formed before launching any pursuit, for only by re-forming could they successfully defend themselves against a counter-charge launched by an as yet uncommitted enemy force. Secondly, to guard against such a counter-attack, it was equally important that a portion of any charging cavalry force – ideally at least one-third of the whole – be held back, out of combat, to act as a reserve to protect the remainder whilst they were a vulnerable, milling mass. Once the troops conducting the original charge had reformed, the reserve could then be committed to the pursuit if necessary, in which case the re-formed body would then adopt the role of the reserve. The majority of cavalry actions were decided by one side or the other failing to obey this cardinal rule.

Many variable factors made each cavalry combat different, most significantly the state of the troops and the terrain: heavy ground or cavalry tired at the end of an action might cause a charge to be delivered at no more than a canter, occasionally at a walk. The enormous impact which might be expected when two bodies of cavalry charged towards each other (for it was dangerous to await an incoming charge at the halt or walk, giving the enemy the advantage of impetus) did not always result in a tremendous crash of falling horses and riders; though charges might be executed in such tight formations that horses and riders might be lifted off the ground by the pressure of their fellows at either side, equally the files of each unit could open to allow the enemy to pass right through, the men fencing at each other as they passed. Against infantry not in square, a cavalry charge was usually lethal (though in exceptional circumstances the infantry could drop flat and let the cavalry ride over them, horses being unwilling to tread upon prone bodies: the French 4th Line, ridden-over at Austerlitz, suffered only 18 dead); against squares, the cavalry was usually impotent, even when wet weather prevented the infantry from firing their muskets. The number of infantry squares broken by cavalry charges may almost be counted on one hand, and then only by exceptional circumstance (such as part of the square being crushed by a falling horse and rider), unless lancers were among the cavalry, when if the rain and consequent wet gunpowder prevented the infantry from firing, the lances could stab away at will without the infantry being able to reply; Austrian

squares were broken at Dresden in this manner, and Prussians at Katzbach, but these were the exceptions rather than the rule. All Napoleonic weapons dealt appalling injuries, but cavalry sabres were especially terrible; as Lasalle wrote of his charge at Medina de Rio Seco (an operation involving but three squadrons but which turned the course of the battle), 'My two regiments of chasseurs surpassed themselves and made a horrible carnage among those disgusting Spaniards . . . I saw sabre wounds eighteen inches long, and severed arms. It was magnificent . . .'

The nature of cavalry charges was often determined by the terrain, varying from a frontage of three-quarters of a mile at Waterloo, to the tactics employed at Ligny where from want of space regiments had to follow each other in column. This also affected the co-ordination of charges, for only in unusual circumstances was cavalry launched in the attack without supporting horse artillery or infantry; against unsupported infantry in squares, the joint deployment of horse artillery almost guaranteed

*A squadron of cavalry in 'column by fours', the usual formation adopted on the march. In this formation the companies of a squadron were spaced equally along the route, with sufficient room to allow the ranks to wheel and form a line of battle facing at right-angles to the line of march. Following squadrons maintained a gross distance (i.e. lead-horse to lead-horse, not the gap between the rear of one squadron and the front of another) of 100 metres (108 yards).*

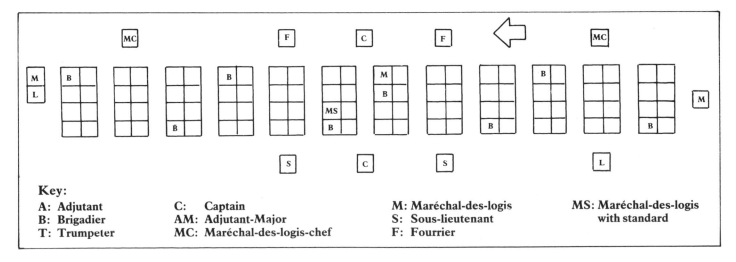

Key:
A: Adjutant
B: Brigadier
T: Trumpeter
C: Captain
AM: Adjutant-Major
MC: Maréchal-des-logis-chef
M: Maréchal-des-logis
S: Sous-lieutenant
F: Fourrier
MS: Maréchal-des-logis
with standard

success, as the infantry were unable to form in anything other than square for fear of massacre at the hands of the cavalry, yet remained most vulnerable to artillery fire. Charges which were unsupported were likely to end in failure, as Waterloo demonstrated. All these factors – discipline, co-ordination, timing and inspiration – depended upon competent leadership, and Napoleon was blessed by a number of the most outstanding cavalry generals of the age, and many others of professional competence. Whilst the peacock Joachim Murat (1767-1815) was the archetypal *beau sabreur*, ostensibly more concerned with the magnificence of his uniform than with any great pretensions as a strategist, he was beloved by the troops for his bravery, audacity and panâche, and was seconded by many generals of great ability: the hussar Lasalle, the heavy cavalrymen François Etienne Kellermann (1770-1835) and Etienne

*One of the greatest cavalry manoeuvres of the Napoleonic Wars was Murat's enormous charge with the massed reserve cavalry which stabilised the situation at Eylau, the employment of some 10,700 sabres in a vast column.*

Marie Nansouty (1768-1815), the cuirassiers Jean Joseph d'Hautpoul (1754-1807) and Jean Louis Espagne (1769-1809), Emmanuel Grouchy (1766-1847) and a host of lesser lights.

As already described, Napoleon's belief in the offensive power of cavlary on the battlefield led him to concentrate the heavy regiments into 'reserve' divisions for use as a *masse de rupture*, striking the enormous, decisive blow which would carve through the enemy; the vast charge at Eylau is a classic example. The lighter regiments, and dragoons, formed the brigades or divisions attached to each *corps d'armée*, with (in 1812) light regiments attached to the heavy reserve to provide their reconnaissance force. This led Napoleon to keep the reserve cavalry with his main army, never with enveloping forces which had to be content with their own medium and light cavalry attached at corps level. Similarly, large-scale raids behind enemy lines were rarely conducted, for whilst these were annoying to the enemy they contributed little to Napoleon's invariable objective: the annihilation of the enemy's field army. Scouting and 'outpost' work was the strict preserve of the light cavalry (and

sometimes dragoons), and required considerable skill both in discovering the enemy's movements and in concealing those of Napoleon's forces, the system of outposts and vedettes (single sentries or scouts) requiring as much care as manoeuvres on the battlefield.

Napoleon paid little attention to the 'minor tactics' of cavalry service: his concern was with the wider application of the force; in fact he never ordered the issue of a cavalry manual to replace the provisional revision of the 1788 manual. Yet he realised the crucial importance of the arm, without which an army was blind and deprived of its most rapid striking-force. The decline in calibre following the losses of 1812 was crucial, and so desperate were his attempts to keep a mounted arm of some description that in the depths of the terrible retreat from Moscow Napoleon organised the 'sacred squadron', a reversion to the 'reformado' practice of the 17th century, by which officers who no longer had any units to command were gathered into impromptu cavalry companies, with colonels acting as NCOs and generals as troop-officers. How true was Napoleon's statement, 'without cavalry, battles are without result.'

# Coastal Defences and Fortifications

The internal defences of the Empire were based upon a series of fortifications along the coastline and borders, with heavily-defended cities at strategic points; but although such bases were of considerable significance, the more fluid style of Napoleonic warfare relegated them from the position of crucial importance which they had held in the earlier years of the 18th century. The instructional text used by the artillery and engineer school of the *Ecole Polytechnique* demonstrated the doctrine of the time: 'an offensive war may . . . be carried on without the use of fortifications, (though recommending the use of field-works were applicable), but that for a defensive war, 'fortresses become essential'. However, the earlier significance of fortified bases was not simply that they provided havens for bodies of troops, who could thus dominate the surrounding country, but that they provided depots for the re-supply of field armies. With the greatly reduced need for such depots – by the French especially, given their policy of 'living off the land' – the importance of fortified bases declined accordingly, except in such areas where living by foraging was impractical. In many areas, the reduction of a fortified garrison was not worth the enormous cost in lives and

resources that a siege inevitably entailed, so the best expedient was not to invest but to detach a force to prevent any overtly offensive moves by the garrison, and simply by-pass the fort. In areas of poor communication, however, where fortresses dominated a major road network or protected a base of wider strategic value, greater efforts were required to maintain the fortifications and, from the enemy's viewpoint, to 'reduce' and capture them: the border-fortresses of Badajoz and Ciudad Rodrigo, and the ports of Danzig and Lisbon, are examples. Despite the change of emphasis occasioned by the Napoleonic art of war, fortresses still exerted some strategic significance: for example, the Italian campaign of 1796-97 revolved around the possession of Mantua; in 1792-93 the tenacious possession of fortresses in north-eastern France served to rally the French field armies; Massena's valiant but unavailing defence of Genoa occupied much Austrian attention while Napoleon marched across the Alps; and heroic stands like that of the Spanish at Saragossa served as symbols of national pride and rallying-calls to resist the invader. But the decline in importance was demonstrated equally: it was Marengo which decided the 1800 cam-

paign, not the continued possession by Austria of many garrisons in north Italy, and in 1814 the French possession of a chain of defence-works along the eastern border of France did not prevent the Allies from side-stepping them and advancing on Paris.

Nevertheless, Napoleon paid considerable attention to the renovation and maintenance of fortified cities along the frontiers and coasts, and indeed throughout all his possessions; as General Maximilien Foy (1775-1825), one of Napoleon's ablest divisional commanders, wrote: 'All Europe has been covered by our redoubts and entrenchments.' The purpose of many of these strong-points was as possible advance bases for offensive manoeuvres, but when France was under threat in 1813 Napoleon found it impossible to utilise them in this manner, and the troops which were blockaded in various large fortresses served only to deprive him of resources which would have been better utilised with the field army; though they did occupy some Allied attention and gain a little time. The great age of fortification-design was at the close of the 17th century, and designs of defence were still based on those of the great engineer Sebastien de Vauban (1633-1707). Certain new developments were added to the Vaubanesque style of fortification, most notably in the increase of 'out-works' (detached defences which delayed the approach of a besieger) and by the enclosure of hitherto-open gun emplacements in 'casemates', roofed galleries which gave the guns and crews greater protection from enemy fire. Carnot contined this practice by advocating in addition the use of *caponiers*, storied structures from which casemated guns could pour enfilade fire along the defence-ditches at the base of the wall, so that every part of the attackers' approach would be open to fire from the defences.

*The fort at Toulon (1793), where Bonaparte first came to prominence, is typical of the style of earthworks which might be erected outside the stone defences of a fortification: the wall (and ramparts) are made of packed earth, held together by wicker hurdles with posts driven into the ground, with 'storm-poles' outside.*

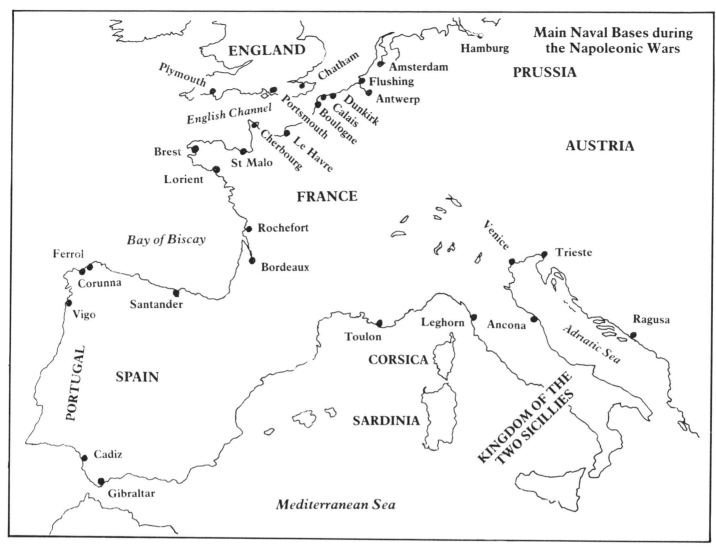

Main Naval Bases during the Napoleonic Wars

As the great expense involved precluded total reconstruction, most existing fortresses were merely improved by the addition of new batteries and outworks. Additional defences could be constructed quickly by using earthworks and gabions (earth-filled baskets) instead of stone, which had the additional advantage of absorbing the enemy's roundshot, which would sink into the earth ramparts without inflicting much material damage.

Coastal defences were equally important, though comparatively few descents on the French coast were ever attempted, and those which were ended in failure, but the cause was as much due to the mismanagement of the attack as to the strength of the defences. The huge Mediterranean naval base of Toulon was captured in 1793 and held by an Anglo-royalist force for three months before being ejected; a similar landing of émigrés at Quiberon in 1795, endeavouring to support royalist risings in the Vendée, met with even greater defeat. A British landing at Ostend (1798), intending to destroy the Bruges-Ostend canal, was catastrophically mis-managed; and the landing at Walcheren in 1809, intended to open a 'second front' and instigate a German uprising, was another disaster which if properly managed would probably have captured Antwerp. Nevertheless, such landings did have the effect of keeping large numbers of troops occupied in coastal-protection duties, who were often needed urgently elsewhere.

In addition to the regular troops, there existed a number of home-defence formations for internal security. For the shore defences there were the units of Canonniers Gardes-Côtes (Coast Artillery), organised by Napoleon into 100 mobile companies under artillery command; and 28 static companies of National Guard, the latter termed Canonniers Sédentaires (Garrison Artillery). Two other varieties of home-service troops existed, the Departmental Reserve Companies and the National Guard. The Reserve Companies (organised in 1805) were used for internal duties which might otherwise have required the use of regular troops or the Gendarmerie (quasi-military police), locally-based and formed in each département (administrative area), but who could be mobilised for active service as in the 'Departmental Legions' which fought in the Peninsular War. The National Guard was resurrected in March 1812, into which men up to the age of 60 could not be conscripted. The force was organised in 88 'cohorts', each comprising one depot, one artillery and six fusilier companies; they numbered a total of about 78,000 men and in January 1813 were incorporated into the army.

93

# Communications, Semaphore and Intelligence

The whole purpose of war, wrote Wellington, was endeavouring to discover what was on the other side of the hill. Thus, intelligence and communications were vital factors for any campaign, though even at the height of his power, Napoleon was never able to overcome the fact that in the field, messages could only be relayed at the speed of a horse and rider.

The basic element in military communications was the Aide-de-Camp mounted upon a fast horse, usually a young and audacious officer who would carry written despatches between the general staff and individual units. Every general officer had a staff of ADCs waiting in turn to carry his messages, a duty both arduous and extremely dangerous; Marbot's attempt to rescue the 14th Line at Eylau, a unit having received no orders to retire due to all the previous messengers having been killed, is an example of how a general's staff could be annihilated in a single battle. One lost message could result in disaster: thus in

very heavy fire a relay of couriers might be sent with duplicate messages, to ensure that at least one reached his destination. Invariably mounted upon the best horses available, and able to commandeer remounts from any unit en route, ADCs were capable of rapid movement: four miles in eighteen minutes was nothing unusual.

Although communications on campaign were dependent largely upon the speed attainable by a horseman, other modes of communication were utilised, most notably the telegraph or semaphore. The first mechanical system of signalling appears to have been a rudimentary semaphore invented by an Englishman named Edgeworth who in 1767 was able to transmit the results of horse-races from Newmarket to London, but the first practical military use was the invention of the 'Tachygraphe' (later 'Telegraph'), devised by the French engineer Claude Chappé (1763-1805). His original device consisted of an upright post upon which was a transverse

bar, with movable arms or discs at the ends, the position of which could be varied to indicate individual letters or words. By a chain of signal-stations at visible distances, a speed of transmission of about 120 miles per hour was possible in good weather. Chappé's device was adopted (at Carnot's behest) in 1792, and a chain of 22 stations was established between Paris and Lille; so efficient was the system that the capture of Condé in 1793 was announced to Paris

*Chappé's original telegraph consisted of a post with movable 'arms' affixed to it, by which messages could be spelled out, each position representing a letter or word. Other patterns of mechanised semaphore existed, however, including one with movable boards arrayed on a 'ladder' frame, the combination of boards similarly spelling words. The telegraph arms (above) are taken from Rev J Gamble's* Essay on Modes of Communication, *1797. The 'ladder' framework is topped by a red 'bonnet of liberty', the republican symbol.*

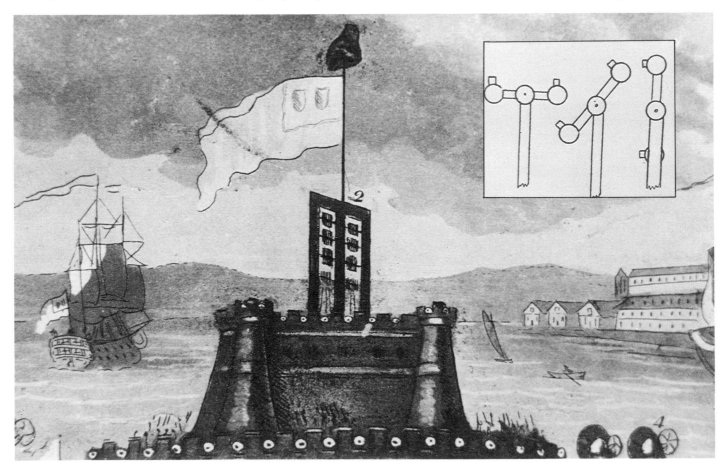

in 20 minutes. In 1793 Chappé was appointed as official *ingénieur-télégraphe*, but the originality of his invention was questioned as other inventors attempted to copy it, and as a result Chappé was seized with melancholia and committed suicide in 1805.

The telegraph service prospered during the Empire, the military application being run by the small but efficient Military Telegraph Service, who manned a series of stations linking Paris with the great cities of the Empire and the naval bases; where practicable on campaign a series of flag-relay posts was established to keep Imperial headquarters in contact with the nearest permanent telegraph-station. However, there were serious shortcomings to the telegraph, which was inoperable in bad weather (especially fog and snow) which necessitated the maintenance of the military postal service which ran a relay of despatch-riders and mail-coaches to transmit the longer despatches. An example of how the telegraph could fail is provided in the 1809 campaign, when Napoleon sent a critical message by telegraph from Paris to Berthier, in command at the front. Half an hour after sending the telegraph signal, a qualifying message was despatched by courier. Due to fog and the slow transmission of the message from Strasbourg onwards, the telegraph message took six days to arrive; whereas the courier reached Berthier two and a half days earlier. Berthier's subsequent misunderstanding of the supplementary message (without having the original despatch which it was intended to qualify) led to two days of utter confusion, with units marching and counter-marching to no effect, and it was only good fortune that the error was not attended by fatal consequences.

When couriers were in danger of being intercepted, messages were relayed in cypher. In the Peninsular War, for example, guerrilla raids were so common that ADCs were not even safe if accompanied by a company of cavalry, and many French despatches fell into guerrilla hands, and were then transmitted to Wellington. The French cyphers were little security, as Wellington's headquarters included Capt George Scovell, who was a brilliant code-breaker; he even cracked the complex 'Great Paris Cypher' which was used for the most important despatches.

*An ADC wearing staff uniform, though many wore regimental uniform or costume unique to the staff of a particular marshal. The colour of the brassard indicated the rank of general to whose staff they were attached. (Print by Martinet)*

Intelligence in the field was gathered firstly by the advance reconnaissance-parties and light cavalry scouts, who even penetrated enemy lines to discover the enemy's composition and location, with great audacity. In addition to intelligence gleaned in this manner and by the interrogation of prisoners-of-war, Napoleon possessed a number of spies, the most audacious of whom was the chameleon Charles Schulmeister. A master of disguise who could alter his appearance by changing his expression and combing his hair, Schulmeister proved an invaluable source of information in the early stages of the Austerlitz campaign, in which he posed as a dealer in tobacco and spirits and insinuated himself into the Austrian general headquarters. The Austrian commander Mack believed him to be an Austrian spy, and thus Schulmeister was privy to much information regarding troop-movements and Allied strategy, which he duly passed to Napoleon. About half way through the campaign Schulmeister was discovered to be an imposter, but amazingly the Austrians let him go after a beating. Another major factor in field-intelligence was the provision of accurate maps; the Topographical Department was invalu-

able in providing accurate information to general headquarters, but never seems to have operated in Spain, where Massena (in particular) had enormous difficulties in having to use inaccurate, outdated and locally-produced cartography such as Lopez's map of Spain.

Aerial observation was used briefly during the Revolutionary Wars, a *Compagnie d'Aërostiers* being created under J.M.J. Coutelle and N.J. Conté in March 1794. The aviation service used captive hydrogen balloons (the gas produced by passing steam over red-hot iron, the use of sulphuric acid being forbidden in the interests of the gunpowder industry), the two-man crew of each balloon ('pilot' and observer) transmitting messages to the ground by flag-signal, luminous balls hung on the basket or messages slid in sandbags down the cables. Such observation was of great assistance in the victory of Fleurus, and though by 1796 France possessed four balloons, of which one was taken to Egypt, Napoleon never believed in the concept and the aviation service was disbanded in 1799.

Internal security was controlled by the Gendarmerie (quasi-military police), the whole under the command of the sinister Minister of Police, Joseph Fouché (1759-1820). One of the period's great survivors, Fouché was an accomplished schemer, serving first Robespierre, then the Directory and Napoleon, all of whom he betrayed for his own ends. He eliminated most of the opposition to Napoleon (both royalist and republican) but was dismissed in 1810 following proof of his plotting with the Bourbons, but remained in command of events by his network of personal agents, which was so invaluable that in 1815 he was reinstated to his former post by both Napoleon and the Bourbons, until finally dismissed as untrustworthy in 1816; he retired in luxury to Trieste on his ill-gotten proceeds, a feared, hated and thoroughly untrustworthy man. Internal security of the Empire was not unbreachable; Allied spies produced some notable coups, and the Gendarmerie was not so vigilant to prevent the famous swindler Collot from inpersonating an *inspecteur aux révues* (general staff inspector) with great panache, turning out the garrisons of numerous towns and obtaining free dinners and free quarter in every one!

# The Medical Services

The weapons of the Napoleonic era caused frightful injury. Sabres might make clean cuts, but the lead musket-ball often flattened and fragmented on impact, whilst a roundshot, even rolling along the ground like a cricket ball, would literally carry away any limb which lay in its path. In general, medical and surgical knowledge was limited, and any wound, no matter how slight, could result in death from neglect or gangrene, with amputation the universal palliative. Anaesthetics and hygiene were non-existent, operations were carried out in the open field and many injured soldiers, if their wounds were inspected at all, received only 'a few words of consolation, or perhaps a little opium . . . all that could be recommended . . . prudence equally forbids the rash interposition of unavailing art, and the useless indulgence of delusive hope.' Disease was even worse than injuries in battle, for a lingering sickness could devastate an army; as Napoleon wrote, 'It is better to fight the most sanguinary battle than to encamp the troops in an unhealthy spot.' (Napoleon appears not to have placed great reliance upon his physicians, writing to Eugène in 1813: 'Above all choose a very healthy soil. Consult the medical men and the natives on this point. Do not permit any exceptions. If you are close to marshes or inundated meadows, you may say what you like, but you are in an unhealthy spot and must go higher up. You will understand that in such places I should lose my whole army in one spring month. I wish you to consult your common sense and the natives rather than the doctors.') Though few European sicknesses ever approached the mortality-rates of troops serving in the West Indies, malarial fevers were an ever-present danger of any siege, and at times had devastating effect; in 1807, out of every 196 French soldiers admitted to hospital, only 47 were wounded, and at the beginning of the 1812 campaign, for example, it was estimated that about half the Bavarian corps fell ill before they had ever fired a shot. 'Guadiana fever' (suffered in Portugal) and the infamous 'Walcheren fever', both the result of stagnant water, were terrible scourges for which the medical establishment had no response; when

asked to investigate the Walcheren outbreak, the British Physician-General declined as 'he was not acquainted with the diseases of soldiers in camp or quarters'! Many doctors could suggest no more effective treatment than inducing bleeding (even for wounded men who had lost blood!) or the 'cure' prescribed by one doctor: 'the best of living and at least two bottles of Madeira per diem.' Small wonder that the medical profession in general had the reputation encapsulated by the cossack Platov's reply when the Czar offered him more surgeons: 'God and your Majesty forbid! The fire of the enemy is not half so fatal as one drug!'

Of all the European armies, the French ultimately had the most enlightened medical system, at least from the Austerlitz period onwards, but in the Revolutionary Wars it was deplorable; as the great surgeon Pierre François Percy remarked in 1799, 'One would believe that the sick and wounded cease to be men when they can no longer be soldiers.' Principally responsible for this appalling state was the fact that in 1792 all medical schools had been abolished in France as 'privileged' establishments; the training schools which had replaced them were largely useless, and only in 1803 were the old facilities resurrected. Fortunately, to remedy these grievous failings, the French army possessed a number of the most gifted medical experts of the era, in Percy, the Physician-in-Chief René Desgenettes (*ci-devant* Baron Des Genettes), and above all Dominique Jean Larrey (1766-1842), surgeon-in-chief of the Imperial Guard and the greatest humanitarian of the age.

Successful treatment of wounds depended upon the early evacuation of casualties from the battlefield, where wounded men might lie for hours, even days, before they received any treatment by which time many would have

*A surgeon of the Guard directing the removal of casualties. Many regimental surgeons wore the uniform of their regiments plus the red velvet facings which identified their role (doctors had black facings and pharmacists green), but many wore the regulation cornflower-blue uniform. (Print by Martinet)*

succumbed to their injuries. Usually, such evacuation was dependent upon fatigue-parties devoid of equipment, so that stretchers improvised from greatcoats were used to transport the wounded to the nearest dressing-station, or to slow-moving carts or *fourgons* to carry them to hospital. In 1793 Percy began despatching surgeons to the battle-front on horseback, and in 1799 designed a four-wheeled caisson with a padded top (nicknamed a *wurst-wagen*), to seat up to eight medical orderlies, who would be driven with their equipment to treat men as soon as they were wounded. The evacuation from the battlefield was completed by Larrey, who designed 'flying ambulances', light, two- and four-wheel sprung carriages with covered roofs and provision for two and four stretchers respectively. These were in existence as early as 1793 but the parsimony of the government prevented any wide-scale introduction. In 1797 Larrey organised full medical-trains, each 'ambulance' comprising 340 men in three divisions of 113, plus a surgeon-in-chief. Each division comprised a surgeon-major, 14 assistant-surgeons, 4 quarter-master

personnel, a military police lieutenant, 6 NCOs, two musicians, 12 mounted and 25 dismounted orderlies, eight 2-wheel and four 4-wheel ambulances and drivers, and four *fourgons* crewed by 4 NCOs, 20 drivers and a trumpeter. Even in Egypt Larrey was able to improvise casualty-evacuation, by slinging panniers on either side of a camel, in which the wounded could ride. Only for the Imperial Guard, however, was such sophisticated treatment widely available.

The army contained three medical branches: surgeons, doctors and pharmacists, all of which were represented in the medical organisation of a field army. Each army headquarters had a surgeon, doctor and pharmacist *en chef* in control of their respective branches. Each division had a surgeon-major and several *aides-major* to supervise the ambulances and field-hospitals, and each regiment its own surgeon-major and several *aides* (assistant-surgeons) to render the battlefield first-aid. The rank-and-file of the medical services were the *infirmiers* or orderlies attached to hospitals and field-ambulances. From 1809 each Corps was authorised to have its own company of 108 *infirmiers*, commanded by a *centenier* ranking as a 2nd lieutenant, with a *sous-centenier* (sergeant-major), sergeants and corporals as NCOs. These operated horse-drawn ambulances, but the service was never comprehensive due to a perennial shortage of trained surgeons, and efficiency depended upon the attitude of the Corps commander, some of whom were greatly interested in the welfare of their men, whilst others embezzled the cash allotted: Massena, for example, diverted it from the medical service to his own 'little savings'.

The first treatment after evacuation from the battlefield was given in a tent or any available building, turned into an operating theatre; so short were resources that in the 24 hours after Borodino Larrey had to perform 200 amputations personally, and in 1813 the situation had deteriorated so much that he had to use straw-filled wheelbarrows to transport the casualties. In general, French hospitals were larger and more efficient than those of other nations; for example, no fewer than 21 had been opened in Warsaw alone by January 1807. Such were the preparations for the 1807 campaign that although there were over 27,000 men in hospital in June 1807, there was

room for 30,000 more; from the period October 1806-October 1808, 421,000 men were admitted to military hospital, of whom 32,000 died, the average time spent in hospital being 29 days. Even better results were obtained for the Guard, whose medical services were run by the magnificent Larrey; for Aspern-Essling and Wagram, out of 1,200 wounded, by August 600 had returned to duty, 250 had been sent home and only 45 had died. Napoleon himself paid great attention to the fate of his wounded; on the retreat from Moscow, he ordered Mortier to 'Pay every attention to the sick and wounded. Sacrifice your baggage, everything for them. Let the waggons be devoted to their use, and if necessary your own saddles . . .', and this attitude was echoed by Wellington, if the story told to Larrey and repeated by him is not apocryphal. At Waterloo, the Duke had noticed him attending the wounded under fire. 'Who is that bold fellow?' enquired the Duke, and being told it was Larrey said, 'Tell them not to fire in that direction; at least let us give the brave man time to gather up the wounded', and doffed his hat; 'I salute the courage and devotion of an age that is no longer ours.'

The resilience of the Napoleonic soldier appears incredible to modern

*A scene repeated on every battlefield: parties of the victorious army search the carnage for wounded men, who were then carried away by whatever means was available, or their wounds treated on the spot. This print by Lameau & Misbach shows French infantry, cuirassiers and hussars (the latter perhaps prisoners-of-war) assisting a surgeon (right) on a snow-covered field.*

eyes, for not only did many survive shock, crude surgery and disgusting conditions, but regarded their wounds with an amazing stoicism. Accounts of great fortitude after injury are legion, but none more remarkable than that of the chasseur colonel Jean Baptiste Sourd on the day before Waterloo. Receiving a sabre-cut on the right arm, he went to Larrey for treatment, who found the injury so severe that amputation was necessary. While Larrey operated Sourd dictated a letter to Napoleon to the effect that he would not accept the rank of general were it offered, but that 'the greatest favour you can do me is to leave me in command of the regiment that I hope to lead to victory.' As Larrey bound the stump Sourd signed the note with his left hand, stood up, mounted his horse and rode off to lead his regiment; and recovered fully.

Though the storming of the Bastille on 14 July 1789 is taken as the beginning of the French Revolution, for the French army, stricken by internal upheaval and deprived by emigration and purges of much of its officer corps, the Revolutionary Wars began in 1792 when an Austro-Prussian alliance (soon after joined by Piedmont) declared itself prepared to restore power to the French monarchy by force. The campaigns which resulted are important in understanding the background to the Napoleonic Wars and the conditions which allowed the rapid rise to supreme power by Napoleon Bonaparte.

The bellicose statements issued by the allied monarchies led the French Legislative Assembly to declare war on 20 April 1792 to pre-empt any attempt to restore the power of the *Ancien Régime* by force. Although the French army was in some degree of turmoil, enough of the old professionalism remained to stiffen the enthusiastic but untrained volunteers and National Guardsmen who formed a major part of France's military service, so that in general the republican armies performed adequately. Fighting began along the frontier with the Austrian Netherlands almost immediately, with wretched French forces being brushed aside by the Austrians with such ease that the French commander, Marshal Rochambeau, resigned command of the 'Army of the North' and was replaced by the renowned Marquis de Lafayette (1757-1834) who had won fame with the French army in the American War of Independence. After the storming of the Tuileries by the Paris mob (10 August 1792) and the depriving of the King of the last vestiges of his power, Lafayette fled to the Austrians and was replaced as commander by General Charles Dumouriez (1739-1823). With part of his army he hastened to support General François Kellermann (1735-1820) and his small 'Army of the Centre' in opposing an 80,000-strong Austro-Prussian army under the Duke of Brunswick which was driving towards Paris. Dumouriez and Kellermann united with 36,000 men to oppose 34,000 of Brunswick's at Valmy (20 September 1792); fortunately for the French the armies never seriously came to grips,

as the Prussians were repelled by a French artillery bombardment. Dispirited, Brunswick withdrew to Germany and temporarily France was saved.

Following Valmy, French fortunes declined despite a victory at Jemappes (6 November 1792) which led to the over-running of the Austrian Netherlands. The execution of Louis XVI (21 January 1793) and a declaration by the French National Convention (November 1792) that they would aid all other states wishing to overthrow their monarchies aroused widespread hostility, and led to France declaring war on Britain, Holland and Spain. In the beginning of 1793 a massed offensive was launched on France from Germany and the Netherlands; Dumouriez was defeated at Neerwinden (18 March 1793) and fled to the allies when falsely accused of treason. The French government was racked with internal dissent and rivalries; Dumouriez's successor Dampierre was killed in action on 8 May and his successor, Custine, was guillotined after being defeated at Valenciennes (21-23 May). Gripped internally by 'the Terror' orchestrated by Robespierre, France's military situation deteriorated rapidly, with a major royalist counter-revolution in the Vendée, and yet another army commander (General Houchard) guillotined for failing to drive the Austrians from northern France. France was saved, however, by two factors: the *Levée en masse* which conscripted virtually the entire male population, and the total reorganisation of the French military machine by the war minister of the Committee of Public Safety, Lazare Nicolas Carnot (1753-1823). A soldier turned politician, he masterminded the reconstruction of the French army and the national war effort, and his role in preparing the way for Napoleon's success cannot be overstated. Carnot was styled 'the organiser of victory', a title which merely does him justice; but though he served briefly as president of the Directory and war minister under the Consulate, his opposition to the establishment of the Empire caused him to be virtually unemployed until 1814, when he was appointed General of Division. Exiled in 1815, he died neglected

by the country he had helped save.

Gradually, French fortunes improved as a result of Carnot's reforms; an Anglo-allied force landed at Toulon, but was repelled largely as a result of a plan prepared by a young Corsican artillery colonel, Napoleon Bonaparte, who was consequently promoted to General of Brigade. A major victory by General Jean-Baptiste Jourdan (1762-1833) at Fleurus (26 June 1794) helped to bring about the fruition of Carnot's plans to clear French territory of foreign armies. The French army swept through the Austrian Netherlands, Holland was invaded and General Jean Victor Moreau (1763-1813) in command of the 'Army of the Rhine and Moselle' made considerable gains in Germany. Despite his great talent he had poor political judgement, was seen as a rival to Napoleon and was exiled, living in the United States from 1804 to 1813, when he returned to Europe as military advisor to the Czar. He was killed at Dresden. In August 1795 a new government was established in France, the Directory, a 5-man council which replaced the National Convention, which was dissolved following a monarchist insurrection in Paris which was crushed swiftly by the rising star, General Bonaparte. Carnot remained in control of the military direction of the nation, and conceived a strategy no longer of national defence but now of conquest, partly missionary in the spreading of the doctrine of 'Liberty, Equality and Fraternity' and partly because France could no longer feed her immense citizen armies. The exhausted Prussia had made peace in mid-1795, so Carnot's target was Austria, against which he planned a pincer movement by French armies under Jourdan and Moreau in Germany, and by the 'Army of Italy' marching north, intending to unite at Vienna.

*The Napoleonic Wars produced many heroes whose deeds were quoted to inspire the nation. Here, Antoine Guillaume Rampon (1759-1842) calls upon his 32nd Demi-brigade to swear on their flag to defend their position at Montelegino, 10 April 1796.*
*(Print after Berthon)*

# The Campaigns in Italy 1796-1797

In February 1796 the 27-year-old General Bonaparte was appointed to command the French 'Army of Italy' in the place of Barthélemy Schérer (1747-1804), an experienced but not competent commander who had served in the Austrian and Dutch armies but was reputedly over-fond of the bottle. The appointment was surprising: Bonaparte was inexperienced in high command, and though he had campaigned in north Italy in 1794 his promotion was regarded as a political favour granted him by Barras (whose cast-off mistress Bonaparte had just married) in return for defending the Convention against a royalist-inspired mob which Bonaparte had dispersed with his famous 'whiff of grapeshot' in the attempted but unsuccessful *coup d'état of 13* Vendemiare. Any of Bonaparte's three senior divisional commanders in the Army of Italy would have been more likely choices for overall command: Jean Sérurier (1742-1819), *ci-devant* aristocrat with 34 years of service in the royal army; Pierre Augereau (1757-1816), a Parisian peasant whose service had been in foreign armies since fleeing the French army after killing an officer who had insulted him; and André Massena (1758-1817), an ex-smuggler and fruit-merchant who had risen through the ranks, a capable general and already the victor of the battle of Loano (1795). To them, the emaciated Bonaparte appeared an unlikely leader; until, as Massena wrote, he put on his general's hat when 'he seemed to have grown two feet. He questioned us on the position of our divisions, of the spirit and effective force of each corps, prescribed the course we were to follow, announced that he would hold an inspection on the morrow and on the following day attack the enemy.'

The Army of Italy was in a wretched state when Bonaparte assumed command on 27 March 1796; in rags, starving, dispirited and infiltrated by royalist agents, their morale could not have been lower. Bonaparte's first task (utilising arguably his greatest skill) was to restore their pride and encourage them for the coming campaign. His proclamation issued on his assumption of command (even if fabricated at a later date as has been suggested) epitomises his style of leadership and the rapport he established immediately with the ordinary soldiers: 'Soldiers! You are hungry and naked; the government owes you much but can give you nothing. The patience and courage which you have displayed among these rocks are admirable; but they bring you no glory – not a glimmer falls on you. I will lead you into the most fertile plains on earth. Rich provinces, opulent towns, all shall be at your disposal; there you will find honour, glory and riches. Soldiers of Italy! Will you be lacking in courage or endurance?' To aid him, Bonaparte had already assembled a group of subordinates who were to figure large in the annals of the Empire: the engineer Berthier as chief-of-staff, the Gascon light-horseman Murat, the gunner Marmont.

The campaign in Italy was part of the overall strategy planned by the Directory, the dominant influence being that of Carnot. The main effort was to be made in Germany, with the French pressure in Italy serving to absorb Austrian attention; and ultimately the Army of Italy could cross the Alps, unite with Moreau's army in the Tyrol and march against Vienna, the final objective. With two smaller French forces protecting his communications, Bona-

*Covered by their artillery along the bank of the Adda, French infantry attempt to cross the causeway in the face of heavy Austrian opposition. 'The bridge at Lodi' occupies a revered place in French military annals. (Print after General Lejeune)*

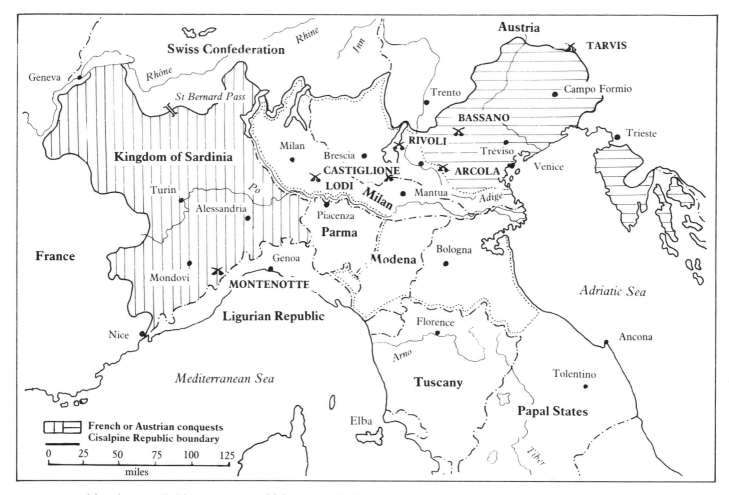

parte was able to use all his meagre resources (about 45,000 men and 60 guns) in the offensive operations he planned against the two allied armies whose separation made them vulnerable: Baron Colli's 25,000 Piedmontese and General Johann Beaulieu's 35,000 Austrians. Bonaparte conducted a thorough overhaul of the disposition of his army, concentrating his small number of cavalry into two divisions and forming a small artillery reserve; then attacked, in classic style intending to drive between the two opposing armies, enabling him to concentrate on destroying one before the other could assist.

Striking north from his headquarters at Nice, Bonaparte interposed his army between Colli and Beaulieu, driving in the Austrian's right flank at Montenotte (12 April). Pressing on with his advance, Bonaparte left Massena to watch Beaulieu whilst he himself pursued Colli; Massena captured the town of Dego on 13 April but then allowed his troops to disperse to forage, and was surprised on the following day by an Austrian counter-attack

which captured all Massena's artillery. Switching his attention, Bonaparte returned from his pursuit of the Piedmontese and recaptured Dego on 15 April. Turning again on Colli, Bonaparte drove the Piedmontese from Mondovi on 21 April. The audacity of the attack, which opened the plains of Piedmont to the French army, knocked the heart from the Piedmontese; Colli sued for armistice on 23 April, and on 28 April the King of Savoy removed Piedmont from the war.

Beaulieu arrayed his forces in a 'cordon defence' along the river Po, yet on 7/8 May, after demonstrating on a wide front to conceal his intentions, Bonaparte plunged across the river at Piacenza, threatening the Austrian line of communication with Mantua, the main Austrian fortress in north Italy. Bonaparte was unable to bring Beaulieu to battle, however, as the cautious Austrian retired before the French. The Austrian rear-guard was left at Lodi, defending the bank of the river Adda, which Bonaparte attempted to cross on

10 May. A long causeway crossing the river was dominated by the Austrian position and swept by artillery, yet the French were desperate to cross. Bonaparte personally sited his artillery along the bank, made an impassioned speech to his infantry, and launched them across the bridge. Initially repelled, with Massena and Berthier at their head the renewed attack carried the causeway and brushed away the Austrian defenders, but the success was limited for Beaulieu had made good his escape. Yet Lodi was hugely significant: it established Bonaparte's reputation with his men, who nicknamed him 'the little corporal' (a corporal's duty being to aim a cannon), and even more important convinced him that the mark of greatness was upon him: 'It was only on the evening of Lodi that I believed myself a superior man, and that the ambition came to me of executing the great things which so far had been . . . only a fantastic dream.' The bridge at Lodi was a watershed in European history; five days later Bonaparte entered Milan in triumph.

# Castiglione – 5th August 1796

The great fortress of Mantua, the key to the Austrian possession of northern Italy, was besieged on 3 June 1796, and was destined to dominate the next eight months of campaigning as Austria was determined that it should be held at all costs. In July two Austrian armies began to march to its relief: 18,000 men under General Peter Quasdanovich advanced to the west of Lake Garda, whilst the main body of 24,000 marched from Trent on Verona, commanded by the new Austrian general-in-chief, Dagobert Würmser (1724-97), a native of Strasbourg who had begun his military career in the French army. To meet a total Austrian offensive of 49,000 men (including another smaller force moving down the Brenta valley) Bonaparte could muster 46,000 men, but a large proportion of these were engaged in occupation duties and in tying down the 12,700 garrison of Mantua. Although the physical condition of the Army of Italy was still wretched, an Italian priest who watched them pass described the transformation brought about by Bonaparte's inspirational leadership: it was amazing, he wrote, 'that these men, dying of hunger, generally small, weak, worn out by fatigue and privation, without clothes or shoes – men that one would take for the dregs of a wretched population – should have conquered the Austrian army, which has everything in abundance . . . and is composed of veterans of great height, robust and inured to war.'

Bonaparte realised that he must concentrate as many men as he possibly could or be submerged by weight of numbers; thus, reluctantly, he ordered that Sérurier lift the siege of Mantua, in the event in such haste that he had to abandon no less than 179 guns in his withdrawal, most of which were captured by the Austrians. Fortunately, the Austrian advance was slow as it had taken Würmser some weeks to re-organise the demoralised troops he inherited from Beaulieu: about 400 officers who had run off in confusion had had to be reunited with their regiments. But once on the march, they recovered their morale and swept away the French outposts, causing Massena to abandon Verona; 'I have never seen the Austrians fight with such a rage; they were all drunk on brandy' was Massena's comment! Bonaparte himself was despondent over his chance of success, but Würmser failed to make the most of his opportunity of uniting his army with that of Quasdanovich, being obsessed instead with the fate of Mantua, which he believed (incorrectly) was ready to surrender. By delaying for even a few days, he gave Bonaparte the opportunity to practice his strategy of the 'central position': to interpose his army between those of his opponents and deal with each in turn. First was the smaller force under Quasdanovich, who was engaged at Lonato on 3 August, suffering heavy losses against Massena, whilst Augereau blunted Würmser's attempt to join his subordinate, in a delaying action at Castiglione on the same day. Augereau's conduct in preventing the union of Würmser and Quasdanovich was never forgotten either by Bonaparte or Augereau himself; whenever the general was criticized in future years, Napoleon would interject, 'but remember what he did for us at Castiglione', whilst Augereau himself built up his worthy deeds into a fiction in which only his resolve prevented Bonaparte from retreating in panic. His bragging perhaps conceals the fact that his stand against Würmser was of vital importance in allowing Bonaparte to deal with each wing of the Austrian

*The battle of Castiglione, 5 August 1796. In the centre background is the castle of Solferino, which anchored the Austrian right, and was assaulted by Despinois's demi-brigades under the command of General Victor Leclerc. (Print after Carle Vernet)*

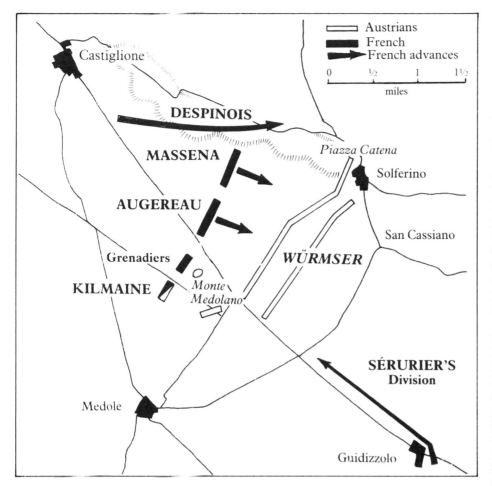

army in turn, as at the height of the fighting only five miles separated the two arms of the Austrian pincer.

With Quasdanovich thrown back in some disarray, Bonaparte realised that he had to defeat Würmser rapidly, for if the Austrian threw himself into Mantua (which had adequate provisions) his force combined with that of the Mantua garrison would be sufficient to defeat the Army of Italy, or at least prevent it from making any further progress; thus, a battle at Castiglione was imperative. The action which resulted is especially significant in the context of the development of Napoleon's art of war, for it proves that even at the age of 26 he had evolved the theories which he would use in many battles in the future. Bonaparte concentrated all his available forces (Massena and Augereau) in the plain of Castiglione, including his somewhat indifferent cavalry force under the Irish General Charles Kilmaine (1751-99); with these forces (totalling some 30,000 including Sérurier) he would engage Würmser's 25,000 in a frontal attack to occupy Austrian attention, Massena on the left and Augereau on the right. They would be seconded by the 4th and 5th *Demi-brigades* under General Hyacinthe Despinois (1764-1848), which were hurrying up at top speed from Brescia. Then, at the best moment, Sérurier's division, also marching up with precise instructions, would fall upon Würmser's left rear, forcing the Austrian to commit his reserve and hopefully weaken his main line by drawing off some of his resources to meet the threat from Sérurier, whose enveloping attack in the classic manner would also cut off Würmser's line of retreat. Then, with the Austrian front weakened, the main French attack would be launched, three grenadier battalions (preceded by a bombardment from Marmont's artillery) would advance in echelon and pierce Würmser's left centre, while the pressure was maintained on every other section of the Austrian line. It would be the classic Napoleonic victory.

Unfortunately, not everything went according to plan. Sérurier had fallen ill and his division was commanded by the Corsican General Pascal Fiorella (1752-1818) who launched his attack rather too early. Bonaparte's initial movement of retiring his front had successfully persuaded the Austrians to advance from their original positions, but once Fiorella was in action there was a delay in Bonaparte's line moving on to the offensive and tying down Würmser's forces. By the failings in timing the manoeuvres correctly, the chance to destroy Würmser comprehensively had been lost. Nevertheless, once Bonaparte had personally urged his main line into action, the remainder of his plan went smoothly enough. Auguste Marmont (1774-1852) was still only a *chef de bataillon* but was so trusted by Bonaparte that he was given complete control of the artillery, and duly rushed up with 18 guns to bombard the selected part of the Austrian line, where the grenadier battalions broke through and folded up the whole of the Austrian left, while Despinois's troops, at last arriving, stormed the Austrian right with great panache. Würmser, escaping capture by seconds, ordered a general retreat, and was able to extricate the greater part of his army, having suffered some 2,000 casualties and lost 20 guns and 1,000 prisoners. In the event, he did well to avoid the destruction Bonaparte had planned. Because Fiorella's attack was early, Würmser had been able to avoid the worst consequences of the envelopment, which in any case was too weak fully to cut the Austrian line of retreat; and thus not all Würmser's resources had been used in protecting his flank, so that the assault on his line by Marmont and the grenadiers had not been as decisive as hoped; and in any case, the assaulting-force was not sufficiently strong for the task in hand. Finally, Massena's and Augereau's troops were so exhausted by days of marching and combat that they were unable to press the pursuit as much as Bonaparte had intended, and the chase was called off after three hours. But despite the imperfections in the timing and execution of the plan, it demonstrates that although Bonaparte was still only learning his trade, the essence of his military system was already in existence; and by defeating the first Austrian attempt to relieve Mantua, the French hold on northern Italy was preserved.

# Arcola – 15th-17th November 1796

The garrison of Mantua was increased to 17,000 by fugitives from Wurmser's army, and Bonaparte renewed the siege on 24 August. In September the French moved north towards Trent, Bonaparte advancing with some 34,000 men, leaving 8,000 to invest Mantua. Desperate to relieve their beleaguered garrison, the Austrians re-grouped and Wurmser also prepared to take the offensive. Despite his previous experiences, he again elected to divide his forces, taking 20,000 men under his own command down the Brenta valley toward Mantua, and ordering General Paul Davidovich with a further 15,000 to defend the Tyrol. Unaware of the Austrian plan, the French encountered the defeated Davidovich at Caliano on the upper Adige and drove him back through Trent (4/5 September); and learning of Wurmser's advance down the Brenta, Bonaparte pursued the Austrian with 22,000 men and overhauled his army by forced march at Bassano on 8 September.

Enveloping both flanks of Wurmser's army, Bonaparte shattered the Austrian force with minimal French loss, capturing some 4,000 prisoners and 35 guns; about 3,000 Austrians escaped east, but Wurmser and 12,000 more forced their way into Mantua, which Bonaparte re-invested on 15 September.

Some weeks later the Austrians attempted a third time to relieve Mantua, the garrison of which was now swollen to around 28,000, which were being contained by only 9,000 French. This attempt was led by the Transylvanian Baron Josef Alvintzi (1735-1810), the victor of Neerwinden in 1794, who moved on Vicenza, east of the Brenta, with 28,000 men, whilst Davidovich with 18,000 more advanced down the Adige, to effect a junction at Verona before driving forward to Mantua. Bonaparte's resources were stretched trying to contain both threats and maintain the siege. He sent Massena and Augereau with 12,000 men to hold up the Austrian

advance-guard, but their progress was slowed by a heavy storm and they encountered the whole of Alvintzi's force at Caldiero on 12 November; the French were pushed back but Alvintzi made little attempt to exploit the check.

The Austrian advance continued in two columns, which with the strong force at Mantua meant that Bonaparte might be caught between three fires. Not sufficiently strong to face two of these forces together, Bonaparte determined to defeat them in detail, and chose to deal with Alvintzi first. Davidovich was still pressing down the upper Adige, so Bonaparte detached some 10,000 men under General Charles Henri Vaubois (1748-1839) to delay him until Alvintzi could be engaged; throughout the three days' fighting which followed, Bonaparte had constantly to keep in mind the threat from Davidovich if Vaubois gave ground too fast. On the night of 14 November Bonaparte advanced with 18,000 men along the south bank of the Adige to force a crossing by pontoon bridge at Ronco, in excess of 4 miles south of Arcola, as if he intended to swing east

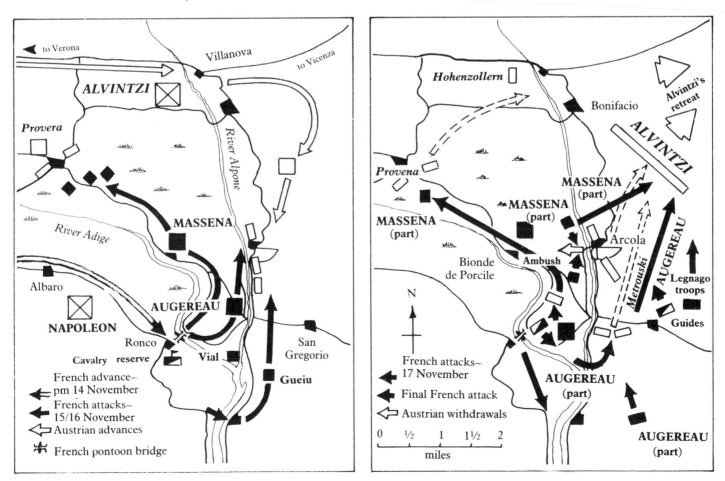

and threaten Alvintzi's communications. Alvintzi, advancing on Verona, sent reinforcements to supplement his garrison at Arcola with its bridge over the river Alpone, and another force under General Johann Provera (1740-1804) to attack Massena at Porcile, where he was stationed to protect Bonaparte's left flank from just such an assault. Bonaparte sent 3,000 men on a flank-march via the river-crossing at Albaredo, under the command of General Jean Joseph Guieu (1758-1817) to attack Arcola from the east, but the marshy terrain delayed the movement until the evening of 15 November. All that day, while Massena held off the attack on Bonaparte's left, the main force attempted to battle its way over the bridge at Arcola, Bonaparte himself almost being drowned when he was pushed into a dyke as he led an attack in person, bearing the standard of the 51st *Demi-brigade*, in an attempt to force the bridge. Throughout the un-availing struggle, Alvintzi's baggage was escaping to the east on the road to Vicenza, to counter the threat against his communications. As the French eventually began to gain the ascendancy, news was received that Vaubois was falling back; unaware of the extent of the damage, Bonaparte called off the attack, and overnight the Austrians reinforced Arcola and occupied Porcile.

On 16 November, no worse news having been received from Vaubois, Bonaparte renewed the assault against Arcola, and though Porcile was recovered in a day-long battle he was still unable to take the vital bridge, and in the evening again withdrew, leaving only a small party north of the Adige. Alvintzi was now in full retreat east, so on 17 November Bonaparte planned a third attempt to cut off whatever remained of the Austrian army west of the Alpone. Massena was ordered to occupy the Austrians in the Arcola area whilst Augereau swung east to capture Arcola from the rear. Massena handled his task with consummate skill; leaving only one unit exposed and the remainder concealed in the marshes and dykes, was able to ambush the Austrian advance which was swept away, Massena storming over the Arcola bridge at last. Augereau had difficulty in forcing a passage of the Alpone, so that some units were sent south towards Legnano to find another crossing; but Bonaparte sent a small party of his Guides to slip across

*Bonaparte encourages his men to greater efforts at Arcola. The episode has passed into the legend of the French army, though the truth is more prosaic: a French officer cried 'if you fall we are lost; you shall not go farther; this is not your place'; and Bonaparte almost drowned when the officer pushed him in the water! (Print by H. Chartier.)*

the river, where they made as much noise as possible. The attention of the Austrians holding Albaredo was thus distracted, allowing Augereau to drive on, capture the place and advance north as planned. Alvintzi, seeing troops approaching at speed, ordered an all-out withdrawal toward Vicenza. The battle cost the French about 4,500 casualties and the Austrians 7,000, but although Alvintzi had made good his escape and countered the perceived threat to his communications, the attempt to relieve Mantua had again failed as Davidovich also retired.

In the new year Alvintzi led a fourth expedition to relieve Mantua, marching down the Adige with 28,000 men, while two diversionary attacks were made against Verona and Legnano. Bonaparte refused to be deflected by the latter movements, and concentrated his army at Rivoli to meet the main threat. On 14 January Alvintzi planned to attack in five columns, three to break the French centre and two to encircle the French flanks; but Bonaparte was reinforced continually as his outlying forces arrived, French strength rising from 10,000 in the early morning to 20,000 by mid-afternoon, so that although his centre was pushed back the flank-attacks were repelled, and a determined counter-attack drove the tiring Austrians from the field. A French pursuit on 15 January completed the destruction of Alvintzi's force, of which half were casualties or prisoners. The fourth attempt to relieve Mantua had been repelled decisively, though one of the subsidiary columns, under General Provera, did evade the watching French forces and reach Mantua, where it was joined by a sally from the garrison in an attack on the besiegers. Sérurier, in command of the besiegers, drove back Wurmser while Bonaparte dealt with Provera (16 January), and with all hope gone Mantua capitulated on 2 February, 18,000 Austrians having died during the siege, mostly of disease.

With the French now in command of north Italy, Bonaparte was able to advance into Austria, where Alvintzi had been replaced in command by the Archduke Charles, who retired before the advancing French. No decisive battle was fought, though Massena smashed an Austrian detachment at Malborghetto on 23 March. Advancing in three columns, Bonaparte united them at Leoben, 95 miles from Vienna on 6 April. Despite his somewhat perilous situation, Bonaparte boldly dictated peace terms without reference to the Directory; Austria accepted them on 18 April, and they were confirmed by the Treaty of Campo Formio in October, by which Belgium became part of France and Austria recognised the satellite Cisalpine Republic in northern Italy. It concluded the astonishing Italian campaign which made Bonaparte's reputation.

# The Campaign in Egypt and Palestine 1798-1801

The expedition to Egypt was conceived by Bonaparte as a way of striking at Britain and furthering his career, Egypt being regarded as the crossroads between east and west: accessible from the Mediterranean, yet an ideal staging-post for an advance into British India. With Austria having been removed from the war by the Treaty of Campo Formio, French resources were available to undertake the Egyptian expedition; and the Directory had an ulterior motive in supporting the scheme as it removed the ambitious, popular and successful Bonaparte from the immediate political scene. He began to assemble his army at Toulon, most of it comprising selected units from the Army of Italy. In May 1798 Bonaparte set sail with around 35,000 men, escorted by Admiral François P. Brueys with 13 ships of the line. Evading the British Mediterranean squadron, Bonaparte captured Malta (12 June) and arrived off Alexandria on 1 July 1798. He seized the port and marched on Cairo.

From the 13th century Egypt had been effectively under the control of the Mameluke beys, a warrior caste which originated in the Caucasus. In 1798 their rule was in the hands of Ibrahim Bey (1735-1817), an ex-slave of European origin, and Murad Bey (1750-1801), joint leaders of the Mamelukes. Though nominally vassals of the Ottoman

Empire, the Mamelukes were sufficiently powerful to govern Egypt in their own way. Consequently, severe opposition to the French landing was guaranteed, and on 21 July they met the French army in the shadow of the Pyramids. Though defeated heavily, the Mamelukes remained troublesome and continued to harrass the French expeditionary forces. The French entered Cairo on 22 July, but the decisive blow of the campaign was struck against them on 1 August, when Admiral Nelson's British fleet destroyed the French ships in Aboukir Bay, which marooned the French expedition in Egypt.

Bonaparte's position was now perilous in the extreme; completely cut off from reinforcements and even without the facility of evacuating his troops, in an inhospitable country, surrounded by a hostile population and with armies gathering to coordinate action against him: a large Ottoman force was being gathered at Rhodes to invade Egypt under the escort of a British squadron, and another was assembled in Syria under the command of Achmed Pasha 'the Butcher'. Undaunted, Bonaparte decided to take the initiative and at the end of January 1799 marched into Syria at the head of 13,000 of his men. Marching along the ancient coast-road across the northern Sinai he captured El-Arish (14/15 February) and Jaffa (7 March),

defences which cost Bonaparte valuable time, and which may have caused probably the most indefensible act of his career. 3,000 Turks in the citadel of Jaffa accepted 'quarter' (a promise that they would be treated in a civilized manner if they surrendered); but Bonaparte, perhaps incensed with the delay or in an attempt to overawe 'the Butcher' with a display of French ruthlessness, ordered the execution not only of these prisoners, but a further 1,400 as well. Excuses that he had no supplies to feed the prisoners, nor men to escort them, or that he found paroled ex-prisoners amongst them (i.e. those having broken the terms of their release, not to fight against the French) are unconvincing for an act of controlled barbarity. Further delay was caused by an outbreak of plague in the French army, and when he recommenced his march Bonaparte had to leave behind 300 sick and a guard of 150, of whom only 36 survived; but English propaganda that he deliberately poisoned his own sick men is untrue and has served to obscure the enormity of the deed committed on the prisoners. The delays enabled the Ottoman defenders of the city of Acre – 'the key of Palestine' – to strengthen the fortifications, aided by a French émigré engineer, Col Phélippeaux, a classmate of Bonaparte's at the Paris Military Academy, and the British naval captain Sidney Smith. As

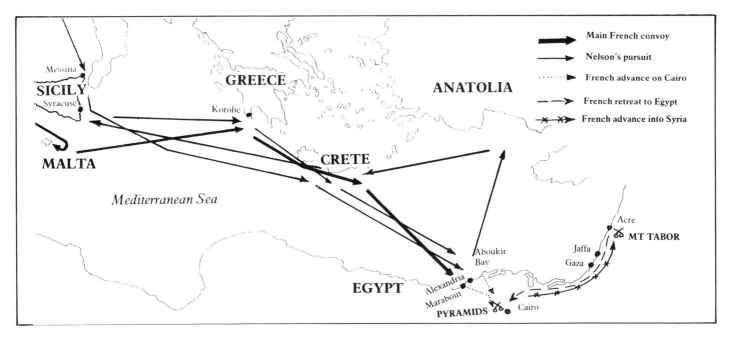

*Cavalry did not play a major role in the Egyptian campaign, though two light regiments and the 3rd, 14th, 15th, 18th and 20th Dragoons were part of the expedition. Here dragoons attack British infantry at Alexandria. (Print after A. Dupray)*

the siege of Acre progressed, the Turks attempted to relieve the city; Bonaparte sent out General Jean-Baptiste Kléber (1753-1800) with a reconnaissance force, which was attacked by overwhelming numbers at Mount Tabor on 16 April. Fighting all day against odds of 17:1, Kléber's force was only rescued by Bonaparte himself, who had marched the 25 miles from Acre, and the Ottoman force was scattered. As plague broke out again, the siege of Acre was abandoned and Bonaparte retreated once again to Egypt, having lost some 2,200 men (mostly to plague) as a result of his fruitless expedition into Palestine. During the retreat back to Egypt, morale sank to a new low; mutiny was threatened, all

but 40 of the army's guns had to be abandoned, and 2,300 men were ill. The failure was partly offset by a major success at Aboukir on 25 July 1799, after the Ottoman force from Rhodes under the aged Mustapha Pasha had landed and entrenched some ten days before. In a stiff assault of the two concentric rings of Ottoman defence, the 18,000-strong invasion force was annihilated for a French loss of some 900 men; for the first time in the campaign the French cavalry, led by the dashing Murat, made a major contribution in helping to destroy the Ottoman force, but were assisted by the stupidity of the Turkish Jannissaries (the elite infantry of the Ottoman Empire) who repeatedly left their defended position in search of French heads as trophies.

Although Aboukir confirmed the French in possession of Egypt, there was clearly no future for the expedition, gradually being whittled away by casualties and disease, and on 22 August Bonaparte turned over command to Kléber and returned to France in a fast

frigate, successfully eluding the British fleet. Though this effectively ended Bonaparte's dream of oriental conqest, the campaign was far from concluded. The French army was incensed by the desertion of their commander (Kléber described him as 'ce petit bougre' in his complaint to the Directory), and were again attacked. Kléber concluded the Convention of El Arish with the Turks and Sidney Smith in January 1800, by which the French agreed to evacuate Egypt in return for passage home; but it was disavowed by Smith's superiors and hostilities recommenced. Kléber won a victory against the Turks at Heliopolis (20 March), only to be assassinated by a knife-wielding fanatic on 14 June. Command passed to General Jacques-François Menou, who was defeated decisively by a British expeditionary force at Alexandria on 20 March 1801. On 31 August Menou capitulated and the surviving French troops were given free passage home, bringing to a close the whole sorry episode of Bonaparte's oriental expedition.

# The Battle of the Pyramids – 21st July 1798

Napoleon was never greatly concerned with 'minor tactics' (the mechanism by which units were handled on the battlefield) which he preferred to leave in the hands of his subordinates, concentrating himself on strategy and 'grand tactics', the planning of campaigns and battles. In Egypt, however, most noticeably demonstrated at the Battle of the Pyramids, he used his only major contribution to the evolution of 'minor tactics', the so-called 'divisional square'. (His other innovation in the Egyptian campaign, the formation of the *Régiment des Dromedaires*, troops carried on camel-back, was basically to remedy his shortage of cavalry and was obviously only applicable to Egypt.) The development of the 'divisional square' was due to the unique character of the enemy he faced in Egypt, which was more akin to that which opposed the Crusaders than anything which might be encountered in Europe. The British general Sir John Moore reported in 1801 that although the individual Ottoman soldier was a stalwart fighter when properly led (as proven by Smith's defence of Acre), under Turkish command the Ottoman army was merely 'a wild, ungovernable mob'. This was equally true of the forces of Egypt, led by the Mamelukes. These had first appeared in Egypt in the 13th century when the then Sultan had imported 1,200 Georgians and Circassians from the Caucasus to form an élite bodyguard. Even after the Turkish conquest of Egypt in 1517 the Mamelukes had remained the dominant power, though nominally subservient to the Turkish governor appointed by Constantinople; they replenished their numbers by the regular importation of youths from the Caucasus and thus formed a warrior caste which maintained total superiority over the native Egyptians. The Mamelukes were trained from boyhood in the arts of war, were all superb swordsmen and riders, but had no conception whatever of any other tactics than a wild charge followed by single combat with the enemy. Colourfully dressed, their equipment (but for their firearms) was medieval: iron helmets, mail-coats and body-armour, javelins and curved sabres. A British officer described the typical appearance: 'Every

Mameluke is formidably armed with a long carbine, two brace of pistols, one in his holsters; the other in his girdle, together with a stiletto and a sabre, well tempered and with the keenest edge possible. He carries at his saddle bow a battle axe and his slave follows with his javelin.' Each Mameluke was accompanied by two *serradj* (servants) on foot. In combat, the Mameluke would fire his carbine from the saddle, then all his pistols, which he would drop on the ground as soon as discharged, to be retrieved by his servants; then would fling his javelins (four-foot sharpened palm-branches) and finally charge with the sabre (sometimes with one in either hand and reins between the teeth); discipline or concerted action with his fellows was quite beyond his comprehension. Yet despite this lack of any tactical sense

whatever, the Mamelukes were perfectly fearless and, individually, the most formidable warriors ever met by the French army, so were very much to be taken seriously. The Mamelukes numbered some 9,000 or 10,000 with about 20,000 dismounted servants; other Egyptian troops included some decent Albanian and Moroccan infantry and mounted spahis, but the bulk of the infantry was of wretched quality, many simply mobs of impressed *fellahin* armed with clubs.

Bonaparte's 'Army of the Orient' consisted mainly of veterans of the Army of Italy, plus a battalion of sailors (*Légion Nautique*) and a rather reluctant battalion of Maltese (*Légion Malte*) enrolled en route to Egypt. The expedition was rather short of cavalry, only 2,700 strong on disembarkation, with regimental strengths of around 400, plus

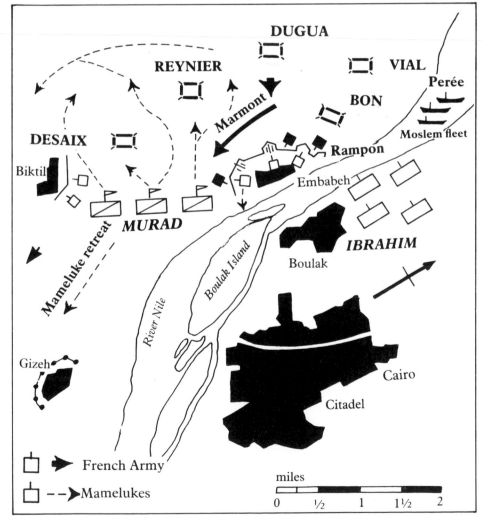

180 mounted Guides for headquarters duties. But despite their experience and the unconventional nature of the enemy, morale among the French forces was poor, worn down by the arid climate, food consisting mainly of dry biscuit, dysentery, opthalmia (which caused temporary blindness) and a shortage of water, wells often being filled in by the hostile Bedouins who hovered around the fringes of the army. Bonaparte drove his army relentlessly on the advance from the sea towards Cairo, realising that any relaxation could result in disaster, but his driving caused complaints bordering on mutiny; some soldiers were so dispirited as to commit suicide. Even the senior officers were discontented, and after Bonaparte rejected an ultimatum to retire their spokesman, General François Mireur, killed himself. A threat to shoot another leader of dissent, General Dumas, brought the troops back to their loyalty.

In these circumstances it was imperative that the Mamelukes should be defeated decisively; hence the development of the 'divisional square' which would guarantee safety not only to the combatant troops but also to the French non-combatants and the vital supply-trains and baggage, which could not be left unprotected due to the marauding habits of the Mamelukes and their followers. In essence, the 'divisional square' was an enlargement of the ordinary square formation adopted by infantry as the habitual defence against cavalry by presenting a hedge of bayonets on each side. In this case, each of Bonaparte's 'squares' was formed as an

*The Battle of the Pyramids: Baron Lejeune's painting illustrates the formation of a 'divisional square', sheltering staff, baggage and non-combatants in the centre. The artillery in action at the corner of the square is covered by flanking detachments of grenadiers* (carabiniers *in the* demi-brigades légères). *The Nile appears at the left of the scene.*

immense oblong, each composed of three *demi-brigades*, a complete *demi-brigade* arrayed in line on the front and rear sides and the third of each division split in half to form the flanking sides. Inside these huge rectangles were gathered the expedition's cavalry, baggage-train, staff and non-combatants, with the artillery positioned at each corner of the rectangle, sometimes protected by parties of grenadiers thrown forward a short distance; in effect, the entire expedition was thus protected by moveable 'fortresses' composed of men, the ideal counter to the wild and undisciplined charges of the Mamelukes.

On 20 July 1798 the presence of the army of Murad and Ibrahim was reported some twenty miles from Cairo; Bonaparte marched his 25,000 men to the vicinity of the village of Embabeh on the banks of the Nile, on the opposite bank of which stood Ibrahim's horde, relegated to spectators by the width of the river. Confronting them was Murad with some 6,000 mounted Mamelukes and 15,000 *fellahin*, the latter installed in Embabeh and the cavalry on Murad's left wing. The Pyramids were visible fifteen miles away and provided Bonaparte with one of his most theatrical

exhortations ever delivered to his troops: 'Remember that from those monuments yonder forty centuries look down upon you!' He advanced his five divisional squares, those of Generals Louis Bon (killed at Acre) and Honoré Vial along the river-bank, Louis Desaix and Jean Reynier into the desert, with Charles Dugua's square (containing Bonaparte) in reserve in the centre. At the extreme right of the French position Desaix detached a small body to occupy the village of Biktil. At 3.30 p.m. the Mamelukes made their massed cavalry charge toward Desaix and Reynier; the squares closed just in time and poured their artillery and musket-fire into the three columns of Mamelukes which lapped around the squares and took off towards the French rear. Assailed by howitzer-fire from the interior of Dugua's square, they galloped back, attempting to drive Desaix's men from Biktil; the French climbed onto the house-roofs until Desaix relieved them. With the Mameluke cavalry thus occupied, Bonaparte launched Vial's and Bon's divisions, covered by the fire of French gunboats on the Nile, towards Embabeh. Within minutes they had stormed into the village, whose defenders broke; unable to escape, at least 1,000 were drowned trying to cross the Nile. By 4.30 p.m. the battle was over, with the Mameluke forces in full retreat; for the loss of 29 dead and about 260 wounded, Bonaparte's divisional squares had accounted for at least 2,000 Mamelukes and several thousand more *fellahin*. By any standards, it was a convincing victory.

# The Campaign in Italy 1799-1800

Whilst Bonaparte was engaged with his campaign in Egypt, the situation had altered dramatically in Europe after the organisation of the Second Coalition against France in December 1798 (Russia, Britain, Austria, Portugal, Naples, the Ottoman Empire and the Vatican). The strategy of the Allies was to attack the French on all fronts: an Anglo-Russian army to drive them from the Netherlands, an Austrian army under the Archduke Charles (1771-1847, the ablest Austrian commander of the age) to attack them in Germany and Switzerland, and an Austro-Russian army under the veteran Field-Marshal Alexander Suvarov (1729-1800) to collaborate with the Austrian General Karl Mack von Leiberich (1752-1828) with his Neapolitan army to recover the ground lost to Bonaparte in the Italian campaigns. Despite the overwhelming numerical superiority of the Allies, France took the offensive on all fronts. In the Netherlands the Anglo-Russian force under the

Duke of York (1763-1827) was unable to make much headway, and withdrew in October 1799; early in the year the French offensive in Germany was repelled, but Massena defeated the Allied forces in Switzerland before Suvarov could march to their assistance from northern Italy. Despite these Allied disappointments, the campaigning in Italy went badly against the French, largely as a result of the ability of the aged Suvarov. Naples fell to the French in January 1799 after the Austrian Mack had fled to French lines to save himself from his mutinous Neapolitan rabble, and a French satellite state, the Parthenopean Republic, was established. Further north Schérer, commanding the French forces, hoped to win a victory over the Austrian army of the Hungarian General Paul Kray (1735-1804) before Suvarov could reinforce the Austrians; but when he engaged Kray at Magnano (5 April 1799) it was Schérer who was defeated, and was replaced by the talented Moreau.

But by now Suvarov's Russians had arrived, more than twice the strength of Moreau, and defeated the French at Cassano (27 April), seizing Milan and Turin as a result. Because of political conflict with the Austrian government, Suvarov had to abandon his pursuit, which gave the French time to reorganise, sending the Scottish émigré General Jacques Macdonald (1765-1840) north from Naples to assist Moreau. Finding himself between the two French armies, Suvarov turned on Macdonald and defeated him at the battle of the Trebbia (17/19 June 1799) and then pressed on to deal with Moreau, who was relieved of his command and replaced by General Barthelemy Joubert (1769-99). Joubert attacked Suvarov at Novi on 15 August but was heavily defeated and killed, but before Suvarov could complete his conquest of northern Italy he was ordered to Switzerland, leaving the Austrian General Michael Melas (1729-1806) to drive the French back across the Alps. Virtually all of Bonaparte's gains of 1796-97 had been erased.

Despite the lack of long-term success in the orient, Bonaparte's victories in Egypt had established him as a popular hero, and upon his return to France he found the Directory in a state of near-collapse. With the complicity of Barras and Ducos (themselves both Directors), the old Jacobin Siéyès and foreign minister Talleyrand, he planned a coup d'état to invest himself with supreme power. (Siéyès had planned to make Joubert the military head of the coup, but transferred his allegiance to Bonaparte after Joubert's death at Novi.) On 9/10 November, by the coup of *18 Brumaire* (the date according to the republican calendar) Bonaparte became virtual dictator of France, dissolving the Directory and replacing it with the Consulate, a triumvirate of three 'Consuls' with Bonaparte as 'First Consul'. (The other Consuls, originally Siéyès and Ducos,

*The French army approaches the hospice of St Bernard on their march across the Alps. This most audacious of marches, in terrible conditions, was made possible by determination and ingenuity: note the cannon-barrels hauled on sleds made from hollowed tree-trunks.*

later the ex-Jacobin Cambacères and the royalist Lebrun, had little actual power, which was concentrated in the hands of First Consul.) As head of state, Bonaparte offered peace to the Allies, but was rebuffed (although Russia had withdrawn from the Coalition), and he prepared to continue the war as he had always fought: aggressively.

During his sojourn in Egypt, the French army in Italy had slipped from the excellence of Bonaparte's earlier campaigns, dispirited by successive defeats and the large number of conscripts who had been drafted into the army. Morale was poor, desertion (or failure to report when conscripted) was common, and some units were almost in a state of insurrection: officers were powerless and murdered when they tried to maintain order. Sérurier wrote that he wished to resign command of his division because he could no longer exercise any authority: 'This manner of serving cannot be suitable for a man of my age.' Attempting to restore heart to his men and victory to the army, Bonaparte created a new formation, the 'Army of the Reserve', which he assembled at Dijon under the command of Berthier (temporarily abandoning his role as chief-of-staff in which he was happiest). The Austrians planned for Kray to contain Moreau in Germany, while Melas with 100,000 Austrians overwhelmed Massena, who commanded the 40,000-strong Army of Italy which now held only the Riviera coast. Bonaparte had two options for the employment of his 'Army of the Reserve': join Moreau in an offensive through Switzerland and Germany against Kray, or invade Italy through Switzerland and catch Melas between himself and Massena. It was the latter course he chose, but to his surprise it was Melas who took the offensive first, and through April 1800 made considerable gains against the Army of Italy, which was split into two sections; with about 12,000 men Massena was driven into Genoa, which was besieged by the Austrians on land, and blockaded by the British navy from the sea, making both resupply and reinforcement impossible. The other part of the army, commanded by General Louis Gabriel Suchet (1770-1826) – one of the most talented of Napoleon's subordinate commanders, whose great skills were probably not employed to their best advantage – was

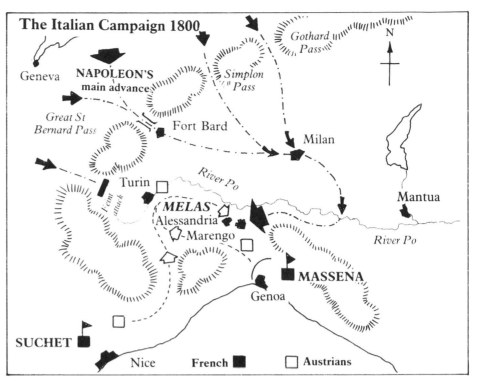

**The Italian Campaign 1800**

pursued by Melas beyond Nice. In view of this depressing situation it is not surprising that Bonaparte felt the need to add 'Soyez gai' ('cheer up') in his despatches to Berthier! Bonaparte planned that Massena would be able to occupy a large proportion of the Austrian resources, leaving him to deal with Melas's main body; but Massena was in the midst of a most terrible siege. Supplies ran out, so that the garrison had to exist on a little horsemeat and 'bread' made from straw, oats and cocoa; Massena's hair turned grey, and the civil population was so unsettled that any assembly of more than three people was fired upon. After appalling privation, Massena surrendered on 4 June, and was permitted to evacuate his garrison behind the river Var.

In May, however, Bonaparte began his advance from Switzerland, crossing the Alps via the Great St Bernard pass, with other troops moving via the Simplon, Mt Cenis and St Gotthard passes, to debouch into the Lombardy plain. He had had the passes surveyed as early as December 1799, and his choice to use the least practicable (the Great St Bernard) as the main channel filled his subordinates with dismay, as it was believed unsuitable for artillery and baggage. It was a perilous ordeal, but one accomplished with remarkably few

difficulties, exercising all the ingenuity of Bonaparte and his army. Deep snow and appalling tracks prevented the conventional use of artillery carriages, so the capable Marmont improvised, transporting his gun-barrels in hollowed-out troughs made from split tree-trunks, dragged by 100 men each, or hauled on sledges with the carriages taken to pieces and carried on stretchers. Waggons were emptied and sent over the passes unloaded, with their supplies following on the backs of mules or men. After ten days of struggling through the snow, braving freezing weather and avalanches, by 24 May the greater proportion of 40,000 men was in the valley of the Po, with Bonaparte himself experiencing all the difficulties of his men; as the official despatch stated, 'The First Consul came down from the top of the St Bernard Pass, sliding and rolling in the snow.' It was an audacious manoeuvre typical of Bonaparte's system of warfare; as he wrote to his brother Joseph on 24 May, 'We have fallen like a thunderbolt; the enemy did not expect us and still seem scarcely to believe it.' All was now prepared for the confrontation with Melas, Bonaparte's plans made; for long before the crossing of the Alps, he had driven a pin into his map and declared, 'I will fight him here'; remarkably, the pin marked the town of Marengo.

# Marengo – 14th June 1800

When assessing the career of a general, the one question which Napoleon always asked was, 'is he lucky?' It is possible that this preoccupation with so unscientific a quality was the result of his own good fortune at decisive moments of his career. For if the battle of Marengo were one of Napoleon's greatest and most decisive victories, without question it was also one of his luckiest.

The operations which led to Marengo were beset with confusion and error; the capitulation of Massena at Genoa tended to disorder any plans which had already been laid. Much of the confusion stemmed from the inherent weaknesses of the staff system, compounded by Berthier who was always happier as a chief-of-staff than as a commanding general, which role he had temporarily adopted; thus he tended to duplicate his own chief-of-staff's work, which resulted in some formations receiving orders twice over and others none at all. The fact that General Jean Lannes received four contradictory sets of orders in 24 hours may in part explain why he rushed into a rash battle on 9 June.

The Austrian general Melas, finding that Bonaparte had manoeuvred so as to sever his communications with Turin, remained somewhat inactive around Alessandria, concentrating his army into one large force; General Karl Ott with 18,000 Austrians marched north from Genoa and ran into Lannes's 8,000 men at Montebello on 9 June. Lannes dashed at the Austrians despite being outnumbered, and reinforced by General Victor's 6,000 men drove off Ott, who retired on Alessandria. Bonaparte ordered his army to advance on Alessandria (and the neighbouring village of Marengo), and on 11 June Bonaparte reconstituted his army to take into account the arrival from France of General Louis Charles Desaix (1768-1800), an aristocrat who had embraced the revolution, served with great distinction in Germany, in north Italy with Bonaparte and in Egypt, where he had fought a successful campaign against Murad Bey during Bonaparte's excursion into Syria. Captured by the British navy when returning home, he was freed just in time to join the French army before Marengo. Allocated a division, he was sent towards Novi to prevent Melas retiring on Genoa. Another division was sent northward to cover the crossings of the river Po, leaving Bonaparte with fewer than 24,000 men. It is characteristic of the weakness of reconnaissance that Bonaparte had no idea either of Melas's intentions (he believed that the Austrians were deliberately avoiding battle) or of their forces; yet consciously weakened his army in the hope that he could prevent Melas from escaping. When Melas took the initiative it was a most profound shock.

Melas believed that a junction of the French 'Army of the Reserve' (Bonaparte and Berthier) and the 'Army of Italy' was imminent (which it was not); thus the Austrian decided to stake all on a full-scale attack on Bonaparte's army which he knew was encamped about Marengo. In the early hours of 14 June a frantic report was rushed to Bonaparte's

*Bonaparte (centre) and his staff (left) attempt to check the flight of French infantry at Marengo, prior to the arrival of Desaix, when the French were under intolerable pressure.*
*(Print after F. de Myrbach)*

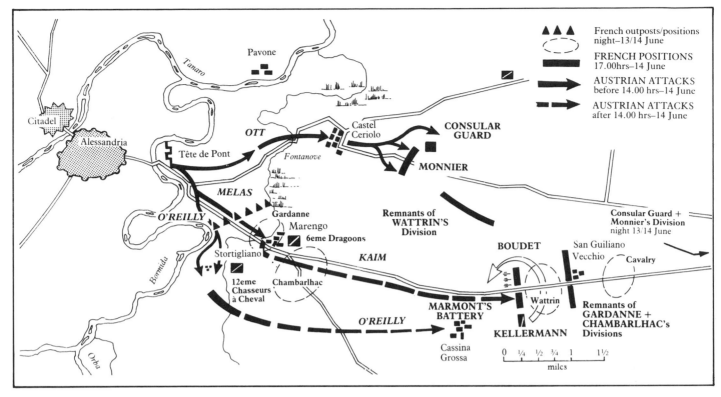

headquarters that three columns of Austrians were streaming out of Alessandria, across the river Bormida and engaging the nearest French units, Victor's division. Not until mid-morning did Bonaparte realise that the attack was serious, but by that time it appeared too late to avert a disaster. At 11 a.m. orders were sent to recall the separated divisions ('for God's sake come up if you still can'), by which time (despite support from Lannes's division and Murat's cavalry) Victor's men were giving ground. Appeals for assistance came from all sides, but Bonaparte's reserve (including the Consular Guard) were sent north, to head-off a threatened out-flanking movement by Ott. By mid-day the Austrians had paused in their advance to reorganise, but despite the respite the French were giving ground at almost every point, and ammunition was running low. So convinced was Melas that the battle was won that at about 3 p.m. he handed over command of the expected pursuit to General Zach and retired to Alessandria for a rest having suffered a minor wound. At that moment, however, Bonaparte's luck came into play with the return of Desaix. Floods had delayed his march that morning, so he heard the Austrian cannonade which announced the beginning of the battle;

not waiting for orders to return, he obeyed the maxim of 'always march towards the sound of the guns', and by 5 p.m. the first of his troops, half-exhausted by their forced march, had begun to arrive. 'This battle is completely lost', declared Desaix; 'but there is still time to win another.'

Bonaparte ordered Desaix to counter-attack immediately, supported by Marmont with his artillery and General François Etienne Kellermann (son of the victor of Valmy) with a cavalry brigade. Desaix advanced with his brigades in oblique order, but almost immediately fell dead to an Austrian shot; his men hesitated, but Marmont's guns opened fire at point-blank range against the flank of Zach's column. An Austrian ammunition-caisson exploded, the concussion temporarily stunning the Austrians; and at this exact moment Kellermann launched his squadrons at the milling Austrian mass. The psychological impact was immense; Zach's men began to flee and panic spread along the whole Austrian line, which began to unravel. Seeing this, the weary French gathered themselves for a final effort and turned the Austrian retreat into a dis-ordered rout. Their losses were about 14,000; those of the French 7,000, or a quarter of their force.

Next evening, the shattered Melas signed an armistice which agreed to the evacuation of much of Lombardy. Moreau's victory at Hohenlinden on 3 December 1800 finally forced Austria to sign the Treaty of Luneville in February 1801; but it was Marengo which had tipped the scales. The 'Army of the Reserve' ceased to exist only nine days after the battle, being merged with the Army of Italy, having performed only about a month of full campaigning, a short but glorious career. Bonaparte's Order of the Day, congratulating the army, stated that 'The day of Marengo will remain famous throughout History' and indeed he always regarded it as one of his most significant victories: his first as head of state and the victory which assured his reputation. Over the years Napoleon 'adjusted' the record to create the impression that the victory was his alone, minimising the part played by the dead hero Desaix and Kellermann (who always resented being cheated of 'his' victory!). Napoleon's career benefited from good luck at vital moments; but there is a case for the view that the Empire was built upon Desaix's bold determination to march towards the sound of gunfire in defiance of his orders. If anyone deserved the laurels of Marengo, it was Desaix.

# Manoeuvres on the Danube – September-October 1805

The year 1805 was the most brilliant in Napoleon's career, and is best remembered for the victory of Austerlitz, which is often regarded as his masterpiece. But though Austerlitz was a major triumph, the events which led to the Convention of Ulm are second to none in history as an example of a victory gained not on the battlefield but by strategic manoeuvre.

On 27 March 1802 peace returned to the whole of Europe for the first time in a decade when the Peace of Amiens was concluded between France and Britain, though it was obvious to many that the cessation of hostilities was only a brief respite. On 2 August 1802 Bonaparte was proclaimed 'First Consul for Life' which was but a short step to his 'election' as Emperor Napoleon I, a move which re-established in France the concept of a dynastic succession. He was crowned Emperor on 2 December 1804, by which date the Empire was once again waging war. Hostilities between France and Britain resumed on 16 May 1803, with the avowed policy of Napoleon being an invasion of southern England, to eliminate his most implacable opponent. The scheme was never truly practicable given the fact that the British navy controlled the English Channel, but Napoleon assembled a vast army on the Channel coast. The bulk of France's military force was thus gathered at the extreme west of the Empire; the only other major

*Jean Lannes (1769-1809); excepting perhaps Berthier, none of the marshals was more highly regarded by Napoleon as a soldier and friend, and few were braver or more capable.*
*(Print after J.-B.-P. Guerin)*

*Louis Nicolas Davoût (1770-1823); one of Napoleon's ablest and most loyal marshals; his Corps was always the model for the army.*
*(Portrait by T. Marzocchi after C. Gautherot)*

force was Massena's army of 50,000 men in Italy. To take advantage of this apparent weakness, the Third Coalition was formed by which Austria, Russia and Sweden joined Britain in determining to crush the perceived French plan for European domination. Their strategy was to fall upon Massena, and then advance in overwhelming force on the northern side of the Alps towards the Rhine and France.

Learning of his enemies' intentions, Napoleon discarded his plans for the descent upon England (even before the defeat of Trafalgar devastated the fleet he had hoped to use to support the invasion), broke up his camps on the Channel coast and marched east on 31 August to face the Austro-Russian menace. Although Napoleon planned his operations with great care and ability, probably the most vital factor was the calibre of his army, which reached the pinnacle of its quality in the 1805 campaign. A large number of veterans of the Revolutionary Wars were still serving and above all, the morale of the army was exceptionally high, following a series of almost unbroken successes. Probably never had Napoleon commanded so fine an army, and he used it to devastating effect.

Set against this matchless army was a

more numerous but unco-ordinated Allied force. On 2 September Austrian forces, around 50,000 strong and commanded by Archduke Ferdinand d'Este (1781-1835?) and General Mack, knowing nothing of the French movements, invaded Bavaria. Deficiencies in the management of the Austrian forces were compounded by the fact that although Ferdinand proved an able commander overall command was vested in the incompetent Mack. A larger Austrian force of around 100,000 men, commanded by Archduke Charles, prepared to attack Massena in Italy, whilst a Russian army of 120,000 under Kutuzov began its slow march westward to join Mack.

On 26 September the French crossed the Rhine, advancing on a wide front, with Mack still unaware that Napoleon had left Boulogne. The advance of the *Grande Armée* was planned meticulously and executed with maximum speed. His complete lack of intelligence of the French movements, and his own incompetence, led to Mack's isolation at the town of Ulm. On 6 October the French reached the Danube, Murat's cavalry demonstrating in front of Mack's forces to keep him occupied, whilst the remainder of the *Grande Armée*, in six huge columns, swung north and went in a wide concentric arc. Napoleon concentrated the bulk of his 210,000 men against Ulm, leaving strong corps to

*Joachim Murat (1767-1815), known from his love of gaudy uniforms as 'the clothes-horse of the Empire'; a dashing cavalry leader, his strategic sense was poor but his élan was much admired by the army.*
*(Print after F. Gerard)*

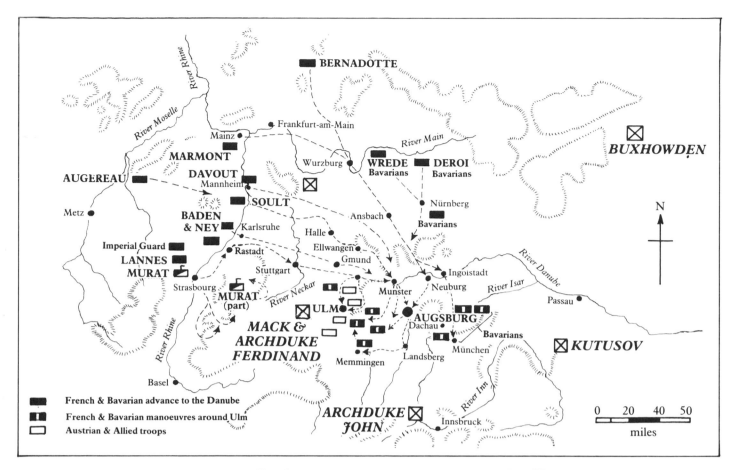

BERNADOTTE

River Rhine

River Moselle

Frankfurt-am-Main

River Main

Mainz

WREDE    DEROI
Bavarians    Bavarians

BUXHOWDEN

MARMONT
DAVOUT

Wurzburg

AUGEREAU

Mannheim

Nürnberg

Metz

SOULT

Ansbach

BADEN
& NEY

Karlsruhe

Bavarians

Halle

N

Imperial Guard

Rastadt

Ellwangen

River Danube

LANNES
MURAT

Stuttgart

Gmund

Ingolstadt

Neuburg

River Isar

Strasbourg

River Neckar

Munster

Passau

MURAT
(part)

ULM

Augsburg
Dachau

MACK &
ARCHDUKE
FERDINAND

Bavarians

KUTUSOV

München

River Rhine

Memmingen

Landsberg

Basel

ARCHDUKE
JOHN

River Inn

Innsbruck

0   20   40   50
miles

French & Bavarian advance to the Danube

French & Bavarian manoeuvres around Ulm

Austrian & Allied troops

guard his rear and watch for the approach of Kutuzov's Russians; it was the most spectacular example of the strategy of envelopment, and it worked to perfection. By the time Mack realised his predicament, he was completely isolated and cut off from reinforcement, the French being firmly astride his line of communication. His position desperate in the extreme, Mack made several attempts to break out from the strangulating encirclement; and bungled a battle at Haslach on 11 October in which overwhelming Austrian forces (25,000) failed to overpower Dupont's single French division (4,000). Three days later Mack despatched another force to break out, but Ney stopped them in a hard-fought battle at Elchingen, in which almost half the Austrian force was destroyed. This convinced Mack that he was hopelessly penned at Ulm, and must treat with Napoleon; but Archduke Ferdinand, wishing to have nothing of surrender, broke out with 6,000 cavalry on 15 October, of whom only some 1,900 got away. On 17 October Mack opened negotiations with Napoleon, and agreed to surrender his remaining forces if no

Russian assistance was received by 25 October. But Mack was so demoralised by this time that he did not even wait for the time to run out, but after learning of the surrender of other detachments capitulated on 20 October, with some 27,000 men. In all, the campaign had cost Austria some 50,000 men out of an original force of about 72,000, and was concluded without a major battle; Ulm was a strategic victory so complete that a serious combat was never necessary to resolve the outcome. Napoleon had outmarched, out-manoeuvred and outthought his adversary, an achievement quite unprecedented.

Following the disaster of Ulm, for Austria the situation only worsened. Archduke Charles attacked Massena in Italy at Caldiero on 30 October, to give him time to retire, but was pursued enthusiastically by Massena. Joining the Archduke John, retiring from the Tyrol, Charles withdrew, but finding his route across the Alps blocked, and harrassed by Massena, he regained Austria via Hungary, south of the Alps, and was thus unable to participate in the action on the Danube which decided the war.

After Ulm, Napoleon advanced east, detaching corps to the south (Ney and Marmont) to prevent Charles from interfering via the Alps, and from early November invaded Austria, having left about 50,000 men behind to protect his communications. By this time the Russians had at last arrived, but were unable to prevent Napoleon from occupying Vienna; Kutuzov fought effective delaying actions at Dürrenstein (11 November) and Hollabrünn (15/16 November). Leaving the Austrian capital on 15 November, Napoleon began to concentrate his remaining forces near Brunn, some 70 miles from Vienna. He had left a further 20,000 men in Vienna, so that his Grande Armée was now reduced to some 73,000 men; the apparent weakness of the force only served to tempt the Austro-Russian commanders into deciding upon a decisive action, rather than waiting to concentrate the largest possible army against the French. By planning to circle Napoleon's right flank and sever his communications with Vienna, the Allied commanders achieved Napoleon's purpose for him.

# Jena-Auerstadt – 14th October 1806

Until the Austrians were crushed at Austerlitz, Prussia had been contemplating joining the coalition against Napoleon. In 1806, her King Frederick William III (1770-1840) attempted to acquire Hanover, in part to redress the balance of power in Germany which had tilted following the proposal to form the Confederation of the Rhine. When negotiations broke down, Frederick William gave Napoleon notice to quit Germany. A Fourth Coalition was formed (Britain, Prussia, Russia and Portugal), and by moving their troops into Saxony, Prussia forced that state to enter the war on their side. In their anxiety to defeat Napoleon, the Prussians exhibited a degree of overconfidence, for which they were made to pay dearly.

Napoleon's *Grand Armée* was still in southern Germany, and he prepared to invade Prussia, concentrating his forces far to the east, in northern Bavaria, close to the Austrian border. For the first time the army could be described as multinational, for it now numbered not only Frenchmen but contingents from the Confederation of the Rhine, Holland and Italy; and as in 1805 the Russians were slow in marching west to aid their allies, so that providing Napoleon struck with his usual speed he would have only Prussians facing him. To meet the

*Grande Armée's* approximate 180,000 men, the Prussians assembled some 130,000 under the overall command of Karl Wilhelm Ferdinand, Duke of Brunswick (1735-1806), who had been in virtual retirement since shortly after his defeat at Valmy. He was seconded by the even more aged Field-Marshal Richard Mollendorf (1724-1806), nominally the senior commander, and by Frederick William III himself.

One of the most remarkable features of the Jena campaign was not the combat which decided it, but the advance launched by Napoleon from north-eastern Bavaria which began on 8 October, proving once again not only the tremendous advantages gained by the French army's ability of marching at top speed but equally in the flexibility of the 'bataillon carré' formation, and in the capacity of each *corps d'armée* to fight an action unaided. The *Grand Armée*, shielded from Prussian view by the usual screen of light cavalry which preceded it, advanced on a front of about 30 miles in three columns, together forming a huge square, travelling through the Thuringerwald (Thuringian Forest) at the rate of about 15 miles per day, the corps of Soult, Ney and the Bavarians on the right, Lannes and Augereau on the left, and Bernadotte, Davoût, the Imperial

Guard and reserve cavalry in the centre. The speed which Napoleon travelled completely confused the Prussians, though Napoleon's plan of engaging them in the general vicinity of Leipzig foundered when no report of the enemy was received from that direction. The flexibility of the 'bataillon carré', however, was nowhere better demonstrated than on this occasion, when Lannes, leading the left flank, encountered Prussian opposition at Saalfeld on 10 October. Rushing into action, he inflicted a minor defeat on the Prussians, in which action Prince Louis Ferdinand of Prussia – was killed bravely duelling with French cavalry. Three days later, Lannes reported encountering large enemy forces near the town of Jena; Napoleon at once set out to join his left wing, and all other corps were ordered to veer west and support Lannes. Joining Lannes at about 4 p.m., the sight which greeted Napoleon convinced him that he was facing the main body of the Prussian army, and that it would probably retire before offering battle in about three days time. In fact, Napoleon had miscalculated totally; Brunswick's main body of 60,000 was in fact retiring north towards Auerstadt (15 miles north of Jena), leaving the Württemberger General Friedrich

*Marshal Joachim Murat, King of Naples (1767-1815) was an inspirational cavalry commander who led from the front.*

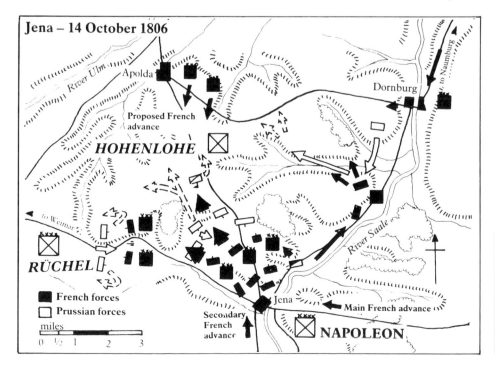

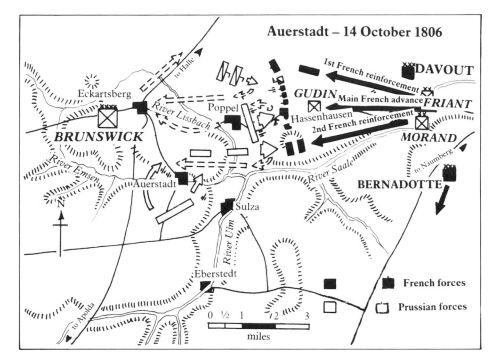

**Auerstadt – 14 October 1806**

to Halle
Eckartsberg
River Lissbach
Poppel
1st French reinforcement
**DAVOUT**
**GUDIN** Main French advance **FRIANT**
Hassenhausen
2nd French reinforcement
**BRUNSWICK**
River Emsen
River Saale
**MORAND**
Auerstadt
to Naumberg
**BERNADOTTE**
River Ulm
Sulza
to Apolda
Eberstedt
N
0  ½  1  2  3
miles

■ French forces
□ Prussian forces

Hohenlohe (1746-1818) with 51,000 men scattered on a wide front to cover Brunswick's withdrawal, and it was these three troops which Napoleon saw.

All night and early next morning the French force-marched to the support of Lannes's V Corps, initially the Imperial Guard, but by 10 a.m. on 14 October the force had doubled to an excess of 50,000 by the arrival of Augereau, with Soult's IV Corps, Ney's VI Corps and the reserve cavalry raising the total to over 90,000.

Davoût's III Corps and Bernadotte's I Corps were sent to execute the classic enveloping movement whilst Napoleon engaged what he believed to be the main body. The first action occurred near Jena as the French pressed forward on the early morning of 14 October, Augereau on the left, Lannes in the centre and the leading elements of Soult's corps on the right; against them, Hohenlohe had only 33,000 men, though he sent urgent messages for help to General Rüchel who had 15,000 more near Weimar. Furious at not being in the forefront of the action, the fiery Alsatian Marshal Michel Ney (1769-1815) launched his VI Corps in an unauthorised attack, which almost brought disaster; charged by massed Prussian cavalry, he was almost isolated and was only saved by the intervention of both Lannes and the reserve cavalry; but though it disordered Napoleon's plans, Hohenlohe failed to take advantage of the confusion, and his chance to save the day passed. Trying to fight a delaying action until Rüchel arrived instead of taking the initiative, Hohenlohe left his infantry in an appallingly exposed position, under French artillery and skirmish-fire, for two hours. The magnificent Prussian infantry was mercilessly shot to pieces, standing as if on parade despite the carnage around them. Thus, when Napoleon ordered an advance, they could not resist and by 3 p.m. the Prussians were in full retreat;

Rüchel's arrival an hour earlier could do nothing to prevent the rout of the Prussians who had survived the terrible punishment. Napoleon believed that he had beaten the enemy's main army, but a shock awaited him when he received dispatches from Davoût.

Since early morning, Davoût's 27,000 men had been heavily engaged against the entire weight of Brunswick's army at Auerstadt, some 15 miles north. Obeying Napoleon's order for an enveloping march to cut off the Prussian line of retreat, Davoût had received no co-operation whatever from the awkward Bernadotte, who resented taking his orders, and who had marched his corps south instead of supporting his companion. Davoût had thus confronted at least 50,000 Prussians, and had defeated them in a desperate battle at Auerstadt. Husbanding his meagre resources, Davoût was able to defeat each Prussian attack in turn, their advances being extremely poorly co-ordinated. Both Brunswick and Mollendorf were mortally wounded, and when Davoût ordered an advance at about 11 a.m., Prussian co-hesion broke. Frederick William III, now in personal command after the wounding of both his field-marshals, ordered the Prussian army to break off the action, and by evening some 13,000 Prussians had been lost, though at a crippling price to Davoût, as at least 40 per cent of his corps was dead or wounded. Bernadotte, realising his error, marched to the sound of gunfire and arrived in late afternoon behind Hohenlohe's already routed troops and hounded the rear of Frederick William's army. The entire Prussian force disintegrated; at Jena and Auerstadt together they lost 25,000 casualties and a similar number captured, a smashing blow which was decisive.

Although only seven days had elapsed since Napoleon began his advance – the most spectacular example of his *blitzkrieg* style of warfare – Prussian resolve was shattered. The *Grande Armée* swept north in pursuit of the remnants of the Prussian army; Napoleon entered Berlin in triumph on 24 October, and the last substantial command, that of the old warhorse Gebhard Blücher (1742-1819), surrendered at Lübeck on 24 November. It was almost seven years before Prussia again dared to take the field against Napoleon.

# Eylau – 8th February 1807

Following the total defeat of Prussia at Jena-Auerstadt, the *Grande Armée* swept northwards in pursuit of the fugitives; King Frederick William fled to Russia. At the end of November Napoleon began to march east to thwart an attempt by Russia to sustain Prussia, holding the line of the Vistula river and occupying Warsaw. Opposing him was General Levin Bennigsen (1735-1826), a German officer who had served in the Russian army since 1773, with some fragmentary Prussian forces and a Russian army nominally commanded by Marshal Alexander Kamenskoi (1731-1807), whose age led him to leave effective command in the hands of his subordinates. Some 32 miles north of Warsaw at the town of Pultusk on 26 December 1806, Bennigsen with about 35,000 men was attacked by Marshal Lannes, later reinforced by Davoût, totalling some 25,000. The battle was hard-fought but

indecisive, and as dusk fell the French retired having suffered about 8,000 casualties. Bennigsen abandoned his positions during the night, having lost some 5,000 men; and on the same day an equally indecisive engagement had been fought against Augereau and Murat at Golymin. Following these two unsuccessful actions, Napoleon determined to suspend the campaign and go into 'winter quarters'.

Campaigning in mid-winter was comparatively rare, as unseasonal weather made movement, foraging and communications extremely difficult. Nowhere was this more apparent than in Poland in 1806-07; roads were either blocked with snow or turned into morasses of mud, and the cold was extreme (over 30° of frost were registered on the night of Eylau, for example). The supply system, always ramshackle, broke down completely (causing Napoleon to institute

his comprehensive overhaul of the system); the French troops, already desperately cold, almost starved. In these dreadful conditions, which rendered manoeuvre difficult in the extreme, it was therefore a surprise when the Russians attacked the outlying French dispositions in late January 1807; Bennigsen now commanded in name as well as fact, old Kamenskoi having been assassinated by a peasant on 9 January. Somewhat unjustly, Napoleon blamed Ney's unauthorised sweep to find supplies for provoking Bennigsen, whereas the fault was probably his own for underestimating the capability and determination of the Russian. Moving out of his winter cantonments, Napoleon hoped to trap Bennigsen, but the evil conditions delayed some couriers (so that Bernadotte's corps arrived two days late for the battle of Eylau), and another with Napoleon's entire plans fell into the hands of patrolling cossacks, which information allowed Bennigsen to escape, extricating his army from an indecisive battle at Ionkovo on 3 February 1807.

Bennigsen turned at bay at the town of Preussisches Eylau on 6 February, with 67,000 men and an immense artillery train of 460 cannon. Napoleon had only 45,000 men and 200 guns, but the corps of Ney and Davoût (26,000) were within marching distance. The only reinforcement available to Bennigsen was a force of 9,000 Prussians under General Lestocq, retiring before Ney. Desperate to gain a single, decisive victory, Napoleon closed upon Eylau on the afternoon of 7 February and a hard fight occurred before the town was cleared of Russians, an action probably started by accident when the imperial baggage-train, oblivious of the enemy presence, wandered into the town in search of lodgings for the night. The fiercest fighting occurred, appropriately, in the town cemetery, which changed hands several times.

The 8 February dawned wretchedly, with heavy snowstorms and howling blizzards which at times blotted out all view. Ney and Davoût were still not in sight, but Napoleon held his positions, gambling upon resisting the Russian attack until they could arrive and outflank Bennigsen. He positioned Soult's corps on the left, Augereau's on the right, and the massed cavalry reserve under Murat in the rear. Bennigsen arrayed his army with an infantry

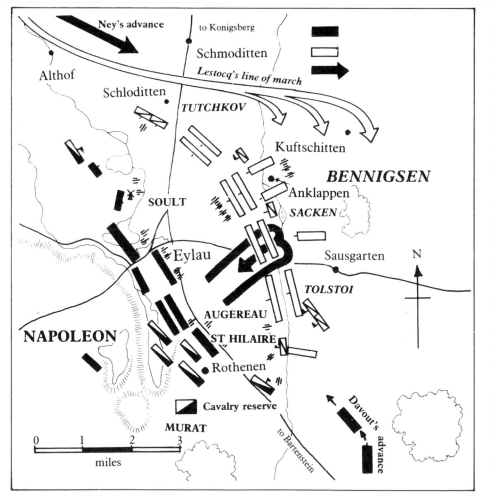

reserve and two massed batteries of 70 and 60 guns in front. Amid the snow and gale, Bennigsen responded to Soult's probing attack about 9 a.m., exerting severe pressure on the French left after a preliminary bombardment; which despite the overwhelming superiority of Russian artillery caused more Russian casualties than French, for when the French artillery replied the dense Russian columns made a far better target than the extended French lines. Already the leading units of Davoût's corps had begun to arrive on the French right, but they were engaged immediately and their progress halted; whilst Soult was taking a severe hammering. To buy time for Davoût and Ney, Napoleon ordered Augereau to advance in the centre with his own corps and St Hilaire's division; Augereau was seriously ill and had pleaded to be relieved, but agreed to stay in command for the day of the battle, and now led his corps to its doom. Blinded by the blizzard, they lost all sense of direction, marched through their own artillery fire and right into the Russian

*Marbot (mounted) attempts to save the 'Eagle' at the last stand of the 14th Line. 36 officers and about 590 other ranks of the regiment were buried in a mass grave at Eylau. (Print after L. Royer)*

70-gun battery.

By 10.30 a.m. Napoleon's position was critical; Soult was hard-pressed, St Hilaire's advance had been halted and Augereau's corps was in tatters; and a large Russian force was seen through the blizzard making for the shattered centre. Augereau's men were thrown back to the cemetery at Eylau, where the remnants began to reform; but one unit had not retired, the 14th Line, which formed square atop a small mound between the armies. Repeated couriers were sent to them but none got through until Captain Marbot of Augereau's staff. By then it was too late: 'I can see no way of saving the regiment' said their commander; 'return to the Emperor and give him the farewells of the 14th Line which has faithfully carried out his orders, and take him the Eagle which he gave us which we can no longer defend . . .'; but Marbot was wounded and the Eagle lost as the 14th went under the Russian attack, which pressed on and penetrated even to the streets of Eylau, Napoleon only escaping by the self-sacrifice of his escort. His only chance of salvation lay with Murat's 10,700 cavalry reserve, and at 11.30 a.m. they launched into one of the greatest cavalry charges in history, led by the flamboyant Murat in person: through the Russian infantry retiring

before them, through the Russian centre in two columns, reformed in a single column in the Russian rear, then charged back through the Russian battery which had destroyed Augereau, with the Guard cavalry covering their return.

The charge was decisive; for a loss of 1,500 men it had bought Napoleon the time he required. Davoût's men pressed on as they came up, until Bennigsen's line was forced back upon itself; but French victory was prevented by the arrival of Lestocq's 9,000 Prussians, who blunted the French advance, and it seemed that the day was again swinging against Napoleon. Then, at last, Ney arrived (the snow having dulled the sound so that he had no idea a battle was in progress), and made some ground on the French left before darkness made a welcome end to one of the most sanguinary of all Napoleonic battles. Bennigsen retired overnight, but Napoleon was in no state to follow: as many as 25,000 French may have fallen, and 15,000 Russians, though the actual casualty-figure is obscured by Napoleon's usual propaganda which announced a major success at paltry cost: 'to lie like a bulletin' was the saying arising from such dispatches! He had succeeded in stopping Bennigsen's winter offensive, but at a terrible cost.

# Friedland – 13th June 1807

The war was renewed after both sides had spent some time in winter quarters, refitting and bringing up reinforcements after the butchery of Eylau. Napoleon captured the city of Danzig after a siege lasting from 15 March to 27 April, and intended to resume the offensive against the Russians on 10 June, but again Bennigsen took the initiative, hoping to overwhelm Ney's corps before Napoleon could concentrate. 90,000 Russians took up prepared positions at Heilsberg, which Napoleon attacked on 10 June, a sanguinary but indecisive combat in which the French frontal assaults showed little finesse and cost heavily. The Russians expected a renewal of battle on the following day, but Napoleon decided to manoeuvre them out of position instead, and consequently Bennigsen retired (leaving his supplies and wounded) when his flank was turned. The Russian continued to withdraw towards the river Alle and his forward base of Friedland. Napoleon believed him to be retiring on Königsberg, and organised a rapid march to cut him off from that fortress, but on the evening of 13 June his reconnaissance parties reported that a large Russian force was concentrating at Friedland. Both forces were small at this juncture; on the morning of the 14th Napoleon mustered only 17,000, the Russians having increased to 45,000 overnight. Both sides hurried up troops as quickly as possible, so that eventually Napoleon's strength grew to about 80,000 and 118 guns, and Bennigsen's to about 60,000 and 120 guns. Napoleon arrived in person about mid-day, and though his staff advised that he wait for Davoût and Murat to arrive, he decided to fight that day, for two reasons: it was the anniversary of Marengo, which seemed a good omen, and (more significantly) Bennigsen's position was parlous in the extreme.

Bennigsen had drawn up his army on the west bank of the river Alle, holding a four-mile line on each side of a stream which flowed due east into the Alle. Were he required to retreat, the entire Russian army would have to funnel in to Friedland, the main crossing over the river, so that an opposed withdrawal would be the most perilous of manoeuvres. Bennigsen had realised the weakness of his position and had given orders for a withdrawal in the evening to the safer east bank of the Alle; but Napoleon moved before he could put the plan into effect. Napoleon intended Ney on the right flank to initiate the assault, crushing the Russian left against the river, whilst the remainder of the French army occupied the Russian right. At 5.30 p.m. a pre-arranged signal by French artillery informed Ney that he must begin his attack, amazing Bennigsen who never expected that any action would commence so late in the day.

Ney's attack rolled forward against the Russian left, but met very severe opposition. As the Russians were forced back against the river, a Russian 'massed battery' opened fire from the far bank of the Alle, and Ney's advance hesitated under the bombardment. Bennigsen sent cavalry from the right and centre to relieve his beleaguered left wing, and had not Napoleon acted in person the French attack might have been repelled. Napoleon had held back in reserve the corps of Marshal Victor and the Imperial Guard, behind his right-centre, and now sent Victor forward to assist Ney, falling upon the flank of the advancing Russian cavalry. Once again the Russians began

*Meissonier's painting '1807' depicts a charge of French cuirassiers saluting Napoleon as they gallop into action. A massed cavalry charge did not win Friedland, or save the day as at Eylau; the 'charge' which was decisive was that executed by the artillery of Victor's division, demonstrating in full the value of mobile artillery gathered in a large battery.*

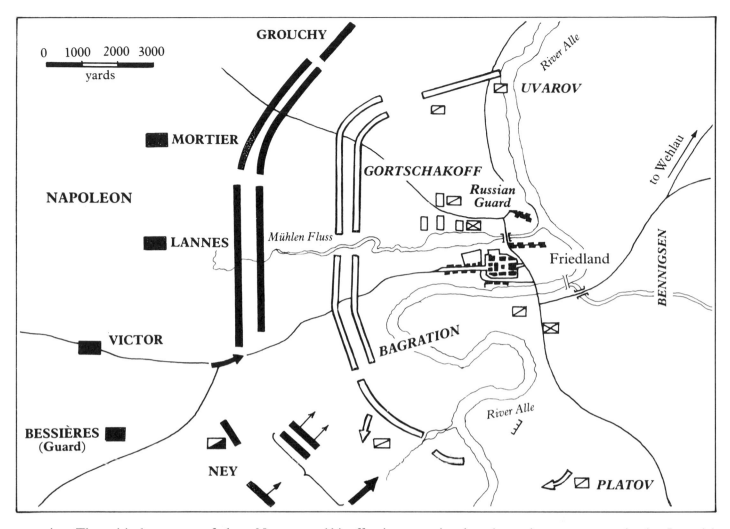

to retire. The critical moment of the battle arrived as the Russians attempted to reorganise their confused mass of units falling back on the river. The commander of Victor's corps artillery, General Alexandre Sénarmont (1769-1810) suddenly realised the opportunity presenting itself, and obtained Victor's permission to bring his guns into action. He gathered a 'massed battery' of 38 guns, mainly 6pdrs but with four 12pdrs, four 4pdrs and 8 howitzers and, obscured by smoke and Russian units from the Russian battery on the far bank, proceeded to 'charge' the Russian army. He opened fire on the mass of Russians at about 450yds, then moved forward his batteries alternately (covering one another) to about 250yds, pouring salvo after salvo into the Russians. Finally, he advanced to within 60 paces; so audacious was the manoeuvre that it was said that Napoleon at first thought that Sénarmont was deserting!

The Russians left was shattered, and Ney renewed his offensive, sweeping the Russian infantry towards the town of Friedland. Bennigsen attempted to relieve the pressure on his left by attacking the French centre and left with his right wing, but the attacks were repelled. His last hope was the Russian Imperial Guard, which tried to stem the flood of Ney's advance on Friedland; the fight was hard and bloody but unavailing, and the Russians began to pour over the river, setting the town on fire to hold up French pursuit. Bennigsen managed to extricate much of his right wing, thanks to the discovery of a ford north of Friedland, and the lethargy of the French cavalry on the left: the absence of Murat was felt keenly. By 11 p.m. the Russian army had left the field, much of it a disordered rabble, covered by the large battery on the east bank of the Alle. Napoleon had lost between 8,000 and 10,000 casualties; Bennigsen had suffered around 20,000 or 25,000 casualties, and had lost 80 guns. Had Napo-

leon chosen to commit the Imperial Guard as the Russians were attempting to retire over the Alle, or had Generals Grouchy and Espagne used their massive cavalry superiority to assail the retiring Russian right, Bennigsen might have been totally annihilated.

Nevertheless, Friedland was the decisive battle which Napoleon had been seeking. On the day after the battle, Lestocq's Prussians evacuated Königsberg, and on 19 June the Russians asked for an armistice. On 7/9 July Napoleon met both the Czar Alexander and King Frederick William of Prussia for a peace-conference upon a raft in the middle of the river Niemen, and concluded the Treaty of Tilsit which humiliated Prussia and compelled Russia to ally herself to France. Napoleon thus became the virtual controller of central Europe, but a deal of his success was owed to the unsung Sénarmont, who at Friedland proved the truth of Foy's maxim, 'the best tactic is to get up close and shoot fast.'

# The Campaigns in Spain 1808-1809

At the end of 1807 only Britain stood between Napoleon and the domination of western and central Europe. Napoleon attempted to counter the threat by the imposition of the 'Continental System', a trade embargo upon British goods, and as Portugal alone continued to deny him he resolved to occupy that country, by marching upon it through the territory of his ally, Spain. Even at this early stage it is likely that Napoleon intended to overthrow the weak Spanish monarchy and replace it with a Bonaparte regime; but it was to prove one of his worst mistakes and result in the 'Spanish ulcer', a running sore which consumed an ever-increasing quantity of the Empire's resources.

Years of corruption and neglect had reduced the Spanish army to a rabble, with the best, 15,000 men commanded by General Marquis Pedro La Romana (1761-1811), loaned to France and deliberately sent out of the way to Denmark. The Spanish King Charles IV and his heir-apparent Prince Ferdinand were apathetic and hated each other, and real power lay in the unscrupulous hands of the Queen's favourite, Manoel Godoy; thus, no common face was presented to Napoleon, who at the end of 1807 sent his ex-secretary and ADC General Jean Andoche Junot (1771-1813) with 30,000 men through Spain and into Portugal, where he occupied Lisbon in December, the Portuguese royal family fleeing to Brazil. To consolidate his hold on the Iberian peninsula, under the pretext of 'protecting' the Spanish coast, Napoleon sent Joachim Murat with 100,000 more French troops into Spain in March 1808. Godoy was overthrown, Charles IV abdicated and Ferdinand was interned in France and compelled to surrender the throne to a nominee of Napoleon's, his brother Joseph. Though unwilling, Joseph Bonaparte relinquished the throne of Naples, where he was replaced by Murat. Although deprived of central leadership, the Spanish population protested vehemently at the virtual annexation of their country, and insurrections began throughout Spain, most notably in Madrid where an uprising on 2 May 1808 was suppressed with enormous brutality. This began the unique character of the Peninsular War, in which the field armies behaved toward each other with a degree of civility, but in the guerrilla war against the population, massacre and atrocity was commonplace. When Joseph Bonaparte was 'elected' King of Spain in June 1808 by pro-French factions, almost the whole country rose in rebellion, swearing loyalty to the exiled Ferdinand; resistance to Napoleon was organised by regional *junta*s with no co-ordination or common aim save the desire to drive out the French.

The Spanish regular army was devoid of capable leadership and rendered largely worthless by years of neglect, though La Romana's reliable nucleus escaped from Denmark and returned home in British ships; but the ordinary population, though undisciplined, was fired with enthusiasm, and those fighting the guerrilla war were formidable, especially as the appalling communications, poor roads and barren country made service in Spain hell on earth for the French army. Napoleon, directing operations from Bayonne, despatched forces to crush the *junta*s, with mixed success; the infirm and incompetent General Gregorio Cuesta (1740-1812), the senior Spanish commander, was predictably defeated at Cabezon, though the citizens of Saragossa with great gallantry successfully withstood a siege. In July 1808 Cuesta took command of the army of the Galician *junta* and on 14 July was duly crushed at Medina del Rio Seco by Marshal Jean-Baptiste Bessières (1768-1813), commander of the Imperial Guard cavalry and one of Napoleon's closest friends and most loyal servants. At Baylen, however, General Pierre Dupont (1765-1840) surrendered his isolated French army of 17,500 to Andalusian troops; those prisoners not massacred were left to rot in prison hulks. This, the first surrender by one of Napoleon's armies, not only stimulated Spanish resistance but lowered French morale, and a further reverse followed. Junot was left isolated in Portugal, and in August 1808, intending to support the growing opposition to Napoleon, a British expedition landed north of Lisbon under the command of Sir Arthur Wellesley (1769-1852), a young general with a spectacular record in

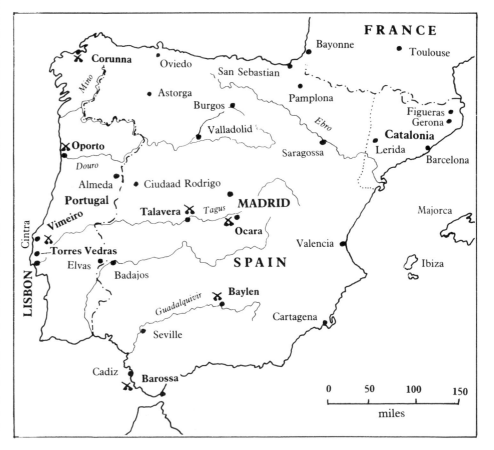

India. On 17/19 August Wellesley defeated Junot twice, at Roleia and Vimiero, but the arrival of the senior but less capable generals Burrard and Dalrymple prevented the annihilation of Junot; against Wellesley's advice they arranged the Convention of Cintra, by which the French were evacuated from Portugal in British ships. 'The Convention that Nobody owns, that saved old Junot's Baggage and Bones' caused such indignation in Britain that all three generals were recalled (only Wellesley to be exonerated) and command of the British expedition passed to Sir John Moore (1761-1809), the light-infantry tactician whose system of training had a major influence on the British army.

In September 1808 Moore was ordered to take 35,000 men into Spain, to co-operate with the Spanish *junta*s, though their leaders were not fully willing to assist and their forces largely useless. As Moore advanced towards Salamanca, Napoleon took personal command of over 200,000 French troops in Spain.

*The battle of Talavera, 28 July 1809, rated by Wellington as one of the bitterest he ever fought. Let down by his Spanish allies, Wellesley had to rely upon his skill and the courage of his British troops to repel repeated French attacks, at a cost of a quarter of the British troops involved.*

Realizing himself abandoned by his allies, Moore wished to retire, but to preserve Anglo-Spanish relations continued to advance, deflecting Napoleon's attention from adminstering the coup de grâce to the Spaniards. In this it may have achieved its object, but it almost destroyed the British army as Moore was compelled to retreat to Corunna, in mid-winter and in appalling conditions; yet the ragged British army was able to turn at bay at Corunna and inflict a heavy defeat upon Marshal Soult on 16 January 1809, before they were evacuated by the British navy, though at the cost of the life of the gallant Moore. A fortnight before the battle, however, Napoleon had left to return to France, believing that the Spanish question was all but settled, and to concentrate upon the coming war with Austria.

Despite the evacuation of Moore's army, Britain remained determined to continue the war in the Peninsula, and had a secure base at Lisbon into which supplies could easily be shipped, given the British command of the sea; though the situation was not hopeful, especially following the fall of Saragossa on 20 February 1809 after a harrowing second siege, which proved that the real resistance in Spain lay with the ordinary people, not with the incompetent and posturing generals and their rabble armies. Wellesley returned to Lisbon to

command the British forces, who were now assisted by an ever-improving Portuguese army, re-trained and re-equipped on British lines. Cuesta continued to be a greater danger to his allies than his enemies and was again defeated, at Medellin (28 March 1809), but Wellesley took the offensive and drove Soult from Oporto and back into Spain, and attempted to co-operate with Cuesta. The Spaniard, predictably, left Wellesley to face the combined forces of King Joseph and Marshal Claude Victor (1764-1841), but the small but stalwart British army beat off repeated French attacks at Talavera (28 July 1809), a victory which won the title Viscount Wellington for the British commander. Given the lack of Spanish support, however, Wellington had no option but go on the defensive and retired on Lisbon again. The year 1809 ended with another heavy Spanish defeat at Ocana on 19 November, Joseph and Soult routing 53,000 Spaniards under General Areizaga (Cuesta's replacement), inflicting 5,000 casualties and capturing 20,000 for a French loss of only 1,700; and in December, after an arduous siege of eight months, the city of Gerona fell to the French. Despite the presence of Wellington's British army in Portugal and the continual harrassment by the Spanish guerrillas, the situation in Spain looked not unpromising for Napoleon.

*(Above):* Eylau, 7/8 February 1807, with Napoleon and staff *(centre and right)*. The firing-line is indicated by the line of cannon in a 'massed battery'. Eylau was marked by blinding snow-storms, but otherwise the lines of troops accurately depict the appearance of a typical Napoleonic battle. *(Print after Swebach.)*

*(Below):* A scene from the later Peninsular War which shows the true appearance of an attack in 'column of companies': a succession of companies deployed in line, one behind the other. The leading company *(right)* wavers as it suffers the musketry of the British.

(Above): Borodino, 7 September 1812. Murat directs operations (centre), the surrender of Russian prisoners is accepted, and Barron Larrey bandages a wounded officer in the centre foreground. (Painting by Baron Lejeune.)

(Below): Waterloo, 18 June 1815. French cuirassiers (foreground), seconded by Grenadiers à Cheval and lancers of the Imperial Guard (mid-ground) execute one of their many brave but unavailing charges against the disciplined musketry of the impenetrable British infantry squares. Hougoumont burns in the background.

135

The Battle of the 'Glorious 1st of June'
(1794), known to the French by the date
of the republican calendar 10 Prairial An
II, in which Lord Howe defeated the
French fleet of Admiral Villaret-Joyeuse.
In the foreground is the French Vengeur
(74 guns), which became entangled with
HMS Brunswick which poured in
broadsides at close range. Vengeur drifted
away, a dismasted wreck, her crew
shouting 'Vive la liberté' as she sank.
(Print by Ozanne)

The battle of Trafalgar, 21 October 1805.
This painting by N. Pocock shows Nelson's
British fleet in two columns breaking the
French line-of-battle, to bring about the
'pell-mell' fight desired by Nelson. The
smaller vessels standing off from the main
engagement are frigates, which did not
normally become involved, being totally
outgunned by ships-of-the-line.

complete machine for its numbers now existing in Europe', and it is probably no exaggeration to state that, under his guidance and incomparable skill, it was the most formidable British army ever seen in continental Europe. By a series of brilliant manoeuvres, Wellington rapidly outflanked the main French defensive line and caused Joseph once again to evacuate Madrid (17 May 1813) and retire to the Ebro. With about 66,000 men, Joseph and Marshal Jean-Baptiste Jourdan (who had been defeated at Talavera along with Joseph) made a stand south of Vittoria. On 21 June 1813 Wellington attacked, and the French army (expecting a frontal assault) collapsed as Wellington turned both flanks and split their centre. It was the most decisive battle of the war, for despite a poorly-organised pursuit the French army was destroyed; Wellington captured all Joseph's treasury (the looting of which caused the delay in the allied pursuit!) and 143 out of his 150 guns. Joseph retired across the Pyrenees in the face of allied pursuit, and Suchet also began his withdrawal from Catalonia. Soult took overall command of the remaining French armies, but his aim was no longer to hold Spain, but to defend France from invasion, and performed as capably as his comparatively meagre resources would allow, using the great natural barrier of the Pyrenees to advantage.

Wellington laid siege to the border fortresses of San Sebastian and Pamplona, but wisely decided not to engage in a full-scale invasion of France until

they had been neutralized. Attempting their relief, Soult counter-attacked, forcing the passes of Maya and Roncevalles despite sterling defences. After several days of heavy fighting in the 'Battle of the Pyrenees', Soult's attack exhausted itself and allowed Wellington to counter-attack which drove back the French with a total of 13,000 casualties against some 7,000 allied. Soon after (31 August) San Sebastian fell, and on 31 October Pamplona. On 7 October 1813 Wellington crossed the Bidassoa; France was invaded. Napoleon by now had realised the enormity of his error in attempting to maintain a hold on Spain in the face of the universal hostility and active resistance of the population, and the Anglo-Portuguese army; in December 1813 he wrote in despair, 'I do not want Spain either to keep or to give away. I will have nothing more to do with that country', but now his concern was with the defence of France, for the liberation of Spain from French forces was but a step in the campaign. Ironically, by maintaining the same scrupulous fairness in dealing with the French population that his army had adopted in Spain and Portugal, not only did Wellington prevent any French guerrilla movement against him, but actually received more co-operation from the French civilian population than did Soult, whose armies were as rapacious in their own country as they had been in Spain.

Soult continued to retire with skill, but was defeated by Wellington at Nivelle (10 November), Nive (9/12

December) and Orthez (27 February 1814), and fell back upon Toulouse to avoid encirclement. The final stage of the Peninsular War, in which the French had no chance of eventual success, reflects with great credit upon Soult, who held off the allies for almost ten months following the débâcle of Vittoria. It was, however, a hopeless fight, and ended with an unnecessary battle, at Toulouse on 10 April 1814. Soult adopted this position in the hope that Suchet might be able to strike north and join him, but Wellington assaulted the city, losing 5,000 casualties against Soult's 3,000, but the French were driven out and Soult retired next day. On the following day, two days after the battle, news was received of Napoleon's abdication on 6 April, the action at Toulouse thus being fought after the official cessation of hostilities. A convention between Wellington and Soult ended the seven years of the Peninsular War.

The war in Spain and Portugal had a profound effect upon Napoleon's destiny, the 'Spanish ulcer' being an unrelieved drain on men and resources. Napoleon's own active contribution was small and thus he conducted the war at long range, via subordinate commanders who, though possessing considerable skill in the persons of Soult and Suchet, lacked the touch of military genius which their main opponent, Wellington, certainly possessed. Logistically the war was a nightmare, with bad roads and communications rendered almost impossible by incessant guerrilla activity. The rapaciously acquisitive behaviour of the French army, which began with the Marshals and extended to the lowest ranks, served only to inflame a population already committed to the annihilation of every Frenchman who crossed the Pyrenees. Under such circumstances and with resources increasingly limited, French defeat was inevitable. Had Napoleon not meddled in the affairs of the Iberian peninsula, the history of his Empire might have been very different.

# The Invasion of Canada 1812

The War of 1812 was occasioned largely by American over-reaction to British over-zealous enforcement of the 'Orders in Council', which responded to Napoleon's 'Continental System'. In pursuance of the policy of attempting to wreck Napoleon's economy, Britain exercised the right to stop and search any vessel of whatever nationality, and to confiscate any goods bound for France or French satellites. The policy did considerable harm to Napoleon's economy but not unnaturally angered many neutral nations, especially the United States, which in any case harboured ambitions to acquire those parts of Canada adjacent to the Great Lakes and the river St Lawrence. Furthermore, in 1811 the United States had come into conflict in the north-west with a confederation of Indian tribes led by the Shawnee chief Tecumseh who attempted to oust the white settlers from the area, and who was supported by Anglo-Canadian fur interests. In November 1811 Brigadier General William Henry Harrison, governor of Indiana Territory, moved with 1,000 troops against the Indian capital of 'Prophetstown', and defeated the Indians at Tippecanoe (8 November).

This campaign brought to a head anti-British sentiment in the USA, which had been simmering for years and had resulted in some bloodshed over the past half decade. These regrettable incidents arose from the British practice of not only stopping vessels in search of contraband, but also from impressing seamen from American ships for service in the Royal Navy (more than 6,200 were forcibly enlisted in this manner). In June 1807 HMS *Leopard* opened fire on the frigate USS *Chesapeake*, killed and wounded several men and boarded to take off four deserters; and in May 1811 the US frigate *President*, pursuing a British frigate with impressed men aboard, overhauled the British sloop *Little Belt* which was devastated by the American gunnery. By mid-1812 the 'war hawks' in the American establishment were in the ascendent, and sought a full-scale conflict during which, they hoped, they might conquer Canada while Britain was fully occupied fighting Napoleon. On 19 June 1812 President Madison duly declared war, ostensibly in defence of the 'freedom of the seas'.

The American military and naval establishment was almost totally unprepared for a major conflict, but the idea of conquering Canada was not as foolish as it might appear. Britain's defences were extremely slim, all her resources being directed towards the war against Napoleon: which in June 1812 did not appear to be progressing very advantageously, as Napoleon was just embarking on his Russian campaign, which most commentators believed would serve only to consolidate his position. The *Grande Armée* appeared an assemblage of immense proportion, and news of Borodino (which contributed to the wrecking of Napoleon's ambitions) was regarded in Britain as a 'calamity of our northern allies. It is unmanly to deceive ourselves with false hopes . . . Where, indeed, will the successes of this man [Napoleon] end?' Consequently, the garrison of Canada was at its lowest strength ever: to defend 1,600 miles of frontier were only four regular battalions, one Veteran Battalion, a permanent regiment of local troops (the Newfoundland Regt) and a few companies of artillery, about 4,450 men in all, scattered along the frontier. Small

*Fought on 13 October 1812 the Battle of Queenston was representative of the amphibious operations used extensively in North America in 1813-15, a war in which neither side emerged with great distinction, save Generals Isaac Brock and Andrew Jackson.*

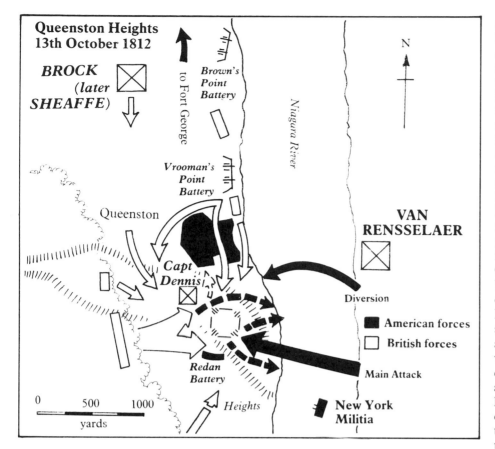

**Queenston Heights 13th October 1812**

BROCK (later SHEAFFE)

to Fort George

Brown's Point Battery

Niagara River

N

Vrooman's Point Battery

Queenston

Capt Dennis

VAN RENSSELAER

Diversion

■ American forces
□ British forces

Redan Battery

Main Attack

0    500    1000

yards

Heights

■ New York Militia

wonder that the South Carolinan congressman John Calhoun could state, 'in four weeks from the time that a declaration of war is heard on our frontiers, the whole of Upper and a great part of Lower Canada will be in our possession.'

To this end, in the first half of 1812 the United States had expanded its regular army greatly, and Congress had authorised the employment of 100,000 state militia should war be declared which, though inexperienced and largely untrained, would be sufficient to swamp the small British garrison. They had, however, not reckoned on two vital factors: though the Governor of Quebec, the American-born Sir George Prevost, was a vaccilator, Britain possessed on the spot a soldier of exceptional talents, Major-General Isaac Brock (1769-1812), a Guernsey man whose last campaign service had been aboard Nelson's fleet at Copenhagen. Secondly, the Canadian militia which was used to support the regulars was far more zealous and effective than its American counterpart; though small in number, Upper Canada's settlers were mostly exiled Tories who had emigrated from the United States after the War of Independence, and who thus

harboured a deep hatred of the USA. Although some of the militia units were unreliable, the majority were as determined as their regular-army comrades.

The war opened with a small American incursion into Canada, which was driven out and on 15 August the British replied with the capture of Fort Dearborn (present-day Chicago), after the surrender of which the garrison was massacred by the Indians who fought with Britain. The following day the American Brigadier-General William Hull surrendered Detroit with some 1,700 men, without firing a shot, when Brock approached with a tiny force of 300 regulars, 400 militia and some Indians (under Tecumseh). With the threat of American invasion thus temporarily neutralised (reinforcements for Hull fell back when they received news of the surrender), Brock moved east to the Niagara frontier where the next American threat lay. To guard the Niagara river (a 36-mile stretch between lakes Erie and Ontario) Brock had only 10 companies of regulars and the local militia (amounting to about 2,000 in all), plus between 200 and 300 Indians. Across the river were American forces

more than twice his strength, a regular brigade of 1,700 under Major-General Alexander Smyth, and another regular regiment plus 2,300 New York Militia under Major-General Stephen van Rensselaer. Fortunately for Brock the two American commanders hated each other, so that when Van Rensselaer took the offensive, Smyth refused to support him. The American decided to throw his men across the Niagara at Queenston, establish a fortified base there and, having thus split Brock's defence-line, launch the invasion proper, and on the night of 12/13 October put his advance parties across the river by boat. Only four companies (two British regular, two Canadian militia) opposed the landing, but their skirmishing and the slowness of the American advance held up Van Rensselaer until Brock could gather his scattered detachments. Brock himself arrived absolutely alone, and attempted with his meagre resources to lead a counter-attack to delay the American advance until the remainder arrived. As his first reinforcement came up, two companies of York Militia, Brock led them in a counter-attack against a battery the Americans had occupied, and was calling 'Push on the York' when he was shot through the breast and was dead within a minute. The counter-attack had to fall back, but Brock's sacrifice was not in vain, for the stiff resistance had exhausted the American regulars and the progress made by the remainder was exceptionally slow. At last two more reinforcements arrived to Brock's forces, and under Brigadier Shaeffe, though still outnumbered, cleared the Canadian side of the river by annihilating the American force, over 900 being captured. From the opposite bank, Van Rensselaer was powerless to help as his advance-guard was cut to pieces, for his militia refused to move despite his frantic pleas; they remained sullen and inactive while the regulars were overwhelmed.

Queenston brought the danger of invasion to an end for the year, and an American expedition at lake Champlain in November, under the inept Major-General Henry Dearborn, failed when the American militia stood on their constitutional rights and refused to cross into Canada. The United States's great opportunity had gone, by a combination of their own ineptitude and the skill of the fallen hero Isaac Brock.

# The Invasion of Russia 1812

The invasion of Russia in 1812 must be counted as Napoleon's greatest error, and the motives behind it are still somewhat obscure. By mid-1811 the position of France was secure; only Britain, Portugal and the dissenting part of Spain were actively opposed to Napoleon, and Russia was neutral. Relations with Russia had deteriorated since Tilsit, as Czar Alexander I was anxious about Napoleon's ultimate intentions for the Duchy of Warsaw, and resented his demands that Russia support the 'Continental System' by banning British trade. In early 1812 the Czar had been negotiating with Britain, and in July renounced the Continental System, but by that time Napoleon's expedition was already on the move. The decision to invade Russia was taken some time in 1811, perhaps in the hope of forestalling renewed hostilities which might occur; but whatever the case, it was a foolish decision and one which ultimately cost Napoleon his crown.

By the spring of 1812 Napoleon had mustered a *Grande Armée* of immense proportions, something between 614,000 and 675,000 men (the figure dependent upon how much of his support and reserve-area troops are included in the total). The name 'the army of twenty nations' was not exaggerated: the expedition was drawn from every state over which Napoleon had any influence,

including one whole Corps of Poles, one of Bavarians, one of Saxons, one of Westphalians, and (to operate on the flanks) one largely Prussian and one wholly Austrian, though neither of the last two formations (Macdonald's X Corps and Schwarzenberg's 'Austrian Auxiliary Corps') were seriously involved in the fighting. Napoleon made extensive logistical preparations, including the planning of supply-depots as the vast army could not live by foraging alone, but the supply-system organised was wholly inadequate for the task in hand. Napoleon never intended a protracted sojourn in Russia, but anticipated (in his usual way) a rapid campaign culminating with a huge battle which would destroy the Russian field army and end hostilities at a stroke. His greatest miscalculation was in underestimating the will of the Russian people to resist the invader irrespective of cost.

The advance began in three main columns, heading in the general direction of Moscow; the actual invasion-force was around 450,000 strong, and reinforcements were received throughout the campaign. Crossing the Niemen on 23 June, the advance was curiously slow; not only was there a vast baggage-train, but Napoleon himself caused many unnecessary delays. A rapid advance in the old style would have taken advantage of

the disunity of the Russian command, their two main armies being commanded by Minister of War Barclay de Tolly (1761-1818), a Livonian of Scottish descent, and General Peter Bagration (1765-1812). Their mutual antipathy led to lack of co-ordination, and the Czar's strategy was greatly confused by his Prussian advisor, Col von Phull, who 'lived in a world of his own imagination and contrived to stumble over every straw that lay athwart in his path.'

As the Russians retired before the advancing *Grande Armée*, they adopted a policy of 'scorched earth', denying to Napoleon the resources of an already impoverished country. Refusing to engage in battle, they drew the invaders after them, lengthening Napoleon's lines of communication which even at this stage were under threat from bands of marauding cossacks. The *Grande Armée* dwindled in strength at every step, from sickness, skirmishes and desertion, and discipline deteriorated accordingly. Napoleon was unable to trap or entice the Russians into battle, so when Barclay and Bagration converged on Smolensk, Napoleon launched a costly frontal assault on 16/17 August, but was unable to prevent the Russians from again renewing their withdrawal. At this stage Napoleon was faced with a choice of withdrawing or consolidating for the winter around Smolensk, or pressing on toward Moscow. Believing that the Russians would fight in defence of

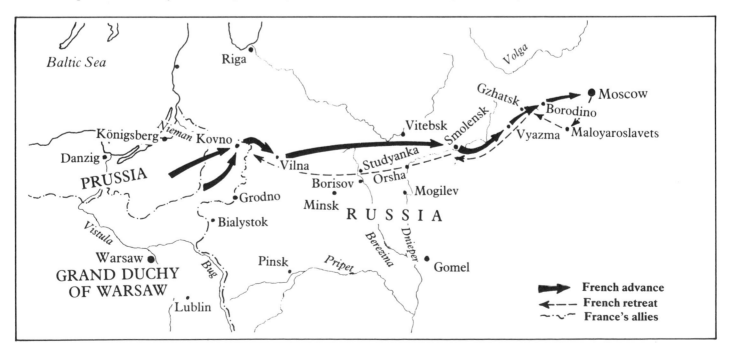

French advance
French retreat
France's allies

*Michel Ney, 'le brave des braves', was not one of the greatest tacticians of the Empire, but none was braver or more inspirational. He alone held together the rearguard on the retreat from Moscow, fighting musket in hand, and was unrecognisable when he staggered out of Russia, bearded and tattered: 'Don't you recognise me? I am the rearguard of the Grande Armée . . . I fired the last shot . . .' (Print after A. Yvon)*

the city, he continued to advance. The march on Moscow, a further 280 miles, given the lateness of the season, would certainly involve the *Grande Armée* experiencing the beginning of the fierce Russian winter, and would stretch supply-lines to an insupportable degree; yet Napoleon continued to advance, believing that 'within six weeks we shall have peace'; it was an amazing error.

With the Russian strategy in chaos, the Czar had to recall the general he openly disliked, the one-eyed, fat and immobile old Kutuzov. But Kutuzov was experienced, shrewd and revered by the men, and he assumed overall command of the Russian forces on 20 August. Until this moment it seems that there had been no deliberate plan to lure Napoleon onward, the Russian withdrawal simply the result of an inability to think of anything else; that Napoleon

walked into the trap was his fault alone. Uniting the armies of Barclay and Bagration, Kutuzov made a stand with about 120,000 men at Borodino, some 60 miles from Moscow, a position hastily fortified by the field-works typical of the Russian army. On 7 September 1812 Napoleon, with around 133,000 men, launched into a series of appallingly-expensive frontal assaults against the Russian positions, tactics which employed no imagination. Davoût proposed a huge flanking manoeuvre, but strangely lethargic, Napoleon attempted only a small flank-attack and a bludgeoning assault on the front of the Russian position. All day the armies battered each other, the *Grande Armée* making only very limited progress, until by 5 p.m. both sides were utterly exhausted and Bagration mortally wounded. About 44,000 Russians and 28-30,000 French had fallen, and during the night Kutuzov withdrew his shattered army.

Kutuzov declared that he would not fight again before Moscow, 'for the loss of Moscow does not signify the loss of Russia'; and Napoleon accordingly occupied the city on 14 September. Almost immediately an immense fire began, started by the Russians to deny Napoleon the use of its resources, and much of the city was destroyed by the

conflagration. Napoleon waited for the Russians to advance again, but after five weeks realised his mistake, and that he could not over-winter in the ruins of Moscow. On 19 October his retreat began, the *Grande Armée* now numbering around 100,000 men. It was the most catastrophic retreat in history; desperately short of provisions, a Russian attack at Maloyaroslavets (24 October) prevented them marching via an area in which supplies still existed, and they began to retrace their steps to Smolensk. Discipline broke down even before the harrying attacks by the cossacks and Russian cavalry became incessant; the first snow fell on 5 November. The army was doomed.

On 13 November Davoût's I Corps was cut off at Vyazma by the Russian advance-guard, and though it was dragged free by reinforcements the Corps was in total disarray – and it was the best in the army. The *Grande Armée* – or what remained of it – was cut in half at Krasnyi on 16/17 November, and though Napoleon was able to rescue the trapped portion, much of the army was now a straggling, orderless mob, dying of starvation, the cold and cossack lances; only the rearguard of the redoubtable Marshal Ney – 'the bravest of the brave' – held together, and then only by the iron will of their commander. Reaching the river Berezina on 26 November, Napoleon had to fight for the next two days to hold off converging Russian forces as the army escaped over two ramshackle bridges, maintained against all the odds by the pontooneers. The river became so choked with bodies that it was said it could be crossed on foot. As the remnants lurched on, Napoleon left the army on 5 December to return to Paris, ostensibly to raise a new army but actually to restore order after the attempted coup by the half-insane General Malet. Murdat briefly assumed command of the wreck, and when he left, the competent Eugène. Berthier reported that 'every human effort is hopeless. One can only resign oneself'; and two days later the rearguard staggered across the Niemen, Ney being the last Frenchman to quit Russian soil. The magnificent *Grande Armée* was reduced to some 20,000 filthy, starving skeletons, plus a mob of demoralized fugitives. From such losses, recovery was impossible.

# The War in North America 1813-1815

After the American invasion of Canada had been blocked in the autumn of 1812, hostilities were suspended for the remainder of the year. From the beginning of 1813, the War of 1812 was waged on several 'fronts', in the west, north and south; despite the large distances between the various theatres, events of one campaign could effect the course of another.

In the west, General Thomas Proctor with a small force of British regulars, Canadian militia and Tecumseh's Indians attempted to prevent a further American incursion like that defeated at Queenston by leading a raid onto American soil to strike the camps at which General William Henry Harrison was training his army. Harrison had been ordered to recapture Detroit, but found himself attacked before he was ready, and suffered a heavy defeat at Frenchtown on the Raisin River (22 January 1813), losing 197 casualties (many of the wounded being murdered by the Indians) and 737 captured. Not until September was Harrison ready to advance, and only when learning of Commodore Perry's victory over the British squadron on Lake Erie on 10 September. Harrison divided his forces and converged on Detroit, accompanied by Perry's squadron. On 29 September Detroit was recaptured, the British retiring before the vastly more numerous American forces, until on 5 October Proctor with 800 troops and 1,000 Indians made a stand at Chatham, in the 'Battle of the Thames'. The American cavalry (Kentucky mounted riflemen) charged the British right, whilst their infantry attacked frontally;

when Tecumseh was killed his Indians fled, leaving only the British troops to face 3,500 Americans. Proctor surrendered with 34 casualties and 477 taken prisoner. Although the victory broke up the Indian confederation (Britain's allies), Harrison's militia was disbanded and his regulars transferred to the nothern front. Enraged, Harrison resigned his commission and retired to civilian life; he later used his fame to assist his passage to the White House.

In the north, the United States planned a double-pronged invasion of Upper Canada. As a preliminary, on 24 April 1813 1,600 Americans captured York (now Toronto); 320 of the invaders were killed or injured when a magazine exploded, their leader Zebulon Pike being among the killed. The expedition withdrew after burning the town, achieving little save hardening Canadian resolve. In late May Colonel Winfield Scott with 4,000 men captured Fort George (on the mouth of the Niagara) in an amphibious attack, the 700 British defenders under General John Vincent retiring before them. The Americans pursued in a careless fashion, and when Vincent rounded on them at Stony Creek (6 June) they were ignominiously routed. Britain was unable to profit, however, for when Sir John Prevost, governor of Upper Canada, attempted an amphibious assault on Sackett's Harbor, the American arsenal on Lake Ontario (28/29 May), the gallant American defence repelled the attack. Heartened by this success, the U.S. sent a force under General James Wilkinson down the St Lawrence, and another

under General Wade Hampton from Lake Champlain in a converging advance on Montreal, where a British army was assembling. The expedition was a farce; Hampton's 4,000 men attacked a small British force on the Chateaugay river on 25 October, but retreated when the British sent buglers into the woods to simulate an enveloping manoeuvre. Wilkinson, with 8,000 men, moved down the St Lawrence by bateaux; at Chrysler's Farm on 11 November his rear was attacked by a tiny British force – 800 men – and the Americans were soundly defeated. Both Hampton and Wilkinson moved into winter quarters whilst the British captured Fort Niagara and burned the city of Buffalo.

Following another disastrous expedition in March, when Wilkinson's 4,000 men were worsted by 600 British at La Colle Mill, he was dismissed and replaced by Jacob Brown, who began a programme of reorganisation and training which greatly improved the wretched quality of the American forces. On 5 July 1814 Brown's renewed invasion of Canada met 1,700 British at the Chippewa River. Winfield Scott's brigade, regulars dressed in makeshift grey uniforms instead of the U.S. blue due to shortage of cloth, were said to have been mistaken for militia by the British, who were defeated when the American regulars thus met them on equal terms. But by now British reinforcements (Penin-

*The battle of New Orleans, 8 January 1815. In this print, the British attack can be seen reaching the American defence-line (the dried-up Rodriguez Canal) in two places.*

sular veterans among them) had arrived in Canada, and though a sharp battle at Lundy's Lane on 25 July was evenly-fought, it was a technical success as Brown retired. After another action at Fort Erie (17 September) the Americans abandoned the position, and with it all thoughts of a further invasion of Canada. Similarly, a British invasion by Prevost from Montreal upon Lake Champlain was turned back at Plattsburg when the British squadron was defeated on the lake by an American force on 11 September. Deprived of his amphibious support, despite his considerable numerical superiority and the presence of Peninsular veterans in his army, Prevost retired and there were no further actions in this theatre.

A British expedition was mounted in the Chesapeake Bay area of the eastern coast, when General Robert Ross landed with some 5,400 Peninsular veterans and advanced on Washington. A makeshift American force attempted to hold up the advance on Bladensburg on 24 August, but was brushed aside, the 6,500 militia bolting whilst the 400 naval gunners and marines made a valiant but unavailing resistance. Next day the British burnt several buildings in Washington, including the Capitol and White House, in retaliation for the burning of York. The raiders then re-embarked and sailed on to Baltimore, intending to repeat the dose, but received far stiffer opposition from the Maryland militia; Ross was killed in one of the attacks, and Fort McHenry withstood a bombardment, inspiring Francis Scott Key to write *The Star-Spangled Banner*. The expedition pulled back on 14 October.

On the southern 'front', contacts had been made between British agents and the Creek Indian nation in Alabama, who in July 1813 allied themselves to Britain and commenced hostilities against the United States. On 30 August 1813 the U.S. garrison at Fort Mims (35 miles above Mobile) was surprised and over half were massacred, and a campaign to combat the Creeks was organised by Colonel (later General) Andrew Jackson. At Tallasahatchee (3 November) and Talladega (9 November) Jackson's volunteer forces inflicted heavy punishment on the Indians, but when the volunteers disbanded the Creeks again became a threat. In February 1814 Jackson was again forced to take the offensive and on 27 March at Horsehose Bend the main Creek force was annihilated. The Creek War ended on 9 August 1814 by the Treaty of Fort Jackson, and Andrew Jackson (a regular army general since May) was given command of the Gulf coast area. In November he seized the British base at Pensacola, in Spanish Florida, which had been used to support the Creeks.

The final campaign of the war was in the New Orleans area, where Britain landed a small expeditionary force of Peninsular men commanded by Sir Edward Packenham, Wellington's brother-in-law. Andrew Jackson assembled an extemporized defence-force at New Orleans, consisting of some 700 regulars, his experienced Tennessee and Kentucky volunteers, some New Orleans militia and an assortment of other volunteers, including Gulf pirates and privateers. Packenham landed on 13 December 1814 and though Jackson was outnumbered he left his defences for a number of harrassing raids – especially on the night of 23/24 December – which raised the morale of his small command. His defence-line was along the Rodriguez Canal, south of New Orleans, which was bombarded by the British for some time before Packenham launched a frontal assault with 5,300 men on 8 January 1815. Advancing unwisely against the American entrenchments, the British lost 2,100 casualties (including Packenham killed) before abandoning the suicidal attack; Jackson lost 7 killed and 6 wounded. A week later the British re-embarked. Like Toulouse, New Orleans was an unnecessary battle, for unknown to the armies the Treaty of Ghent had been signed on 24 December, which guaranteed the territorial integrity of both the U.S.A. and Canada, bringing to a close a sad and unnecessary war.

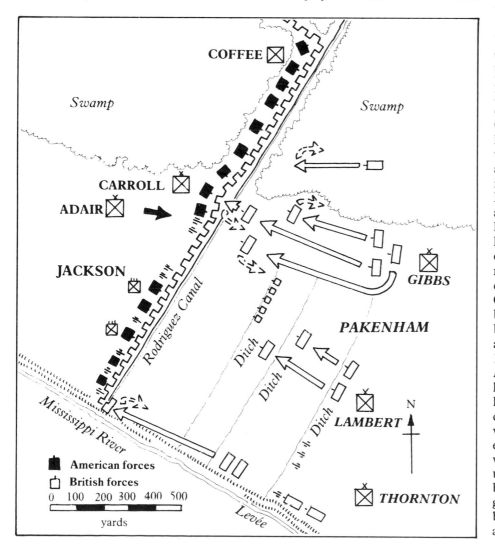

American forces

British forces

0  100  200  300  400  500

yards

# Lützen, Bautzen and Dresden 1813

To all intents and purposes, the *Grande Armée* was destroyed in Russia; the forces which remained on the eastern frontier comprised only the wreck of the *Grande Armée* – scarcely more than a mob of fugitives – together with troops from the detached garrisons which had not been committed in to the Russian campaign. The Russians did not pursue, choosing to wait out the winter before resuming hostilities, which gave Napoleon an opportunity to form a new army.

The political repercussions of the débâcle in Russia were vast. The Prussian contingent of the *Grande Armée*, commanded by General Johann David Yorck (1759-1830) had largely been concentrated on the left wing, under Marshal Macdonald, and was falling back from the Riga area when Yorck negotiated a treaty with the Russians. By the Convention of Tauroggen (30 December 1812) the Prussian contingent became neutral in the war, which most Prussians desired, still smarting from their humiliation in the 1806 war and at Tilsit. King Frederick William III initially disowned the Convention, but it forced him to desert Napoleon for the allied camp. Fleeing to Silesia, he mobilised his forces and instituted both an assembly of volunteers and conscription, and after concluding an alliance with the Czar declared a 'war of liberation' against Napoleon in March.

Eugène de Beauharnais, in command of Napoleon's forces in the east, left French garrisons at Danzig and Thorn on the Vistula, and at Stettin, Kustrin, and Frankfurt on the Oder, and withdrew what remained to Magdeburg on the Elbe, which with reinforcements received in January brought the strength to 68,000. Schwarzenberg's Austrian 'reserve corps', which had formed the right flank of the *Grande Armée*, withdrew first to Warsaw and then into Bohemia. As the campaigning season of 1813 drew nearer, a Sixth Coalition was formed against Napoleon, with Britain and Russia at the nucleus, plus Portugal, Spain and Prussia. An experienced and powerful Allied army was thus ready to press in upon Napoleon's eastern defence-line.

Napoleon assembled a new army at amazing speed, some 200,000 of the planned 700,000 being intended for the German front; but the forces thus assembled were woefully inexperienced and desperately short of equipment, a situation which deteriorated even further as the 1813 campaign progressed. The new army was assembled in part by conscription, including the impressment of ever-younger soldiers, culminating with the 15- and 16-year-olds known as the 'Marie-Louises' (after Napoleon's second, Austrian empress), but who fought remarkably well given their lack of training and experience; though they were far less resilient than the veterans lost in previous campaigns, being unable to march at the sustained pace for which Napoleon's armies had become famous, for example. Every conceivable means was employed to assemble the new *Grande Armée*; veteran troops were recalled from Spain (in particular the dragoon regiments, which became the nucleus of the new army's cavalry as the others had been virtually annihilated in Russia), the National Guard was mobilised, the *Artillerie de Marine* (naval artillery) was transformed into combat infantry regiments, discharged men were recalled and even pensioned invalids whose disabilities were not severe. The greatest shortage was in trained and experienced leaders at company and battalion level, but despite this the new army was a formidable one, whose morale was still surprisingly high.

In April Napoleon moved east to join Eugène along the Elbe, where at this point the Prussian forces numbered around 80,000; the Russians had about 120,000 in Prussia and Saxony. The Confederation of the Rhine still remained

*Napoleon at Lützen, 2 May 1813. Lützen was one of the most famous battlefields in Europe, the site of the last battle of the great Gustavus Adolphus against Wallenstein and Pappenheim in 1632. Visible in the mid-ground here is Napoleon's 'massed battery' of 70 guns, which bombarded the Allied line before the advance of the Young Guard broke their centre.*
*(Aquatint by Couché after Bovinet)*

loyal to Napoleon, but most of their armies had been as devastated in Russia as had the French. Napoleon planned a typical offensive, to penetrate the Allied cordon of defence and defeat their various contingents in detail, before they could combine against him. To this end he moved on Leipzig in three columns, preceded by a strong advance guard, but faulty reconnaissance (largely the result of the inexperience of his cavalry) failed to reveal fully to Napoleon that on his south flank lay some 75,000 Allied troops under the command of General Ludwig Wittgenstein (1769-1843), the son of a Prussian general in Russian service. Wittgenstein was in command of the Allied forces with the Prussian Gebhard Blücher (1742-1819); the joint headquarters of the Allied monarchs (Czar Alexander I and King Frederick William II) was at Dresden. On 1 May, as Napoleon pressed on to bring the Allied forces to battle, Ney's III Corps and the Guard cavalry commanded by Bessières ran into stiff opposition at Weissenfels, where the young French conscripts beat off the Russian cavalry in fine style, though Marshal Bessières was killed by a cannon-ball.

On the following day, as Napoleon was at Lützen, Wittgenstein fell upon an apparently isolated French force on the road south of the town. Ney went to their assistance and was joined by Napoleon, who behaved with the skill and flair of improvisation which had been absent for some time. More of the French army came up during the course of the afternoon bringing their strength to around 110,000, against the Allies' 73,000. Bringing up strong forces on either flank, Napoleon declined to commit the Imperial Guard until early evening. Massing 70 guns, Napoleon shattered the Allied centre with an assault by the Young Guard, supported by the Old, and by 7 p m the Allies were in full retreat, having lost around 18,000 men, about the same as Napoleon. Napoleon's desperate shortage of cavalry prevented any immediate pursuit; but the victory of Lützen had gained him the initiative.

This was confirmed at Bautzen on 20/21 May. Napoleon occupied Dresden (7/8 May) and followed the retreating Allies east of the Elbe, until Wittgenstein was ordered by the Allied sovereigns to make a stand. The Allies had something short of 100,000 men and 450 guns;

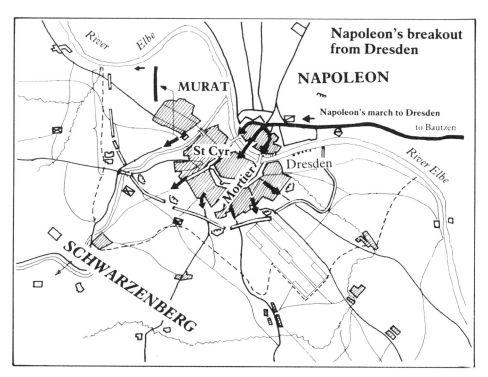

Napoleon commanded 115,000, with a further 85,000 under Ney approaching from the north. Napoleon planned a classical battle of envelopment, his army pinning Wittgensetin frontally whilst Ney was to fall upon the Allied flank and rear, cutting their line of retreat. It was a brilliant plan, but not for the first time failed due to the inability of a subordinate to grasp the initiative, Ney failing completely to cut the Allies' line of retreat. In two days of heavy fighting, though Wittgenstein was defeated by the frontal attack plus Ney's flank-movement, he was able to retire into Silesia with 20,000 casualties (the same as Napoleon), and live to fight again. Unable to pursue for want of cavalry and from general exhaustion, Napoleon agreed to an armistice on 4 June, pending the possibility of negotiations.

Both sides used the results to re-organise and re-equip, but though the break was valuable to Napoleon, it was decisive to the Allies; for now Sweden entered the war behind Crown Prince Bernadotte, Napoleon's ex-marshal, and on 12 August Austria declared war. Thus, when hostilities resumed on 16 August Napoleon faced the 'Army of Bohemia' (230,000 under Schwarzenberg), the 'Army of Silesia' (195,000 under Blücher, who had replaced Wittgenstein), and the 'Army of the North' (110,000 under Bernadotte). The Allies'

plan was to defeat Napoleon's outlying formations before uniting to engage the main force; on 23 August Bernadotte defeated Oudinot at Grossbeeren, and on 26 August Blücher defeated Macdonald at the Katzbach.

Napoleon was endeavouring to catch Blücher when he learned from Marshal St Cyr that Schwarzenberg's army (with the Czar, the Emperor and King Frederick William) was advancing on Dresden. On 22/25 August St Cyr managed to repel the first Austrian advance, and the main Allied attack was planned for the following day, by which time Napoleon and his forward elements had entered Dresden to bolster St Cyr. After heavy fighting on the 26th the Allies had made little progress, and overnight Napoleon's strength rose to 120,000 as Victor and Marmont's corps came in, against which Schwarzenberg had 170,000. On 27 August Schwarzenberg planned to batter in the centre of Napoleon's line, but Napoleon intended to smash the Allied flanks, and it was Napoleon's plan which worked; but the defeat was not decisive and Napoleon expected a renewal of the fight next day. Having suffered 38,000 casualties, however, (to the French 10,000), Schwarzenberg decided to retire, and made good his escape. Among the dead at Dresden was the brilliant Moreau, who had returned from America as advisor to the Czar.

# Leipzig – 16th-19th October 1813

Following the victory at Dresden, the pursuit of the Allied forces was appallingly mis-handled, largely due to Napoleon's own inactivity. General Dominique Vandamme (1770-1830), pursuing with his own Corps without the support he should have received, ran into overwhelming Allied forces whilst attempting to cut the Austrian line of communication at Kulm on 29/30 August. He extricated part of his command but was captured with 13,000 of his men. This was a severe blow to Napoleon: for not only did the battle of Kulm change 'into a cry of joy the despair which was spreading through the valleys of Bohemia' as the Czar's aide described, negating the victory of Dresden, in Vandamme Napoleon lost one of his most loyal supporters, a general who had stated that 'I who fear neither God nor Devil, tremble like a child when I approach him.'

After Kulm, the situation deteriorated further for Napoleon as the 1813 campaign drew towards its climax; on 6 September Ney, who had replaced Oudinot, was defeated by Bernadotte's Swedes at Dennewitz whilst attempting to take Berlin. This reverse persuaded Napoleon to re-group west of the Elbe, intending to use Leipzig on the river Elster for his base of operations, but these plans had to be abandoned when both Blücher and Bernadotte bridged the Elbe, their forces moving on Leipzig from the north whilst Schwarzenberg's Austrians advanced from the south, intent on crushing Napoleon between them. Although Napoleon succeeded in gathering some 195,000 men his army was weary, short of equipment and ammunition, and the Confederation of the Rhine was falling apart; Bavaria withdrew from the organisation in early October, and declared war on Napoleon. By 15 October Napoleon had gathered some 122,000 men in the environs of Leipzig, where he had determined to make a stand, and hoped to defeat in detail the various Allied forces before they could overwhelm him. The 'Battle of the Nations' which took place over the next four days was the largest of the Napoleonic era, Napoleon's forces rising to 195,000 men and 700 guns and the Allied armies, initially 257,000 strong,

to 365,000 men and 1,500 guns.

The battle began when Schwarzenberg sent Barclay de Tolly with 78,000 men to attack the south of the city on 16 October, but the advance was ill-organised and a French counter-attack recaptured all the lost ground. At the same time, Blücher's Prussians assailed Marmont's positions in the north of Napoleon's defensive perimeter, but though Marmont was outnumbered two to one the French held their ground around the town of Mockern. An Austrian attack to the west of Leipzig, intending to surround Napoleon, was turned back by IV Corps under General Henri-Gatien Bertrand (1773-1844), and

at the end of the first day's fighting Napoleon had successfully repelled the assaults on his positions; though the approach of massive Allied reinforcements (and only limited French support) made Napoleon's situation increasingly perilous. Had he succeeded in defeating either Blücher or Barclay de Tolly decisively on the first day, the Allied stranglehold around his army might have been smashed: but being unable to concentrate the bulk of his forces against either one or the other, for fear of leaving a fatal gap in his defences, Napoleon could not do more than hold his own.

The following day was spent largely in reorganisation by both sides, Napoleon arranging his defences within the Leipzig perimeter, and the Allied army being reinforced by the arrival of Bernadotte's

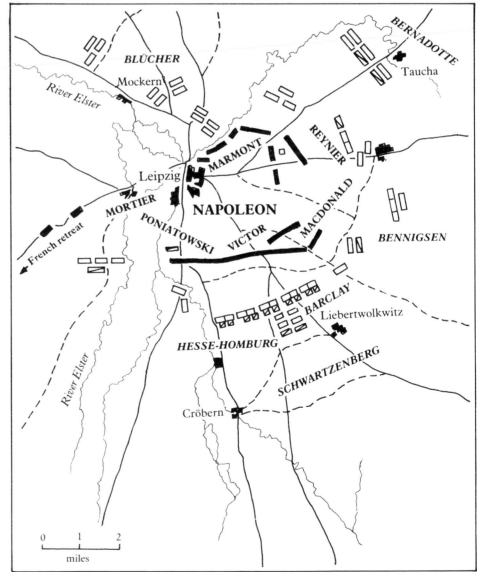

*Jean-Baptiste Jules Bernadotte (1763-1844). Though an ardent republican (with 'Death to Tyrants' tattooed on his arm!) he was elected Crown Prince of Sweden in 1810, after his career as a French marshal ended in disgrace at Wagram. His 'Army of the North' fought against Napoleon in 1813-14. (Print after F. Kinson.)*

'Army of the North' and Bennigsen's Russians, which added more than 100,000 men to the combined army. Now Napoleon had not only the Prussians to the north and Austrians and Russians to the south with which to contend, but Swedes in the east. Though his line of retreat to the west was still open, he was otherwise surrounded. The situation was made even worse by his shortage of ammunition, which ran desperately low even before the renewed fighting on 18 October; as Napoleon wrote to Eugène, 'If on the eve of the 18th I could have had 30,000 cannon balls, I would be master of the world today.'

On 18 October the Allies launched a concerted offensive of over 350,000 men against all points of Napoleon's perimeter. Such pressure was impossible to resist, and after the defection of the Saxon corps from Napoleon's army, his only course of action was to cut his way clear, over the Elster to the west. After nine hours of bitter fighting, which spread into the centre of the city itself, Napoleon gave orders for retreat. Despite their huge advantage of numbers, the Allied commanders were slow in following up their success, and Napoleon's forces still remained in good heart; but for a tragic error the evacuation of the Leipzig positions would have proceeded without a hitch. However, the premature demolition of the only bridge over the Elster by a nervous engineer corporal marooned 20,000 of the French rear-

guard on the Leipzig side of the river, including both Marshals Macdonald and Poniatowski, and Generals Lauriston and Reynier (whose Saxon corps had just deserted to the Allies). Both generals were captured, whilst the marshals attempted to swim the Elster, during which the injured Poniatowski was drowned. Although the battle was a massive defeat for Napoleon, he was lucky that the Allies had not pressed him harder and prevented his escape; as it was he lost 73,000 men to the Allies' 54,000 and much of his equipment. From the 'Battle of the Nations', Napoleon's eventual downfall was assured.

The French retreated to the south-west towards Frankfurt-am-Main, and on 30/31 October at Hanau the Bavarian army of General Karl Wrede – Napoleon's comrades at the beginning of the month – attempted to block his retreat, but with a flash of his old genius

*The French rearguard fights to keep open the line of retreat from Leipzig on 18 October; the ill-clad troops at right are Prussian landwehr (militia) wearing makeshift uniforms and wooden shoes. (Print after F. de Myrbach.)*

Napoleon swept Wrede aside, thanks largely to the fire of a 'massed battery' of 50 guns which burst from a dense forest to bombard the Bavarian lines. But in addition to the approximate 6,000 casualties sustained at Hanau, Napoleon lost some 10,000 stragglers who fell out with exhaustion and were captured on his line of retreat, so that of his great army which had fought at Leipzig he reached France with only some 70,000 men in formed units. Although Allied pursuit halted temporarily at the Rhine, the climactic battle of Leipzig had cost Napoleon control of Germany, and now the frontiers of France were in jeopardy.

# The 1814 Campaign to Montmirail and Château Thierry

During the winter of 1813-14, Napoleon was faced with the task of mustering yet another army. Only a supreme optimist could have held out any hope for France in the circumstances, but Napoleon was confident; as he wrote to Marmont in November, 'At present we are not ready for anything, but by the first fortnight in January we shall be in a position to achieve a great deal.' Yet the situation *was* desperate; more than 300,000 Allied troops were poised to cross the Rhine, against which France had fewer than 80,000 exhausted and tattered men to defend the entire 300-mile eastern frontier. A further 100,000 were still in Germany, but all were widely-separated and besieged, incapable of uniting or of returning to assist in the defence of France. On the southern frontiers, Wellington was driving steadily northwards from Spain, and Eugène in Italy was barely holding his own, precluding any serious transfer of resources from either front to assist the war in the east. The Confederation of the Rhine had collapsed, so that France could no longer call upon the resources of the German states, the French economy was nearing

exhaustion, Belgium and Holland were becoming mutinous and there was growing discontent even among the marshalate.

But Napoleon was not the man to be discouraged, no matter how bleak the picture; probably his optimism was partly due to his character, and partly to memories of what had been achieved in 1796-97, when the situation had looked equally bleak. As he had once turned a demoralised, half-starved army into the conquerors of Europe, he could do so again, and for a few brief months in the winter and spring of 1814 his energy and vigour returned, so that he resembled at times the 'little corporal' of Italy. Napoleon's health was not good (he suffered from an array of ailments which would have discouraged even the strongest constitution) and at times – such as the immediate aftermath of Dresden when the pursuit of the Allies was totally unco-ordinated – he seemed to sink into a torpor of lethargy, a marked contrast to the tireless energy of his greatest days. But at this desperate hour the old fire and capacity for unremitting toil returned, his will to succeed driving him

on as of yore. Resurrecting the old cry of the early revolutionary wars, '*la patrie en danger*', Napoleon set to with enthusiasm, working his ministries and staffs ceaselessly, to create a new army for the defence of the nation. No fewer than 936,000 conscripts and discharged reservists were called up in the winter, including 150,000 men not officially due for service until 1815; the National Guard was formed into combatant units, gendarmerie, customs officials and forest rangers were all swept up into the new battalions in an attempt to give some seasoned solidity to the mass of untrained conscripts. The Young Guard, which was to become the centre of the Empire's resistance, was hugely expanded, denuding the ordinary units of some of their experienced men, losses which could not be filled and consequently lowering the calibre of the remainder of the army. Drafts were called from the Italian and Spanish fronts to form the cadres of the new units (even though these theatres of operations could ill afford to spare anyone, and government newspapers poured out an incessant stream of hysterical propaganda, exhorting the citizens to take up arms against the monsters who were assembling on the frontiers, ready to devour '*la patrie*'. A measure of the desperation which all this involved is the fact that apparently Napoleon considered a mass issue of pikes to compensate for the shortages of proper weapons. The reconstruction of the French army during the winter of 1813-14 was a major achievement, but it was a shadow of the excellence of old; most of the conscripts never reported (only about 120,000 mustered), the drafts from Italy failed to arrive, and shortages of horses and weapons left the cavalry and artillery in a poor state. Napoleon's last foreign ally, Denmark, left the war in January 1814, and even Murat defected to the Allies in an attempt to retain his throne of Naples, ending Napoleon's scheme from a drive from Italy towards Vienna, as of old, to relieve the pressure on the Rhine.

Napoleon planned a diplomatic offensive, offering (among other concessions) to restore Ferdinand to the throne of Spain, and hoping that dissention in the Allied camp would bring about a peace advantageous to France. The Allies, in

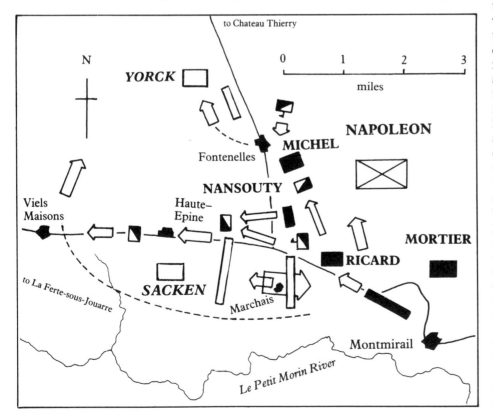

fact, *were* divided about how best to proceed: Britain and Austria were concerned about the balance of power in post-war Europe and were prepared to make peace if France could be returned to her natural boundaries; Bernadotte was unwilling for Sweden to invade France, as he hoped the peace would cause Napoleon's deposition and himself be invited to take over as Emperor (an absurd idea as he was regarded throughout France as a black traitor); the Czar and King Frederick William were uncertain, but the Prussian 'war party' (led by Blücher) was so vociferous that both Russia and Prussia came down upon the side of renewed conflict. Nevertheless, the Allies offered peace if Napoleon would consent to a restoration of France to her 1792 boundaries, ie without the Netherlands. Napoleon rejected the offer out of hand, and the war re-commenced.

The Allies planned a three-pronged offensive against France, Schwarzenberg with 210,000 men from the upper Rhine, Bernadotte with 60,000 from the Netherlands and Blücher with 75,000 from Lorraine, all heading for Paris. In the old style, Napoleon prepared to defeat each in turn before they could effect a union, aiming first to crush Blücher before he could rendezvous with Schwarzenberg. On 29 January Napoleon attacked 25,000 of Blücher's dispersed army

at Brienne, with about 30,000 French, mostly raw conscripts, and forced back the Prussian by threatening his flank. Blücher counter-attacked at La Rothière almost immediately, assembling around 116,000 Allied troops in the vicinity against Napoleon's 40,000; Napoleon intended to withdraw but was dragged into a fierce combat amid the snow, until he disengaged at nightfall, each side having lost around 6,000 men. The Allies pushed on towards Paris.

Napoleon now turned on Blücher and performed a series of manoeuvres which recalled his greatest achievements: the so-called 'Five Days' of victory. On 10 February Napoleon learned that Blücher's 'Army of Silesia' was strung-out upon its line of march, so with about 30,000 men determined to fall upon its parts and annihilate them in detail, beginning with General Olssufiev's 5,000 Russian at Champaubert. With an inferiority of 6 to 1 Olssufiev should have retired at once, but

expecting Blücher's assistance decided to fight, and was annihilated, losing 4,000 men. Next day Napoleon marched west to engage the next detachment, the corps of Yorck and General Dmitri Sacken (1790-1881), son of the Russian general who had fought at Eylau and in 1812. Initially with only 10,500 men (basically the invincible Guard) Napoleon detached a portion to watch for the arrival of Yorck, containing Sacken's 18,000 with the remainder at Montmirail until reinforcements brought his total to around 20,000, when he counter-attacked and routed Sacken's corps, whilst Yorck's leading elements (only about 3,000 engaged of the 18,000 total) were turned back by the newly-arrived corps of Mortier. On 12 February, in the third battle in as many days, Napoleon and Mortier engaged Yorck's rearguard as they retired through Château-Thierry on the Marne. They attempted to make a stand but Ney crashed through them and occupied hills overlooking the river, complicating the Allied retreat, but most managed to extricate themselves, though with considerable loss. In the three days of fighting the Allies had lost some 10,750 men against 3,450 by the French, and having thoroughly battered Blücher's army Napoleon decided that he must now transfer his attention to Schwarzenberg's army, after launching a final thrust at the retreating Blücher.

# The 1814 Campaign from Vauchamps

Following the defeat of Yorck and Sacken at Château-Thierry, Napoleon spent the next day in the town before sending Mortier and part of the Guard in pursuit. The delay enabled the Allied force to break contact, but before Napoleon turned to deal with Schwarzenberg he aimed one last blow at Blücher, who was advancing with the corps of the Prussian general Friedrich Kleist (1762-1823) towards Montmirail. Blücher, with perhaps 20,000 men, ran into French outposts at Vauchamps where Marshal Marmont was posted. Blücher's cavalry was roughly handled before he discovered from a prisoner that Napoleon was approaching in person, bringing the French forces to around 25,000; Blücher disengaged immediately. The French cavalry of General Emmanuel Grouchy (1766-1847) attempted to cut Blücher's line of retreat, but the sodden ground hindered deployment and most of the Russo-Prussian forces got away, Napoleon halting the pursuit to rest his exhausted men. Blücher had lost 7,000 men and a vast quantity of baggage, whereas Napoleon had lost only 600 men. With the threat from the 'Army of Silesia' thus temporarily neutralised, Napoleon was free to turn against Schwarzenberg.

The 'Army of Bohemia' was now threatening Paris from the south-east, so Napoleon hastened back to the Seine; some of his weary units force-marched 60 miles in under two days. Upon his approach, the Austrians began to withdraw, leaving the Prince of Württemberg to cover the retreat at Montereau. Marshal Victor was late in arriving and received a temporary suspension as a punishment, but on 18 February the French launched a massive attack, following a bombardment by a 'massed battery', which captured the town. The Austrians lost about 6,000 casualties against the French 2,500, but it was fortunate that Schwarzenberg decided to retire 40 miles, as Blücher had regrouped his forces and was again pressing on, forcing Napoleon once again to switch his attention to the 'Army of Silesia' which by 27 February was only 25 miles from the capital. Leaving Macdonald to attempt to stave off Schwarzenberg, Napoleon moved north. As soon as it was evident that Napoleon had again turned on Blücher, the 'Army of Bohemia' recommenced its march on Paris: despite his victories, the scale of the task was proving too much even for Napoleon's re-born skill.

As Blücher advanced along the Marne with 85,000 men, Napoleon struck swiftly and drove them over the river Aube. Blücher planned to hold his position on the plain of Craonne and envelop Napoleon's flank with a huge force under the Austrian-born Russian general, Ferdinand Winzingerode (1770-1818); but Napoleon hit first, at Craonne on 7 March, pinning Blücher frontally while Ney assailed the flank. This time the plan failed, the co-ordination bad; Ney was roughly handled and Blücher disengaged successfully, having sustained 5,000 casualties to Napoleon's 5,400, and withdrew towards Laon, where he had now massed his whole force, some 85,000 against 47,500. Napoleon sent Marmont with 9,500 men to turn Blücher's left flank whilst he engaged the Prussian frontally, but Marmont was slow in moving and was overwhelmed by Yorck, and saved from total destruction only by two small parties of Frenchmen: a baggage escort of 125 Old Guardsmen who held the Festieux Defile, turning back the Prussian cavalry, and 1,000 men under Col Etienne Fabvier who counter-attacked on his own initiative and allowed Marmont to escape. The outflanking having failed, Napoleon withdrew in the evening, having lost a further 6,000 men.

Napoleon retired to Soissons, the situation becoming more hopeless by the day. Learning that the Allies had occupied Rheimes, he decided on a rapid march to recapture the city, which was accomplished on 13 March, the isolated Russian corps of St Priest being routed and its commander killed; now Napoleon stood across the communications between Blücher and Schwarzenberg. Napoleon was heartened temporarily ('I am still the man I was at Wagram and Austerlitz', he declared), though his forces were weary and dwindling: 'the

*The final action of the 1814 campaign: Russian infantry storms an outlying defence-work at Montmartre, 30 March 1814. Napoleon had ordered Joseph Bonaparte to put Paris into a state of defence prior to the Allied advance, but little had been done to fortify the approaches to the city. Consequently, after the brave stand at Clichy little stood in the way of the Allied forces.*

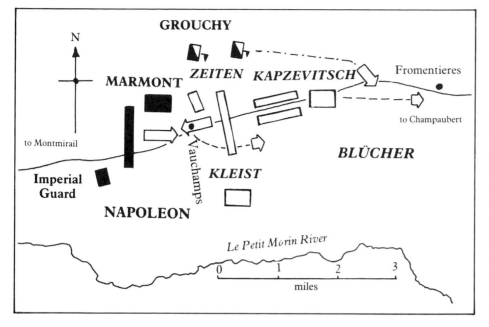

GROUCHY

N

MARMONT  ZEITEN  KAPZEVITSCH  Fromentieres

Vauchamps

to Montmirail  to Champaubert

BLÜCHER

Imperial
Guard  KLEIST

NAPOLEON

*Le Petit Morin River*

0    1    2    3
miles

Young Guard is melting like snow.' His only chance was to threaten Schwarzenberg's communications and thus compel him to abandon his march on Paris, but his dispatches were intercepted and his plans revealed, and the Allies decided to ignore his manoeuvre and drive on. Napoleon's last blow was struck at Schwarzenberg at Arcis-sur-Aube, on 20 March, driving back the Austrian's advance-guard; but overnight reinforcements brought the Allied total to 80,000 men, facing only 28,000 French. Schwarzenberg suspected a trap and did not attack with his overwhelming strength until mid-afternoon on 21 March, by which time Oudinot's rearguard had held their position long enough for the remainder of the French to withdraw back across the Aube. Technically it was

a French success, but Napoleon profited little. On 25 March Schwarzenberg defeated the corps of Marmont and Mortier at La Fère-Champenoise, in which the National Guard acquitted themselves like veterans, but were slaughtered in the process, barely 500 of the original 4,000 rearguard escaping. Clearly, Napoleon could no longer bring about a union with Marmont and Mortier, who were now attempting to defend Paris, nor could he prevent the Allies from reaching the capital. On 28 March the Armies of Bohemia and Silesia united in front of Paris, at least 107,000 strong, against which Marmont and Mortier mustered about 28,000. The capital was in a poor state of defence, but on 30 March Marshal Moncey and the Paris National Guard made a brave stand at Clichy, but were driven back to Montmartre, held by Marmont, which was stormed by the Allies. At the end, Lieut Viaux of the 2nd Grenadiers of the Guard, convales-

cing in Paris, gathered about 20 companions and tried to defend the area unaided; his body was found under a tree, sword in hand, surrounded by Prussian corpses.

It was the end. In the early hours of 31 March Marmont opened negotiations, and Paris was occupied. After 22 years of warfare, the Allied nations had achieved their goal, yet still Napoleon refused to admit defeat, heartened by his Guardsmen crying 'À Paris! À Paris!' He summoned the marshals to receive their orders, but Ney quashed his hopes of continuing the fight: 'The army will not march.' 'The army will obey me', retorted Napoleon; to which Ney replied, 'The army will only obey its generals.' The news that Marmont and his corps had defected to the enemy was the last straw; on 6 April Napoleon abdicated in favour of his son, but the Allies would have none of it. They had 145,000 men in Paris, against Napoleon's weary 60,000 at Fontainebleau, and the heart had finally been beaten out of the French resistance. The marshals were betraying Napoleon, his army was utterly exhausted, and the populace seemed to want only peace. The peasantry remained apathetic to Napoleon's call for a *levée en masse*, and to his credit he had refused the offer of local leaders to raise guerrilla corps if they showed Jacobin tendencies; 'If fall I must, I will not bequeath France to the revolutionaries, from whom I have delivered her.' Noth-ing but total abdication would satisfy the Allies, which Napoleon signed 11 April, being ratified on the 16th. Since he had almost been captured by cossacks at Maloyaroslavets, Napoleon had worn a bag of poison around his neck, and took it on 12 April; but it had lost its efficacy and he survived, to be given by the Allies the 'kingdom' of Elba, 600 soldiers and an income of two million francs a year. King Louis XVIII ascended the throne of France, and the Allies gathered at Vienna to re-draw the map of Europe.

The 1814 campaign was one of Napoleon's most brilliant, but he was fighting the inevitable from the beginning; his foes were overwhelming, the country was exhausted, and the marshals ready to betray him partly from self-interest and partly in the belief of the greater good of France. These facts were not realised by Napoleon until too late; but even now he was not yet finished.

*Auguste Frederic Louis Viesse de Marmont, duc de Raguse (1774-1852). Napoleon's artillery expert, Marshal Marmont was a valuable and capable subordinate until wounded at Salamanca. He served throughout the 1814 campaign but his defection to the Allies resulted in the verb raguser, to betray, entering the French language. In 1815 he joined the Bourbons and voted for the execution of Ney.*
*(Print after J.B.P. Guérin)*

# Ligny – 16th June 1815

Napoleon was conveyed to his new realm, the tiny island of Elba, on 20 March 1814. He was to remain there for less than a year, brooding over the injustice of his fate. The harsh royalist rule in France was unpopular, and despite everything the sentiments toward Napoleon were generally favourable, especially among his old troops. On the night of 26 February 1815 Napoleon embarked with stealth and transported his 'army' (the 'Elba Battalion' formed from the most diehard of the Old Guard) to land at Golfe de Juan on 1 March, and then set about re-conquering his Empire. His overtures to the garrison at Antibes were rejected, but at Grenoble he was met with wild enthusiasm; his forces swelled to 14,000 men and he advanced on Paris. Marshal Ney, given the task of arresting him, promised his new master Louis XVIII that he would bring Napoleon to Paris in an iron cage. In the event, the entire force assembled by Ney joined their old commander, followed by Ney himself. A number of Napoleon's old Marshals, including some of his most valued, wanted nothing more to do with him and followed the King into exile when it became obvious that nothing could stop Napoleon from re-occupying Paris. Almost every ordinary soldier in France flocked to march once again under the 'Eagles'; the only defections were senior officers, the whole of which

(in Wellington's words) were 'not worth a damn'. Once again, Napoleon's charismatic leadership had turned the situation upside-down. When confronting Ney's 'royalist' forces at Laffrey, south of Grenoble, Napoleon advanced alone towards the levelled muskets of the 5th Line: 'Soldiers of the 5th, you can shoot your Emperor if you dare! Do you not recognise me as your Emperor? Am I not your old general?' The cries of '*Vive l'Empéreur!*' which followed were deafening. As Napoleon said, 'Before Grenoble I was an adventurer; at Grenoble I was a ruling prince.' Whatever his failings, the power of Napoleon's personality was quite phenomenal.

Though it had been greatly reduced by the Bourbons, the structure of Napoleon's old army was still in place; thus, the cadres were available to reform the old regiments, but from the outset Napoleon had difficulty in building his forces to an acceptable level in the short time he knew he had available. The Imperial Guard was re-created from the small Royal (ex-Imperial) Guard and the Elba Battalion, but though a large expansion of the Young Guard was planned only four regiments were formed in time to take the field, recruited from discharged veterans and members of the line. Napoleon instituted a recruiting campaign ('enlist volunteers and attract old soldiers . . . beat the drums, parade

the flags . . . do everything possible to arouse enthusiasm', but although he assembled 188,000 men with another 100,000 in depots and up to 300,000 ready training, equipment and supplies were short. His immediate command, the 'Army of the North', numbered around 124,000, every man of whom he was going to need.

As soon as Napoleon's escape from Elba was announced, the Allies meeting at the Congress of Vienna declared him an outlaw, and formed the Seventh Coalition to oppose him again, promising to field between 500 to 800,000 men, financed by Britain, to restore Louis XVIII yet again. Their plan was to assail France on all fronts, but the execution of such a scheme would obviously take a considerable time. The only forces immediately available were an Anglo-Netherlands army of about 95,000 and a Prussian army of around 124,000 in Belgium. Schwarzenberg had 210,000 men along the Rhine, and 75,000 Austrians were in north Italy; Barclay de Tolly's 167,00 Russians were moving slowly west but would be long in arriving. The only ally Napoleon had was Murat, who in an

*Napoleon gives orders for the final advance to break the Prussian army at Ligny, about 7.30 p m on 16 June; the ADC wears hussar uniform. At the right may be seen the 'bonnets à poil', the Imperial Guard waiting with ordered arms for the command to advance.*
*(Print by J. Grenier)*

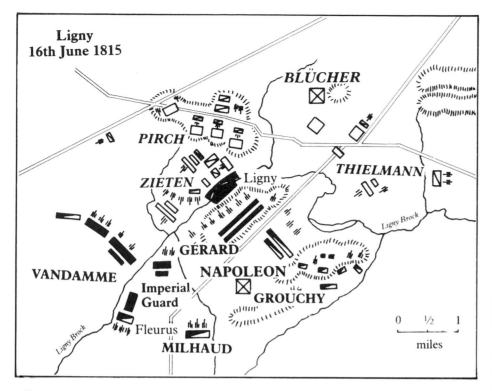

**Ligny**
**16th June 1815**

BLÜCHER

PIRCH

ZIETEN    Ligny    THIELMANN

*Ligny Brock*

GÉRARD

VANDAMME    NAPOLEON

Imperial
Guard    GROUCHY

Fleurus    0    ½    1

*Ligny Brock*    MILHAUD    miles

effort to regain favour marched into central Italy, but was beaten by the Austrians at Tolentino (2 May), and was rebuffed by Napoleon when he fled to France and requested a field command. Knowing the delay which would result before the full weight of the Allies could concentrate, Napoleon adopted his usual tactic of 'defeat in detail': he would take the offensive, shatter the forces in the Netherlands and hope that his success would compel the Allies to make a negotiated peace. It was a bold plan, but Napoleon made a serious error in appointing Davoût as Minister of War and

Governor of Paris; the Marshal's tactical skills should have been employed with the field army, for which Napoleon's principal deputies were the impetuous Ney and Grouchy, appointed as the last of the marshals on 15 April. Soult, a more capable general than either, was hopelessly mis-cast as chief-of-staff.

The two Allied armies in Belgium, commanded respectively by the Duke of Wellington (who had returned from the Congress of Vienna) and old Blücher, were taken by surprise at the speed of Napoleon's advance, the French dashing on from Charleroi to drive a wedge between the Allies. In the now-traditional manner, Napoleon planned to contain one Allied force with a minority of his army, and crush the other by achieving 'local superiority', before turning upon the first to repeat the dose. The Prussian army under Blücher had concentrated rather in advance of

*General Dominique Joseph René Vandamme, comte d'Unsebourg (1770-1830). One of Napoleon's most loyal subordinates, he was possibly unlucky not to receive the bâton of a Marshal, though his rough manner, bad language and unreserved financial dishonesty counted against him: three times he was relieved of command for looting or financial irregularities.*

Wellington's Anglo-Netherlands force, and it was thus Blücher who was selected to feel the first blow of the 'Army of the North'. Napoleon sent two corps under Ney towards Quatre Bras, to engage Wellington's army in a holding action, while the left wing under Grouchy attacked Blücher at Ligny. With Blücher thus fully occupied, Napoleon would envelop his right flank (thus cutting his communications with Wellington) and redouble the attack with the French reserve and the Guard, and drive them towards Namur where they would be in no position to aid Wellington, on whom the attack would then switch.

Surprised by the swiftness of the French advance, Blücher had assembled some 84,000 men along some low ridges at Ligny. At about 2.30 p m on 16 June Napoleon launched his attack with some 80,000 men, engaging him frontally while the corps of General Vandamme assailed the Prussian right, and soon heavy and bitter fighting was in progress. The enveloping attack on the right, however, never materialised as the corps designated for it, commanded by Jean-Baptiste Drouet, comte d'Erlon (1765-1844), became confused by conflicting orders; unsure whether to support Ney or Napoleon, d'Erlon wandered ineffectively between the two. However, Blücher began to give ground and Napoleon was about to launch the Guard to shatter the Prussians when a dark mass of troops appeared to the left rear of the French. Fearing a Prussian outflanking move, Napoleon held back, until it was discovered that the troops were in fact d'Erlon, who was approaching by the wrong route and thus unable to participate in the battle. It was thus late evening before Napoleon was able to renew the assault, giving him little time before nightfall to complete the destruction of the Prussian army. The Prussians duly broke under the pressure, and Blücher, leading a cavalry charge, was ridden-over and left for dead. His chief-of-staff, General Augustus Gneisenau (1760-1831), with no knowledge of the whereabouts of his chief, ordered a withdrawal. The Prussians had definitely been beaten, losing 25,000 men to Napoleon's 11,000, but the defeat was not decisive, and the lateness of the day and the slowness of the French pursuit allowed them to get away reasonably unhindered. It was Napoleon's last victory.

# Quatre Bras – 16th June 1815

While Blücher was out of commission after his fall at Ligny, command of the Prussian forces devolved upon Gneisenau, who was an experienced and capable chief-of-staff who made an ideal foil for old 'Marshal Vorwärts', as the fiery Blücher was known to his men; whereas Blücher was all impetuosity, Gneisenau was a cool, calculating individual. His assumption of command on the evening of Ligny, however, could have had dire consequences for the Allied armies, for he was unaccountably distrustful of Wellington and (as Fortescue commented), as 'ignorant of the meaning of good faith' as was Napoleon! His natural inclination was to retire the Prussian army on Namur, leaving Wellington to face Napoleon alone, which was exactly as Napoleon had planned should happen. However, perhaps influenced by Blücher's insistence on keeping his promise to support Wellington come what may, he directed the Prussian army to retire upon Wavre instead, thus maintaining a tenuous contact with the Anglo-Netherlands army. When Blücher duly reappeared on 17 June, battered but bolstered by copious doses of gin and rhubarb, he had thus nothing to do but continue the movements already instituted by Gneisenau.

Wellington's army was but a shadow of the magnificent creation he had commanded in the Iberian Peninsula. The nucleus was formed of reliable British infantry, but the remainder was a polyglot mixture of very varied quality. The territory taken from France in 1814 had been formed into a united Kingdom of the Netherlands (Belgium and Holland), whose troops comprised much of Wellington's army; these included some seasoned campaigners (such as the Nassau regiments), but most of these had until a year before been fighting *with* Napoleon. The remainder were inexperienced militiamen, and the other forces in the army were not much better: the Duke of Brunswick had loyally brought his army, but few were veterans of his 'Black Legion' of earlier years, but were mainly young soldiers, and much of the Hanoverian army which was present was similarly inexperienced. Even by blending the veterans with the others, Wellington could not rely on

much of his army, and the situation was complicated by his nominal second in command being the young Prince William of Orange (1792-1849), who had served as Wellington's ADC in the Peninsula but who was totally inexperienced in command, and though well-meaning appeared extremely incompetent. Wellington's description of it as 'an infamous army' was not inaccurate.

Marshal Ney was given the left wing of Napoleon's army and ordered to seize the crossroads at Quatre Bras, on the Charleroi/Brussels road, thus severing the communications between the two Allied forces, and to occupy Wellington's attention while Napoleon dealt with Blücher at Ligny. The Anglo-Netherlands army had been surprised by the speed of the French advance – 'Napoleon has humbugged me, by God!' was Wellington's comment – and thus only slim forces were available to resist Ney's probing. As the bulk of Wellington's army prepared to march south from Brussels, where they were concentrated, on the evening of 15 June Ney had encountered the Netherlands troops of Prince Bernard of Saxe-Weimar who held up his advance on the crossroads. Even on the morning of the 16th Ney did not hurry,

though opposed by only some 8,000 Netherlanders, who put up sterling resistance (stiffened by the presence of the Nassauers); whatever the failings of the Netherlands troops in the following days, their stand at Quatre Bras helped to save the campaign. Only at 2 p m did Ney make a serious attack, with the 20,000 strong corps of General Honoré Reille (1775-1860), and immediately began to make progress despite the sterling defence of the Netherlanders. At mid-afternoon Wellington arrived in person, followed at last by some of his British troops, raising Allied strength to 17,000. The position was still desperate, and Wellington sent the Brunswick corps in support of the beleaguered Nassauers. The Duke of Brunswick was killed rallying his men; and when the Prince of Orange brought up a brigade of Netherlands cavalry, the whole lot fled in disorder before ever meeting the French.

Ney sought to call up his second corps in support of Reille, but d'Erlon's men were not there; a confusion in orders had sent them marching toward Ligny. In a furious rage, Ney ordered their recall (which resulted in d'Erlon fighting in neither battle, a grievous loss of resources to the French), and then launched a massive attack upon the faltering Anglo-Netherlanders. François Etienne Kellermann led his French cavalry towards

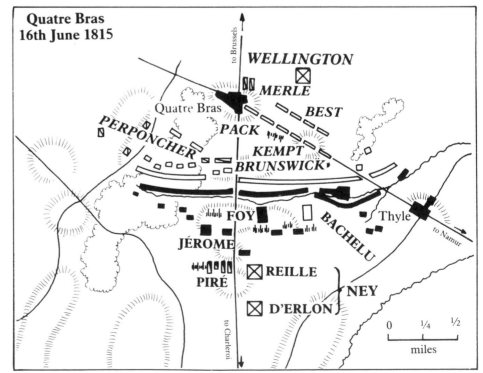

the crossroads, and almost captured Wellington himself, who only escaped by leaping his horse over the 92nd Highlanders, whose musketry drove back the French, but the fighting became even more savage. The 42nd Highlanders were caught by French cavalry in the act of forming 'square' and completed the manoeuvre trapping a large number of Frenchmen inside, all of whom were killed. The British 44th was unable to form square, but stood back-to-back to repel the French. More British troops were arriving all the time, and the formidable veteran Sir Thomas Picton (1758-1815) formed his battalions in square to drive off the French. The Prince of Orange, resenting Picton's 'interference', ordered the battalions into line; consequently they had little defence against the French cavalry, and only one battalion survived in good order when they were duly over-run. The French attack almost succeeded in breaking the Anglo-Netherlands force, but as the day wore on more and more Allied troops came up, so that Wellington was now reinforced to a total strength of around 36,000 and 70 guns,

*The British infantry was the most significant factor in the Waterloo campaign. This engraving after Lady Elizabeth Butler's painting portrays the 28th (North Gloucestershire) Regt at Quatre Bras, as the British squares beat off repeated French cavalry attacks. One error which should be noted is that the regiment is depicted wearing the 1812-pattern shako, whereas the 28th retained the earlier 'stovepipe' cap.*

giving him a theoretical numerical superiority (though many of his troops were either scattered or with shaken morale). However, he was sufficiently confident that at 6.30 p m he launched a counter-attack against the tiring French, and was able to regain almost all the ground lost by the time that fighting ended for the day at around 9 p m.

In terms of casualties, the French had the better of the battle of Quatre Bras, suffering some 4,000 to the Allied loss of 4,800 (including 2,275 British); but in the wider context, it was Wellington's day, Ney's slowness in forcing the attack early on the 16th, and the severe confusion which had afflicted d'Erlon's

command, had saved the Allies. Had Ney attacked more strongly and sooner, when the Allies were at their weakest, or had d'Erlon been available even when Wellington's supports had come up, the crossroads could have been taken and the Anglo-Netherlands army severely mauled. As it was, Napoleon's plans were already falling apart. D'Erlon eventually returned to Ney's command, but despite being thus heavily reinforced, on the following day Ney still made little offensive action until the afternoon. This delay gave Wellington ample time to withdraw his forces behind a screen of cavalry and horse artillery, to a position further along the Brussels road. Napoleon supervised the pursuit, but pouring rain and the early start enabled the Anglo-Netherlands force to conduct their withdrawal with only minor skirmishing. Wellington fell back to a position he had selected as early as 15 June, a ridge he had noticed as early as 1814, which intersected the Charleroi/Brussels road at right-angles, just at the hamlet of Mont St Jean. A short way further along the Brussels road was the village of Waterloo.

# Waterloo – 18th June 1815

The position chosen by Wellington was tactically sound; although the forest of Soignies was at his rear, which would have obstructed a withdrawal, he intended to stand and fight, secure in the belief that Blücher would aid him. The ridge of Mont St Jean dominated the battlefield, for although it was not precipitous it provided sufficient cover on the reverse slopes for the Anglo-Netherlands army to be largely concealed from Napoleon's view. A lane which ran along the ridge, crossing the Charleroi/Brussels highway, was sunken in places, and thick hedges provided a further defence. The position was anchored by three outposts: at the right, the farm and château of Hougoumont; in the centre, the walled farm of La Haie Sainte; and at the left the hamlets of Papelotte, La Haie and Frischermont. All these were garrisoned (by the British Guards, the King's German Legion light battalions and the Nassauers respectively). Wellington's two main corps, commanded by General Sir Rowland Hill (1772-1842) his Peninsular War deputy and the Prince of Orange were placed along and behind the ridge, with the main cavalry force under the Earl of Uxbridge (1768-1854) as a central reserve. A strong force was placed away to the right to prevent any out-flanking manoeuvre, though such was unlikely as it would have tended to drive Wellington toward Blücher, which was the opposite of what Napoleon intended. Wellington's dispositions set the scene for the most famous battle of modern history.

Napoleon concentrated his forces behind Ney's wing, which was pressing on from Quatre Bras, but to continue to harrass the Prussians he detached Marshal Grouchy with 33,000 men. Blücher's plan was to concentrate his army around Wavre, hold off any renewed French attack and support Wellington with as many men as he could. Napoleon's tactics were to be a simple frontal assault on the Allied position, and to hold the village of Plancenoit on his right flank in case any Prussians came up; in his last battle Napoleon showed little skill, making no attempt to utilise manoeuvre instead of just bludgeoning forward, and delegated far too much responsibility to Ney, who acted as virtual battlefield commander.

Napoleon's apparent lack of skill resulted partly from ill-health (Larrey believed that he suffered an epileptic fit on the night before the battle) and partly from a contemptuous under-estimation of his opponents. As Napoleon's forces began to assemble on the morning of 18 June, Marshal Soult (who knew about Wellington and the British army from bitter experience) advised that Grouchy be recalled immediately as a stiff fight was in prospect. Napoleon rounded on him: 'Because you have been beaten by Wellington you consider him a good general, but *I* tell you that Wellington is a *bad* general and the English are *bad* troops. The whole affair will not be more serious than swallowing one's breakfast.' Describing the coming battle as an *affaire de déjeuner* was probably a way of bolstering the morale of his generals; but equally is evidence for Napoleon's delusions that he was still invincible. It led him into using unimaginative tactics, caused the most concentrated slaughter of the era,

and ruined him at a stroke.

Napoleon assembled a 'massed battery' to bombard Wellington's line, but it had to be sited a considerable distance away, the long range and Wellington's 'reverse slope' tactic considerably neutralising its effect. With 72,000 men and 246 guns against Wellington's 68,000 (only one-third British) and 156 guns, Napoleon began his 'breakfast' about 11.30 a m when Jérôme Bonaparte led his division of Reille's corps against Hougoumont, an attack intended to divert Wellington's reserves and leave his centre vulnerable. In fact, it had the reverse effect; for Napoleon had not reckoned on the calibre of the British Guards holding the château who, despite being grossly out-numbered and the buildings set on fire, clung on grimly throughout the day, repelling every French attack in vicious hand-to-hand fighting. Far from diverting Wellington's reserves, more and more French troops were siphoned from Napoleon's centre in an attempt to take the château, even after its possession became largely irrelevant to the main battle. French mismanagement and the

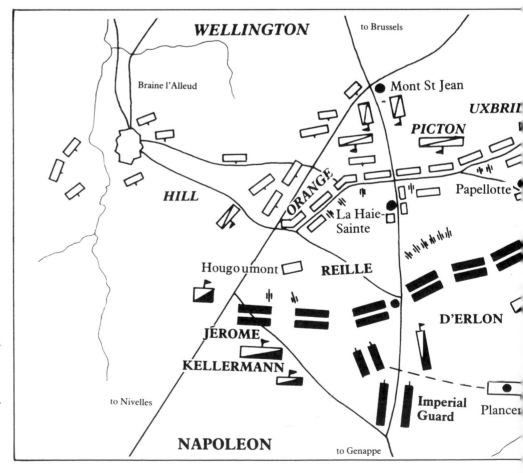

few companies of Guards totally wrecked Napoleon's plan of battle.

At about 1.30 p m the first main assault of the Allied line was made, when d'Erlon's corps was thrown towards the ridge. Shortly before, Napoleon received knowledge that Prussian forces were advancing on his right, so directed that a defence-line be established at Plancenoit, to resist any Prussian advance. But Blücher's progress was slow, hindered by roads turned into quagmires by the recent incessant rain, a partially-blocked road at Wavre, and by the pressure of Grouchy's wing of the French army. All day Grouchy battled against Blücher's rear-guard at Wavre, which resisted valiantly, outnumbered two to one, allowing the bulk of the Prussian army to march east towards the sounds of gunfire at Mont St Jean. Grouchy's subordinate commanders pleaded that he, too, march towards the gunfire, but Grouchy was no Desaix; he obeyed his orders to the letter, so that when Napoleon did send him a frantic appeal for assistance in late afternoon, it was too late to be of any use.

D'Erlon sent forward his corps in vast, unmanageable columns, which were a prime target for the Allied artillery; raked by gunnery, the attack ground to a halt when it encountered Picton's British veterans along the ridge, during which fighting Picton was killed. As the French hesitated, Uxbridge ordered a counter-attack by the British heavy cavalry, the Household and 'Union' brigades, which turned all except one French division into a shambles, capturing two 'Eagles' in the process. The British troopers careered on, out of control, through the mass of fugitives and into Napoleon's 80-gun 'massed battery', sabreing the gunners and riding-down anyone in their path, but then were fallen on by French cavalry, and being disorganised and exhausted were cut to pieces. The charge had cost Wellington almost half his effective cavalry, but had neutralised Napoleon's first main attack. All this time, the German Legion had been clinging bravely to La Haie Sainte, the outpost at the centre of Wellington's line.

At about 3.30 p m Ney mistook an inconsiderable re-alignment of Wellington's line as a sign of withdrawal, and

*Michel Ney, Prince de la Moskova, (1769-1815). 'Bravest of the brave', the red-haired Ney was one of the most celebrated of Napoleon's marshals, a lion-hearted man who was an ideal corps commander when working under supervision, but was limited as a strategist.*

impetuously ordered forward the French cavalry. Napoleon at this moment was preoccupied by the appearance of Blücher's advance-guard, which was now engaged with the French defenders of Plancenoit on the right flank, and Ney was left to conduct the attack on his own, incredibly without the support of artillery or infantry. It was a series of quite amazing charges, executed over sodden ground and ultimately at a walk, so that perhaps as many as 10,000 French cavalry were employed on a 700-yard front, conditions impossible for manoeuvre. The British infantry calmly formed square and poured volley after volley into the milling mass of horsemen, some of Allied artillery holding their positions despite the danger and creating ramparts of dead Frenchmen and horses in front of their batteries. Never did the French cavalry behave with greater bravery, but from the outset they had little chance; Ney sacrificed them for almost nothing. The attacks were finally pulled back by Napoleon himself at about 5.30 p m, the remaining French cavalry covering the withdrawal of the shattered regiments. By now, however, heavy casulaties had been sustained by Wellington's army;

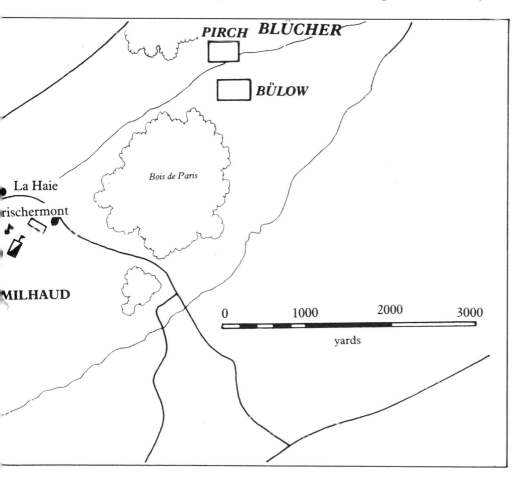

some Netherlanders and Hanoverians began to melt away, including a whole regiment of Hanoverian cavalry (the Duke of Cumberland's Hussars, which about-faced and rode into Brussels with the news that Napoleon had won!), and the mounting casualties caused gaps to appear in the line, which were filled by units moved in from the reserve. In Wellington's words, it was 'hard pounding'; and the outcome depended upon which side could pound the longest.

At 4.30 p m Wellington could hear a cannonade from his far left, indicating that the Prussians were at last in action, and at this stage the fighting was escalating around Plancenoit into a bitter combat; Blücher had arrived in person to command his leading corps, those of Bülow and Pirch, and for a short time they drove the French from the village. Napoleon directed the Young and Middle Guard to his right flank, and they re-took Plancenoit at bayonet-point; Napoleon's position was stabilised for the moment, but only at the cost of almost all his reserves. Wellington's extreme left had been held securely by Saxe-Weimar and his Nassauers, repeated French attacks being repelled; but as evening wore on and the first Prussians began to arrive to give Wellington direct support (rather than just attacking Napoleon's right flank) a tragic error occurred. The Nassauers (some still wearing the uniforms in which they had fought for Napoleon two years previously) were mistaken for French by the Prussians, and Saxe-Weimar believed that he was being attacked by Grouchy; fierce fighting occurred between the two Allied forces and the Nassauers were finally forced by weight of numbers from the defensive positions they had held all day, though inflicted heavy loss on the Prussians in the process. When the enormity of the error was recognised the Nassauers returned to their original positions, but were so exhausted that they could take no further part in the battle.

Before this came the most critical phase of the action, as the gallant German Legion in La Haie Sainte ran out of ammunition just as Ney at last co-ordinated an attack. The French smashed in the gates of the farmyard and the German Legion tried to hold them off with bayonets alone. At this juncture the Prince of Orange put in his meddlesome hand, ordering two more German Legion

battalions to advance in line and support the farm; one was annihilated by French cavalry as it tried to form square. At last, the 42 surviving riflemen evacuated La Haie Sainte, which fell into French hands, allowing Ney to bring up artillery to blast the Allied line at close range. The already-damaged, inexperienced battalions began to waver, and a complete rout was probably only prevented by Wellington deploying the light cavalry brigade of Sir John Vandeleur in a single line behind them. Brigade commander Colin Halkett begged Wellington to let him withdraw his men from the incessant bombardment, but knowing the effect that such a movement would have on the foreign contingents, Wellington replied

*Nothing is so indicative of the fall of the Empire as Hippolyte Bellangé's picture of the last stand of the Old Guard around their 'Eagle' at Waterloo. Others may have deserted Napoleon; the Old Guard remained loyal to the death.*

that 'every Englishman on the field must die on the spot we now occupy.' And die they did; some battalions were so shattered that two had to combine to form a single square, whilst the 27th Regt held its position, but 'dead in a square'. Now was the moment for Napoleon to commit his reserves and smash the Allied line; but most of them were already fighting at Plancenoit. Ney's pleading for more men became more frantic: 'do you think I can make them?' was Napoleon's reply. Gradually the French pressure on Wellington's centre began to slacken, as the first elements of Zieten's Prussian corps came up on Wellington's immediate left, allowing him to transfer units from his flank to bolster the devastated centre; and increasing pressure was being exerted upon Napoleon's right as more and more Prussians came into action, so that Napoleon was now barely holding his own.

All that Napoleon had left was the Old Guard, which he still held back, plus the battalions of the Middle Guard not already committed to Plancenoit. It was his last resort, and the situation so desperate that all had to be gambled. Led first by Napoleon himself, and then by Ney, two immense columns marched up to the west of La Haie Sainte (mistakenly not against the most shaken part of Wellington's line), accompanied by those forces still capable of providing support. The larger column headed for the British Guards, lying prone concealed amid the corn. Wellington was there in person, and ordered them to stand up when the French were barely 40 yards away. As they fired into the head of the French column, the British 52nd Light Infantry wheeled to enfilade their flank. The French fell in huge numbers before the column dissolved and they began to recoil down the slope. The second, smaller column had some initial success but there the Netherlanders counter-attacked, and that too broke and fled. The invincible Imperial

Guard had been vanquished for the first time in its history, and their defeat was the signal for a mass rout of Napoleon's army. Seeing the destruction of the Guard, the incredulous cry 'La Garde recule' ran down the French lines, followed by 'Sauve qui peut'. Judging the moment to perfection, Wellington raised his hat to signal his whole line to advance in pursuit, or at least those units still able to move. They swept down upon the retreating French army as the Prussians, singing Luther's hymn 'A mighty fortress is our God', erupted from the blazing shambles of Plancenoit. All that remained were some battalions of the Grenadiers of the Imperial Guard, who fell where they stood in square, attempting in vain to cover the retreat of the fugitives. As night drew on, Wellington and Blücher shook hands by Napoleon's command-post, the aptly-named inn of *La Belle Alliance*.

Waterloo was one of the most appalling carnages of all time: as one British survivor remarked, whereas after a battle it was usual to ask 'who's dead?', after Waterloo he asked 'who's alive?' The Allies had lost about 22,000 men (15,000 from Wellington's army) and Napoleon perhaps 40,000. Although Grouchy was able to disengage and retire in good order, and though the worthy Davoût had considerable forces around Paris, Napoleon's career was over, his political credit exhausted. His support melted away, and within three weeks he abdicated for the last time. The Napoleonic age effectively ended in the gathering dusk of Sunday, 18 June 1815, on the

slopes running down from the ridge at Mont St Jean. The scene of the conflict proved beyond doubt the validity of Wellington's remark, that after a battle lost, nothing is half so melancholy as a battle won.

Napoleon was exiled to the rocky island of St Helena, an unhealthy and remote spot in the Atlantic ocean, where he lived out the remainder of his life, not in discomfort but for a man like him in depression, deprived of all but a few servants, under a British governor he considered harsh; lonely, embittered and attempting to vindicate his conduct by writing unreliable memoirs. He never returned alive to Europe, but died at his house, Longwood, on 5 May 1821, a sad figure at the end. The eagle's flight was stilled, but he left Europe a changed place, and history would never record a greater soldier.

The final act of the Napoleonic legend occurred in 1840, when Napoleon's body was disinterred and returned to France for a state funeral at *Les Invalides*, where Marshal Moncey (governor of the hospital) and General Petit (whom Napoleon had embraced at Fontainebleau in 1814) presided over those members of his army still able to reassemble to pay him their last respects, dressed for the last time in the uniforms which had made Europe tremble, older and wearier but no less devoted. Their ranks thinned as the years progressed, but some survived to within living memory: Lieut Markiewicz of the Polish lancers of the Guard, born in 1794, who fought in Russia in 1812 and charged at Waterloo, was still alive in 1902. Despite the criticism Napoleon has received since his death, his men never forgot him: like Grenadier Noisot, who erected a bronze monument to Napoleon near Dijon, and ordered that he should be buried nearby in a standing position, so that he might mount Guard on his Emperor for all eternity. Napoleon founded no great dynasty, but achieved immortality.

*Napoleon's return to France, 15 October 1840. It is interesting that Napoleon's remains were brought home in state and with great emotion from St Helena by the last of the Bourbon kings of France, who forgot the past and the fate of his ancestors sufficiently to recognise Napoleon's greatness. From that day the legend has never faded. (Painting by Eugene Isabey)*

# Chapter Eight: THE FRENCH NAVY

In sharp contrast to the triumph of the French army and the dominance of Napoleon on mainland Europe, the French navy enjoyed few successes. In the earlier 18th century they had generally proved inferior (in terms of effectiveness if not *matériel*) to the British fleet, which was basically a result of the differing priorities of the two nations. France was a leading continental power to whom maritime success (though important for trade and colonial affairs) occupied a secondary position to operations on land. Britain, being primarily a maritime power, looked to naval success first and military operations second. Though the ships of the French navy might even be superior to those of the British, the legacy of British naval superiority, especially in the calibre, morale and seamanship of her sailors, was never overcome despite Napoleon's desire that France become the leading naval as well as military power. The effects of the mentality of the navy of the *Ancien Régime*, including the attitude of prudence to conserve *matériel*, and the effects of the purges of the republican period which deprived the navy of its most competent leadership, were never surmounted, so that Napoleon's navy was very much the most inferior part of his military strength.

Napoleon's naval policy was directed towards two strategies: by using the navy to support land forces, and in waging the 'war of commerce'. In neither was he successful, despite expending huge resources: he ensured that newly-built French ships were at least the equal of their British counterparts, and strengthened and improved the naval bases at Brest, Rochefort and Toulon, and began constructing a new one at Antwerp, 'a pistol pointed at the heart of England'. In support of the land forces, the French navy failed to emulate their comrades in the army. The most significant use of naval transport was in the Egyptian campaign, the oriental expedition successfully crossing the Mediterranean (capturing Malta en route, against negligible opposition); but the crushing defeat at Aboukir Bay effectively decided the outcome: no matter how many victories were won on land, the British domination of the Mediterranean and the virtual annihiliation of the French fleet meant that not only was the expedition deprived of re-supply from France, but was effectively marooned in Egypt. An attempted invasion of Sicily by Murat was repelled in 1810, and the only real success of an operation depending upon seaborne transport was the capture of Capri.

In the 'war of commerce' little more good fortune was enjoyed. Napoleon's avowed aim was to strangle Britain's ability to continue the war by annihilating her trade, but found his navy quite unequal to the task. Of the two basic methods, the active blockade of British ports and the ravaging of British merchant-fleets on the high seas was quite impossible; for the French navy was itself blockaded in its own harbours, and even when naval units did slip out their chances of winning a major victory against the British fleet were slim. By far the most practicable method of damaging British trade was by closing the ports into which British goods might be shipped, hence the 'Continental System' imposed by the Berlin Decrees (21 November 1806) and supplemented by the decrees of Milan and Fontainebleau, which declared all British goods to be contraband. The system had mixed effect; France itself suffered from the lack of import of British goods (for example, she imported 1,368,000kg of British cotton yarn in 1806!), though Napoleon's management of the economy was remarkable in making France virtually self-sufficient, for example in the substitution of sugar beet instead of cane sugar. For Britain, the Continental System proved little more than an irritation. Napoleon's prophecy that British ships would 'wander the high seas, which they claim to rule, seeking from the Sound to the Hellespont a port that will receive them' was never fulfilled; in 1806 British exports totalled £40,874,000; they fell only to £37,245,000 in 1807 (after the imposition of the Continental System), and leaped to £47,371,000 in 1808. Despite the trade embargo, a vast smuggling industry maintained the flow of British goods to continental Europe, which not all Napoleon's customs services or inshore vessels could halt; in fact, his economic sanctions had little more effect than the republican government's measures against British trade in the period before 1800. It is estimated that the total effect of France's 'war of commerce' against Britain between 1793 and 1800 (when no fewer than 3,466 British merchantmen were captured by French naval units and privateers) was to stop a mere 2½ per cent of British trade. In reply, British naval supremacy virtually annihilated French overseas trade. Despite the undoubted bravery of French seamen, Napoleon's naval policy was a dismal failure.

---

## French Naval Strength
1793 Disposition of the main serviceable line-of-battle ships

**At Brest:**
**ready for sea:** 1 110-gun ship, 1 80-gun, 10 74-gun ships.
**Fitting-out:** 1 120-gun ship, 1 110-gun, 3 80-gun, 2 74-gun.
**In good condition:** 1 80-gun ship, 11 74-gun.

**At Toulon:**
**ready for sea** 1 120-gun ship, 1 80-gun, 4 74-gun.
**Fitting-out:** 1 80-gun ship, 6 74-gun.
**In good condition:** 1 120-gun ship, 1 80-gun.

**At Rochefort:**
**ready for sea:** 3 74-gun ships.
**Fitting-out:** 1 74-gun ship.
**In good condition:** 6 74-gun ships, 1 unspecified rate.

---

*French sailors board a British Warship with which the French ship has become entangled. Boarding-parties were usually armed with cutlasses, short pikes, pistols and axes.*

161

# Admirals and Officers

Like the army, the French navy suffered severely from the purges of the aristocracy which were instigated by the early revolutionary government; but, unlike the army, the navy never truly recovered from the damage done at this time, doubtless due in part to the concentration upon France's role as a continental rather than maritime power, which had tended to neglect the navy at the expense of the army.

Prior to the revolution, French naval officers came from two very distinct backgrounds, the aristocracy and the commercial merchant trade. Whilst a similar fusion of these opposing social and educational backgrounds was workable in the army, where (for example) the middle- and lower-class commissioned ranks were often concentrated in the technical branches, (artillery, engineers) and in the less exalted infantry regiments, at sea the combination was more difficult. The 'aristocratic' officers in particular were known for possessing largely a theoretical knowledge of seamanship, whereas the experienced ex-merchant officers excelled in the practice of handling their ships, arising from years of service at sea. (Throughout the period, French naval officers were generally better in theoretical knowledge than the British naval officers to whom they were opposed, but in practical seamanship there was no comparison, the British being far in advance.) The conflict between the 'aristocratic' officers (who often occupied the higher ranks) and the ex-merchant officers (known as 'blue officers') led to intolerable situations aboard ship, the more experienced men on occasion refusing to take orders from their less-competent superiors, leading to insubordination and badly affecting the capability of fleets in general.

The purges of any officers with aristocratic or even vaguely 'privileged' backgrounds which occurred in the early revolutionary wars made the situation even worse, as not only the genuine aristocrats were hounded out of office but many of the most capable senior and middle-ranking officers as well; of those serving in 1790, perhaps as few as 25 per cent were still on active duty by June 1791. The stupidity of this purge is perhaps best demonstrated by the disbanding of the Marine Artillery, the highly-trained gunnery corps, which (because of their degree of training) was considered 'elitist' and therefore politically suspect; so instead of trained specialists, gunnery was vested in the hands of those who were politically reliable but technically incompetent. Given that the French navy had never been as well-trained or capable as its main European rival, Britain, the damage caused at this time was so severe that, despite all Napoleon's concern with providing excellently-built ships for his navy, the French maritime service never recovered.

In the structure of the French navy's commissioned ranks, naval officers were graded on military lines (further evidence that the navy was regarded as the junior service to the army). From 1795, naval officers were even ordered to wear the same distinctions of rank as their army counterparts, though the titles of the various ranks had maritime connotations. The highest rank was that of Admiral, which corresponded to a General-in-chief in the army (an army or corps commander); the next was a Vice-Admiral (corresponding to a *Général de division*), and then Rear-Admiral or *Contre-Amiral* (*Général de brigade*). After these 'general

*A naval junior officer of c 1798, wearing the uniform of his rank, which resembled that of the army: dark blue, with red 'stand-and-fall' collar and cuff-flaps, gold epaulettes and a bicorn hat. Higher ranks had embroidered facings. He holds a 'speaking trumpet', the device for projecting the voice.*

## The Allied Navies

Napoleon's allied and satellite states contributed effectively to his naval forces. The following are examples of allied naval strength:

**Spain (in 1792)**
72 ships-of-the-line (112 to 58 guns), only 56 of which were in seaworthy condition; 41 frigates; 109 sloops and smaller vessels.

**Batavian Republic (in 1801)**
2 76-gun ships, 8 68-gun ships; 1 44-gun frigate, 2 32-gun frigates, 2 24-gun frigates, 4 18- to 20-gun sloops, 93 brigs or gunboats, 4 galleys, 3 guardships, 2 coasters, 2 transports.

**Kingdom of Holland (in 1806)**
1 90-gun ships, 3 76-gun ships, 4 68-gun ships; 6 40-gun frigates, 6 32-grun frigates, 3 20-gun sloops, 2 22-gun sloops, 7 brigs, 2 galleys, 70 schooners, 207 gunboats, 94 transports.

**Kingdom of Italy in 1806**
inherited the naval forces of Venice. 3 frigates.

**Kingdom of Naples:**
nothing larger than sloops and gunboats.

*Vice Admiral Pierre Charles Baptiste Sylvestre de Villeneuve, 1763-1806. Napoleon's most famous naval commander entered the French navy at the age of 15, serving under de Grasse in the West Indies. In 1793 he was suspended from active service for his aristocratic connections, but restored two years later.*

officers' came *Chef de Division* (commodore: commander of a small squadron of ships-of-the-line), then *Capitain de Vaisseau* (lit. 'captain of a ship-of-the-line'), *Capitain de Frégate* (lit. 'frigate-captain'), with lieutenants and ensigns as the lowest ranks. *Capitaine de Frégate* replaced the earlier rank of *Major de Vaisseau* in 1795, the latter being thought to have elitist, aristocratic connotations, and *Enseigne* replaced the earlier *Sous-lieutenant*. As in the army, such terms as *Capitaine de Vaisseau* (like *Général de Brigade*, etc.) were not necessarily terms of appointment but of rank; i.e. a *Capitain de Vaisseau* was not necessarily the actual commander of a ship-of-the-line, such titles being retained even when detachments of seamen were employed in operations on land.

The higher administration of the navy resembled that of the army, with separate departments existing for administration, provision of stores, hydrographical surveys, supplies and medical matters; in rank, the officials thus employed resembled those of their army counterparts. A further administrative grade was that of *Préfet maritime* (maritime prefect), and the whole organisation was under the supervision of the minister of Marine,

Admiral Decrès being the most capable occupant of this post. The administration of the navy, however, at times served only to compound the inherent weaknesses of the service. Political dissension and jealousy wracked the higher echelon of the army (including the mutual jealousy of the marshals), but a further complication was apparent in maritime affairs when officers inexperienced at sea insisted on interfering in matters of which they knew little. Evidence of this is provided in the Trafalgar campaign, when Admiral Villeneuve (an experienced and professional sailor) was harrassed by General Lauriston (a soldier), who persisted in telling Villeneuve what he should do despite being nominally under Villeneuve's command. For reasons of protocol, Villeneuve had to send his despatches and communications to Decrès, the Minister of Marine; but Lauriston, being an ADC to Napoleon, not only sent libellous letters regarding Villeneuve to Decrès, but also to Napoleon direct. The result of this was not only that Villeneuve's best advice was over-ridden despite his knowledge of his profession, but that Napoleon decided that 'Villeneuve is a wretch who must be discharged with ignominy', a most unjust charge upon an admiral who was only concerned in doing what he considered best. Villeneuve's defeat at Trafalgar (after being compelled to put to sea at a time he knew was not advantageous) led to his being disgraced, so that when he was released from British captiviy and allowed to return home to France his only solution was to commit suicide by stabbing himself six times through the heart. Much of the confusion and bad administration of the French naval command was self-inflicted, and could easily have been prevented.

There were, nonetheless, many fine naval officers, from the lowest ranks upwards; Captain Jean Jacques Lucas of the 74-gun *Redoutable* is an example, who turned his ship and crew into one of the most efficient in the French navy. It is interesting to note the interchange of career between officers of Napoleon's command. Whilst it was exceptionally rare for British naval officers to hold a command on land, a number of naval officers attained considerable distinction on land, in both French and Spanish service. Vice-Admiral Count Baste, for

example, the tough but surly commander of the Seamen of the Imperial Guard, was killed whilst commanding an infantry brigade at Brienne. Admiral Juan Porlier, a Spanish officer who fought at Trafalgar, made his greater name as a leader of guerrillas against Napoleon (nicknamed *El Marquesito* from the fact that he was La Romana's nephew), whilst Miguel de Alava, who also served in the Spanish forces at Trafalgar, became Wellington's favourite liaison officer and was present as Spanish attaché at both Quatre Bras and Waterloo, a singular distinction of being present at the greatest sea and land battles of the Napoleonic era.

*French naval officers had an extremely elaborate, laced uniform, but when at sea more often wore 'undress', as illustrated in this engraving of Admiral Goudon, c1802, very similar to the style worn by the army.*

# Crews and Shipboard Life

Life at sea was hard and dangerous; as the proverb stated, he that would go to sea for pleasure would go to hell for a pastime. Living conditions at sea were grim for all nationalities, but in the French service they appear to have been particularly bad, cleanliness having a very low priority in the French navy. Perhaps this point has been over-emphasized as a result of the extreme cleanliness observed in the British Royal Navy, about which many foreign observers remarked; a French clergyman in 1777 described the English as 'a people to

*Gunnery NCO: there was no prescribed uniform for ordinary naval crews; most wore a tailless loose blue jacket, loose blue or white trousers, and a tarred straw or leather 'round hat'. The gunners wore an army-style uniform: bicorn hat and blue surtout with scarlet facings (and gold rank-lace on the collar). He carries a 'portfire'.*

whom cleanliness is a kind of instinct', and even Napoleon commented upon it on his way to St Helena, when conveyed there by the British Navy. Conversely, British officers were often very struck by the dirtiness of French warships, which cannot but have had an adverse effect upon morale, and may have been due in part to the sentiments of the early revolutionary period when clean and smart clothing was regarded as somehow elitist and thus unpatriotic. (Even the *Garde du Directoire* protested at being made to smarten their appearance: 'Well, what next? Is Liberty, then, to become an empty word? Are waist-coats and breeches to become an apple of discord thrown into Patriots' midst to divide them and strengthen the Royalists? Not in the accoutrements, but in the heart, lies the sanctuary of Republicanism.') This no doubt was responsible for the much worse health record of the French navy when compared to that of the British, though the revolting French practice of burying their dead in the ship's ballast must have been particularly culpable for the spread of infection. So severe was the health problem among the French navy that in Villeneuve's fleet during its sojourn at Cadiz during the Trafalgar campaign, no fewer than 1,700 seamen were sick, ashore in a temporary camp, about one-sixth of the total; and a further 300 had deserted.

Existing in French service was a separate naval artillery service, which provided trained gunners, but being regarded as 'privileged' it was disbanded in September 1792. Like the suspension of 'aristocratic' sea-officers, it took some years for the folly of the practice to be appreciated, and as the naval officers began to be reinstated from about 1795, so a new maritime artillery service was recreated in 1795, and in May 1797 squadrons of trainee gunners were formed.

The existence of such units enabled the gunnery of the French navy to be restored to competence, though it was usually believed that in this respect as in many others, the overall standard of French naval ability was inferior to that of its main rival, the British navy. The lack of training, experience and general seamanship of the French navy throughout the period generally served to more than cancel out the advantages they enjoyed over the British navy in superior ship-design.

The duties of ships' crews were very similar in all navies, most companies of seamen being divided into the main body, and the specialist tradesmen such as sail-makers, carpenters and artificers, who normally worked by day but did not stand watches at night, hence the use of the term 'idlers'. The most skilled of the non-tradesmen were those whose duties were aloft amid the yards, who served the sails, a perilous task in heavy seas. The skills involved were exactly the same as those practiced in the merchant service, though the numbers of men involved were usually very different. Naval ships always carried very much larger crews than those required of merchant vessels (though privateers, not naval vessels *per se*, equally kept large crews), in order that sufficient men were available both to sail the ship and fight. As such large numbers of men were required, naval crews often contained a far higher proportion of untrained crew or 'lands-

---

### Crews of French ships during the Napoleonic Wars

Crew-statistics were variable according to circumstance, often being under 'establishment'

| Ship | Crew |
|---|---|
| 120-gun ship-of-the-line | 1,098 |
| 110-gun ship-of-the-line | 1,037 |
| 80-gun ship-of-the-line | 840 |
| 74-gun ship-of-the-line | 690 |
| 40-gun frigate | 330 |
| 38-gun frigate | 320 |
| 36-gun frigate | 300 |
| 32-gun frigate | 275 |
| 28-gun frigate | 200 |

| Ship | 1793-1802 | 1803-1815 |
|---|---|---|
| **French naval losses** | | |
| 120 guns | 2 | 1 |
| 110 guns | 1 | — |
| 80 guns | 9 | 7 |
| 74 guns | 39 | 28 |
| 72 guns | — | 1 |
| 50 guns | 1 | 1 |
| 44 guns | 8 | — |
| 40 guns | 18 | 62 |
| 38 guns | 6 | 1 |
| 36 guns | 54 | 3 |
| 32 guns | 7 | 4 |
| 31 guns | — | 1 |
| 30 guns | 1 | 3 |
| 29 guns | — | 1 |
| 28 guns | 15 | 4 |
| 26 guns | 7 | 2 |
| 24 guns | 7 | 2 |
| 22 guns | 13 | 5 |
| 20 guns | 23 | 7 |
| Fewer than 20 | 167 | 319 |

men' than those of merchant ships, for whom most seamen had to be experienced at their trade. With the larger crews, the duties of naval sailors when not in action were usually less arduous than those of merchant ships (there being more men available to perform the necessary tasks), but this was more than off-set by the horror of naval combat.

Battle at sea was an even more terrible experience than battle on land, for at sea there was no escape, and not only the enemy but the elements had to be combatted. The most desperate time, in fact, was often after the conclusion of a sea battle, when a dismasted or leaking ship was easy prey to bad weather; typical of the ravages of a storm under these conditions is the fate of the Franco-Spanish ships captured at Trafalgar by the British; of the 18 captured 'prizes' (minus *Achille* which blew up at the conclusion of the action) only six survived the storm

*A gun-crew, as portrayed by Mettenleitner in a German print. The nationality is ostensibly British, but the artist would only have been able to see French seamen, an identification reinforced by the long-tailed coat of the artilleryman and the ignition by match instead of flintlock.*

and the succeeding days of bad weather. Aboard ship, combat was a living hell as the crews 'fought' their guns, loading and firing in an atmosphere of almost total darkness below-decks; badly-lit to begin with, the clouds of powder-smoke obscured vision and created choking conditions, and even worse was the inability to recognise danger from the enemy. Few sailors would be able to see the enemy vessels approach through the gun-ports (which were sometimes closed until the guns were actually run-out for each shot), the first intimation of death and injury being when the enemy's round-shot came smashing through the woodwork, bringing destruction wherever they passed. Serving the upper-deck guns was better in terms of visibility and atmosphere, but the men here were exposed to additional danger of musketry from the enemy's 'fighting-tops', marksmen being situated amid the sails to shoot down on the decks of the enemy ships alongside. When ships collided, their spars and rigging often becoming entangled, it was not always possible to continue to fire broadsides, in which case (or when the enemy ship was judged to be sufficiently wrecked to be incap-

able of an effective defence), parties of 'boarders' would be thrown onto the enemy's deck, seamen armed with cutlasses, pistols and boarding-pikes, when the most fierce hand-to-hand combat would occur until either the boarders were repelled or the enemy crew surrendered. It was in action that the discipline of the ship's crew counted above all else, and this was another reason why the British navy was generally superior to the French. French naval discipline (as in the army) had been greatly relaxed upon the Revolution, corporal punishment being banned: but though British methods of enforcing discipline were savage, the result was a far superior calibre of crew.

For those wounded in battle, the prospect of treatment was no better than in the army, for although each ship of consequence carried a surgeon and assistants (who formed an independent department within the naval administration), the wounded were normally removed into the bowels of the ship, the 'cockpit', where the crudest of surgery would be performed in stygian gloom, amputation and caulking with boiling pitch being the universal palliative to wounds.

# 'Marines', Artillerie de la Marine and Naval Engineers

By definition, 'marines' were basically soldiers who served aboard ship, ready to execute minor amphibious landings and to assist in the defence of the ship in close combat, serving as sharpshooters and in boarding-parties; and, in some navies, of guarding against any possibility of mutiny among the crew. Though such marine units existed in many European navies, France had no *Infanterie de Marine* as such, the only military units in the maritime service being the artillery companies who were used to supply trained gunners to the naval service. (Four 'marine infantry' regiments were created in 1792, but only as garrisons for ports and naval arsenals, each regiment of two battalions of 9 companies, including one of grenadiers; but these were disbanded after two years.) Consequently, all amphibious operations had to be undertaken either by units of proper sailors, or by army detachments who were not trained for service at sea. The result of using such inexperienced personnel could be disastrous, as in the occasion when Napoleon ordered part of the Boulogne flotilla (assembled for the invasion of England) to pass in review before him as part of their amphibious training. The incident demonstrates clearly that Napoleon never understood the basic nature

of maritime service, which resulted in his interference in naval tactical and strategic concerns being generally only a hinderance to those who did understand the essence of warfare at sea. His insistance on a review of sloops loaded with troops, despite an onshore gale on this occasion, was catastrophic; Admiral Eustache Bruix (1759-1805), an experienced seaman, was dismissed on the spot and exiled to Holland for protesting, and the result was as he had predicted: more than 20 vessels were driven ashore by the gale and over 2,000 men drowned simply on Napoleon's whim and as a result of his ignorance.

The maritime artillery service (titled under the *Ancien Régime* 'Corps royal des canonniers-matelots') was disbanded in 1792, two regiments for garrison duty being formed in the same year, but of brief duration. The folly of this disband-

*The Elba Battalion landing at Golfe Juan in 1815, a typical scene of disembarkation from a fleet. The Elba Battalion was Napoleon's bodyguard in exile, comprising six companies of Old Guardsmen, 100 artillerymen and a 'crew' of 21 Seamen. They formed the nucleus of the re-created Imperial Guard in 1815. (Print after F. P. Reinhold.)*

ment became obvious, and the marine artillery was re-instituted in October 1795, assembled on army lines in seven *demi-brigades* of three batallions each. The corps was re-structured as the *Artillerie de Marine* in 1803, when the 21 battalions were reduced to 12, formed in four regiments, to which were added four companies of *ouvriers* (artisans) and four of cadets. Although detachments of this force served at sea (at Trafalgar, for example), they became increasingly employed on land, in Portugal and in the 1812 Russian campaign. In February 1813 they were transferred from the jurisdiction of the Ministry of Marine to the War Ministry. The four regiments were gathered from where they had been stationed in scattered detachments and sent to Germany to fight as infantry, where they behaved conspicuously well, serving at Lützen, Bautzen, Dresden, Leipzig and Hanau; over 17,300 were employed in Germany in the campaign of this year, but lost so heavily that they had to be broken up and reorganised into individual companies.

Other naval departments were those which existed for duties of administration and supply, whose personnel normally served on land, and were organised and titled in military fashion; in the

administration, for example, there exis-ted *ordonnateurs*, *commissaires principaux*, *commissaires ordinaires*, *aide-commissaires*, etc, whose grade is obvious from their title. Dockyards were supervised by *con-trôleurs des grands ports*, and the supply-service officials were graded as *direc-teurs*, *sous-directeurs*, *contrôleurs*, *aides-contrôleurs* and *employés principaux* and *ordinaires des vivres de la marine*.

It was not uncommon throughout Europe for units of sailors to be formed for service on land, usually in 'specia-list' roles such as engineers or artillery. In French service these were largely employed as engineers (or infantry *in extremis*), including garrison duty to relieve combatant soldiers for service with the field army; though naval engi-neer units also took the field. In 1809, for example, the army's central engineer 'park' for the campaign against Austria included a battalion of specialist naval pioneers, 800 strong, and a labour bat-talion of seamen, 1,200 strong. Units of seamen could be formed for specific duties; for example, the *Bataillon de flotille* for garrison service at the camp of Boulogne in 1808. Naval battalions normally wore a version of maritime uniform, with the glazed or varnished 'round hat' and infantry equipment, the whole ensemble resembling that of the undress uniform of the Seamen of the

Imperial Guard, minus the shako. In addition to these *ad hoc* battalions there existed a proper corps of Naval Engineers (*Génie Maritime*), to which the corps of hydrographical officers (*ingenieurs hydro-graphes*) was attached. In January 1808 a separate corps of Artificiers was formed (*Ouvriers Militaires de la Marine*), origin-ally six companies (later 18, each of 207 men and 2 officers), initially stationed at Brest, Toulon, Rochefort, Lorient, Genoa and Antwerp, the main French naval bases. These were formed into a battalion in 1812.

The most valuable of the battalions of Seamen were those of the Imperial Guard, whose calibre was far above that of the ordinary companies; as Napoleon wrote, 'I would rather have 100 men like them than all your naval battalions.' Their organisation demonstrates how naval terminology was retained even on land: when originally formed in 1803 the Guard battalion was organised in five 'crews' (*equipages*) of five squads each, under a *Capitaine de Vaisseau* and a *Capitaine de Frégate*. Like the naval artil-lery, they rarely served as a complete battalion; in 1811, for example, two com-panies were serving as marines at Toulon, one at Brest, one at Antwerp and one in Spain. Their versatility is demonstrated in the duties they performed, their train-ing at sea giving them unique capabilities with the field army: in the Austerlitz campaign they manned a small flotilla on the Danube, and in December 1806 one detachment built a boat-bridge over the Vistula while others operated a ferry across the river. After Eylau a company built a bridge from 40 captured river-boats at Marienwerder, and a midship-man and six seamen were sent to Danzig upon an intelligence-gathering mission, after which the corps manned eight boats on the Friche-Haff, the inland sea bet-ween Danzig and Königsberg. Around the island of Lobau they piloted river-craft armed with fieldpieces, and organi-sed a system of communication along the Danube. In 1810 they were sent to Spain in an engineer role, and were regarded as too valuable (given their unique talents) to be committed to action, until during Massena's retreat in 1811 they were regarded so highly as to be assigned to the rearguard. In 1812 they used their naval gunnery skill to form a battery of artillery with Russian cannon captured at the Kremlin.

*A corporal of the* Artillerie de Marine, *c1813, when deployed as infantry in the campaign in Germany. The corps wore artillery uniform, dark blue with madder-red facings. This man wears a combination of uniform-styles as was common at this date, retaining the old-fashioned long-tailed coat replaced officially in 1812 with the lapelled jacket, plus the 1812-pattern shako with a plate bearing an anchor and a red pompom.*

# Ships of the Line

The main naval units were the 'ships-of-the-line', the 'battleships' which in action would participate in the 'line-of-battle' (hence the name), those which were capable of engaging the enemy fleet in a major action. Smaller vessels, frigates and less, did not normally participate in the 'set-piece' naval battles of the era. 'Line-of-battleships' were normally classified, or 'rated', according to the number of guns they mounted, though this was not necessarily a universal guide to their classification, as only proper cannon were counted in the reckoning; the short-barrelled anti-personnel and anti-rigging guns known as 'carronades' were not normally included in a ship's rating. In addition, some ships might carry less than the number of guns that they were able; it was usual to refer to a ship by the number of guns for which it was 'pierced', i.e. by the number of gun-ports whether or not all were operational. When a ship was very lightly armed, or had its guns stored in the hold (as it might if on transport duty, or when used as a floating barracks in harbour) it was said to be *en flûte*. The system of rating was not totally rigid, nor was the definition of what was a 'ship-of-the-line' (for example, some heavily-armed frigates were almost as powerful as the weaker battleships), but in general the rating of ships was as follows: a '1st rate' was a ship with 100 guns or more (exclusive of carronades; and note that some '100-gun' ships might actually mount about 104). These were the most powerful of naval units, 110- and 120-gunners being the largest used in French service, though the Spanish navy used even more massive vessels, up to the giant 130-gun *Santissima Trinidad* which fought at Trafalgar. A '2nd rate' ship carried 98 guns, and the term '3rd rate' covered

most of the remaining ships-of-the-line, 80-, 74-, 70-, and 64-gunners. '4th rates' were the line-of-battleships between the ordinary size and the larger frigates, carrying 50 or 60 guns. '5th rates' were the frigates, with 44, 36 or 32 guns; '6th rates' were the smaller vessels of 28, 24 or 20 guns, and below them the 18-gun sloops and smaller gunboats. It is interesting to note that by this definition (correct to 1802), the French fleet at Trafalgar had no 1st or 2nd rates at all, the ships-of-the-line all having 74 or 80 guns; the Spanish fleet had four 1st-raters, the British three 1st-raters and four 2nd-raters, and all other ships (like the French) mounting between 64 and 80 guns. Even in 1793, before the fleet had suffered from the ravages of war, the French navy included only eight 1st-raters (*Républicain*, 110; *Sans-Culotte*, 120; *Commerce de Marseilles*, 120; *Côte d'Or*, 120; *Majestueux*, 110; plus three 110-gunners not in seaworthy condition, *Révolutionnaire*, *Invincible* and *Terrible*).

French ships in general were well built, but not always well-maintained. At the outbreak of war many of the ships-of-the-line were in want of repair, and some totally unserviceable, and the standard of maintenance was far below that of the British navy. In this respect, it is interesting to note the condition of Villeneuve's fleet when in harbour at Cadiz, prior to the attempted break-out through the British blockade to the Mediterranean, ending in the action at Trafalgar. Of Villeneuve's 18 French ships-of-the-line, he reported that only five were fit in all respects for service. Some needed docking to have their keels scraped or re-coppered (the adhesion of marine organisms tended to slow the speed of a ship through the water, whilst the boring teredo worm could literally

eat out the bottom of a ship); most were short of sails and rope (spare sets of canvas would normally be carried, as a ship might have its sails ripped to shreds in battle), one had a damaged mizzen-mast and *Swiftsure* was leaking at the rate of six inches per hour. French ships were often built slightly longer and sleeker than British ships, the reduced width giving them superior handling at sea, and reducing the amount of 'roll' in the water; but such advantages of design were more than cancelled by the inferiority of French crews when compared to those of the Royal Navy. Desertion was always a major problem (300 of Villeneuve's men had run off in Cadiz, for example), originating in the appalling mismanagement of the naval service in the early revolutionary period; the exodus or suspension for political reasons of 75 per cent of the trained sea-officers led to the desertion of experienced seamen, who realised the danger in which they were placed by serving in ships with half-trained crews and inexperienced officers. Unlike the army, sailors had no opportunity to line their pockets from the proceeds of looting, and as the republican government could neither adequately clothe them, feed nor pay them, there was little incentive to remain in the service. The impressed men drafted aboard served only to reduce still further the overall competency of the service.

The overall result of this mal-administration was that even the best squadrons in the French navy were often badly-handled, especially in the earlier period when the results of the purge of officers had not been overcome. In June 1793, for example, Admiral Justin Bonaventure Morard de Galles (1741-1809) reported of the Brest squadron: 'I have sailed in the most numerous fleets but never in a year did I see so many collisions as in the month this squadron has been together.' (Ironically, though he joined

## Armaments of ships-of-the-line in French service

| Ship | Main deck guns | 2nd deck guns | 3rd deck guns | Quarterdeck guns | Forecastle guns | Poop guns |
|---|---|---|---|---|---|---|
| 120-gunner | 32 × 36pdrs | 34 × 24pdrs | 34 × 12pdrs | 14 × 8pdrs | 6 × 8pdrs | 4 carr |
| 110-gunner | 30 × 36pdrs | 32 × 24pdrs | 32 × 12pdrs | 12 × 8pdrs | 4 × 8pdrs | 4 carr |
| 80-gunner | 30 × 36pdrs | 32 × 24pdrs | — | 12 × 12pdrs | 6 × 12pdrs | 6 carr |
| 74-gunner | 28 × 36pdrs | 30 × 24pdrs | — | 12 × 8pdrs | 4 × 8pdrs | 4 carr |

('carr' = carronades, all of 36-pdr size)

the navy as a marine in 1757 and took twenty years to rise to the rank of lieutenant, in November 1793 Morard de Galles was arrested and cashiered for being a suspected aristocrat! He was reinstated in March 1795.) Even by 1805 the situation had not improved very greatly, as Villeneuve reported to Decrès about his own ships: 'The fleet looked well in harbour, but in the gale things were very different. The few sailors were lost among the soldiers, who were seasick and could not remain in the batteries but encumbered the decks. It was impossible to work the ships. Spars were broken and sails carried away, as much by clumsiness and inexperience as through bad materials supplied by the dockyards.' Though Napoleon did his best towards tackling the most glaring inadequacies of the French navy, as far as he was able given his limited knowledge of maritime affairs, the net result was that throughout the period the inefficiencies remained. It is interesting to note that in his ambitious ship-building programme, in the later years Napoleon attempted to increase the size of the ships-of-the line,

*The 'line-of-battle': the French fleet at Trafalgar, 21 October 1805. The French ships-of-the-line are firing broadsides towards the British, who are already heavily engaged. Of especial note is the condition of the sails on the leading French ships, with holes ripped in by British gunnery. (Engraving after Robert Dodd.)*

away from 3rd-raters and towards 100-gun 1st-raters with three gun-decks, perhaps as a result of the advantages which the British 3-deckers had at Trafalgar over the French 2-deckers. By late 1814 he planned to have 36 ships-of-the-line in the Mediterranean (including Italian ships), 28 on the Atlantic coast (including six 3-deckers), 30 at the Scheldt and 10 at the Texel. Napoleon did make earnest attempts to improve discipline and training, and instituted permanently-assigned ships' crews, but morale never really recovered from the ravages of the early years.

The main line-of-battleships normally acted in concert, in squadrons of four or six upwards, and were generally employed against the enemy's main fleet; commerce-raiding was more the preserve of faster ships, like frigates or corvettes. A constant supply of new ships-of-the-line was required, especially in the Trafalgar period and before, as the losses of major ships were considerable, and although those of the Dutch navy were taken into French service, the supply of captured ships-of-the-line was minute (only one British battleship was captured and not ultimately recovered throughout the period). What made the situation worse for France was that on occasion large numbers of capital ships were lost in one action, which served to wreck temporarily the maritime forces of a particular area. Thirteen were lost at Toulon in 1793; seven at the 'Glorious First of June'; four foundered in a gale in January 1795; 11 were lost at Aboukir Bay; two at the surrender of Malta; nine at Trafalgar and four in the aftermath in November 1805; four off San Domingo in February 1806; five at Cadiz in 1808; four at Basque Roads and two at Frontignan in 1809.

# Frigates, Armaments and Stores

The smaller ships of the French navy were responsible for much of the damage inflicted upon the British merchant trade. Despite the comparative weakness of the smaller ships when compared to the ships-of-the-line, they were on balance the most effective part of the French maritime force. Although the existence of the line-of-battleships was responsible for imposing a heavy burden upon the resources of the British navy, which had to blockade the French fleets in port under all weathers, arduous and unsatisfactory duties, this was essentially a negative method of combatting the British, by simply sitting in harbour and threatening to come out. The more positive tactic of commerce-raiding was that for which the frigates and smaller vessels were more ideally equipped, being faster-sailing and thus able to chase and overhaul all but the very swiftest of merchant vessels. The frigates had far more relevance than merely disrupting the enemy's commerce, however; they were invaluable attachments to any squadron of line-of-battleships, being described as the 'eyes of the fleet'. In essence they fulfilled the same function as the light cavalry on land: scouting ahead of the fleet to discover the whereabouts of the enemy, and carrying messages between fleets or from battle-fleet to home ports, being so swiftly-moving that they could easily out-distance any ship-of-the-line. Thus, a frigate was not

normally in danger from the enemy's battleships, as they could simply sail away before the enemy could bring them to action; the threat instead came from the enemy's frigates, which similarly would accompany their squadrons of ships-of-the-line. The frigates were thus capable of fulfilling a dual function (scouting/communications and raiding), and were thus probably the most useful elements of the navy.

Frigates normally carried their armament upon a single main gun-deck (1st-raters usually had three gun-decks and other ships-of-the-line two), with secondary armament on the quarterdeck and forecastle. French frigates in particular were superbly-built and exceptionally good sailers, and Napoleon paid considerable attention to the improvement of design, as following the destruction of the battle-fleet at Trafalgar his frigates were virtually the only ones of his ships continually employed in offensive operations. The successes of the large and heavily-armed American frigates against their weaker British opponents in the War of 1812 caused Napoleon to order that new French frigates be constructed, or similar design and similar armament to the American. In 'rating' of guns, frigates normally ranged from 28 to 40 guns, though the larger frigates might mount up to 44 guns. Many of the most effective commerce-raiders, however, were smaller (and more manoeuverable)

than the frigates. These vessels came in a variety of names and designs, with guns ranging from the 28 of the smaller frigates down to single-gun 'gunboats'. Corvettes were the largest of the smaller ships, flush-decked vessels with a single gun-deck. Schooners were two-masted ships with square-rigged sails; cutters or sloops were single-masted vessels of about 18 tons. Several varieties of small ship of Mediterranean origin were used by the navy in that area: xebecs (also 'schebeck'), two- or three-masted craft with 'lateen' (triangular) sails, also propelled by oars; polaccas (three-masted vessels with lateen sails), settees (single-decked ships with long prow and lateen sails), and tartans (lateen-rigged coastal boats, propelled by oars). Fast-sailing *chasse-marées* were used in the English Channel to raid the British coastal merchant trade, and a further variety of warship was the 'bomb ketch', a small vessel with a single gun in the centre of the deck, a mortar which flung high-angle shells or 'bombs' like the mortars used for siege-work on land.

Naval guns were essentially like those used on land, though were generally much heavier in weight of shot, at least aboard the ships-of-the-line. 36-gun frigates and below carried 12pdrs as their main armament (the largest guns normally used by field artillery on land), but the larger frigates and line-of-battleships carried 18, 24, and 36pdrs, in addition to a number of 12pdrs. For secondary armament 8 and 6pdrs were used, plus the carronade, a short-barrelled weapon invented at the Carron ironworks in Scotland in 1779, and adopted by the French navy before the revolutionary wars (though never employed as effectively as were the carronades aboard British ships). Known as a 'smasher', the carronade had a much shorter range than the ordinary naval cannon (for which the length known as a 'gunshot' was judged to be about 1¼ miles), but fired either a 36lb shot or grapeshot for

*Among the most fierce combats at sea were so-called 'boat-actions', in which a frigate's longboats would be filled with sailors and marines and rowed towards small enemy vessels or merchantmen at anchor, which would then be boarded and captured after quelling the resistance of the crew. Such captured vessels were said to have been 'cut-out'.*

anti-personnel and anti-rigging use. Employed at the shortest range, carronades could inflict the most appalling damage upon an enemy ship, smashing its woodwork or slaughtering its crew. Artillery projectiles were similar to those used on land, roundshot being the principal weapon, though explosive shells were sometimes used. There were in addition types of shot which were almost exclusively maritime in use, notably 'grapeshot'. This term is often applied to 'heavy case-shot' used on land, but true grape-shot consisted of a number of iron balls stacked around an iron pillar and enclosed in a tarred canvas bag; its purpose was both anti-personnel and anti-rigging. Other types of shot were designed primarily for cutting in shreds an enemy's sails: lang-ridge (iron bars in a case), bar-shot (roundshot linked by a fixed bar to spin through the air and scythe through sails and rope), expanding shot (bar-shot with an expanding bar which lengthened in flight), chain-shot (roundshot linked by chain for the same reason) and even knife-blade shot (balls with expanding sharp blades attached). Grevious casualties were caused by any of these projectiles hitting the woodwork of a ship, when splinters would be flung around like shrapnel. Another expedient adopted at sea (or when firing upon ships from land) was 'hot-shot', when round-shot were heated red-hot in ovens prior to firing; when imbedded in a ship's woodwork they would smoulder for hours, eventually setting alight to the ship; fire was always the most feared hazard at sea, and not even dousing with cold water would necessarily prevent a hot-shot from starting a fatal conflagration.

Naval guns were similar in design to those of land-service artillery, though (especially in the British navy) ignition was often by means of a flintlock screwed onto the gun-barrel when action was imminent, obviating the need for lighted

matches (always dangerous near woodwork and gunpowder) though flintlock-ignition was rare in French service, and then only latterly. Gun-carriages were smaller than those of field artillery, and ran on small wheels or 'trucks', recoil being controlled by a complex system of ropes and pulleys attached to the sides of the ship, allowing the guns sufficient movement to be run out through the gun-ports for firing, and pulled back inboard for loading, when the ramrods usually had to be poked out through the gunports to be inserted in the barrel. The British use of flexible ramrods permitted the guns to be loaded even when tight against the enemy ship; French ramrods were not flexible and thus when jammed against a British ship a French warship was unable to use her lower-deck guns, a great disadvantage.

Vast quantities of stores were required by every naval ship, ranging from casks of fresh water to cheese and biscuit (which should have remained edible for years), to meat (both salted and pickled, and livestock kept aboard to provide fresh meat); but the quantity and quality was often poor, with rotten food and foul water increasing the chances of sickness.

*The transfer of stores from a sloop-of-war to a moored 'hulk'. Old ships-of-the-line, with masts and usually most guns removed, were utilised as floating storeships, barracks or prisons; in this case the ship has had its gunports glazed into windows, and the upper deck has been fitted with a piked roof, from which chimneys protrude.*

Re-supply of French ships was a problem throughout the era, especially for those squadrons stationed at the main base of Brest, for the area was both sparsely-populated and poor from a viewpoint of obtaining supplies. Timber was impossible to find locally (due to the activities of generations of ship-builders), and food was also equally difficult to obtain. When in 1797 the French navy could have taken advantage of the mutinies in the British fleet, the fleet at Brest could only be provisioned for fifteen days instead of the usual six months, and the situation at Texel was little better. In the Trafalgar campaign, when Villeneuve was at Cadiz, the Spanish authorities (equally short of supplies) only agreed to release the barest necessities for the French fleet, and then only after Villeneuve had paid for them in cash!

## Armaments of French frigates

| Ship | Main deck | Quarterdeck | Forecastle |
|---|---|---|---|
| 40-gunner | 28 × 18pdrs | 10 × 8pdrs, 2 carronades | 2 × 8pdrs, 2 carronades |
| 38-gunner | 26 × 18pdrs | 10 × 8pdrs, 2 carronades | 2 × 8pdrs, 2 carronades |
| 36-gunner | 26 × 12pdrs | 8 × 6pdrs, 2 carronades | 2 × 6pdrs, 2 carronades |
| 32-gunner | 26 × 12pdrs | 4 × 6pdrs, 2 carronades | 2 × 6pdrs, 2 carronades |
| 28-gunner | 24 × 8pdrs | 6 carronades | 2 × 6pdrs |

(All carronades of 36pdr variety)

# Transports, Amphibious Operations and Strategy

French naval strategy during the period fell into two sections: the destruction of British commerce and in support of land operations. Virtually all naval campaigns were conducted in accordance with these aims, or in defence of the French merchant trade. In support of land campaigns, amphibious operations were required, involving the conveyance of troops by sea, though French 'overseas' operations were limited in number and success, the only major transportation of troops being that which conveyed the 'Army of the Orient' to Egypt in 1798, though there were in addition operations mounted in the Caribbean.

There were no specially-designed troop-transports in use at this period, except for those of small size intended for basically inshore work. For conveying troops any distance by sea, either merchant ships or warships were utilised (ships-of-the-line and frigates), including those with guns removed, sailing *en flûte*. Conditions aboard such ships, when packed with troops in addition to their ordinary crews, were even more unsanitary than usual, especially when the soldiers suffered from sea-sickness as a result of their first experience of sailing. Ships under these circumstances were rarely able to function effectively, the troops aboard getting in the way of the seamen's normal duties, so that a ship transporting troops was not fully capable of resisting an attack. When arriving at their destination, on occasion troops could be disembarked at a port, but more usually had to be landed upon an enemy coast by means of longboat, rowed ashore to the beach, which in heavy surf could be extremely hazardous. Horses for cavalry and artillery when landed in this manner were usually hoisted out of the ship's hold by an improvised crane and simply flung over the side into the sea, and left to make their own way to shore. Sea-voyages were frequently very costly in terms of horses, the appalling conditions below-decks often causing a large number to die during transportation.

The most sophisticated preparation for an amphibious operation were those made for the projected invasion of England, when a vast number of small vessels was assembled on the Channel coast ready to land a French army on the southern coast of England. Many existing vessels were gathered, but a vast number specially constructed for troop-transportation, based at seven embarkation points: Boulogne, Étaples, Wimereux, Ambleteuse, Calais, Dunkirk and Ostend. The fleet was enormous, and in August 1805 consisted of the following: 18 *prames* (Dutch *praam*, a flat barge), together capable of transporting 2,040 men or 890 horses; 3 bomb-ketches (150 men); 10 packet-boats (380 men, 56 horses); 6 sloops (780 men); 265 gun-brigs (34,450 men); 365 gunboats (36,805 men, 714 horses) 349 pinnaces (23,034 men); 19 caiques (light skiffs, 570 men); 81 transport-ships (8,349 men, 233 horses); 405 horse-transports (24,245 men, 6,596 horses); 80 artillery transports (1,260 men); 246 staff and baggage-transports (2,315 men, 246 horses); 102 'Newfoundland boats' (1,224 men); 209 whalers (1,363 men); plus 55 Dutch gun-brigs (7,150 men), 207 Dutch gun-boats (20,700 men, 414 horses), and 23 other vessels at Boulogne (345 men). The grand total was 2,343 vessels capable of transporting 167,590 men and 9,149 horses, the largest armada yet assembled for an amphibious operation. The amount of work and resources which went into assembling this fleet (and improving the harbours, especially at Boulogne which prior to this was infamous) was a most useless expenditure, as the plan had very little chance of success given the dominance of the Royal Navy.

Other amphibious expeditions fared little better, though the transporting of the Egyptian expedition was a conspicuous success; but soured when the fleet was destroyed at Aboukir Bay, leaving the army marooned in Egypt. The fleet employed in transporting the 'Army of the Orient' was vast: 224 chartered merchantmen convoyed by 13 ships-of-the-line and 6 frigates and smaller vessels, carrying 24,000 infantry, 4,000 cavalry and 3,000 artillerymen. Other operations were not given the backing they perhaps deserved, and served only to cause the French considerable losses. Most bizarre was the raid led by the American adventurer Tate against western Britain in 1797; intended to burn Bristol, or traverse Wales and burn Liverpool, the expedition actually landed at Fishguard on 22 February 1797 and surrendered on the following day at the first appearance of British home-defence forces. Both the frigates used to transport the raid were captured on their way home. It was incredible that such ill-conceived schemes should ever have been considered, especially given the calibre of the troops employed, described by Hoche as '600 men drawn from all the prisons in my district and gathered in two forts on islands from which they cannot escape. I have added to them 600 galley slaves (who are still in irons)'! An attempt to invade Ireland by Hoche and Morard de Galles in December 1796 never even got ashore, bad weather and incompetent seamanship resulting in chaos as French signalling by gunfire became confused with distress-guns fired by a grounded ship and a bombardment by a British frigate! Slightly more effective was the invasion of Ireland at Killala Bay under General Humbert in August 1798, intended to support the Irish rebellion (which had largely been crushed before the French arrived). Transported by four frigates, Humbert and 1,150 men and four guns landed unopposed and routed a small but unprofessional British force at Castlebar on 27 August, but were compelled to surrender at Ballinamuck on 8 September when the promised reinforcements were intercepted en route by the Royal Navy.

France's colonial operations were largely restricted to the Caribbean, and in particular to Haiti or San Domingo. This French colony had been in a state of social revolt and anarchy for years, and a slave uprising in 1794 gave Britain a chance to move in. British forces were evacuated in 1797 and nominal French control re-established by Pierre Toussaint l'Ouverture (1743-1803), 'the black Napoleon', a local statesman and general of considerable skill. His moves towards Haitian independence caused Napoleon to initiate an expedition to recover the island, which was led by his brother-in-law General Victor Leclerc (1772-1802), husband of Pauline Bonaparte). Initially the campaign was successful, Toussaint l'Ouverture being captured and sent to France (where he

*An invasion-barge: 'The Great Raft now afloat in Brest Harbour'. This somewhat fanciful print (published by C. Thompson, 1798) reflects the attempts made to design vessels for the invasion of Britain. Such floating castles were not feasible, especially when including batteries of 48pdr guns, bombproof magazines, drawbridges for disembarkation, and propulsion by paddle-wheels powered by windmills!*

died in prison of starvation and neglect), but Leclerc died of the yellow fever which carried off about 25,000 French troops on the island. Continuing guerrilla war (the Negroes now led by Jean Jacques Dessalines, later Emperor Alexandre I until his assassination) made the situation intolerable and, having suffered horrendous casualties, the French withdrew in 1803 leaving civil war to flourish in Haiti. Other French or allied colonies fared little better. Cape Town (originally Dutch but partly garrisoned by France) fell to a British expedition in 1806, and in 1809 Admiral Villaret de Joyeuse surrendered Martinique and St Lucia to Britain after a spirited defence. An Anglo-Spanish force helped the eastern (Spanish) part of Haiti throw off the domination of the French-speaking Negroes of the west in 1808-09. In 1810 further French out-posts were captured by Britain, the islands of Mauritius and Réunion, which had served as bases for French raiders against British commerce in the Indian Ocean.

The other French amphibious operations of the period were those in the Mediterranean theatre, the most notable success being Murat's capture of Capri in October 1808. The island was weakly-defended by British 'foreign corps' (under the command of Napoleon's eventual gaoler, Hudson Lowe, 1769-1844), which succumbed to Murat's landing with 2,000 men in 60 transports, escorted by a frigate, a corvette and 36 gunboats. This minor operation was the most successful French amphibious landing of the Napoleonic Wars, which is a measure of the failure of the others, most notable of which was Murat's attempted invasion of Sicily in September 1810, when he assembled a fleet of 300 transports and 60 gunboats to transport about 35,000 men; the Neapolitan navy consisted of only 1 frigate and 1 corvette! Napoleon was sceptical about the operation, and in the event only 3,000 Neapolitans got ashore (who were quickly driven away or captured by the British and Sicilian forces), the commander of Murat's French forces wisely not allowing them to embark for a hopeless operation.

# Naval Tactics

Naval tactics could be classified into two sections: the intentions of each side, and the methods employed once combat was initiated. For much of the 18th century, French naval tactics were markedly different from those of the British, the French emphasizing caution and conservation of resources. It was not the practice of French fleets to engage in combat unless victory could bring a tangible result other than the destruction of the enemy; conversely, to the British the sinking or capture of enemy ships was an end in itself, and thus while the French would often try to avoid combat, the British would attack if there existed the slightest chance of success. These different priorities resulted in differing methods of attack; the French in general attempted to disable the enemy's masts and rigging, to prevent them pursuing at the conclusion of the action; whereas the British concentrated their gunnery upon the enemy's hull, either to sink the ship or, more likely, to wreck their gun-decks and decimate the crew so as to be incapable of further resistance. The British tactic was especially costly in terms of the lives of the enemy crew, but was generally successful in shattering the enemy's will or ability to continue the fight. The French emphasis on conserving ships and *matériel* continued from the earlier 18th century into the revolutionary and Napoleonic period, but did not meet with universal approval as a number of French admirals were in favour of much more offensive tactics. The internal conflict thus caused is perhaps best demonstrated in an incident involving Admiral Charles Magon, Villeneuve's third-in-command at Trafalgar; it was said that when Villeneuve broke off the action against Calder's fleet off Cape Finisterre, Magon was so outraged at what he considered Villeneuve's over-prudent handling of

*'Breaking the line' or 'crossing the "T"': a representation of the most effective naval tactic employed in the Napoleonic Wars, concentrating the fire of the attacker against the most vulnerable part of the enemy ship, the lack of bulkheads allowing shots from stern or bow to smash the entire length of the vessel. Here, HMS* Victory *breaks Villeneuve's line-of-battle at Trafalgar.*

the fleet that when Villeneuve's ship passed he not only hurled abuse from his own quarterdeck towards his superior, but threw at the flagship anything upon which he could lay his hands, including his own telescope and wig!

Ships-of-the-line were floating artillery-platforms, and their best utilisation was to bring as many guns to bear upon the enemy as possible, which meant firing by 'broadside', i e with the sides of the ship facing the enemy, as few guns were positioned to fire forward or astern. The need to concentrate the power of the ship's guns in this way led to the evolution of the 'line-of-battle', in which both fleets assembled in parallel columns ('line ahead'), drew toward each other and exchanged broadsides until one or another became disabled or chose to break away. The maintenance of the line-of-battle became something of a shibboleth in the mid-18th century; as a British manual of 1744 noted, 'the line of

battle is the basis and formulation of all discipline in sea fights . . . universally practiced by all nations that are masters of any power at sea. It has had the test of long experience, and has stood the stroke of time, pure and unaltered, handed down by our predecessors.' The rigid enforcement of the 'line of battle' (to the extent of court-martialling a captain who deliberately broke it) was a negative tactic in which a decisive result was almost impossible to achieve. (The one truly decisive action which was fought at this period in which linear tactics were used was Aboukir Bay, but was exceptional in that the French fleet was caught at anchor and was bombarded by the British who sailed along a parallel course.)

It had long been recognised that the most effective bombardment of a ship was to 'rake' it, firing upon it from bow to stern at right-angles, known (from the respective position of the ships) as 'crossing the "T"'. This had a double impact: the 'target' ship was virtually unable to reply to the attacker's gunnery, except

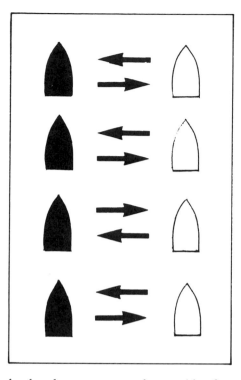

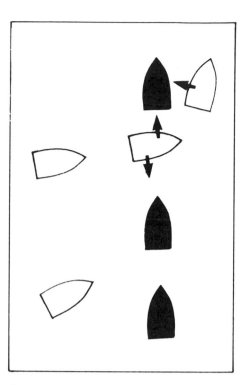

*The continuing theories of naval combat, simplified to a great degree in a diagram which illustrates the two basic manoeuvres. (Left): the 'line of battle': two fleets sailing in roughly parallel courses, exchanging broadsides, in which almost half the guns on each ship could be brought into action, a parity of weaponry which generally resulted in neither side achieving a convincing victory. The alternative was as (Right): 'breaking the line' or 'crossing the "T"', which could bring about a decisive result. The attacking fleet approaches the enemy's 'line of battle' more or less at right angles, the enemy's broadsides during the approach being rendered less effective by the attacking fleet presenting a smaller target by approaching head-on. Once into the enemy's 'line of battle' the attackers could wreak appalling havoc, 'raking' the stern of one enemy ship and the bow of another, these shots passing through the entire length of the enemy, which might put a ship temporarily out of action.*

by her bow- or stern-chasers (the few guns which aimed forwards or to the rear), and secondly the attacker's shots would pass longitudinally down the enemy ship, carving a swathe of havoc from stern to bow or vice-versa, with no bulkheads to impede their progress. A ship 'raked' in this way might lose so heavily in crew and guns as to be disabled. From this evolved the tactic of 'breaking the line', in which one fleet cut through the line-of-battle of the other; for while on the approach the attacker would have to suffer the broadsides of the enemy, the target would be comparatively small (by attacking head-on), and once having cut the line could rake the enemy before laying alongside and 'broadsiding' in the usual manner. This tactic had been practiced before it reached its zenith with Horatio Nelson, for example at Camperdown, but the development from the basic tactic was the 'melée' battle in which the bulk of one fleet would concentrate upon part of the enemy's, which would be destroyed by weight of numbers before the remainder of the enemy could reverse their course and join the battle. Coincidentally with Nelson's perfecting of the theory was the publication in 1804 of John Clerk's *Essay on Naval Tactics* which recommended that an attacking fleet should cut the enemy line-of-battle and concentrate upon destroying the

rear by weight of numbers, while a smaller portion of the attacking fleet held off the enemy van, which would take a considerable time to tack and return to help the beleaguered rear. This is exactly what happened at Trafalgar: the Franco-Spanish rear was overwhelmed when their line was broken before the van was able to assist. Nelson's plan he described to his captains as 'the "Nelson touch", it was like an electric shock . . . It was new – it was singular – it was simple!' and worked to perfection: 'It will surprise and confound the Enemy. They won't know what I am about. It will bring forward a pell-mell Battle, and that is what I want', for in a melée he knew that the superior seamanship and gunnery of the British would be more than a match for the French; as was proved at Trafalgar.

In combat at sea, despite the long range of the guns, fire was often reserved until about 400 yards from the enemy, so as not to waste shot. The methods of firing varied according to circumstance: the entire guns on one side of the ship could fire simultaneously (the classic 'broadside'), or each gun fire as it bore upon the target (such as when raking the stern or bow of a ship). The direction at which the gunnery was aimed could be varied only in the vertical plane, by elevating or depressing the individual gun-barrel or by timing the moment of

firing in accordance with the 'roll' of the ship; the roundshot could also be made to ricochet off the surface of the sea to strike the enemy low on the hull. Ships rarely sank during sea battles unless they caught fire and blew up, fights more often being decided by boarding when opposing ships became locked together, either deliberately or when the masts crashed down and rigging became entangled. Boarding was normally reserved until the enemy was in a parlous state, though the deterioration in French naval skills in the aftermath of the Revolution caused the deficiencies to be concealed by ordering: 'Disdaining skilful evolutions, our seamen should think it more fitting to attempt those boarding actions in which the French always conquer', a ridiculous way of endeavouring to hide the fact that they were largely incapable of performing 'skilful evolutions'! When a ship became unable to sustain the fight, it would strike its colours as a signal of surrender; though a French directive of February 1794 prescribed the death penalty for any captain who surrendered before his ship was sinking, and the same punishment was accorded a captain who deliberately broke the line of battle. With such inability to handle their ships and the retention of outdated tactics, it is not surprising that the French were consistently out-generalled.

# Chapter Nine: THE NAVY'S CAMPAIGNS

The French navy was not in an effective state to fight a maritime war upon the out-break of hostilities in 1792, due to the mediocre condition of the fleet: of the 76 ships-of-the-line, only 27 were actually in commission in January 1793, against which her enemies could muster 113 British, 76 Spanish, 49 Dutch, 6 Portuguese and 4 Neapolitan (though not all of these were in commission). The demoralization of the naval personnel was even worse, with three-quarters of the officers 'purged' for supposed aristocratic or privileged backgrounds, the seamen miserably treated, mutinous, under-strength and with desertion endemic, so that had all the ships-of-the-line been seaworthy, less than half could have been manned and equipped.

In the late summer of 1793 the French fleet of Admiral Morard de Galles put to sea off the Atlantic coastline, but avoided battle with the British Channel fleet of Admiral Lord Howe (1726-99); the fleet was stricken by mutiny and forced to return to Brest, and in November Morard de Galles was temporarily suspended from duty. The other main French naval base, Toulon, where the Mediterranean fleet was stationed, was seized in mid-August 1793 by an Anglo-Spanish expedition which occupied the town. This one blow virtually halved the effective strength of the French navy; some of the ships captured at Toulon were removed and taken into British service, and others were destroyed when the Allied position became untenable and the Toulon area was evacuated in December; in all at least thirteen service-able ships-of-the-line were lost and twenty smaller vessels, and some of those which were re-possessed by the French were no longer in a seaworthy condition. Had the Allies done their duty capably, the whole fleet would have been carried off or destroyed before the French counter-attack recovered the port, and France's loss would have been even more grievous than it was; the British loss of control of the Mediterranean after Spain changed sides can largely be attributed to the failure to destroy the whole of the Toulon fleet when the opportunity was there.

The main sea battle of this period occurred in an attempt to avert famine in France. The 1793 harvest had been bad and the problem was accentuated by the unrest of the Revolution. Large quantities of grain were purchased in the United States and in April 1794 a fleet of 125 merchant ships set sail for France, and the Brest squadron, now commanded by Admiral Louis Villaret de Joyeuse (1748-1812), was ordered to sail out and escort them in. Britain knew of the convoy and Howe was ordered to intercept it, so sailed to Brest where he found Villaret de Joyeuse still in port. When the French did come out, Howe was present with 26 ships-of-the-line. Villaret de Joyeuse also had 26 ships-of-the-line, and Howe intercepted them some 400 miles off Ushant on 28 May 1794. The two fleets manoeuvred in close proximity, sporadic fighting being inconclusive despite Howe's attempt to break the French line-of-battle on 29 May (prevented by his signals being obscured by gunsmoke). Both sides suffered some damage, some ships dropping away and others coming up, so that Howe had 25 ships against the French 26 when the decisive action was fought on 1 June. Howe ordered each of his ships to break the French line where they could, and although not all were able to achieve it, those which did brought about a mêlée in which the French suffered severely, no fewer than 13 ships being dismasted (against 11 British), though when they began to break off the action after about 90 minutes fighting (which had begun at 8.30 a m) some of their wrecked vessels were taken in tow and escaped. One French ship sank (*Vengeur*) and six others were captured; including the captured crews the French losses were at least 7,500 against 290 British dead and 858 wounded. Tactically, the 'Glorious First of June' was a stunning British success, but strategically Villaret de Joyeuse had achieved his objective, as the merchant convoy arrived safely.

The situation improved little for France over the next few years. A trip by Villaret de Joyeuse from Brest to Toulon in the winter of 1794-95 ended in disaster with the wrecking in a storm of 4 ships-of-the-line; and the French West Indian trade was ravaged by the Royal Navy. The luckless Villaret was also the victim of another defeat off Ile de Groix (near Lorient) on 23 June 1795, when his Brest squadron was attacked by Admiral Lord Bridport, in which another three French ships-of-the-line were lost. Had France not gained the Spanish and Dutch fleets she might well have ceased to be a maritime power. The only success scored by France at this period was the capture of the Dutch fleet in the Texel, which was achieved by the French *army*: frozen-in by the appalling winter of 1794-95, the Dutch ships were captured by French cavalry which rode over the ice to take possession!

*One of the bravest French naval officers, Admiral Charles Magon fought with great valour aboard his flagship* Algéciras *at Trafalgar, despite several wounds; when his ship rammed and was captured by HMS* Tonnant, *he was found dead by the poopdeck ladder.*

| The French navy suffered severely prior to 1796 from actions in which multiple losses occurred. | | | |
| --- | --- | --- | --- |
| | ships-of-the-line | frigates | smaller vessels |
| Toulon, August 1793 | 4 | 9 | 6 |
| Toulon, Dec 1793 | 9 | 3 | 2 |
| San Fiorenzo, Feb 1794 | — | 2 | — |
| '1st of June' 1794 | 7 | — | — |
| Calvi, August 1794 | — | 2 | 3 |
| Wrecked, Jan 1795 | 4 | — | — |
| Genoa, March 1795 | 2 | — | — |
| Lorient, June 1795 | 3 | — | — |
| Other actions | 4 | 26 | 66 |

# The Naval War from 1796 to Algeciras

Throughout the period, the 'war of commerce' continued, with the French overseas merchant trade being almost annihilated by the Royal Navy. Much of this desultory warfare was conducted on both sides by 'privateers', privately-owned ships operating under a 'letter of marque' which allowed them to practise legalised piracy against enemy shipping. Often fast-sailing, armed more heavily than ordinary merchantmen and with larger crews (ensuring that they could board and overpower a merchant crew), the privateers had a considerable effect on the commercial war, and on occasion even engaged small naval vessels.

In 1796 the British navy's main task was in blockading the French naval bases of Brest and Toulon, and also watched the actions of the Spanish and Dutch fleets. The blockade was not completely effective, and in September Admiral Joseph de Richery (1757-99) slipped out of Toulon with a small squadron, sailed to Newfoundland where he disrupted trade, and returned safely. In the Mediterranean the balance of power tilted sharply from mid-August when Spain signed the Treaty of San Ildefonso with France (19 August), joining them in the war against Britain.

French military campaigns were already denying Britain the use of Mediterranean bases (Leghorn, for example, was evacuated in June), and the fact that the Spanish fleet was hostile caused Britain to evacuate the area, bringing to an end the harrassment of commerce conducted along the Franco-Italian coast, and the co-operation with Allied land forces. The Spanish fleet (26 ships-of-the-line) from Cadiz and Cartagena sailed to Toulon, joining the French fleet; the combined total of 38 ships vastly outnumbered the 14 ships of Sir John Jervis, who ordered the evacuation of the British garrison on Corsica. Jervis transferred the activities of the Mediterranean fleet to the Atlantic coasts of Spain and Portugal, sending Captain Horatio Nelson (1758-1805) back to evacuate the British garrison of Elba in December. Unable to defeat the British at sea, France had won command of the Mediterranean by diplomacy and as a result of her victories on land.

Less successful was an attempted invasion of Ireland under General Louis Lazare Hoche (1768-97), for which some 17 ships-of-the-line, 13 frigates, 20 transports and some smaller vessels were assembled at Brest, commanded by

Admiral Morard de Galles. The crews of many of these ships were ill-trained, and the troops to conduct the invasion were appalling, including many foreign deserters 'by which means it will be possible to rid France of many dangerous individuals' as the plan stated! The absurd scheme ended when bad weather prevented the landing even of those troops which reached Bantry Bay; five ships were lost to the weather and five transports and a frigate were captured by the British as they sailed home.

Hoche devised another scheme for a renewed invasion in 1797, to be supported by the Spanish and Batavian (Dutch) fleets. Admiral Don José de Cordova sailed from the Mediterranean for Brest and a planned junction with the French fleet, with 27 ships-of-the-line and 12 frigates. Jervis's former Mediterranean fleet, 15 strong, was cruising off the Portuguese coast to prevent such a move, and met the Spanish on 14 February off Cape St Vincent. Cordova's ships were in two groups, between which Jervis sailed, then turned on the larger group and a regular mêlée ensued, the escape of the Spaniards being prevented by Horatio Nelson's HMS *Captain* which broke away from the fleet without orders and sailed into the path of the Spanish. In the fight which followed, four Spanish ships were captured (two in rapid succession

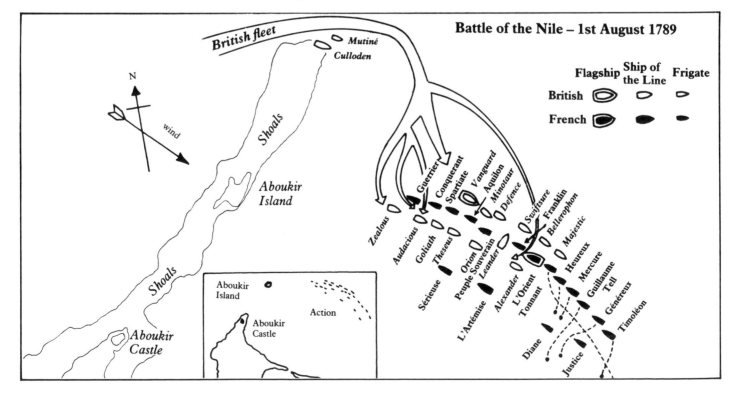

Battle of the Nile – 1st August 1789

by Nelson himself) and ten others were badly damaged; total Spanish losses were around 5,000 men, as against 73 British killed and 227 wounded. The Battle of St Vincent marked the end of the Spanish threat to Britain, and confirmed the advantages over a formal 'line-of-battle' of a 'pell-mell' fight in which the superior seamanship and gunnery of the Royal Navy gave them a huge advantage over their opponents. The surviving Spaniards limped into Cadiz, where Jervis blockaded them. In October 1797, still in pursuance of the plan to invade Ireland, the Batavian fleet of Admiral Jan Willem de Winter sailed from the Texel to join the French fleet at Brest. Despite disruptions caused earlier in the year by the British naval mutinies at Spithead and the Nore, Admiral Adam Duncan with 16 ships attacked the Batavians (26 ships including 15 ships-of-the-line) off Camperdown (north of Haarlem) on 11 October. Duncan

*The first battle of Algeciras (6 July 1801) was the worst day for the Royal Navy during the period; not only did the French fleet of Charles Alexandre de Linois hold its own, but HMS Hannibal struck a sandbank and was captured, the only British ship-of-the-line to be captured and not re-taken between 1793 and 1814. Revenge was gained six days later.*

attacked in two columns, splitting the Dutch line into three, and in a fiercely-contested melée the Dutch lost 9 ships-of-the-line and two frigates captured, but the British fleet was so damaged by the savagery of the fight that they were in no condition to pursue the remainder. The invasion of Ireland was finally attempted by the French alone, most half-heartedly, by General Jean Humbert who landed a small force at Killala Bay in support of the Irish rebellion, on 22 August 1798. The plan was ill-conceived and the force ill-managed, and surrendered before the intended reinforcement could be ferried from France. When this fleet did sail, it was intercepted by Sir John Borlase Warren on 12 October; of the nine French vessels, only two frigates escaped.

News of Bonaparte's Egyptian expedition caused Britain to return to the Mediterranean, in the shape of a small fleet under Horatio Nelson, now an Admiral. The French evaded his search and landed the expedition safely in Egypt, but on 1 August 1798 the fleet of Admiral François Brueys d'Aigalliers (1753-98) was caught entirely unprepared, at anchor in Aboukir Bay. Nelson divided his fleet into two columns, one standing to seaward and the other sailing between the French line and the shore, an audacious manoeuvre risking running

aground in the shallows; but caught between two fires, the French fleet was destroyed as the British ships cruised down the line, battering each French vessel in turn. By dawn on 2 August Brueys was dead (killed when his flagship, *l'Orient*, exploded) and of his 13 ships-of-the-line and four frigates, only two and a frigate escaped. It was a catastrophic defeat which marooned the French army in Egypt and destroyed their control of the Mediterranean.

From this time, the British navy was completely in the ascendant. France endeavoured to combat their 'war of commerce' by encouraging the formation of the 'Armed Neutrality', in which Russia, Denmark, Sweden and Prussia combined to protect their shipping from the British trade war (in which all neutral ships were compelled to stop at British command, any goods intended for France or French satellites being confiscated). British reaction was immediate: to forestall the Neutral League from actively supporting France, in March 1801 a British fleet commanded by Admiral Sir Hyde Parker (1737-1807), with Nelson as second-in-command, was despatched into the Baltic. Ignoring orders from Parker, on 2 April 1801 Nelson with 12 ships sailed into Copenhagen harbour, and in a savagely-contested five-hour battle destroyed the Danish fleet, carrying away 12 prizes. Nelson wished to continue to Revel and destroy the Russian fleet, but an armistice brought an end to the campaign, the 'Armed Neutrality' collapsing after the annihilation of Denmark's naval strength.

One further action of note occurred in the period prior to the temporary cessation of hostilities, when Admiral Sir James Saumarez (1757-1836) intercepted a small French force off Algeciras on 6 July 1801. The fight was severe but inconclusive, and Saumarez withdrew to carry out repairs whilst the French admiral, Linois, sent to Cadiz for Spanish assistance. The combined Franco-Spanish fleet mustered 9 ships-of-the-line and 3 frigates; the British, 6 ships-of-the-line, a sloop and a Portuguese frigate. On 12/13 July Saumarez attacked again (at night); the Franco-Spanish fleet was badly damaged, one Frenchman captured and two Spaniards blew each other up, engaging each other in the dark by mistake. British naval supremacy was again confirmed.

# Trafalgar – 21st October 1805

The campaign of Trafalgar resulted from Napoleon's use of his naval resources as merely an assistance to his military campaigns. After the renewed outbreak of hostilities in May 1803, Napoleon ordered the assembly of an enormous force concentrated at Boulogne, the 'Army of England' numbering 160,000 men, with which he planned a descent upon the south coast of England. After the construction of a vast fleet of invasion-barges and troop-transports, he was ready from March 1805 to execute the operation, but for one factor: the squadrons of the Royal Navy which not only controlled the English Channel but were actively blockading his own fleet in their harbours. His strategy was simple: he would lure away part of the British fleet and mount the invasion before they were able to return. This would require the French fleet to slip out of Toulon and Brest, evade the British fleet, and with their Spanish allies from Cartegona and Cadiz, sail for the West Indies. Having decoyed the British fleet in pursuit, the Franco-Spanish forces would unite in the Caribbean, quickly return to Europe in sufficient strength to defeat the remaining British channel squadrons, and protect the invasion-fleet during its short trip across the English Channel.

Overall command of the Franco-Spanish fleet was to rest with Vice-Admiral Pierre de Villeneuve (1763-1806), who was probably the best seaman available; but he was not allowed independence of action by Napoleon, and was opposed by perhaps the greatest naval tactician in history: Horatio Nelson. Under such circumstances, and given the innate superiority of the Royal Navy over their French counterparts, the odds were weighted heavily against Napoleon's fleet from the beginning, though their campaign did open auspiciously. On 29 March 1805, under cover of bad weather, Villeneuve sailed out of Toulon, heading for Gibraltar and the Atlantic beyond. Learning that the French had evaded the British blockade, Nelson miscalculated Villeneuve's intention and took his fleet further into the Mediterranean, awaiting the French off Sardinia; thus he was hopelessly behind Villeneuve when he finally learned (18 April) that the French had already passed through the straits of Gibraltar. Nelson waited to ensure that Admiral Sir William Cornwallis (1744-1819) was protecting the Channel approaches before setting off in pursuit of Villeneuve, who had picked up the Spanish fleet of Admiral the Duke of Gravina (1756-1806) from Cadiz en

route. Faulty intelligence took Nelson towards Trinidad, whereas in fact Villeneuve had turned back towards Europe as soon as he learned that Nelson was upon his trail. Learning this, Nelson dispatched a fast brig back to England – which actually overtook the Franco-Spanish fleet – to alert the defences of the Channel, and on 22 July off Cape Finisterre Admiral Sir Robert Calder (1745-1818), commanding the blockade of Brest, intercepted the returning fleet in an indecisive action, after which Villeneuve put into Ferrol and Corunna. Disgusted at having missed his opportunity of bringing the French fleet to battle, Nelson left his ships on station and returned home for a short holiday. Already, Napoleon's invasion plan had effectively been countered, and he began to shift the *Grande Armée* eastwards for the campaign which would culminate in Austerlitz. By charges of cowardice, Napoleon bullied Villeneuve into putting to sea again – for little strategic purpose – and the Franco-Spanish fleet sailed to Cadiz, shadowed by the British squadron of Admiral Sir Cuthbert Collingwood (1750-1810). Learning of this brief foray, and certain that Villeneuve would again put to sea, Nelson rejoined the fleet aboard his flagship HMS *Victory*. Having lost confidence in his senior

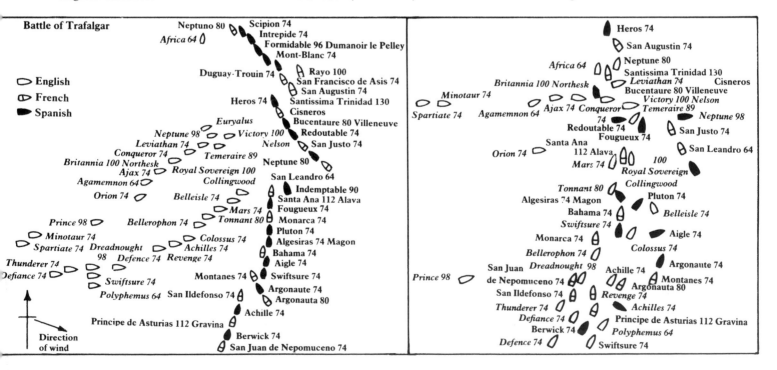

admiral, Napoleon sent a replacement to assume command of the Franco-Spanish fleet, but learning of it the unfortunate Villeneuve, stung by the charge of cowardice and to preserve his position again put to sea: once again, Napoleon's interference had forced his admiral, against his better judgement, to leave port at a time disadvantageous to him and thus play into Nelson's hands. Nelson had deliberately withdrawn his main fleet, in the hope of deceiving Villeneuve, which is exactly what happened: on 19 October the 'Combined Fleet' left Cadiz, intending to make for the Mediterranean to raid Malta's supply-convoys and harbour in Toulon, but unaware that the British fleet was just over the horizon. Nelson marshalled his 27 ships-of-the-line and cut off Villeneuve from the Mediterranean.

About 6 a.m. on 21 October the two fleets were in sight of each other off Cape Trafalgar, Villeneuve with the 33 ships-of-the-line of the 'Combined Fleet' trying to regain Cadiz without a fight, but there was little chance that he could outsail the superior British fleet. Nelson had discussed his tactics with his captains –

his 'band of brothers' – and determined that instead of forming a conventional 'line of battle' would apply what he termed 'The Nelson Touch', and split the enemy fleet at right-angles. The concept was not Nelson's invention, but he was responsible for deliberately setting out with a plan which 'will surprise and confound the enemy. They won't know what I am about. It will bring on a pell-mell battle, and that is what I want'; for he knew that once the action devolved into a series of ship-to-ship encounters, the superior British seamanship and gunnery would win the day. By attacking in two columns, he would separate the enemy fleet and allow their van to escape, whilst he brought his entire fleet to bear upon the centre and rear, knowing that the van would take hours to reverse its course and help its beleaguered fellows; it was, in effect, a naval version of the 'strategy of the central position': to overwhelm a major part of the enemy force by achieving 'local superiority'.

The tactic worked to perfection. With Nelson's signals 'England expects that every man will do his duty' and 'Engage

the enemy more closely' flying on HMS Victory, leading the windward column, and played into action by the band of HMS Tonnant with 'Britons Strike Home!', the second column led by Collingwood's HMS Royal Sovereign broke into the Franco-Spanish line about mid-day, shortly followed by Victory three ships ahead of the initial break, heading straight for Villeneuve's flagship Bucentaure. Villeneuve's van was isolated, and the centre and rear of the 'Combined Fleet' was duly overwhelmed as French and Spanish ships found themselves fighting two and even three British ships at once. By about 4 p.m. no fewer than 15 ships of the 'Combined Fleet' were out of action, either captured or drifting as shot-riddled hulks. Their only success had occurred about 1.30 p.m. when a marksman aboard Redoutable had mortally wounded Nelson whilst he was walking upon Victory's quarterdeck, but Redoutable was shot to a wreck, and Bucentaure captured, and with it Villeneuve. Admiral Dumanoir, commanding the French van, finally was able to reverse his course and enter the battle, but by then it was too late, and after losing two ships Dumanoir broke off and ran, as did the mortally-wounded Gravina with what he could salvage from the rear. At 5.30 p.m. the French ship Achille, which had been blazing since her own marksmen had set her sails alight by the flashes of their muskets, blew up with a tremendous explosion, which effectively marked the end of the battle. The 'Combined Fleet' had lost 18 ships (though only four of the 17 prizes survived the furious storm which occurred that night) and 14,000 men, for the loss of 1,500 British sailors and no ships, though the loss of Nelson was a tragic blow to the Royal Navy. It was the most crushing defeat which effectively ended Napoleon's naval power, for although the invasion-plan had been postponed even before Trafalgar, the destruction of the fleet meant that it could never again be contemplated seriously.

# Naval Operations following Trafalgar

Following Trafalgar, Napoleon made earnest attempts to increase the strength of his navy, hoping eventually to build so many ships that he could overpower the British by weight of numbers: 'We shall be able to make peace with safety when we have 150 ships of the line.' Despite the campaigns on land, he never lost sight of the need to increase the fleet and improve the dockyards, and despite steady losses throughout the period the resources of the Empire were such that an ambitious building-programme could be undertaken; 19 ships-of-the-line per year were constructed at Antwerp, for example, and by 1814 France had 79 battleships and 39 more under construction. Toulon was made the principal naval base, at the expense of Brest and Rochefort, and the navy improved so much in quality that the British Admiral Sir Edward Pellew reported in 1811, 'I have never seen a French fleet in half the order that the Toulon one is in. They have, I am sorry to say, adopted too many of our arrangements.'

Nevertheless, until such time that France could overpower Britain by weight of numbers, they rarely risked a full-scale 'fleet action', and morale never really recovered after Trafalgar. From then to the end of the Napoleonic Wars, Britain lost only 12 ships-of-the-line, all to wreck or accidental fire and not one to enemy action; in fact the only one lost to the French after the resumption of hostilities in 1803 was HMS *Calcutta* (54 guns) a month before Trafalgar. This domination of the sea allowed British operations to progress unhindered; there was no attempt to prevent the evacuation of Moore's army from Corunna, for example, or to disrupt the passage of supplies to the Peninsular army via Lisbon. It has even been suggested that one reason for British reverses during

*Thomas Cochrane's attack with fireships, Basque Roads, 11/12 April 1809, under the overall command of Admiral Gambier. Fireships were expendable vessels filled with combustible material, sailed by skeleton crews who evacuated the burning vessel in the immediate presence of the enemy. A fireship would cause panic in an enemy anchorage, causing the enemy's ships to cut their cables and run in confusion.*

the early stages of the War of 1812 was that their crews and training had become lax from lack of serious opposition, until they encountered the American navy.

There was, however, considerable naval activity in the post-Trafalgar period, beginning with the successful British descent upon Calabria to disrupt French plans for the invasion of Sicily. Elements of the main battle-fleet were used by Napoleon in the 'war of commerce', though with little of the success he envisaged; deploying the ships-of-the-line in small numbers made them considerably less effective. Admiral Leissègues evaded the British blockade of Brest with 5 ships and began to attack British commerce in the West Indies, until caught by Admiral Sir John Duckworth's squadron in February 1806 at Santo Domingo; three French ships were captured and the other two went aground. French and allied colonies fell to British expeditions without serious opposition, and a perceived attempt by Napoleon to enlist the support of the Danish fleet led to a second British expedition against Copenhagen, which in 1807 sailed away with virtually the entire Danish fleet,

including 16 ships-of-the-line and 10 frigates. In the Mediterranean, France had a minor success in the capture of Capri, but the attempt to invade Sicily ended in humiliation.

As the French navy refused to engage in a major 'fleet action', the British were compelled to find other methods of engaging the main French forces, which led to the most audacious raid upon Basque Roads. Taking advantage of the temporary absence of the British blockaders, Admiral Willaumez slipped out of Brest in February 1809 with 8 ships-of-the-line, intending to join the Lorient and Rochefort squadrons and together cruise to the Caribbean. The Lorient squadron (3 ships-of-the-line, 3 frigates) was intercepted by the British, who captured the frigates, and thus deprived of support Willaumez ran for the safety of Basque Roads (or Isle d'Aix, an anchorage near Rochefort), where he was joined by the Rochefort squadron, bringing the French fleet to a strength of 11 ships-of-the-line and 4 frigates. They were immediately blockaded in by the British under Admiral Lord Gambier (1756-1833), who had 11

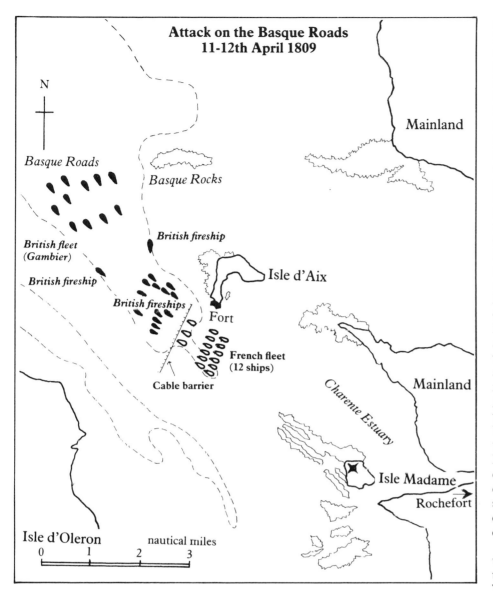

## Attack on the Basque Roads
## 11-12th April 1809

N

Mainland

*Basque Roads*

*Basque Rocks*

*British fireship*

*British fleet
(Gambier)*

Isle d'Aix

*British fireship*

*British fireships*

Fort

*French fleet
(12 ships)*

Cable barrier

Mainland

*Charente Estuary*

Isle Madame

Rochefort

Isle d'Oleron

nautical miles

0    1    2    3

ships-of-the-line, 8 frigates and 18 smaller vessels. The anchorage occupied by the French was deemed impregnable; the area was edged with shoals, making navigation perilous, and an enormous cable, supported on buoys, formed a boom between the French anchorage and the open sea which apparently made any attack upon the fleet impossible. The boom was over-looked by an island citadel which mounted 30 guns, and was constantly patrolled by 70 small boats. Between the boom and the main French fleet were anchored three frigates. Admiral Allemand (who had replaced Willaumez) believed himself secure; but the British navy had other ideas.

Gambier sent a message to the Admiralty that the position might be attacked by fireships, and Britain's most

daring frigate-captain, Thomas Cochrane (1775-1860, later Earl of Dundonald) was selected to plan and lead the attack. He joined Gambier on 26 March with his frigate and 12 fireships, plus the inventor William Congreve with a supply of his explosive rockets which had been used against Copenhagen in 1807. For the attack on the Roads, Gambier allocated a further 6 frigates, 11 brigs, 8 fireships and 3 'bombships' (small vessels loaded with 1,500 barrels of gunpowder), but because of the narrow waterway and shoals was unwilling to risk any ships-of-the-line. Consequently, Cochrane had only a weak force with which to execute the operation, which he timed for the night of 11 April. Keeping his frigates back, Cochrane marked either side of the entrance to the narrows with a fire-

ship, to guide in the remainder, preceded by the two bombships, which ran into the boom-cable and destroyed it when they exploded. Several of the 20 following fireships (whose skeleton crews had been taken off by the frigates) drifted through the severed cable on the tide, and towards the French lines. The three frigates cut their cables and drifted in towards the French ships-of-the-line; they in turn cut their cables and, in darkness and great confusion, ran aground. By first light on 12 April only 2 French ships-of-the-line and a frigate were capable of manoeuvre, the remainder stuck fast. Cochrane attacked immediately with his frigates; Gambier was initally unwilling to risk his larger ships, but eventually sent in some support. Two of the help-less French ships surrendered, and two others and a frigate were burned, but at high water the remainder were re-floated and drifted up the Charente estuary, where the British dare not pursue. The action had not been as decisive as it might have been had Cochrane been given the support he urged (Gambier was severely criticised for his conduct but was vindicated by an enquiry), but though less than half the French fleet had been lost the blow to morale was crushing; one French commander was court-martialled and shot! Once again, it served to emphasize the complete mastery of the sea achieved by the Royal Navy over the main French battle-fleet.

This dominance was re-asserted by the lack of French naval opposition to the British descent upon the island of Walcheren in the Scheldt estuary in August-September 1809, some 200 transports carrying 40,000 troops, escorted by 35 ships-of-the-line and 11 frigates. The expedition was intended to open a 'second front' in northern Europe by causing a rising in north Germany, but this never materialised and the British forces were appallingly mis-handled, an opportunity to capture Antwerp being missed, and 4,000 of the British troops died from the infamous 'Walcheren fever' before the expedition was withdrawn. For the rest of the period, the Royal Navy supported the land campaigns, British control of the sea making possible the transfer of Wellington's base from Lisbon to Santander, but despite the lack of action by the French battle-fleet, only in 1813 were the French privateers and commerce-raiders really mastered.

# US-British Frigate Actions

In comparison with the large 'fleet actions' of the Napoleonic Wars, the naval actions of the War of 1812 were insignificant in size, though not in the impact that they had upon the general state of the war. The United States navy was tiny: at the outbreak of war only 3 large frigates (66 guns), 4 ordinary frigates, 9 corvettes and brigs and about 100 gunboats, though it is a mistake to regard the largest of these as 'frigates' in the normal sense. Strongly-built and fast, they were vastly more heavily armed than their British counterparts, and it is this factor, allied with the fact that the level of seamanship and gunnery of the United States navy was similar to that of the Royal Navy, which resulted in several disasters for a British navy which had become used to regarding itself as invincible. In contrast to the often dismal performance of the US army, the navy covered itself with honour in a series of hard-fought actions.

Naval affairs – in the presence of the British claims to right of search of neutral vessels in an attempt (quite successful) to counter Napoleon's Continental System – had contributed to the outbreak of war in 1812, and the need to blockade any port of importance to Napoleon stretched the resources of the Royal Navy. Thus, the huge imbalance in the sizes of the British and US navies was not immediately significant, as the main actions were fought between single ships; at the outbreak of war Britain had only 1 ship-of-the-line and 6 frigates along the eastern American seaboard. One of the first clashes occurred on 23 June 1812 off Chesapeake Bay when HMS *Belvidera* (36 guns) engaged two American frigates and two smaller vessels, and was hard-put to escape. The USS *Essex* (32) captured the small HMS *Alert* (16) on 13 August, but on 19 August came the first major action, off Nova Scotia, when USS *Constitution* (44) – the famed 'Old Ironsides' – devastated HMS *Guerrière* (38) in a two-hour battle. On 17 October the 18-gun sloops USS *Wasp* and HMS *Frolic* battered each other off Virginia, but though *Frolic* was smashed into submission *Wasp* was so badly damaged that she had to strike her colours when the 74-gun HMS *Poictiers* arrived. On 25 October the USS *United States* (44),

under the command of Stephen Decatur, crippled and captured HMS *Macedonian* (38), and on 29 December *Constitution* captured HMS *Java* off Bahia, Brazil. This latter action, completing a most successful naval year for the United States, illustrates the disparity between ships which at first glance appeared almost equal: the 44-gun *Constitution* had a broadside weight of 1,490lb, whereas the 38-gun *Java* had a broadside of only 1,034lb; the American's crew was also much larger, 485 to 377; in 'single combat', when the proficiency of crews was about equal, this was decisive. This series of defeats led to an increase of British naval strength (soon almost 100 Royal Navy ships, including 11 line-of-battle ships and 34 frigates, were engaged in the blockade of the US coast), and also to the realization that the US navy was a far sterner proposition than had been thought.

The comparative weakness of US naval strength allowed them only one policy: for individual ships to elude the blockade and attempt to damage British commerce, in which they were assisted by a large number of American privateers. On 24 February 1813 the USS *Hornet*, cruising in Brazilian waters, encountered HMS *Peacock* (the old USS *Wasp*, re-christened when commissioned in British services) and sank her in 11 minutes. American naval vessels and privateers continued to wreak considerable havoc on British commercial shipping; as *The Times* noted in March, Britain had lost 'Five hundred merchantmen, and three frigates! Can these statements be true; and can the English people hear them unmoved?'; and it was even said that the American success put heart into the French navy, whose crews now no longer went into action convinced that the British were invincible. On 1 June, however, came perhaps the most famous of the 'frigate actions' of the War of 1812, when Captain Philip Vere Broke of HMS *Shannon* (38) was watching the Boston coast, hoping for a contest with a US frigate, confident in the excellence of the gunnery of his crew, among the best in the Royal Navy and trained to the highest degree. In Boston harbour lay USS *Chesapeake*, commanded by Captain James Lawrence (late of the *Hornet*).

Broke issued a formal challenge, and Lawrence sailed out, eager to fight. The whole action lasted only 15 minutes; so accurate was Broke's gunnery that his first broadsides severely damaged *Chesapeake*'s rigging, killed her sailing-master and mortally-wounded Lawrence, who begged 'Don't give up the ship!' as he was carried below. As *Chesapeake* fell on board *Shannon* Broke in person led a boarding-party and within five minutes had captured the ship; *Shannon* had lost 24 killed and 58 wounded, to 61 and 85 respectively aboard *Chesapeake*. It was a stunning victory; *Chesapeake* was taken as a prize to Halifax, and British morale was restored after having been considerably shaken.

The United States suffered a further blow on 14 August when their brig *Argus* (16), which had transported the American ambassador to France and had stayed to cruise in the Channel, was caught by the sloop HMS *Pelican* (18), was raked with fire and surrendered before she was boarded; but on 3 September HMS *Boxer* (12) was captured by USS *Enterprise* (14) off Maine. Despite the fact that US naval ships continued to evade the blockade and damage British commerce, their weakness was such that they were unable either to prevent British descents upon the American coast, or to drive away the blockading squadrons, so that the cumulative effect on US trade was to bring the Treasury close to bankruptcy. So effective were the US raiders, however, that convoys became the only safe way of proceeding for British merchant ships, and naval actions still occurred: on 29 April 1814 USS *Peacock* (named to commemorate the vessel sunk by *Hornet*) took the 18-gun HMS *Epervier* off the Florida coast, on the same day that the privateer *Perry* took HMS *Ballahou* (4). On 21 March, after a 17-month cruise which terrorized British shipping in the Pacific, USS *Essex* (32) was captured by HMS *Phoebe* (36) and HMS *Cherub* (20) near Valparaiso after a sanguinary battle which caused 89 dead and 70 wounded aboard *Essex* for the loss of 5 British sailors killed and 10 wounded. On 28 June USS *Wasp* (the second ship so named) (18) took HMS *Reindeer* (18) in the Channel, and on 1 September sank HMS *Avon* (18), but disappeared in October, never to be seen again. Several frigate actions occurred after the official conclusion of peace, including the capture

of Decatur's USS *President* after a gallant fight on 15 January 1815, and the USS *Constitution*'s capture of the vastly inferior HMS *Levant* (22) and HMS *Cyane* (20). The last frigate action of the war of 1812 occurred on 23 March when HMS *Penguin* (18) was taken by USS *Hornet* off Tristan da Cunha.

In addition to operations on the high seas, some naval actions occurred on the island lakes. At the outbreak of war Britain possessed several small warships here, whilst the United States had none, but in a remarkably short time an 'inland navy' was constructed to meet that of the British. Though the naval forces of both sides were small (20-gun ships were generally the largest involved), the fights were not without influence on the course of the war. On 10 September 1813 the turning-point of the war in the northwest occurred with the Battle of Lake Erie, in which Captain Oliver H. Perry's US 'fleet' (2 20-gun ships, 1 6-gun, 1 3-gun, and 5 1-gun boats) met and defeated Captain Robert Barclay whose British force comprised 1 20-gun ship, 1 17-gun, 1 13-gun, 1 10-gun, 1 3-gun and 1 1-gun vessel. After Perry's flagship *Lawrence* was put out of action he transferred to *Niagara*, broke the British line-of-battle Trafalgar-style and the entire British squadron

*The defeat of USS* Chesapeake *(Capt. James Lawrence) by HMS* Shannon *(Capt. Philip Bowes Vere Broke) on 1 June 1813 was the result of the excellence of gunnery and seamanship instilled by Broke into his crew, and greatly restored British morale after defeats in which British captains had tended to be over-confident.*

surrendered. The action shook Indian allegiance to Britain and opened the way to a renewed American offensive, in which Perry's lightest boats co-operated to good effect with the military forces.

Perhaps the most decisive action of the war was the battle fought on Lake Champlain on 11 September 1814, when a hastily-built British squadron of four ships (1 37-gun, 1 16-gun, 1 11-gun and 1 10-gun) and 12 2-gun galleys commanded by Captain George Downie engaged Captain Thomas Macdonough's US squadron protecting the American position before Plattsburg, in a co-ordinated land and water-borne advance. The US forces were inferior (1 26-gun ship, 1 20-gun, 1 17-gun and 1 7-gun, plus 10 galleys) but had a preponderence of heavier guns, and Macdonough was experienced in the conditions of the lake. The British squadron went into

action as their troops advanced on land, but suffered a raking fire from the American long guns in the approach; the battle was contested keenly for two hours until Macdonough swung round his flagship *Saratoga* by means of a stern anchor and delivered a shattering broadside against Downie's *Confiance*; Downie was killed and his wrecked flagship struck her colours, to be followed by the remainder of the squadron after some gunboats manned by militia had fled. The attack on land was misdirected and was called off. Despite the small numbers of vessels and combatants involved, the battle ensured that no further threat of invasion of the United States from the north was possible, and had considerable effect upon the peace conference at Ghent when news was received there in late October.

At least until the battle of New Orleans, the British had had rather the best of the War of 1812; but at sea, given the enormous disparity of numbers and despite the fact that Britain's main pre-occupation was with the war against Napoleon, the United States navy did far better than could possibly have been envisaged, and gave the hitherto invincible Royal Navy greater shocks than ever the French were able to achieve.

# French-British Frigate Actions

At the outbreak of war, France had almost twice the number of frigates possessed by Britain, including many of the larger and more heavily-armed variety. Despite this initial imbalance, France's loss of frigates when compared with those of Britain was totally out of proportion: between 1793 and 1801 the Royal Navy lost 36 frigates, only six of which were taken by the enemy (including one seized in neutral Smyrna and one by mutiny); in the same period France lost 103, of which 84 were lost in action, 18 wrecked and one chopped up for firewood in Malta. Many of these were taken by greatly superior forces, such as those captured at Toulon, rather than in single-ship duels, though it was the latter which produced some of the hardest-fought actions. As the French enjoyed little success, the British began to penetrate their anchorages in 'boat-actions', in which frigate-crews would row in longboats, under cover of darkness, and seize anchored French vessels. Typical of these was the attack by 180 British seamen and marines upon the French corvette *Chevette* near Brest in July 1801. After a six-mile row the boats approached *Chevette* (whose crew was swelled by soldiers to 339) who greeted them with grapeshot, but undaunted the British swarmed aboard and after a ferocious hand-to-hand fight in which 11 British and 92 Frenchmen were killed, took possession of the corvette and sailed her away.

The audacity displayed by the British navy in countless such minor fights gave them a huge morale advantage over their opponents. Some of the incidents were astonishing, such as the capture of the Spanish frigate *Gamo* in May 1801 by the British sloop *Speedy*. *Gamo* mounted 32 guns and had a crew of over 300; *Speedy* (commanded by Thomas Cochrane) had a crew of 60 and carried only 14 4pdrs. Nevertheless, it was Cochrane who chased the Spaniard, boarded with his entire crew (save two seamen and the surgeon) and captured it! In 1807 HMS *Quebec* (32), assisted by the 74-gun *Majestic*, captured the island of Heligoland which became the main base for the smuggling of British goods into Germany in defiance of the Continental System; such was the domination of the area by the Royal Navy that Heligoland was held by only 400 men, despite being only some 35 miles from a coastline which Napoleon considered French. Despite this overwhelming superiority in naval capability, the smaller French warships continued to harrass British merchant shipping, necessitating the use of convoys; but despite the imbalance, the French refused to countenance the use of the submarine invented by the American Robert Fulton, unless he operated it as a privateer, expressing a fear that 'The English, who are ingenious with destructive machines, would soon be using similar devices', and commenting that 'the code of war . . . justly inflicts punishment on those who are naturally inclined to behave in such an atrocious manner.' Fulton then offered his invention to Britain, whose opinion was voiced by Lord St Vincent: 'Such ways of waging war are useless to those who already possess command of the sea.'

Such was the morale of the British frigates that their over-confidence in their ability to overpower any foreign vessel of whatever size was the best hope France possessed of victory: their most notable success was at Mauritius in 1810 when four British frigates injudiciously took on five French, two of the British being burned and two captured. Not until the British came into contact with

*British over-confidence led to the only major French naval success, at Ile Bourbon (Réunion) in 1810, when 4 British '36's' attacked a superior French squadron.*

the vastly stronger American frigates, however, did they suffer any serious reverses in the 'frigate war'.

Many frigate-actions were hard-fought and of considerable duration. A typical incident was the fight between the French *La Piedmontaise* (50) and HMS *St Fiorenzo* (36) in the East Indies in March 1808; the following is an extract from the despatch of Lieut William Dawson, first officer of Capt Nicholas Hardinge of the British ship:

'On the 6th . . . saw a frigate bearing N.E. We immediately hauled our wind in chase, and made all sail . . . and at five shewed our colours, which the enemy took no notice of. At forty minutes past 11 p.m. we ranged alongside him . . . and received his broadside. After engaging till fifty minutes past 11 p.m., within a cable's length, the enemy made sail a-head, out of range of our shot . . . continuing to come up with him till daylight . . . At twenty-five minutes past six re-commenced the action at the distance of half a mile, gradually closing with him to a quarter of a mile. The fire was well-directed and constant on both sides, though that of the enemy slackened towards the latter part of the action. At a quarter past 8 p.m. the enemy made all sail away; our main topsail yard being shot through, the main royal-mast, and

*The French* Didon *(44, Capt. Milins) was captured on 10 August 1805 after being battered into 'a perfect wreck' by HMS* Phoenix *(36, Capt Thomas Baker).*

both the main top-mast-stays, the main-spring-stay and most of the standing and running rigging, and all our sails shot to pieces, and most of our cartridges fired away (as our guns were directed at the hull he was not much disabled about his rigging), we ceased firing, and employed all hands in repairing the damages sustained . . . at nine p.m. on the 8th . . . we bore down upon the enemy under all sail; he did not endeavour to avoid us till we hauled athwart his stern, for the purpose of gaining the weather-gauge, and bringing him to close fight, when he hauled up also, and made all sail; but perceiving that we came fast up with him, and that an action was inevitable, he tacked, and at three we passed each other . . . and re-commenced action within a quarter of a cable's length. With grief I have to observe, that our brave Captain was killed by a grape-shot the second broad-side . . . The enemy . . . after an hour and twenty minutes close action, struck their colours, and waved their hats for a boat to be sent them . . . She had three hundred and sixty six Frenchmen on board, and nearly two

hundred Lascars, who worked their sails . . . In the action she had 48 killed and 112 wounded. The *St Fiorenzo* has thirteen killed and 25 wounded . . . The enemy was cut to pieces in his masts, bowsprit, and rigging; and they all went by the board during the night . . .'

The final action of the Napoleonic Wars at sea occurred on 30 April 1815, when the 40-gun *Melpomène* was captured off Ischia by HMS *Rivoli* (74), ironically named after one of Napoleon's most noted victories (a French ship captured by Britain in February 1812), some six weeks before the Napoleonic age ended in the carnage near Mont St Jean. Twenty-three years of war had produced a Europe very different from that existing before the French Revolution, but in the process had been the cause of untold suffering and human misery. Much of what Napoleon achieved in his less warlike activity was of lasting value, but was ultimately betrayed by his unbounded ambition and eventual self-delusion. As Wellington remarked, 'It is a very common error . . . to believe that there are no limits to military success', a fact which seems always to have escaped Napoleon. As stated by a veteran of the wars of which Napoleon was the cause, 'the crimes of politicians were atoned for by the blood of soldiers.'

# *Appendices*

## Order of Battle, Army of Italy, April 1796

**Headquarters:** General Bonaparte, commander in chief
General Berthier, chief of staff
General Chasseloup, chief engineer
**Division Massena** (resembled a corps d'armée but had no separate headquarters):
Division la Harpe: 14th, 70th, 99th & 1st light *Demi-brigades*, 1 bn 21st *Demi-brigade*: total 9,400
Division Meynier: 51st, 55th & 84th *Demi-brigades*; 3rd & 8th light *Demi-brigades*; 1 bn 21st *Demi-brigade*: total 8,620 (Massena took personal command after Maynier was removed from command)
**Division Sérurier:** 19th, 46th & 56th *Demi-brigades*: total 9,450
**Division Augereau:** 39th & 69th *Demi-brigades*: total 6,200
**Brigade Rusca:** 4th & 18th light *Demi-brigades*: total 2,600. (Originally part of Augereau's division, detached 5 April to form liaison between Massena and Sérurier)
**Cavalry:** General Stengel: total 3,500
**Artillery and Engineers:** total 3,800
**Division Macquard, Division Garnier:** total 6,800
**1st-3rd Coastal Divisions** (lines of communication troops): total 10,500
**16th Light Demi-brigade:** total 1,400

**Grand total:** 62,270 men, 60 fieldpieces, 24 light mountain guns; effective strength deducting lines of communication troops: 41,570; in the field, deducting sick: 37,600

---

## Order of Battle, Army of the Reserve, 14 June 1800
(At Marengo unless stated otherwise)

**Desaix:** Division Gardanne: 3,638
**Lannes:** Division Chambarlhac: 5,287
**Victor:** Division Monnier: 3,614
Division Watrin: 5,083
Division Boudet: 5,316
Consular Guard: 1,232 (including 250 mounted *Guides*)
**Duhesme:** Division Loison: 5,304 (at Piacenza)
Division Lapoype: 3,462 (at Ponte-Curone)
Division Lorge: 4,400 (at Créma)
Division Gilly: 3,300 (at Milan)
**Moncey:** Division Chabran: 3,373 (on the river Po)
Division Turreau: 1,000 (at Turin)
Division Bethancourt: 500 (at Arona)
Reinforcements en route: 3,468

**Cavalry (Murat):** Harville: 500 (heavy cavalry)
Kellermann: 1,551 (dragoons)★
Rivaud: 699 (*chasseurs*)★
Champeaux: 420 (hussars)★
Duvignau: 1,112 (heavy cavalry, en route from Milan); 850 *chasseurs* and 420 hussars at Piacenza
Reinforcements en route: 1,424
**Marmont:** Foot Artillery: 1,466
Horse Artillery: 283
**Marescot:** Engineers: 269

★total of two regts detached at Spinetta

---

## Order of Battle, Grande Armée, Austerlitz 1805

Headquarters: Emperor Napoleon, commander in chief
Marshal Berthier, chief of staff

**Imperial Guard:** Marshal Bessières (5,500, 24 guns)
Hulin: Grenadiers à Pied
Soulès: Chasseurs à Pied
Lecchi: Grenadiers, Royal Italian Guard
Ordener: Grenadiers à Cheval
Morland: Chasseurs à Cheval
Savary: Gendarmerie d'Elite, Mamelukes
**I Corps:** Marshal Bernadotte (13,000, 24 guns)
Advance Guard: 27th Léger
1st Div (Rivaud): 8th, 45th, 54th Line
2nd Div (d'Erlon): 94th, 95th Line

**III Corps:** Marshal Davoût (3,800, 9 guns)
2nd Div (Friant): 108th Line, Voltigeurs of 15th Léger (1st Bde)
33rd Line, 15th Léger (2nd Bde)
48th, 111th Line (3rd Bde)
Attached: 4th Dragoon Div (Bourcier) (2,500, 3 guns):
15th, 17th, 18th, 19th & 27th Dragoons
**IV Corps:** Marshal Soult (23,600, 35 guns)
1st Div (St Hilaire): 14th, 36th Line; 10th Léger
2nd Div (Vandamme): 4th, 28th, 43rd, 46th, 55th, 57th Line; 24th Léger

3rd Div (Legrand): 3rd, 18th, 75th Line; 26th Léger;
    Tirailleurs du Po; Tirailleurs Corses
Light Cavalry Div (Margaron): 8th Hussars, 11th & 26th
    Chasseurs
3rd Dragoon Div: 5th, 8th, 12th, 16th, 21st Dragoons
**V Corps**: Marshal Lannes (12,700, 20 guns)
    Div Caffarelli: 17th, 30th, 51st, 61st Line; 13th Léger
    Div Suchet: 34th, 40th, 64th, 88th, Line; 17th Léger
    Light Cavalry Div (Treilhard): 9th & 10th Hussars, 13th &
    21st Chasseurs
**Grenadier Div:** General Oudinot (5,700)

**Cavalry Reserve:** Marshal Murat (7,400)
    1st Heavy Div (Nansouty): 1st and 2nd Carabiniers; 2nd,
    3rd, 9th & 12th Cuirassiers
    2nd Heavy Cavalry Div (d'Hautpoul): 1st, 5th, 10th & 11th
    Cuirassiers
    2nd Dragoon Div (Walther): 3rd, 6th, 10th, 11th, 13th,
    22nd Dragoons
    Light Cavalry Div (Kellermann): 2nd, 4th & 5th Hussars;
    5th Chasseurs
    Light Cavalry Bde (Milhaud): 16th & 22nd Chasseurs

---

## Order of Battle, Grande Armée, 1 June 1809

**Imperial Guard:** Old Guard (Gen Dorsenne): 3,048
    Young Guard (Gen Curial): 6,068
    Cavalry (Gen Walther): 1,849

**2nd Corps**
**(Gen Oudinot):** 1st Div (Tharreau): 4,582
    2nd Div (Claparède): 6,267
    3rd Div (Grandjean): 7,090
    Portuguese Legion: 1,604
    Light Cavalry (Colbert): 1,768
    Artillery (Villeneuve): 1,288
**3rd Corps**
**(Marshal Davoût):** 1st Div (Morand): 8,544
    2nd Div (Friant): 9,456
    3rd Div (Gudin): 10,588
    4th Div (Puthod): 5,109
    Light Cavalry (Pajol): 1,962
    Artillery, engineers: 625
**4th Corps**
**(Marshal Massena):** 1st Div (Legrand): 4,436
    2nd Div (Carra-St-Cyr): 7,123
    3rd Div (Molitor): 6,761
    4th Div (Boudet): 5,534
    Light Cavalry (Marulaz): 1,520
**7th Bavarian Corps**
**(Marshal Lefebvre):** 1st Div (Louis of Bavaria): 8,002
    2nd Div (Wrede): 5,863
    3rd Div (Deroy): 7,464
**8th (Wurttemberg) Corps**
**(Gen Vandamme):** 1st Div: 8,490
    Div Wölwarth: 952
    Div Dupas (French): 3,580
    Div Rouyer: 5,488
**9th (Saxon) Corps**
**(Marshal Bernadotte):** 1st Div (Zerschwitz): 7,825
    2nd Div (Polenz): 7,806
    Danzig garrison: 2,855
    Glogau garrison: 1,879

**10th (Westphalian) Corps**
**(King Jerome):** 1st Div (Bercterode): 7,658
    2nd Div (Gratien): 6,606 (Dutch)
    Garrisons of Stettin, Magdeburg, Stralsund and
    Custrin in addition
**Reserve Cavalry Corps**
**(Gen Bessières):** 1st Heavy Div (Nansouty): 3,585
    2nd Heavy Div (St-Sulpice): 1,812
    3rd Heavy Div (Arrighi): 1,608
    1st Light Div (Lasalle): 1,434
    2nd Light Div (Montbrun): 2,464
**Armée d'Allegmagne Reserve**
**(Gen Junot):** 1st Div (Rivaud): 4,556
    2nd Div (Despeaux): 8,528
    3rd Div (Lagrange):
    3rd Div (Beaumont):    4,702
**Army of Italy**
**(Eugène):** 1st Corps (Macdonald): 1st Div (Broussier): 7,850
    2nd Div (Lamarque): 6,318
    3rd Cavalry Div (Pully): 1,470
    2nd Corps (Grenier): 1st Div (Seras): 7,850
    2nd Div (Durutte): 8,404
    3rd Corps (Baraguay d'Hilliers): 1st Div (Rusca): 4,820
    2nd Div (Severoli):
    8,265 (Italian)
    Grouchy's Corps: Div Fontanelli: 4,522
    Div Pacthod: 6,175
    Light Cavalry Div (Sahuc): 1,290
**Army of Dalmatia**
**(Gen Marmont):** 1st Div (Claparède): 5,279
    2nd Div (Clauzel): 4,468
**Polish Army**
**(Prince Poniatowski):** 1st Div (Zayonchek): 8,147
    2nd Div (Dombrowski): 3,017

---

## Order of Battle, Grande Armée, 1812

Headquarters (Marshal Berthier): Bn de Neuchâtel; Gendarmerie (1 sqdn); Guides (1 coy)
**Imperial Guard** (Marshals Bessières & Mortier):
    1st Div (Delaborde): 4th, 5th & 6th Tirailleurs, 4th, 5th & 6th Voltigeurs (12 bns)
    2nd Div (Roguet): Fusiliers, 1st Voltigeurs, 1st Tirailleurs, Flanqueurs (10 bns)

## Order of Battle, Grande Armée, 1812 (continued)

3rd Div (Lefebvre): 1st & 2nd Chasseurs; 1st, 2nd & 3rd Grenadiers (10 bns)
Attached: Portuguese Chasseurs, 7th Chevau-Légers (7 sqdns)
     Italian Vélites, Spanish Engineers (3 bns)
     Div Claparède: 1st, 2nd, 3rd & 4th Vistula Legion (12 bns)

**I Corps** (Marshal Davoût):
1st Div (Morand): 13th & 17th Léger, 30th Line (15 bns)
2nd Div (Friant): 15th Léger, 33rd & 48th Line, Regt Joseph-Napoleon (17 bns)
3rd Div (Gudin): 7th Léger; 12th, 21st & 127th Line; 8th Confederation Regt (18 bns)
4th Div (Desaix): 33rd Léger, 85th & 108th Line (14 bns)
5th Div (Compans): 25th, 57th, 61st & 111th Line (20 bns)
Cavalry (Girardin): 1st, 2nd & 3rd Chasseurs, 9th Polish Lancers (16 sqdns)

**II Corps** (Marshal Oudinot):
6th Div (Legrand): 26th Léger, 19th, 56th & 128th Line, 3rd Portuguese Regt (16 bns)
8th Div (Verdier): 11th Léger, 2nd, 37th, 124th Line (16 bns)
9th Div (Merle): 123rd Line, 1st, 2nd, 3rd & 4th Swiss, 3rd Croatian Regt (17 bns)
Cavalry: 7th, 20th, 23rd & 24th Chasseurs, 8th Chevau-Légers (20 sqdns)

**III Corps** (Marshal Ney):
10th Div (Ledru): 24th Léger, 46th, 72nd, 129th Line, 1st Portuguese Regt (16 bns)
11th Div (Razout): 4th, 18th & 93rd Line; 2nd Portuguese,, Illyrian Regt (18 bns)
25th Div (Marchand): 1st, 2nd, 4th, 6th, 7th Württemberg Regts, 1st & 2nd Württemberg Light Infantry, 1st & 2nd Württemberg
     Jägers (18 bns)
Cavalry (Wollwarth): 11th Hussars, 6th Chevau-Légers, 4th & 28th Chasseurs, 1st, 3rd & 4th Württemberg Cavalry, Württemberg
     Leib-Chevaulegers (31 sqdns)

**IV Corps** (Eugène):
Italian Guard (Lecchi): 6 bns, 6 sqdns
13th Div (Delzons): 8th Léger, 84th, 92nd, 106th Line, 1st Croatian Regt (16 bns)
14th Div (Broussier): 18th Léger, 9th, 35th, 53rd Line, Regt Joseph-Napoleon (16 bns)
15th Div (Pino): 1st & 3rd Italian Light Infantry, 2nd & 3rd Italian Line, Dalmatian Regt (16 bns)
Cavalry: 9th & 19th Chasseurs, 1st & 2nd Italian Chasseurs

**V Corps** (Prince Poniatowski):
16th Polish Div (Zajonczak): 3rd, 13th, 15th & 16th Polish Line (12 bns)
17th Polish Div (Dombrowski): 1st, 6th, 14th & 17th Polish Line (12 bns)
18th Polish Div (Kamieniecki): 2nd, 8th & 12th Polish Line (9 bns)
Cavalry (Kaminski): 1st, 4th & 5th Polish Chasseurs, 12th Polish Lancers, 13th Polish Hussars (20 sqdns)

**VI Corps** (Marshal St Cyr):
19th Bavarian Div (Deroy): 1st, 4th, 8th, 9th & 10th Line, 1st, 2nd & 6th Light Infantry (13 bns)
20th Bavarian Div (Wrede): 2nd, 3rd, 5th, 6th, 7th & 11th Line, 2nd, 4th & 5th Light Infantry (15 bns)
Cavalry (Preysing): 3rd, 4th, 5th & 6th Chevaulegers (16 sqdns)

**VII Corps** (General Reynier):
21st Saxon Div (Lecoq): Regts Friedrich, Clemens, Anton; Liebenau Grenadier Bn; 1st Light Infantry (10 bns)
22nd Saxon Div (Gutschmidt): Regts König, Niesemeuschel; Grenadier Bns Anger, Spiegel, Eychelberg; 2nd Light Infantry (9 bns)
Cavalry: Regts Polenz, Clement; Saxon Hussars (16 sqdns)

**VIII Corps** (Jérôme):
23rd (Westphalian) Div (Tharreau): 2nd, 3rd, 6th, 7th Line; 2nd & 3rd Light Infantry (13 bns)
24th (Westphalian) Div (Ochs): Westphalian Guard, 5th Line, 1st Light Infantry (6 bns)
Cavalry: 1st & 2nd Hussars, Guard Chevaulegers (12 sqdns plus 1 coy Garde du Corps)

**IX Corps** (Marshal Victor):
12th Div (Partouneaux): 10th & 29th Léger, 44th, 125th, 126th and Provisional Line regt (14 bns)
26th Div (Daendels): 1st-4th Berg Regts, 1st-3rd Baden Regts, Baden Light Infantry, 8th Westphalian Regt, Hessen-Darmstadt
     Regts Leibgarde, Leib and Guard Fusiliers (8 bns)
28th Div (Girard): 4th, 7th & 9th Polish Line; Saxon Regts. Low and Rechten (13 bns)
Cavalry: (Fournier) Saxon Regt Johann, Berg Lancers, Hessen-Darmstadt Chevaulegers, Baden Hussars (14 sqdns)

**X Corps** (Marshal Macdonald):
7th Div (Grandjean): 5th, 10th & 11th Polish Line; 13th Bavarian Line, 1st Westphalian Line (16 bns)
27th (Prussian) Div (Yorck): 1st, 2nd, 3rd, 5th & 6th Combined Line; 9th Regt; East Prussian Jägers (18 bns)
Cavalry: 1st & 3rd Prussian Combined Hussars; 1st & 2nd Prussian Combined Dragoons (16 sqdns)

**XI Corps** (Marshal Augereau):
30th Div (Heudelet): 1st, 6th, 7th, 8th, 9th & 17th Provisional Regts (22 bns)
31st Div (La Grange): 10th-13th Provisional Regts (14 bns)
32nd Div (Durutte): Regts Belle-Ile, Walcheren, Rhé, 7th Confederation Regt, 1st & 2nd Mediterranean Regts (19 bns), Würzburg
     Chevaulegers (1 sqdn)

33rd Div (Destrées): 5th-7th Neapolitan Regts, Neapolitan Guard (10 bns), Neapolitan Guard cavalry (4 sqdns)

34th Div (Morand): 22nd Léger, 3rd, 29th & 105th Line, 3rd-6th Confederation Regts, Saxon Regt Maximilian, 4th Westphalian Regt (27 bns)

Cavalry: provisional dragoon regt (4 sqdns)

**I Cavalry Corps** (General Nansouty):
1st Light Div (Bruyers): 7th & 8th Hussars, 16th Chasseurs, 9th Chevau-Légers, 6th & 8th Polish Lancers, 2nd Prussian Combined Hussars (28 sqdns)

1st Heavy Div (St Germain): 2nd, 3rd & 9th Cuirassiers, 1st Chevau-Légers (15 sqdns)

5th Heavy Div (Valence): 6th, 11th & 12th Cuirassiers, 5th Chevau-Légers (15 sqdns)

**II Cavalry Corps** (General Montbrun):
2nd Light Div (Sébastiani): 11th & 12th Chasseurs, 5th & 9th Hussars, 10th Polish Hussars, Prussian Combined Lancers (23 sqdns)

2nd Heavy Div (Wathiez de St Alphonse): 5th, 8th & 10th Cuirassiers, 2nd Chevau-Légers (15 sqdns)

4th Heavy Div (Defrance): 1st & 2nd Carabiniers, 1st Cuirassiers, 4th Chevau-Légers (15 sqdns)

**III Cavalry Corps** (General Grouchy):
3rd Light Div (Castel): 6th Hussars, 6th, 8th & 25th Chasseurs, 1st & 2nd Bavarian Chevaulegers, Saxon Regt Albert (28 sqdns)

3rd Heavy Div (Doumerc): 4th, 7th & 14th Cuirassiers, 3rd Chevau-Légers (15 sqdns)

6th Heavy Div (Lahoussaye): 7th, 23rd, 28th & 30th Dragoons (16 sqdns)

**IV Cavalry Corps** (General Latour-Maubourg):
4th Polish Light Div (Rozniecki): 2nd, 3rd, 7th, 11th, 15th & 16th Lancers (18 sqdns)

7th Heavy Div (Lorge): Saxon Garde du Corps and Zastrow Cuirassiers, 1st & 2nd Westphalian and 14th Polish Cuirassiers (18 sqdns)

**Austrian Auxiliary Corps** (Prince Schwarzenberg):
Cavalry (Frimont): 22 sqdns dragoons, 32 sqdns hussars

Div Bianchi: 8 infantry bns, 2 grenadier bns

Div Siegenthal: 8 infantry bns, 1 Jäger bn, 2 Grenzer bns

Div Trautenberg: 4 infantry bns, 1 Jäger bn, 2 Grenzer bns

---

## Order of Battle, 'Army of the North', 1815

Imperial Guard (Gen Count Drouot):
1st-4th Grenadiers, 1st-4th Chasseurs, 1st & 3rd Tirailleurs, 1st & 3rd Voltigeurs, Guard cavalry, Guard engineers, 9 foot and 4 horse batteries

**I Corps** (Gen Count d'Erlon):
1st Div (Allix): 28th, 54th, 55th, 105th Line
2nd Div (Donzelot): 13th Léger, 17th, 19th, 31st Line
3rd Div (Marcognet): 21st, 25th, 45th, 46th Line
4th Div (Durutte): 8th, 29th, 85th, 95th Line
1st Cavalry Div (Jacquinot): 7th Hussars, 3rd Chasseurs, 3rd & 4th Chevau-Légers
Artillery: 5 foot and 1 horse battery

**II Corps** (Gen Count Reille):
5th Div (Bachelu): 2nd Léger, 61st, 72nd, 108th Line
6th Div (Jérôme): 1st Léger, 1st-3rd Line
7th Div (Girard): 11th & 12th Léger, 4th & 82nd Line
9th Div (Foy): 4th Léger, 9th, 93rd & 100th Line
2nd Cavalry Div (Piré): 1st & 6th Chasseurs, 5th & 6th Chevau-Légers
Artillery: 5 foot and 1 horse battery

**III Corps** (Gen Count Vandamme):
8th Div (Lefol): 15th Léger, 23rd, 37th and 64th Line
10th Div (Habert): 22nd, 34th, 70th, 88th Line; 2nd Swiss Regt
11th Div (Berthezène): 12th, 33rd, 56th & 86th Line
3rd Cavalry Div (Domon): 4th, 9th & 12th Chasseurs
Artillery: 4 foot, 1 horse battery

**IV Corps** (Gen Count Gérard):
12th Div (Pêcheux): 6th Léger, 30th, 63rd & 96th Line
13th Div (Vichery): 48th, 59th, 76th & 96th Line
14th Div (Hulot): 9th Léger, 44th, 50th & 111th Line
7th Cavalry Div (Maurin): 6th Hussars, 8th Chasseurs, 6th, 11th & 16th Dragoons
Artillery: 4 foot and 1 horse battery

**VI Corps** (Gen Count Lobau):
19th Div (Simmer): 5th, 11th, 27th & 84th Line
20th Div (Jeanin): 5th Léger, 10th & 107th Line
21st Div (Teste): 8th Léger, 40th, 65th & 75th Line
Artillery: 4 foot and 1 horse battery

**I Cavalry Corps** (Gen Count Pajol):
4th Cavalry Div (Soult): 1st, 4th & 5th Hussars
5th Cavalry Div (Subervie): 11th Chasseurs, 1st & 2nd Chevau-Légers
Artillery: 2 horse batteries

**II Cavalry Corps** (Gen Count Exelmans):
9th Cavalry Div (Strolz): 5th, 13th, 15th & 20th Dragoons
10th Cavalry Div (Chastel): 4th, 12th, 14th & 17th Dragoons
Artillery: 2 horse batteries

**III Cavalry Corps** (Gen Kellermann):
11th Cavalry Div (L'Héritier): 8th & 11th Cuirassiers, 2nd & 7th Dragoons
12th Cavalry Div (Roussel d'Hurbal): 1st & 2nd Carabiniers, 2nd & 3rd Cuirassiers
Artillery: 2 horse batteries

**IV Cavalry Corps** (Gen Count Milhaud):
13th Cavalry Div (Wathier): 1st, 4th, 7th & 12th Cuirassiers
14th Cavalry Div (Delort): 5th, 6th, 9th & 10th Cuirassiers
Artillery: 2 horse batteries

83,758 infantry
20,959 cavalry
10,028 artillery and 350 guns
1,384 engineers

# Chronology

## 1792

20 April – *France declares war on Hapsburg Empire.*
15 May – *France declares war on Piedmont (Sardinia).*
26 June – *First Coalition organised.*
5 September – *'September Massacres' in Paris; start of 'The Terror'.*
20 September – *French (Dumouriez & Kellermann) defeat Prussians (Brunswick) at Valmy.*
21 September – *National Convention established.*
22 September – *Abolition of French monarchy; introduction of republican calendar.*
22 October – *Prussians leave France.*
6 November – *French (Dumouriez) defeat Austrians at Jemappes.*

## 1793

21 January – *Execution of Louis XVI.*
1 February – *France declares war on Britain and United Provinces.*
9 March – *France declares war on Spain.*
10 March – *Outbreak of revolt in the Vendée.*
18 March – *Austrians (Saxe-Coburg) defeat French (Dumouriez) at Neerwinden.*
5 April – *Dumouriez defects to Allies.*
6 April – *Committee of Public Safety established.*
28 June – *Allies take Valenciennes.*
27 August – *Allies occupy Toulon.*
16 September – *Bonaparte takes command of artillery besieging Toulon.*
15/16 October – *French (Jourdan) defeat Austrians (Saxe-Coburg) at Wattignies.*
16 October – *Execution of Marie Antionette.*
28/30 November – *Prussians (Brunswick) defeat French (Hoche) at Kaiserslautern.*
19 December – *French re-occupy Toulon.*
22 December – *French (Hoche) defeat Prussians (Brunswick) at Fröschwiller.*
23 December – *Vendéan revolt ended by battle of Savernay.*
26 December – *French (Hoche) defeat Austrians (Wurmser) at Geisberg.*

## 1794

24 April – *Battle of Villers-en-Cauches.*
18 May – *French (Souham) defeat Allies (Saxe-Coburg) at Tourcoing.*
1 June – *British fleet defeats French at Battle of 1st June.*
26 June – *French (Jourdan) defeat Allies (Saxe-Coburg) at Fleurus.*
27 July – *Execution of Robespierre.*
29 August – *French recapture Valenciennes.*

## 1795

23 January – *French cavalry captures Dutch fleet.*
16 May – *Peace of Basle between France and Prussia.*
23 June – *French fleet defeated off Lorient.*
16/20 July – *French (Hoche) defeat émigré landing at Quiberon.*
22 July/16 August – *British capture Cape of Good Hope.*
1 October – *Annexation of Austrian Netherlands to France.*

5 October – *Coup d'etat of 13 Vendémiare (Bonaparte's 'whiff of grapeshot').*
27 October – *Establishment of Directory.*
24 November – *French (Massena) defeat Austrians at Loano.*

## 1796

1 March – *Bonaparte appointed to command Army of Italy.*
26 March – *Bonaparte assumes command of Army of Italy.*
12 April – *French (Bonaparte) defeat Austrians (Beaulieu) at Montenotte.*
13 April – *French (Bonaparte) defeat Piedmontese at Millesimo.*
14/15 April – *French (Bonaparte) defeat Austrians (Beaulieu) at Dego.*
21 April – *French (Bonaparte) defeat Piedmontese (Colli) at Mondovi.*
28 April – *Piedmont leaves war by armistice of Cherasco.*
10 May – *French (Bonaparte) defeat Austrians (Beaulieu) at Lodi.*
15 May – *Bonaparte enters Milan.*
4 June – *Commencement of first siege of Mantua.*
16 June – *Austrians (Archduke Charles) defeat French (Jourdan) at Wetzlar.*
9 July – *Drawn battle between French (Moreau) and Austrians (Archduke Charles) at Malsch.*
3 August – *French (Bonaparte) defeat Austrians (Quasdanovich) at Lonato.*
5 August – *French (Bonaparte) defeat Austrians (Wurmser) at Castiglione.*
19 August – *Treaty of San Ildefonso (Franco-Spanish alliance).*
24 August – *Austrians (Archduke Charles) defeat French (Jourdan) at Amberg.*
24 August – *French (Moreau) defeat Austrians (Latour) at Friedberg.*
3 September – *Austrians (Archduke Charles) defeat French (Jourdan) at Würzburg.*
5 September – *French (Bonaparte) defeat Austrians (Davidovich) at Caliano.*
8 September – *French (Bonaparte) defeat Austrians (Wurmser) at Bassano.*
12 November – *Austrians (Alvintzy) check French (Bonaparte) at Caldiero.*
15/17 November – *French (Bonaparte) defeat Austrians (Alvintzy) at Arcola.*
21/27 December – *French attempt to land at Bantry Bay.*

## 1797

14 January – *French (Bonaparte) defeat Austrians (Alvintzy) at Rivoli.*
2 February – *Mantua surrenders to French.*
14 February – *British fleet (Jervis) defeats Spanish (Cordoba) at St Vincent.*
22/24 February – *Abortive French landing in Wales.*
23 March – *French (Massena) defeat Austrians at Malborghetto.*
18 April – *French (Hoche) defeat Austrians (Werneck) at Lahn.*
16 May – *Bonaparte occupies Venice.*
11 October – *British fleet (Duncan) defeats Batavians (de Winter) at Camperdown.*
17 October – *Treaty of Campo Formio (France/Austria).*

## 1798

12 April – *Bonaparte appointed to command Army of the Orient.*
26 April – *Creation of Helvetian Republic after French invasion of Switzerland.*
19 May – *Bonaparte sails for Egypt.*
10 June – *French occupation of Malta.*
21 June – *Irish rebellion defeated at Vinegar Hill.*
1 July – *Bonaparte lands at Alexandria.*
21 July – *French (Bonaparte) defeat Mamelukes at the Pyramids.*
25 July – *French occupy Cairo.*
1 August – *British fleet (Nelson) defeats French (Brueys) at Aboukir Bay.*
22 August – *French land at Killala Bay.*
25 August – *French (Humbert) defeat British (Lake) at Castlebar.*
5 September – *France introduces conscription.*
8 September – *Humbert surrenders at Ballinamuck.*
21 October – *Revolt suppressed in Cairo.*
15 November – *British take Minorca.*
29 December – *Formation of Second Coalition.*

## 1799

23/29 January – *French occupy Naples and establish Parthenopean Republic.*
20 February – *Bonaparte invades Palestine.*
7 March – *French storm Jaffa.*
12 March – *Austria declares war on France.*
19 March – *French besiege Acre.*
25 March – *Austrians (Archduke Charles) defeat French (Jourdan) at Stockach.*
5 April – *Austrians (Kray) defeat French (Schérer) at Magnano.*
17 April – *French (Bonaparte) defeat Turks (Achmed) at Mount Tabor.*
27 April – *Austro-Russians (Suvarov) defeat French (Moreau) at Cassano.*
17 May – *French raise siege of Acre.*
4/7 June – *Austrians (Archduke Charles) defeat French (Massena) at Zurich.*
17/19 July – *Austro-Russians (Suvarov) defeat French (Macdonald) on the Trebbia.*
25 July – *French (Bonaparte) defeat Turks (Mustapha) at Aboukir.*
15 August – *Austro-Russians (Suvarov) defeat French (Joubert) at Novi.*
23 August – *Bonaparte sails for France.*
27 August – *Anglo-Russian expedition (York) lands in Holland.*
16 September – *French (Brune) defeat Anglo-Russians (York) at Bergen-op-Zoom.*
25 September – *French (Massena) defeat Russians (Korsakov) at Zurich.*
2 October – *Anglo-Russians (York) defeat French (Brune) at Bergen-op-Zoom.*
6 October – *French (Brune) defeat Anglo-Russians (York) at Castricum.*
9 October – *Bonaparte lands in France.*
18 October – *Anglo-Russians agree to evacuate Holland.*
9/10 November – *Coup d'état of 18 Brumaire; Consulate established.*
14 December – *Bonaparte appointed First Consul.*

## 1800

**20 March** – *French (Kléber) defeat Turks at Heliopolis.*
**5 April** – *Austrian offensive begins in Italy.*
**20 April** – *Siege of Genoa opens.*
**3 May** – *French (Moreau) defeat Austrians (Kray) at Stockach.*
**5 May** – *French (Moreau) defeat Austrians (Kray) at Möskirch.*
**15 May** – *Bonaparte begins crossing the Alps.*
**16 May** – *French (Moreau) defeat Austrians (Kray) at Ulm.*
**4 June** – *Massena surrenders Genoa.*
**9 June** – *French (Lannes) defeat Austrians (Ott) at Montebello.*
**14 June** – *French (Bonaparte) defeat Austrians (Melas) at Marengo.*
**19 June** – *French (Moreau) defeat Austrians at Hochstadt.*
**5 September** – *Malta surrenders to British.*
**3 December** – *French (Moreau) defeat Austrians (Archduke John) at Hohenlinden.*

## 1801

**9 February** – *Peace of Luneville (France/Austria).*
**8 March** – *British Army lands in Egypt.*
**21 March** – *British (Abercromby) defeat French (Menou) at Aboukir.*
**2 April** – *British fleet (Nelson) defeats Danes at Copenhagen.*
**17 June** – *End of Armed Neutrality following Copenhagen.*
**6 July** – *British and French fleets fight drawn battle at Algeciras.*
**12 July** – *British fleet (Saumarez) defeats Franco-Spanish at Algeciras.*
**2 September** – *French Army of the Orient surrenders.*
**14 September** – *French evacuate Egypt.*
**1 October** – *Signing of preliminaries of Peace of Amiens.*

## 1802

**25 March** – *Peace of Amiens concluded (Britain/France).*
**2 August** – *Bonaparte appointed First Consul for life.*
**11 September** – *Piedmont annexed to France.*
**15 October** – *Switzerland annexed to France.*

## 1803

**16 May** – *Britain declares war on France.*
**1 June** – *France occupies Hanover.*
**9 October** – *Franco-Spanish alliance concluded.*

## 1804

**18 May** – *Napoleon proclaimed Emperor.*
**19 May** – *Creation of the Marshalate.*
**2 December** – *Napoleon's coronation.*
**14 December** – *Spain declares war on Britain.*

## 1805

**30 March** – *Villeneuve sails from Toulon.*
**26 May** – *Napoleon crowned King of Italy.*
**4 June** – *France annexes Genoa.*
**7 June** – *Eugène de Beauharnais appointed Viceroy of Italy.*
**22 July** – *British fleet (Calder) checks French (Villeneuve) off Ferrol.*

**9 August** – *Formation of Third Coalition when Austria joins Britain and Russia.*
**27 August** – *Grand Armée leaves Channel coast for Germany.*
**5 September** – *Austria invades Bavaria.*
**25 September** – *Grand Armée crosses Rhine.*
**17 October** – *Austrians surrender to Napoleon at Ulm.*
**21 October** – *British fleet (Nelson) defeats Franco-Spanish (Villeneuve) at Trafalgar.*
**30 October** – *French (Massena) defeat Austrians (Archduke Charles) at Caldiero.*
**14 November** – *Napoleon enters Vienna.*
**16 November** – *French (Napoleon) defeat Russians (Bagration) at Oberhollabrunn.*
**2 December** – *French (Napoleon) defeat Austro-Russians (Kutuzov) at Austerlitz.*
**26 December** – *Treaty of Pressburg (France/Austria).*

## 1806

**1 April** – *Joseph Bonaparte declared King of Naples.*
**20 June** – *Louis Bonaparte declared King of Holland.*
**27 June** – *British capture Buenos Ayres.*
**4 July** – *British (Stuart) defeat French (Reynier) at Maida.*
**12 July** – *Formation of Confederation of the Rhine.*
**6 August** – *Holy Roman Empire dissolved.*
**6 October** – *Formation of Fourth Coalition.*
**7 October** – *France invades Saxony.*
**10 October** – *French (Lannes) defeat Prussians (Louis) at Saalfeld.*
**14 October** – *French (Napoleon & Davout) defeat Prussians (Hohenlohe & Brunswick) at Jena and Auerstadt.*
**25 October** – *Napoleon enters Berlin.*
**7 November** – *Prussians (Blücher) surrender to French (Bernadotte) at Lübeck.*
**21 November** – *Berlin Decrees instigate Continental System.*
**10 December** – *Treaty of Posen (Franco-Saxon alliance).*
**18 December** – *Napoleon enters Warsaw.*
**26 December** – *French (Lannes) and Russians (Bennigsen) fight drawn battle at Pultusk.*

## 1807

**7 January** – *British 'Orders in Council' respond to Berlin Decrees.*
**8 February** – *French (Napoleon) defeat Russians (Bennigsen) at Eylau.*
**26 May** – *French capture Danzig.*
**10 June** – *French (Napoleon) defeat Russians (Bennigsen) at Heilsberg.*
**14 June** – *French (Napoleon) defeat Russians (Bennigsen) at Friedland.*
**7 July** – *Treaty of Tilsit (Franco-Russian alliance).*
**16 August** – *Britain invades Denmark.*
**7 September** – *Danish fleet surrenders to Britain.*
**20 October** – *French declares war on Portugal.*
**29 November** – *Portuguese royal family embarks for Brazil.*
**30 November** – *France occupies Lisbon.*

## 1808

**2 May** – *Anti-French riot in Madrid.*
**6 June** – *Joseph Bonaparte declared King of Spain.*

**19 July** – *Spanish (Castaños) defeat French (Dupont) at Baylen.*
**20 July** – *Joseph Bonaparte enters Madrid.*
**1 August** – *Wellesley lands in Portugal.*
**17 August** – *Wellesley defeats French at Roleia.*
**21 August** – *British (Wellesley) defeat French (Junot) at Vimiero.*
**30 August** – *Convention of Cintra.*
**4 November** – *Napoleon enters Spain.*
**30 November** – *French storm Somosierra pass.*
**4 December** – *Napoleon enters Madrid.*
**21 December** – *British (Paget) defeat French at Sahagun.*
**24 December** – *Moore begins retreat to Corunna.*
**26 December** – *British defeat French at Benevente.*

## 1809

**16 January** – *British (Moore) defeat French (Soult) at Corunna.*
**24 January** – *Napoleon leaves Spain for Paris.*
**20 February** – *French (Lannes) captures Saragossa.*
**28 March** – *French (Victor) defeat Spanish (Cuesta) at Medellin.*
**9 April** – *Creation of Fifth Coalition.*
**9 April** – *Austria invades Bavaria.*
**16 April** – *Austrians (Archduke John) defeat French (Eugène) at Sacile.*
**20 April** – *French (Napoleon) defeat Austrians (Archduke John) at Abensberg.*
**21 April** – *French (Napoleon) defeat Austrians (Hiller) at Landshut.*
**22 April** – *French (Napoleon) defeat Austrians (Archduke Charles) at Eckmühl.*
**22 April** – *Wellesley assumes command of Anglo-Portuguese army at Lisbon.*
**23 April** – *French (Napoleon) storm Ratisbon.*
**12 May** – *British (Wellesley) defeat French (Soult) at Oporto.*
**13 May** – *Napoleon enters Vienna.*
**21/22 May** – *Austrians (Archduke Charles) defeat French (Napoleon) at Aspern-Essling.*
**14 June** – *French (Eugène) defeat Austrians (Archduke John) at Raab.*
**5/6 July** – *French (Napoleon) defeat Austrians (Archduke Charles) at Wagram.*
**12 July** – *Franco/Austrian armistice.*
**28 July** – *Anglo-Spanish (Wellesley) defeat French (Victor) at Talavera.*
**29 July** – *British amphibious landing at Walcheren.*
**16 August** – *British capture Flushing.*
**19 October** – *Treaty of Vienna and Peace of Schonbrunn (France/Austria).*
**19 November** – *French (Soult) defeat Spanish (Areizago) at Ocana.*
**9 December** – *British evacuate Walcheren.*
**11 December** – *Surrender of Gerona.*

## 1810

**5 February** – *French besiege Cadiz.*
**9 July** – *Napoleon annexes Holland.*
**9 July** – *Fall of Ciudad Rodrigo.*
**21 August** – *Bernadotte elected Crown Prince of Sweden.*
**18 September** – *Abortive French invasion of Sicily.*
**27 September** – *British (Wellington) defeat French (Massena) at Busaco.*
**10 October** – *Massena's advance halted by lines of Torres Vedras.*

## 1811

5 March – *Massena begins retreat from Portugal.*
5 March – *Anglo-Spanish (Graham) defeat French (Victor) at Barrosa.*
11 March – *Fall of Badajoz.*
3 April – *British (Wellington) defeat French (Reynier) at Sabugal.*
5 May – *Anglo-Portuguese (Wellington) defeat French (Massena) at Fuentes de Oñoro.*
16 May – *Anglo-Spanish (Beresford) defeat French (Soult) at Albuera.*
28 October – *Anglo-Portuguese (Hill) defeat French (Girard) at Arroyo dos Molinos.*
23 December – *Napoleon begins military preparations against Russia.*

## 1812

9 January – *French (Suchet) defeat Spanish (Blake) at Valencia.*
19 January – *Anglo-Portuguese (Wellington) storm Ciudad Rodrigo.*
6 April – *Anglo-Portuguese (Wellington) storm Badajoz.*
18 June – *United States declares war on Britain.*
20 June
*Sixth Coalition formed.*
24 June – *Napoleon invades Russia.*
22 July – *Anglo-Portuguese (Wellington) defeat French (Marmont) at Salamanca.*
23 July – *French (Davoût) defeat Russians (Bagration) at Mogilev.*
13 August – *Wellington enters Madrid.*
16 August – *British capture Detroit.*
17 August – *French (Napoleon) defeat Russians (Barclay de Tolly) at Smolensk.*
19 August – *French (Napoleon) defeat Russians (Barclay de Tolly) at Valutino.*
7 September – *French (Napoleon) defeat Russians (Kutuzov) at Borodino.*
14 September – *Napoleon enters Moscow.*
15 September – *Start of great fire of Moscow.*
19 September – *Wellington besieges Burgos.*
13 October – *Anglo-Canadians (Brock) defeat Americans at Queenston.*
19 October – *Napoleon evacuates Moscow.*
22 October – *Wellington abandons siege of Burgos.*
24 October – *French (Eugène) defeat Russians (Kutuzov) at Maloyaroslavets.*
2 November – *French re-occupy Madrid.*
16/17 November – *French (Napoleon) defeat Russians (Kutuzov) at Krasnyi.*
26/28 November – *French (Napoleon) defeat Russians (Kutuzov) at the Berezina, and continue their retreat.*
5 December – *Napoleon quits the army in Russia.*
30 December – *Convention of Tauroggen (Russia/Prussian army).*

## 1813

4 March – *Russians enter Berlin.*
16 March – *Prussia declares war on France.*
2 May – *French (Napoleon) defeat Allies (Wittgenstein) at Lützen.*
20/21 May – *French (Napoleon) defeat Allies (Wittgenstein) at Bautzen.*
23 May – *Wellington advances into Spain.*
12 June – *French evacuate Madrid.*
21 June – *Anglo-Portuguese (Wellington) defeat French (Joseph & Jourdan) at Vittoria.*
26 July/1 August – *Anglo-Portuguese (Wellington) defeat French (Soult) at Sorauren.*

12 August – *Austria declares war on France.*
23 August – *Allies (Bernadotte) defeat French (Oudinot) at Grossbeeren.*
26 August – *Allies (Blücher) defeat French (Macdonald) at Katzbach.*
26/27 August – *French (Napoleon) defeat Allies (Schwarzenberg) at Dresden.*
30 August – *Allies (Ostermann-Tolstoi & Kleist) defeat French (Vandamme) at Kulm-Priesten.*
31 August – *Wellington storms San Sebastian.*
6 September – *Allies (Bernadotte) defeat French (Ney) at Dennewitz.*
10 September – *US squadron defeats British on Lake Erie.*
3 October – *Allies (Blücher) defeat French (Bertrand) at Wartenberg.*
7 October – *Wellington crosses the Bidassoa and invades France.*
16/19 October – *Allies (Schwarzenberg, Bernadotte and Blücher) defeat French (Napoleon) at Leipzig.*
18 October – *Bavaria and Saxony join Allies.*
30 October – *French (Napoleon) defeat Bavarians (Wrede) at Hanau.*
10 November – *British (Wellington) defeat French (Soult) at Nivelle.*
9/12 December – *British (Wellington) defeat French (Soult) at Nive.*

## 1814

11 January – *Murat signs peace with Allies.*
29 January – *French (Napoleon) defeat Allies (Blücher) at Brienne.*
1 February – *Allies (Blücher) defeat French (Napoleon) at La Rothière.*
10 February – *French (Napoleon) defeat Allies (Blücher) at Champaubert.*
11 February – *French (Napoleon) defeat Allies (Blücher) at Montmirail.*
12 February – *French (Napoleon) defeat Allies (Blücher) at Château-Thierry.*
14 February – *French (Napoleon) defeat Allies (Blücher) at Vauchamps.*
18 February – *French (Napoleon) defeat Allies (Schwarzenberg) at Montereau.*
27 February – *British (Wellington) defeat French (Soult) at Orthez.*
27 February – *Allies (Wittgenstein & Wrede) defeat French (Oudinot) at Bar-sur-Aube.*
7 March – *French (Napoleon) defeat Allies (Blücher) at Craonne.*
9 March – *Allies (Blücher) defeat French (Marmont) at Laon.*
13 March – *French (Napoleon) defeat Allies (St Priest) at Rheims.*
20/21 March – *Allies (Schwarzenberg) defeat French (Napoleon) at Arcis-sur-Aube.*
25 March – *Allies (Schwarzenberg) defeat French (Marmont & Mortier) at La Fère-Champenoise.*
30 March – *Allies (Schwarzenberg) defeat French (Marmont) at Paris (Montmartre).*
31 March – *Allies enter Paris.*
6 April – *Napoleon abdicates at Fontainebleau.*
10 April – *Anglo-Spanish (Wellington) defeat French (Soult) at Toulouse.*
3 May – *Louis XVIII enters Paris.*
4 May – *Napoleon lands on Elba.*
25 July – *Drawn battle of Lundy's Lane.*
24 August – *British (Ross) defeat Americans at Bladensburg; occupy Washington and burn White House.*

14 September – *British (Ross) repulsed at Baltimore.*
1 November – *Congress of Vienna opens.*
24 December – *Treaty of Ghent (Britain/USA).*

## 1815

8 January – *Americans (Jackson) defeat British (Packenham) at New Orleans.*
26 February – *Napoleon escapes from Elba.*
1 March – *Napoleon lands in France.*
13 March – *Allies outlaw Napoleon.*
20 March – *Napoleon returns to Paris.*
25 March – *Seventh Coalition formed.*
31 March – *Murat declares war on Austria.*
2 May – *Austrians (Bianchi) defeat Murat at Tolentino.*
15 June – *Napoleon invades Netherlands.*
16 June – *Allies (Wellington) defeat French (Ney) at Quatre Bras.*
16 June – *French (Napoleon) defeat Prussians (Blücher) at Ligny.*
18 June – *Allies (Wellington & Blücher) defeat French (Napoleon) at Waterloo.*
18 June – *French (Grouchy) defeat Prussians (Theilmann) at Wavre.*
22 June – *Napoleon's second abdication.*
7 July – *Allies enter Paris.*
15 July – *Napoleon surrenders to HMS Bellerophon.*
7 August – *Napoleon sails to St Helena on HMS Northumberland.*
13 October – *Murat tried and shot.*
17 October – *Napoleon lands on St Helena.*
7 December – *Execution of Ney.*

# Glossary

The following words were all in use during the Napoleonic Wars, or have been applied later to military terms relative to the period; not all were French in origin.

**Adjoint:** assistant adjutant; assistant
**Adjutant:** junior administrative officer or warrant officer
**Adjutant-chef:** senior adjutant
**Adjutant-commandant:** adjutant-general after 1800
**Adjutant-general:** staff colonel often serving as corps or divisional chief-of-staff
**Adjutant-major:** staff officer (usually with rank of major)
**Adjutant-sous-officier:** senior warrant officer
**Amalgame:** tactical amalgamation of regular and volunteer units
**Arme blanche:** cavalry sabres; generic term for cavalry
**Artillerie à Cheval:** horse artillery
**Artillerie à Pied:** foot artillery
**Artillerie légère:** light (ie horse) artillery
**Artillerie volante:** fast horse artillery, all gunners mounted
**Aspirant:** cadet
**Avant-train:** gun-limber
**Banquette:** firing-step behind a parapet
**Batardeau:** dam to retain water in a fortress-ditch
**Battery:** orig a gun-emplacement; later a company of 6 to 8 guns
**Bonnet:** triangular fortification placed in front of a ravelin
**Bonnet à poil:** fur grenadier-cap
**Bonnet de police:** forage-cap
**Bricole:** rope or strap for manhandling a cannon; a gun fired 'en bricole' when the shot struck a sloping revetment
**Brigade:** formation of two or more battalions
**Brigadier:** cavalry corporal
**Briquet:** short infantry sabre
**Butin:** personal kit (colloquial: orig 'booty')
**Cabinet:** Napoleon's household staff
**Cadenettes:** tresses of plaited hair hanging from the temples, worn by hussars
**Canister:** artillery ammunition: lead balls in a tin container
**Cantinière:** sutleress
**Caponnière:** covered communication-trench from an enceinte to a detached work; casemated fortification projecting across a ditch to deliver flanking-fire
**Caporal:** infantry corporal
**Carabinier:** type of heavy cavalry; grenadier of light infantry
**Carnets:** Napoleon's notebooks for records of unit-strengths, etc
**Cartouche:** cartridge-box
**Casemate:** chamber in a fortress-wall
**Cavalier:** raised battery on a fortification
**Centenier:** 2nd lieutenant in the *infirmier* companies
**Chapeau chinois:** lit 'chinese hat': percussion instrument comprising bells on an ornamental pole
**Charoual:** mamcluke-style baggy trousers
**Chasseur:** lit 'hunter': light troops
**Chasseur à Cheval:** light cavalry
**Chasseur à Pied:** light infantry
**Chef de bataillon:** battalion-commander (term of rank rather than appointment)
**Chef de brigade:** brigade-major
**Chef de musique:** bandmaster

**Chef d'escadron:** cavalry squadron-commander
**Cheval-des-frises:** barricade made of stake- or blade-studded beams
**Chevau-léger:** light horse (German, 'chevauleger')
**Chevau-leger-lancier:** lancer
**Coehorn (or Coehoorn):** mortar named after its designer
**Coffret:** ammunition-chest
**Cohort:** battalion of National Guard
**Colback (also 'colpack'):** fur busby or hussar cap
**Commissaire ordinaire:** assistant-commissary
**Commissaire ordonnateur:** commissary-in-chief
**Conducteur:** artillery driver
**Corps:** generic term for any military formation
**Corps d'armée:** self-contained tactical unit of several divisions
**Corps d'observation:** detached formation protecting communications, watching enemy etc
**Crochet:** miniature parallel trench
**Cuirass:** breastplate
**Cuirassier:** armoured heavy cavalry
**Cul de singe:** slang term for cloth patch at rear of a fur grenadier-cap
**Czapka:** square-topped Polish-style cap (also 'Shapska', 'Tchapka', etc)
**Demi-brigade:** infantry unit, originally of one regular and two volunteer battalions; later, any *ad hoc* infantry formation
**Division:** tactical formation of two or more brigades; unit of two infantry companies; two field-pieces with attendant vehicles
**Dolman:** tail-less braided jacket as worn by hussars
**Dragon:** dragoon
**Dragoon:** 'medium' cavalry; orig mounted infantry
**Eclaireur:** cavalry scout
**Ecoute:** small mine-gallery
**Emigré:** French royalist refugee serving in the army of another nation
**Enceinte:** fortress wall
**Envelope:** continuous enceinte
**Epaulement:** breastwork
**Esplanade:** open space between a citadel and the nearest buildings
**Etat-major:** staff
**Fantassin:** infantryman
**Fanion:** small marker-flag
**Farrier:** cavalry pioneer or one who cared for unit's horses
**Fascine:** brushwood bundle used in fortification
**Fausse-braye:** low outer rampart
**Fellahin:** Egyptian peasant infantry
**Fixed Ammunition:** artillery projectile with wooden 'sabot' affixed
**Flanqueurs:** light infantry, especially Young Guard
**Flèche:** arrow-shaped earthwork fortification
**Fourgon:** heavy transport waggon
**Fourrier:** quartermaster-corporal
**Fraises:** sharpened palisade poles projecting horizontally or downwards from a fortification-wall
**Fusil:** musket
**Fusil dépareillé:** composite musket composed of spare parts of different patterns
**Fusil d'honneur:** presentation-musket awarded for outstanding service
**Fusilier:** ordinary infantryman

**Gabion:** earth-filled wicker basket used in fortification
**Gabion-farci:** gabion rolled in front of an engineer to shield him from enemy fire
**Garde du Corps:** royal bodyguard or household cavalry
**Garde d'honneur:** light bodyguard cavalry; escort units of cities or areas
**Garde Nationale:** national guard; home-defence units
**Gendarme:** orig any armed man, but by this time a quasi-military police or security soldier
**Grand-Quartier-Général:** general headquarters
**Grenadier:** élite infantry, orig armed with hand-grenades
**Grenadier à Cheval:** horse-grenadier of the Imperial Guard
**Grenzer:** Austrian border-troops
**Grognard:** lit 'grumbler', nickname for Old Guard infantry
**Grosse-bottes:** lit 'big boots', nickname for Guard Horse Grenadiers
**Guerite:** sentry-box sited on ramparts
**Guides:** light cavalry escort
**Guidon:** cavalry standard
**Habit-veste:** jacket
**Hussard:** hussar; light cavalry styled on Hungarian originals
**Infirmier:** medical orderly
**Infirmier-brancardier:** stretcher-bearer
**Inspecteur aux Revues:** general staff inspecting officer
**Intendant:** commissary
**Invalides:** military hospital founded by Louis XIV; final resting-place of Napoleon
**Jäger:** lit 'huntsman'; German rifle corps
**Kurtka:** Polish lancer-jacket
**Lancier:** lancer
**Légion:** orig a self-contained miniature army, a unit comprising infantry, cavalry, artillery, etc, but later used indiscriminately
**Lentille:** flat woollen disc worn as ornament on shako
**Levée en masse:** mass-conscription
**Lunette:** triangular fortification on or beyond a glacis; small fortification sited at one side of a ravelin.
**Mameluke:** Egyptian warrior caste, some incorporated in Imperial Guard
**Mantlet:** wooden screen protecting diggers at head of a sap
**Maréchal-des-logis:** cavalry sergeant
**Maréchal-des-logis-chef:** cavalry sergeant-major
**Maréchal-ferrant:** cavalry farrier or shoeing-smith
**Ordre mixte:** formation for attack combining both column and line
**Ouvrier:** artisan
**Parallel:** siege-trench running parallel to the besieged fortification
**Park:** artillery reserve
**Pelisse:** furred over-jacket worn by hussars
**Péloton:** platoon
**Pioneer:** pioneer
**Picquet:** infantry outpost or sentinel
**Pokalem:** undress cap of 1812-pattern
**Pontonnier:** pontoon-builder

**Porte-drapeau:** colour-bearer
**Porte-étandard:** cavalry standard-bearer
**Porte-aigle:** 'Eagle'-bearer
**Prolonge:** rope attaching cannon to team to obviate repeated unlimbering
**Pupilles:** cadets
**Queue:** pigtail-hairstyle
**Raquettes:** 'flounders' or knots on end of cap-cords
**Raupenhelm:** leather crested helmet of German style
**Ravelin:** triangular detached fortification in front of a fortress-wall
**Redan:** V-shaped fortification
**Revetment:** retaining-wall of a fortification
**Sabot:** wooden 'shoe' on 'fixed' ammunition
**Sabre:** cavalry sword; also, a cavalryman
**Sabretache:** decorative leather case suspended from a sword-belt

**Sapeur:** engineer or pioneer
**Saucissons:** lit 'sausages'; long, thin fascines
**Shabraque:** decorated horse-cloth
**Shako:** peaked, cylindrical cap
**Spencer:** short-tailed jacket
**Sous-centenier:** sergeant-major of an infirmier company
**Sous-lieutenant:** sub- or 2nd-lieutenant
**Tambour:** drum; drummer; small, palisaded fortification
**Tenaille:** small fortification in a ditch in front of a wall
**Tenue de route:** marching order
**Terreplein:** wide upper part of a rampart
**Tête de colonne:** lit 'head of column': regimental colour-party, musicians, *sapeurs*, etc; colloquially known as the 'clique'
**Timonier:** wheel-horse

**Tirailleur:** skirmisher or sharpshooter
**Toise:** French unit of measurement, used for calculating fortifications; 6.395 English feet
**Train d'Artillerie:** artillery transport service
**Train des Equipages:** transport corps or 'equipment train'
**Trou de loup:** lit 'wolf-pit'; cone-shaped pit used as anti-personnel trap, usually six feet deep, five to six feet wide at surface
**Trunnions:** lugs projecting from cannon-barrel, securing it to the carriage
**Vedette:** cavalry scout or outpost
**Vélite:** cadet or trainee NCO
**Vivandière:** sutleress
**Voltigeur:** lit 'vaulter'; light infantry company of line regiment
**Wurst-wagen:** lit 'sausage-waggon'; caisson with padded seat on top

---

# *Index*

Note: as Napoleon features throughout the book, there is no entry below for the
Emperor; numbers in italics indicate illustrations.